D1598532

Entangling Alliances

Entangling Alliances

Foreign War Brides and American

Soldiers in the Twentieth Century

Susan Zeiger

NEW YORK UNIVERSITY PRESS

New York and London

NEW YORK UNIVERSITY PRESS
New York and London
www.nyupress.org

Library of Congress Cataloging-in-Publication Data

Zeiger, Susan, 1959–
 Entangling alliances : foreign war brides and American
soldiers in the twentieth century / Susan Zeiger.
p. cm.
Includes bibliographical references and index.
ISBN-13: 978-0-8147-9717-4 (cloth : alk. paper)
ISBN-10: 0-8147-9717-2 (cloth : alk. paper)
1. War brides—United States—History—20th century. 2. Military spouses—
United States—History—20th century. 3. Soldiers—Family relationships—
United States—History—20th century. 4. Soldiers—Sexual behavior—
United States—History—20th century. 5. Intercountry marriage—United States—
History—20th century. 6. United States—History, Military—20th century. I. Title.
U766.Z45   2010
306.8088'35500973—dc22   2009041513

New York University Press books are printed on acid-free paper,
and their binding materials are chosen for strength and durability.
We strive to use environmentally responsible suppliers and materials
to the greatest extent possible in publishing our books.

Manufactured in the United States of America
10 9 8 7 6 5 4 3 2 1

In loving memory of Adina Back,
sister-historian, beloved friend

Contents

Acknowledgments

In his evocative poem on an ancient journey, a poem that is a favorite of mine, C. P. Cavafy offers these directions to the would-be traveler: "When you start on your journey to Ithaca, /then pray that the road is long, / full of adventure, full of knowledge . . . visit hosts of Egyptian cities, /to learn and learn from those who have knowledge." My journey to the end of this book has included all of these—time, adventure, and learning from others wiser than myself—in ample measure. I am deeply grateful to the students and teachers, librarians and archivists, friends and family who have shaped my knowledge and enriched my life along the way.

From the beginning, administrators, staff, and faculty colleagues at Regis College were gracious in their patience and support. My particular thanks go to Regis colleagues Christine Padgett, who shared with me the moving story of her mother, a French war bride; Armine Bagdasarian, interlibrary loan director, who cheerfully and tirelessly gathered reference materials from near and far; Deans Pamela Menke and Lee Hogan; and my friend Wendy Lement, Professor of theater, who collaborated with me on a war brides oral history and theater project in the early days of my research. Without grant support the book simply never would have come into being, and I remain humbly grateful for this assistance. A faculty fellowship award from the National Endowment for the Humanities allowed me to launch the project, and a sabbatical grant and a Virginia Kaneb Award from Regis College helped to sustain it. A year's residency at Harvard University's Charles Warren Center for Studies in American History enriched my conception of the book's main themes. I am thankful to the many Warren Center colleagues who read, listened to, and commented brilliantly upon earlier iterations of my ideas, faculty sponsors Carol Oja, Nancy Cott, and Lizabeth Cohen and co-fellows Kimberley Phillips and Susan Carruthers in particular.

Librarians and archivists also provided immeasurably valuable assistance. I thank the archival staff of the Young Women's Christian Association for directing me to an important diary and other war bride documents that were the seed of this project. The National Archive and Records Administration (NARA), which houses the nation's military, State Department, and immigration records, was the sine qua non for this book. Two NARA archivists require special thanks. Richard Boylan was my expert guide through the military records of the Vietnam War, who bent over backward to assist me. Mitch Yockelson, who shares my passion for World War I, was my partner in crime on this project, directing me to invaluable sources I would never have found on my own, but also to colleagues who could share their own expertise. Michele Thomas, a war bride daughter and the editor of an extraordinary website, has undertaken the gathering and archiving of war bride news links, testimony, and photographs that have informed and enriched my understanding of this history. Her website, The American War Bride Experience: GI Brides of World War II (http://www.geocities.com/us_warbrides/) is a starting point for anyone interested in this subject.

Chris Cappozola, Ruth Feldstein, Uta Poiger, Grey Osterud, Andy O'Connell, Marilynn Johnson, Conrad Wright, Marilyn Halter, and Judy Smith gave wonderful comments on segments of the manuscript. The Immigration and Urbanization seminar, hosted by the Massachusetts Historical Society, generously invited me to present a version of chapter 3. My peace history allies Frances Early and Harriet Alonso listened to my ideas, inspired me, and cheered my efforts. Grey Osterud, a brilliant reader and developmental editor, both smoothed and sharpened portions of the manuscript and championed its global perspective. The marvelous Marilyn Young made meticulous comments on chapter 6 at two crucial stages and helped to shape my thinking. My debts to Susan Ware, adviser, friend, and mentor, cannot be repaid or overstated; from the beginning she challenged me to conceptualize the project in its broadest terms and pushed me to complete it when my momentum flagged. Her support, as always, has been indispensable.

I am grateful as well to Deborah Gershenowitz of New York University Press, whose enthusiasm for the project was abundant from our earliest conversation forward. Debbie read the manuscript with care and keen intelligence, as did two anonymous reviewers for the press. Their comments all made the book much stronger. None of the individuals named is responsible for its flaws.

The people who love me most know how much I have counted upon them in the nearly ten years it took to write this book while juggling other responsibilities—and certainly dropping balls from time to time, no doubt. My parents, Herb and Honey Zeiger, my first and still greatest fans, are dear to my heart. My amazing sons, Dan and Micah, small boys when I started this project, have been magically transformed into young adults along the way. Their friendship, intelligence, and good humor have inspired and motivated me. My cherished husband, Jeffrey Katz, published an excellent self-help book on back pain and scores and scores of research articles during the time that it took me to complete this one project, but he always shared his time, ideas, and support lovingly and unstintingly. He served as chief statistical adviser as well. This book and almost everything else that is best in our lives would be impossible without him.

I dedicate the book to the memory of my beloved friend and graduate school colleague Adina Back, who influenced my scholarship in so many ways. Adina died far too young, but everyone she ever met was deeply touched by her joy in living and her passion for all that is true and just.

Introduction

In the fall of 2007, *Newsweek* featured a cover story on marriages between Iraqi citizens and American military personnel that had taken place in the years since the U.S. invasion. The article appeared at a time, opinion polls showed, that American support for the war had reached a new low; calls for a full troop withdrawal were mounting, and the war would soon become a major factor in the presidential campaign.[1] But for the foreseeable future, Americans were "married to Iraq" whether they liked it or not, the title that *Newsweek*'s editors had given their story. For the cover they chose an arresting and somehow unsettling image. A stunning woman, dark-eyed and olive-skinned, stares gravely at the camera, "a native Iraqi," Dr. Zena Majeed. The viewer's eye is pulled to her face, and to the swirling embroidery and beadwork of her purple gown. Her American husband, Lieutenant Colonel Richard Allinger, stands behind her in army dress uniform, gazing soberly ahead. The photograph starkly encodes difference: male and female, military and civilian, light and dark, disciplined and sensual, American and foreign. So too does the article's text: "For all the forces pushing Americans and Iraqis together in this war, . . . even greater ones are driving them apart." Iraqis and their American liberators were divided by a "chasm" of differences, according to the authors—language, history, politics, religion, and violence. This "abyss of religious and cultural misunderstandings" was "hard to cross," even for the small handful of intercultural couples who had ventured to marry. The article's conclusion was a pessimistic one: "Sadly, even as these relationships continue and deepen, so does America's tragic relationship with Iraq."

Like a crystal ball, the magazine implied, intercultural marriages can be read to "tell us" the meaning of the war—what we are doing in Iraq and what might come of our troubled relationship to that nation.[2] Whether they realized it or not, the *Newsweek* writers and editors were engaged in a discursive practice with a long history.

In each of the major wars of the last century—World War I, World War II, the Korean War, and the Vietnam War—overseas military service placed U.S.

military personnel in sustained contact with young women of both allied and enemy nations. In each of these wars, U.S. soldiers returned home with thousands of foreign-born wives and children. Tens of thousands of allied war brides were officially recognized as a new category of immigrant, their numbers peaking in the aftermath of World War II but continuing through the Cold War era. Thousands of former "enemy" women—Germans, Italians, and Japanese—also met and married U.S. soldiers under conditions of postwar occupation. In undertaking responsibility for the foreign wives brought home by American servicemen, the state recognized the war bride as a consequence, welcome or not, of U.S. foreign military commitments.

A central contention of this book is that such intercultural relationships have served an important function in U.S. history: war bride marriages are a multifaceted prism through which Americans have sought to make meaning on a popular level of their relationships with other countries. It is the unique way that the war bride blends gender, sexuality, race, nationalism, and foreign relations that makes these marriages such a rich field of interpretation. My own work is part of an evolving historical discourse in global women's studies that explores how women and women's sexuality have been mobilized in the context of war, and especially postwar eras, as a means to enact social ends such as national purification, revenge, or social healing— processes that usually, though not invariably, oppress or stigmatize women.[3] By making the uses and constructions of gender a topic of inquiry within the history of foreign relations, scholars have broadened and even reconceptualized the field.[4] The study of war brides belongs to that effort.

Those who have considered war brides in the past have been drawn to their stories for very different reasons. One is the impulse to humanize or personalize war. Love in a war zone speaks to many people of the remarkable human capacity to choose life even in the midst of death and chaos. Novelist John Horne Burns, an intelligence officer in the Mediterranean theater during World War II, articulated this view in his best-selling novel of 1947, *The Gallery*: "In a war one has to love, if only to assert that he's very much alive in the face of destruction. Whoever has loved in wartime takes part in a passionate reaffirmation of his life." It is revealing that the authors of a major study of World War II brides chose this passage from Burns as the epigraph to their work.[5] Love across national boundaries, love that is capable of overcoming profound obstacles or deep differences, is for many a special sign of hope; it intimates the possibility of human reconciliation and mutual understanding. This perspective is behind much of the writing by war brides and those who identify closely with them, often war bride daughters.[6] Such personal accounts come from a second and equally strong impulse. Telling war bride stories is a form of grassroots women's history—a collective effort to gather and disseminate war bride testimony that has helped to make this study possible. Authors and editors of these projects express a desire to add women's voices to the history of war, attending to a previously neglected dimension of war experience. While the practice of telling individual stories can be a powerful corrective to standard histories of war, introducing war's human side, it also runs the risk of atomizing that history or, worse, even sentimentalizing it.

Feminist theory provides a contrasting framework for thinking about war brides. The exchange of women across boundaries of tribe or nation is an ancient human practice, carried out to resolve boundary disputes, build political alliances, or denote the close of warfare between groups. For all these reasons, as Cynthia Enloe has shown, "marriage has . . . been treated as serious business by the makers of foreign policy." The bride is the "spoil of war" that goes to the victor, an assertion of power over rival males that upholds patriarchy on many levels. In British North America, for example, marriages between male European trappers and Indian women were "a means of cementing alliances on a frontier that still eluded secure imperial control." Furthermore, such a marriage "gave a white man a sense that he was superior, that he was saving a woman from the deplorable condition of savagery." This belief "bolstered" white men's sense of the "moral rightness" of the colonial enterprise.[7] In a modern context, the American soldier who meets and marries a local woman in a military base community overseas might be seen to represent, in one of its forms, the power that the United States asserts over foreign lands and people, especially over women. This perspective has provided a theoretical underpinning to the important work of feminist activists around the globe who connect U.S. overseas military bases with the subjugation of women, and with social problems such as trafficking, AIDS, and military prostitution.[8]

An alternative point of entry for considering war brides is the history of the term itself. Viewing war brides across the dimension of time, one can begin to see the term's dynamic quality as well as its complexity. The earliest identifiable use of the phrase to denote an intercultural marriage in the context of U.S. military operations comes from the Mexican border conflict of 1914.[9] But in fact, the phenomenon of soldier marriage in foreign war can be traced back to the first overseas military expeditions of the United States in Cuba and the Philippines. No one thought to call these intercultural relationships "war bride marriages" or regarded them as a unique category of matrimony. Their existence is revealed only incidentally, as an artifact of military occupation. In Cuba, where Americans carried out their first experiments in the management of civil affairs in a colonial context, military government was established on a regional or "departmental" basis. One of the tasks assigned to the sanitary affairs officer was to make an accounting of births, deaths, and marriages in his region of command. With American efficiency and attention to detail, several of these officers recorded the marriage statistics in their department broken down into racial and national categories. It is from these records that we learn that one "Negro" and twenty-one white Americans married Cuban women between May 1899 and April 1900. Nothing more is known about these couples, but these women are likely to have been the nation's first identifiable foreign war brides.[10]

"War bride" had a different meaning entirely at the start of World War I—the mirror image of its later connotation. The phrase was used to describe an American wife, usually a newlywed, waiting chastely at home for the return of her soldier, like an American Penelope. By marrying her husband on the eve of his departure for war, she demonstrated her emotional courage and her loyalty to her husband as well as the nation. Waiting was a form of women's war work in this construction, crucial to men's morale.[11] Later generations would wring their hands over such impetuous "gangplank marriages"—unions of young men and young women contracted in the feverish atmosphere of war mobilization—but in World War I, the American war bride stood as a model of patriotic womanhood.

This meaning of the term lingered into the 1920s (in an American stage play, for example, and even a popular Yiddish musical of the postwar years).[12] But it was overtaken, and soon overwhelmed, by a new usage that surfaced early in 1919. The demobilization of the American Expeditionary Force at the close of World War I gave rise to the war bride as a new category of female immigrant. "War bride" now referred to the foreign wives that doughboys had taken by the thousands while serving overseas, "the petite chic *demoiselles*, ever ready . . . to whisper a '*je t'aime*' to a strapping Yankee come over to drive away the Hun."[13] The army was responsible for formulating the term in its new meaning and defining its initial parameters. By the time that Americans first encountered this new species of American wife in the flood of newspaper and magazine stories that accompanied the women's arrival, war brides had already begun to acquire some of the material privileges that would later characterize their position. As the preceding quote suggests, they had acquired as well the sexualized aura and the imprint of difference that would surround them for decades to come in American popular understanding and public debate.

By the end of World War II, "war bride" was a relatively privileged category of immigration accompanied by a number of important features, including a non-quota immigration status, expedited naturalization, room, board, and medical care under military auspices in the period before departure, free transport en route to the United States, and, within the United States, free transport to the husband's city of residence. The foreign wife earned this special status, of course, not through her own initiative or volition but by virtue of being selected by an American serviceman. While the military had the primary role in developing policies that defined the category of war bride, other institutions also made key contributions. The National American Red Cross, an important player across this history, worked closely with the military, sometimes in parallel and sometimes at odds with it, to shape the outlines of who and what constituted a war bride. Congress also took part. A series of war bride bills passed in the late 1940s and early 1950s delineated the rights that attached to the foreign wives of soldiers and outlined the limitations of those rights. Once established, the term took on a life of its own, and it turned out to be flexible, used, for instance, to embrace and rehabilitate former enemies in Germany through military marriages during the early years of the Cold War. It was adaptable as well by some women and couples as a tool for family reunification and economic survival—women from Eastern Europe and Italy, for example, who were married prior to war and utilized the military's policy of providing free transportation for soldiers' wives to unite immigrant families long separated by war and migration. But war bride was also a contested status, sought by and denied to many husbands and wives in intercultural war marriages, most notably, African American GIs with white European wives, and white and black GIs with Japanese wives or fiancées.

This book traces the rise, and then the demise, of the war bride over the course of the twentieth century, both as a special category of female immigrant and as a cultural construction. The history of war brides consists of at least two stories, separate but intertwined, and traced here in alternating chapters. The first, centered overseas, analyzes the development of intercultural marriage against the backdrop of war and the evolution of army policy in regard to marriage. Military policies, the book shows, played a crucial role in shaping the wartime and postwar fabric of gender and sexual relations. Soldier marriage never took place anywhere in a vacuum. Instead, it existed in a matrix of warfront interaction between American soldiers and local women that encompassed courtship and dating, consensual and coerced sexual intercourse, informal and commercial prostitution, and sexual assault and the transmission of sexual disease. Managing relationships between soldiers and women—"fraternization" in military parlance—became a major concern of the U.S. military in every theater of war. It was a source of friction with allied leaders and a cause of conflict with local communities. The "problem" of marriage, alongside the related problems of bigamy, desertion, and extramarital pregnancy, demanded action from military officials. The specific decisions that they made at different moments and in different places had unforeseen and often profound ramifications for women, both foreign-born and U.S.-born, who married or wished to marry American servicemen.

One of the most important factors in the structuring of soldier marriage has been race. The state's repression and condemnation of interracial relationships was a feature of war bride marriage for much of the century. In World War I, for instance, U.S. military and civilian authorities took a paternalistic stance toward white soldiers, determined to "protect" them from sexually promiscuous foreign women. But this attitude was reversed in the case of "colored troops," as military officials warned allies of the sexual danger that African American servicemen allegedly posed to the white women of other nations. By World War II, racial ideology in the United States had begun to face resistance by activists of color and their white allies, who challenged racial segregation in the military and at home, as well as "oriental exclusion" in immigration policy. Yet despite the state of flux in race relations in the 1940s and 1950s, the U.S. government, with the urging of the armed services, maintained its segregationist policies in soldier marriage. These included initially excluding Asian women from the GI Brides Act and denying the marriage requests of black and white interracial couples on the grounds that "miscegenous unions" were illegal in many U.S. states. Deeply held views about racial inferiors and superiors continued to underlie American military engagement in the Cold War. The legacy of biracial relationships in the Vietnam War, as it involved Vietnamese women, American men, and their "Amerasian" children, is one further indication of the centrality of race in analyzing gender relationships in wartime and postwar periods.

The second story, one set primarily in the United States, revolves around the American response to war brides as immigrants and as soldiers' wives. Anyone fascinated by war brides soon finds him- or herself in good historical company. Decade after decade, intercultural war marriages were scrutinized by journalists, fiction writers and Hollywood filmmakers, social workers and marriage counselors, psychologists and sociologists, courts and juries, political leaders and the public as they struggled to understand the consequences of "international intercourse" for their nation. In time I came to see that this discussion *about* war brides was at the heart of the study. In each period, the discourse was shaped by the contemporary concerns of foreign, domestic, and immigration policy and gender relations. This was apparent, for example, following World War I, when the prevailing xenophobia and nationalism of the United States were reflected in a pronounced hostility to European wives. War brides in the 1920s were stigmatized as prostitutes or "gold diggers," women who had taken advantage of innocent American "boys." After World War II, in contrast, soldiers' marriages were linked to the nation's newfound global leadership. As U.S. leaders courted relationships across the globe, war brides were a reassurance of the nation's ability to woo and win the admiration and loyalty of foreign others in the context of the emerging Cold War. In this sense, war bride marriages have had both a cultural and a political function, helping Americans to construct and comprehend their relationships with foreign countries and with foreign newcomers to the United States as these questions were redefined across the century.

Most important, perhaps, the story of war brides is embedded in the comparative history of *post*wars, an important but largely neglected dimension of the social and cultural history of the twentieth-century United States.[14] War disrupts and disorders relationships, communities, landscapes, bodies, structures of power, and even systems of meaning. Much of the "reconstruction" work that societies undertake in postwar eras, I would argue, relates to the restoration or renegotiation of this intangible social, emotional, and cultural infrastructure. War brides have been one vehicle for reckoning with war and its consequences, though never in a one-dimensional way. Consider the trope of disease and healing that has been central to the historical debate about war brides. Postwar anxieties about the nation's integrity and security have been projected onto war brides, seen concretely, for example, in the long-standing view of the women as bearers of infectious or sexual diseases, and, metaphorically, of the women as parasites, leaching vigor from the national body. This view surfaced most acutely after World War I, when the "foreignness" of French brides converged with anti-immigrant sentiment. At other historical moments, Americans have looked to war brides as an aid in the recuperation of the nation's homecoming soldiers, men sometimes broken emotionally or physically and often seen as threatening to the social order. After World War II, for example, Americans turned to white, English-speaking war brides to help recover the balance of power in gender relations disrupted by the war. When American women have been rebuked in postwar moments for excessive independence, materialism, and love of luxury, or for overreaching expectations of American men and marriage, foreign brides have frequently been held out as model wives or partners, happily satisfied with whatever their veteran-husbands could offer them and more than willing to proffer them leadership in their family lives. As this suggests, the discourse about war brides has also been about proper American manhood and men's relationships with women—and, by extension, about the maturity, responsibility, and leadership of the nation in its relations with other countries.

A final unifying focus of the book is the social and subjective experience of women who became war brides. Most men and women in intercultural marriages returned from war, started families, and built lives in the United States. Some of these marriages were tragic mistakes, deeply regretted by one or both parties, but many more seemed to provide companionship and emotional satisfaction, a measure of security and financial stability, or sometimes all of these. In this sense, war bride marriages were much like other postwar American marriages, and not the exotic or aberrant relationships that so interested reporters and the public. War brides' personal narratives and oral histories are an intriguing counterpart and sometimes counterpoint to the stories constructed *about* them.[15] Evidence from across the study, for instance, indicates that American soldiers were frequently attracted to foreign girlfriends or wives for their "old-fashioned" or "feminine" qualities, for their difference from American women. Yet in their self-narration, women often frame their decision to go out with Americans in contrasting terms, as a defiance of conventional gender roles and an embrace of American-style personal freedoms. War brides over time have used narrative to construct a complex and even contradictory identity, one that blends elements of autonomy (from family and patriarchal control) with themes of dependence (on American husbands and/or the U.S. government). Giving voice to their stories helps to uncover further dimensions of war experience from the perspective of women. It allows us to probe the inner, emotional life of men and women in relationships, in wartime and beyond, and to examine the interplay between personal and public meaning in the construction of identity.

The ending of the book traces both continuity and significant change in soldiers' overseas marriage from the Cold War forward. In the aftermath of the Korean War, war bride marriage as amicable "international intercourse" was no longer a useful metaphor for interpreting the morass of foreign relations, global ambitions, and wrenching self-doubt that came to characterize U.S. foreign policy. With the opening of permanent U.S. bases throughout Europe and Asia, the overseas marriage of U.S. personnel became a way of life within the military. So too did the sprawling "camptowns" that provided sex and other R & R services to American troops in South Korea, the Philippines, Okinawa, Vietnam, Thailand, and elsewhere. When intercultural marriages occurred in these contexts, as they did by the tens of thousands over the Cold War decades, Americans reached back to an earlier historical tradition, stigmatizing these foreign and nonwhite wives as prostitutes and economic "parasites," an attitude intensified by American racism. The privileges attached to war bride marriage were quietly withdrawn as the faces of brides came more fully to reflect the global reach of U.S. foreign policy. Equally important for the demise of the war bride was the nature of U.S. military engagement during the Cold War. As "withdrawal" replaced triumph in these Cold War conflicts—wars that lacked not just victory but even conclusion—the political and cultural outlines of postwar reconstruction necessarily shifted. There were no happy endings here. The dynamic can be seen most clearly in Vietnam. U.S. leaders and cultural producers had little interest in highlighting Vietnamese-American marriage as a resolution to the nation's greatest foreign-policy debacle of the twentieth century—although, ironically, the patterns of intercultural marriage in the Vietnam War in many ways paralleled those of earlier wars and earlier waves of postwar "war brides."

In the end, this book tells a story of deep and continuing uneasiness with internationalism on the part of Americans. This uneasiness has grown alongside our growing international involvements—those "entangling alliances" that the first president famously warned against so early in the nation's history. The study of war brides across the twentieth century reveals the multiple ways that this unease was connected with and expressed through relationships of gender.

1

"Cupid in the AEF"

U.S. Soldiers and Women abroad in World War I

Mad'moiselle from Armentieres,
Parlez-vous.
Mad'moiselle from Armentieres,
Parlez-vous.
Mad'moiselle from Armentieres,
She hadn't been hugged in a thousand years,
Hinky-dinky parlez-vous.

. . .

With her I flirted, I confess,
But she got revenge when she said yes,
Hinky-dinky, parlez-vous.[1]

"American or French Girls, which is best?" The American Expeditionary Force (AEF) edition of the *Chicago Tribune* posed this question to its doughboy readership in November 1918, soon after the armistice. As it turned out, American soldiers had strong and varied opinions on the subject, and their responses filled the "letters" column for weeks. Many rose to the defense of American womanhood, praising the home front sweethearts they soon hoped to see. Others, like this anonymous American officer, cast a strong vote for the French: "If the American girl is jealous of the French girl today, she has good reason to be. . . . If [American] girls do not change and learn to be more attentive and appreciative of our men than they have been in the past, they are going to have more time for knitting. . . . the fellows . . . will go out with their little French girls when they want a really interesting evening."[2]

This seemingly lighthearted exchange of letters in fact highlighted several important but subterranean features of the American experience in the First World War. First, the letters acknowledged a reality that the U.S. government worked hard to obscure during the months of fighting: that American soldiers were indeed having intimate relationships with local women in the context of military service overseas. This reality clashed with the carefully managed image of the AEF as the world's "cleanest" army, an underpinning of the Wilson administration's war effort. The idealization of the American soldier in World War I, "the knight in the crusade for democracy," demanded "rigid prescription for upright behavior overseas."[3] Evidence of intercultural intimacy was unsettling to many Americans, who had been assured that the American doughboy would stay chaste and sober in France, saving himself for the American sweetheart he had left behind. Public outrage was acute for this reason when the American press circulated an outlandish rumor in the spring of 1919 that 200,000 American soldiers planned to stay in Europe and settle down with French wives and lovers.[4]

Of course, the French woman who could give an American soldier "a really interesting evening" was precisely the kind of woman that soldiers' families and moral reformers most wanted the men to avoid. In American political and cultural discourse, France and other European countries were alien places that threatened the moral standards and certitudes of the United States. Foreign women had long been seen as both sexually desirable and readily available, women of loose moral conduct and erotic sophistication. This was the view, for example, of reformers in the nineteenth-century anti-immigrant and antiprostitution campaigns, and later, of evangelical citizens who demanded government action to "protect" American soldiers from prostitution in foreign lands. As American doughboys deployed in Europe began to interact with local women, this view also animated the initial responses of AEF leaders: that the women were "gold diggers" or prostitutes scheming to take advantage of naïve American "boys."

For the leaders of the U.S. military effort in World War I, relations between U.S. soldiers and local women posed a largely unprecedented set of questions with military, diplomatic, and domestic implications. AEF leaders were unprepared for the range of policy problems they were asked to face, from the licensure of brothels to the resolution of paternity disputes. Marriage, the most public and visible of these problems, was among the most vexing. Many within the military establishment advocated a ban on soldier marriage overseas. There were many reasons to support marriage, however. What proved to be most significant was pressure from Allied leaders, who were outraged by mounting evidence of out-of-wedlock pregnancy and fears for the future of young women abandoned by American "boyfriends." General John Pershing, commander in chief of the AEF, ultimately took a stand in favor of marriage for U.S. troops under his command and created policies to facilitate intercultural marriage. Pershing acted to extend protection not to American soldiers or to foreign women but to the reputation of the armed services and the American state. At the conclusion of the First World War, more than 5,000 American soldiers were wed to foreign wives—the first foreign "war brides" recognized by the U.S. government. The state had established the legal right of American soldiers to marry and developed procedures for them to do so—though not without qualifications or reservations. All together, the U.S. military's first steps toward resolving these concerns set the stage for soldier marriage to foreign women in subsequent military conflicts.

"Pure and Clean Through and Through": Military Service and Moral Reform in the Progressive Era

World War I brought the modern military draft to the United States, created a wartime apparatus of federal agencies with extensive political and economic authority, and eventually propelled nearly 2 million Americans, including uniformed women, into military service overseas. It was a transforming event in American history by any measure. From the vantage point of 1914, however, Americans viewed the cataclysm across the Atlantic as neither the "Great War" nor the "war to end war," but the "European War." The conflict seemed so foreign, so distant from American concerns, that Army War College scenarios on file as late as April 1917 posited no major role for American troops overseas.[5] When the American Expeditionary Force was created in May 1917 and the Selective Service Act passed, many Americans worried about what might happen to their nation, and to their young men, in a foreign war.

While American families were certainly and appropriately fearful that their sons might lose their lives in battle, they fretted as well about the moral and psychological dangers of military service, "lewd women" and strong drink in particular. Historically, military encampments had held a reputation as a "corrupt and immoral environment," a perception dating back to the Civil War and earlier. World War I reawakened these concerns. Among evangelicals and conservative moral reformers—groups that viewed Wilson's foreign crusade with considerable skepticism—the fears were especially pronounced. One Oregon mother put Secretary of War Newton Baker on notice: "We are willing to sacrifice our boys, if need be . . . but we rebel and protest against their being returned to us ruined in body and ideals"—a coded phrase referring to promiscuity and sexually transmitted disease.[6] Congressional debate of the Selective Service Act in May 1917 echoed these public concerns. Many insisted that military service required the maturity and stability of older men and posed excessive danger to the young. These critics succeeded in setting the draft age at a relatively high twenty-one, with the purpose of protecting vulnerable youths.[7]

Many Americans worried in particular about the impact that *foreign* military service might have on young soldiers. France was, to many, an especially disturbing destination. In Anglo-American culture, the twin reputations of France as a center of high culture and low life had coexisted since the end of the eighteenth century. "No American should come to Europe under thirty years of age," Thomas Jefferson had cautioned; the young, he feared, would succumb too easily to its overpowering moral and social temptations, a characterization that paralleled the self-image of the American nation as a young, boyish innocent facing the corruption of old Europe. France offered many temptations to American innocents. The brothels, dance halls, and gambling houses of Paris were legendary in the American imagination by the second half of the nineteenth century, their reputation spread through underground guidebooks such as *Paris at Night* (1875), which described the intricate social scale of the French sex industry, the *loquettes* and *cocottes*, and where and how sex could be purchased. Mainstream mass publications for the middle class picked up on this theme, titillating their readers with accounts of the French demimonde. From the last quarter of the nineteenth century forward, historian Harvey Levenstein explains, Americans considered France the "capital of naughtiness" in the world. This reputation helps to explain why a YMCA leader might warn an American official in 1918 that "America has as much to fear from the French women of Paris" as from its German foe.[8]

American moral reform organizations that carried out international work further fed public anxiety over the fate of American youths in a foreign war. Women in the international "purity" campaign took the lead in highlighting the problem of prostitution overseas. Some took the analysis even further, describing the interrelationship between militarism, sexual promiscuity, alcohol consumption, and the degradation of foreign women. As evidence of military corruption, leaders of the international Woman's Christian Temperance Union (WCTU) pointed to the British army in India, for example, where native prostitutes serviced troops in regulated brothels. Closer to home in the United States, the recent border war with Mexico furnished compelling evidence of war's corrupting influence. Widespread and negative publicity in the American popular media, as well as the Christian press and reform publications, gave a lurid account of the drinking and prostitution that were practiced by U.S. troops. The "vice problem" in the Mexico campaign of 1916 was so concerning that it prompted Secretary of War Newton D. Baker to commission an extensive investigation.[9]

While U.S. civilian and moral reformers worried hypothetically about the impact of foreign military service on American troops, American military leaders had already made a number of firsthand observations of the moral behavior of regular army troops in foreign deployments. There prostitution was regarded as a fact of army life. In Cuba, Haiti, and the Philippines, relationships between American soldiers and local women were endemic but not discussed beyond the close confines of regular army circles.[10] Interestingly, one incident that threatened to open these relations to wider public view was a sex scandal that involved a prominent army officer in 1906—none other than John J. Pershing, the soon-to-be leader of the world's cleanest army. When President Roosevelt nominated Pershing for brigadier general, Pershing's political enemies spread a rumor that he had lived with a Filipina mistress during his service with the U.S. First Cavalry in the Philippines and had fathered several "half-breed" children with her. Pershing's career was salvaged by the woman's sworn denial of the charges and by the unstinting support of Pershing's wife.[11] But the controversy, whether unfounded or not, uncovered a universe of intercultural interaction between American soldiers and women overseas.

As President Wilson crafted a vision of the new conscript army to share with the American people, the prior problems of troops abroad and the vigorously expressed concerns of moral reformers shaped his approach. Wilson's evocation of a fighting force "pure and clean through and through" was remarkably idealistic even by Wilsonian standards.[12] Several factors, all of them intertwined with Progressive Era ideology, contributed to this vision. First and foremost was his own progressive reform outlook and that of his war cabinet, particularly his secretary of war Newton D. Baker, who earlier, as mayor of Cleveland, had placed the positive moral guardianship of young people at the center of his concerns.[13] Political considerations also played a role, chiefly President Wilson's need to steer unsettled public opinion in support of the European war; an army with high moral standards was an important condition of war support for many American voters, especially evangelicals. Likewise, progressive leaders in medicine and public health were determined to build an army that was "fit to fight" both physically and morally. The campaign against venereal disease in the Army Medical Department dovetailed with the concerns of moral reformers and evangelicals.

The Wilson administration's main policy response to concerns about the moral and sexual health of the troops was a vigorous "social purity" program aligned with the opening of military training camps across the country. The program had two parts: a law enforcement effort to repress prostitution and drinking surrounding the camps, and an extensive infrastructure of soldier recreation, education, and diversion to take the place of less healthy activities. The master strategist in this campaign was Raymond Fosdick, appointed by Secretary Baker to head the newly formed Commission on Training Camp Activities (CTCA) under the aegis of the War Department. A social investigator in his youth and a former resident of the Henry Street settlement in New York City's Lower East Side, Fosdick had outstanding progressive reform credentials. Fosdick had also been the chief investigator of moral conditions in the Mexican border war and arguably knew more about sex in the armed services than almost any other American civilian. Despite the realistic and startling report he had produced for the War Department, Fosdick was insistent that "sexual vice" could be suppressed in the military. The American soldier's "inherent sense of decency," he insisted, was an "invisible armor" of protection—though one, apparently, that needed much attending to. Some congressional and military leaders ridiculed the CTCA, but Wilson and Baker sincerely believed in the program's efficacy. Fosdick was dispatched to France alongside the earliest of Pershing's troops to establish an equivalent "army welfare" program for the AEF.[14]

The Wilson administration's "clean army" campaign derived crucial support as well from the army's Medical Department and its own vigorous efforts to suppress venereal disease. The impulse to apply science and efficiency in addressing social problems was another key dimension of the Progressive Era long recognized by historians. In World War I, military medical leaders created a strong and effective alliance with the nation's leading antivenereal organization, the American Society for Social Hygiene, to advance the case for a comprehensive "social purity" campaign among American troops. The program they crafted placed primary emphasis on the suppression of sexual relations, while for the first time distributing prophylaxis kits.

Military officials urged American soldiers to practice sexual abstinence, both as a patriotic duty and as a public health measure. Bulletin 54, required reading for all AEF personnel, asserted that "sexual continence is the plain duty of members of the A.E.F., both for the vigorous conduct of the war and for the clean health of the American people after the war." Medical research was marshaled to underscore and reassure that "sexual intercourse is not necessary for good health and complete continence is wholly possible."[15]

As the United States prepared to launch a full-scale military force for Europe in the summer of 1917, military and civilian leaders drew upon a pre-established set of beliefs to help construct an expeditionary army. Domestic political pressure from families and reformers for a "chaste" armed services; assumptions about American (male) innocence and foreign (female) immorality; and prior experiences with foreign people and populations in the fledgling American empire all profoundly influenced wartime policies related to the social and moral lives of American troops. Despite all this prior consideration, the AEF, under the command of General John J. Pershing, was unprepared for the range of social relationships that would emerge almost as soon as Americans disembarked on European shores.

"Franco-Yanko Romance"

The American doughboys were "no hermits" overseas, according to writer and First World War veteran Dixon Wecter. As early as November 1917, just months after the arrival of U.S. forces, a journalist commented on the rising phenomenon of "Franco-Yanko Romance." "The French girls like the American boys," he reported, and apparently their feelings were reciprocated. Romances like one between a U.S. Army enlisted man and a young French factory worker were typical. Recuperating from an illness in an army hospital in Orleans, Private Robert Scudder was sufficiently recovered to sit in the park one Sunday; there he saw and spoke with a French girl, who was on a promenade with a group of friends. The next Sunday they had a planned rendezvous at the Joan of Arc statue and went on a date to the movies, and soon she took him home to meet her parents. "I thought a lot of her because she seemed to be a very good girl, a home girl," Scudder wrote. By mid-January, he had asked her to marry him.[16]

AEF commanders sought to minimize the opportunities for contact between army personnel and local women. But with Americans posted in scores of cities and towns throughout France and England, it proved impossible to segregate soldiers. Relationships with local women were widespread and took a variety of forms. Social class background and military rank frequently determined how American men encountered women overseas, and the social class of the women they met. For working-class enlisted men like Robert Scudder, the streets, parks, and cafés of France were the mother lode of dating opportunities. In towns and cities, groups of American soldiers gathered on the streets and attempted to flirt with young women passing by. The cultural conditions of French urban life, with its public sociability, were conducive to such casual meetings. French women frequented the nation's cafés and theaters, reopened after the first six months of the war—though their convivial behavior was scrutinized and sometimes criticized by the French guardians of morality, especially the church.[17] In small villages, where enlisted men were billeted in farmhouses and family dwellings, social contact was easier still, though often more closely supervised. One journalist described a "typical scene"—three marines teaching "the old French father, the pretty daughter, and the flapper cousin" how to play American poker in the family's farmhouse kitchen.[18] With few young Frenchmen around, Americans could monopolize the attention of country girls and their urbanized cousins.

Officers and men of upper-class background might go out with women they encountered in public, but many were introduced to French and British women of better families through mutual acquaintances or friends. Officers also billeted in the homes of respectable bourgeois French and English families, where they shared unavoidable intimacy with the women of the house and were integrated into the social affairs of the community. An army captain from Minneapolis, for example, stationed in England, was introduced to and fell in love with the schoolmistress in the small town where he was posted.[19]

The military workplace was another site for relationships to develop. In a pattern that would continue going forward, U.S. military bases and headquarters reshaped economic, social, and gender relations in the communities where they were situated. In World War I, European women began to work side by side with American military and civilian personnel as stenographers, typists, and file clerks in the large bureaucratic offices and enormous hospital and supply centers that supported the war effort abroad. One American soldier met his French sweetheart while working with her at the giant American salvage plant run by the Services of Supply at Tours; another, an MP, fell in love with an Italian worker for the YMCA in Rome while guarding her office.[20] The diary of an American woman, a civilian typist, traced in absorbing detail the emergence of an office romance between an American lieutenant and a French clerical worker, a relationship that eventually became a marriage. U.S. Army nurses were barred from dating American enlisted men, but no such restrictions were placed on foreign nurse's aides or hospital volunteers who were sometimes attached to American hospital bases. Paul Withington, a Harvard-trained physician, fell in love with an Irish "VAD"—a young female volunteer—working at his base hospital.[21]

Many other interactions between American soldiers and local women revolved around the commercial sex trade. The military was rigorously careful in its public communications to maintain a code of silence on this subject that clashed so incongruously with the notion of the world's cleanest army. Ironically, however, almost everything that historians know about prostitution and the military during World War I comes from army reports, where the topic received abundant though internal attention. Undercover AEF investigators studied the "vice situation" among American troops in Paris, Bordeaux, Tours, Grenoble, Nantes, and Saint-Nazaire, for example. In Tours, a "wide open town," inspectors saw extensive "debauched" behavior, officers carousing with women believed to be their mistresses, enlisted men partying, drinking, and caressing women of "ill-repute" in public places. Colonel Walker, head of the venereal disease section under the AEF's Office of the Chief Surgeon, himself accompanied American MPs on their rounds over several evenings, where he observed the lower rungs of the red-light district, including the brothels reserved for African American troops.[22] Having sex with a prostitute was almost certainly the most common way for an American soldier to engage in sexual relations in the AEF and among the most common intercultural interactions of any kind for American troops.

By the close of the war, intercultural relationships were a flourishing phenomenon. Even *Stars and Stripes*, the AEF newspaper, acknowledged this, at least tacitly, when the paper advertised a French and English phrase book, "Compree? Je t'aime," described as "16 pages of snappy love stuff." This guide to amorous conversation offered the doughboy Romeo priceless pickup lines—for only five francs! The advertisement questioned soldiers: "Haven't you always wished for a little book that told you how to say in French— 'Where are you going, Bright Eyes? Where do you live?'" and, more directly, "'When can I come to see you?'"[23]

But what did these intercultural couplings mean for the individuals involved? Terse military records seldom provide access to the emotional realm in which such wartime relationships flourished. The motives of American soldiers are especially difficult to document, though possible to surmise from a small but growing number of published personal accounts.[24] It is likely that American men who went out with French women were, to varying degrees, lonely, frightened, bored, lustful, or curious. Journalists observed that the doughboys saw French women as attractive, fun-loving, and attentive to Americans. One marine corporal and his "buddies" found it effortless to pick up "a peachy French blonde apiece" and spend an enjoyable evening running up a food and wine bill at a "swell" restaurant. Other Americans regarded French women, especially those in the countryside, as unattractive but conveniently proximate. Having endured the "rigors of the front," these men were eager to be sexually serviced, one private recounted, and "most of the boys had a very low boiling point anyhow" after months of war. The sexual reputation of French women may have contributed to their allure, creating a curiosity factor for some men who sought their company. Curiosity drew a shy and sheltered young man from Indiana to explore the streets of Paris one night; once there he found the women kind and sympathetic. "They were witty and delighted to talk the little American they knew. . . . I thot they were all beauties," he told his diary, though with some embarrassment he turned down their repeated invitations to accompany them indoors. In more sustained relationships, the type that most often produced marriages, Americans eschewed women with "bad reputations" and sought "respectable" partners who cared for them and provided some of the comforts they missed from home. The high representation of immigrant servicemen among American soldier-husbands points to another motive for men to seek the company of women overseas, the ordinary but pressing work of finding a spouse, a particular challenge in immigrant enclaves in the United States with a highly imbalanced sex ratio.[25]

For their part, European women had many reasons to be attentive to American men in uniform. Intimacies with American soldiers could be bartered for a range of resources and opportunities, some more and some less tangible, Colonel Walker's investigators found. They learned, as well, that some women were intrigued by the Americans and desired their company. Juliette and Andree, born in Algeria and widely traveled, "were in love with Americans and were going to America as soon as possible." Vivienne's interest in Americans combined financial need with a striking political sensibility. A well-bred woman whose family fortunes had collapsed with the war, Vivienne occasionally entertained American officers, whom she appreciated for their money as well as their attitude toward women: "She said that the trouble with France is that the women are slaves of the men," and if French women were to achieve the status of American women, "the only hope is in universal suffrage."[26] Though the war opened greater access to public spaces and new social freedoms to young women in Britain and France, it did not legitimate any "wider claims" to citizenship, historian Susan Grayzel has shown. The financial resources that American soldiers could provide were all the more important in this context of political and economic inequality.[27]

Wartime interviews with Allied women highlighted the immense upheaval of the war, the way it shattered lives and disrupted traditional patterns of social class, gender, and family life. For two sisters, Aimee and Renee, the war instigated a downward spiral of loss and economic instability that also led ultimately to relationships with American soldiers. The women reported that "they had lived at St. Quentin, and . . . a German aero-bomb had struck their home and killed their mother, father, and baby brother. After this they were taken to Germany and made to work at gardening. Along with eleven others they escaped into Switzerland, and after the Armistice they had been repatriated at Evian." Since that time they had worked as chambermaids in Grenoble, but the pay was so poor, only five francs a day, they could not support themselves. In this context, American soldiers looked like a solution to their problems, if only a temporary one. There were numerous American *permissionaires* in town, servicemen on leave, and the sisters began to go out with them. Aimee and Renee were alarmed by the impending departure of American troops, who represented meals, company, and gifts to supplement their meager earnings.[28]

To many local women, American soldiers also looked like "good prospects for a well-to-do marriage." British "Tommies" had previously captured the hearts and hands of many French maidens. But American "Sammies," more glamorous newcomers, were better paid than British "Tommies" and spent their francs lavishly, at least to French eyes. High war mortality meant that marriage opportunities for French women to French men were diminished; this was particularly true for single women in the cohort born between 1891 and 1900, where the sex-ratio imbalance was most pronounced. The French system also did relatively little for women who had lost their providers, even as widows were praised and celebrated as patriotic and self-sacrificing mothers of the republic. These widows, left to fend for themselves, were women like Madame Derancey, a Parisienne, who dated a U.S. army captain after her husband was killed in the war. One historian has estimated a minimum of 600,000 war widows in France in the early 1920s. For a widow, especially one left with young children, a relationship with an American could represent hope for the future.[29]

The war front was a realm of power, exploitation, opportunity, need, and desire; in the absence of more numerous and diverse personal reflections it is only possible to guess at the complex mixture of motives that lay behind the intercultural relationships of World War I. Scarcity, social disruption, fear, and loneliness were the substrate in which relationships between American soldiers and European women took form. But the sources hint as well at the "normalcy" of many of these interactions, as men and women went about the ordinary business of getting their needs met despite the war.

Predatory Females and Innocent American Boys: The AEF Campaign against Foreign Women

If soldiers and women saw various opportunities in their relations with the other, AEF leaders saw nothing but trouble—trouble in the form of venereal disease, breakdown of discipline, bad public relations, and overall moral decline. Repeatedly through the war and demobilization, AEF leaders tried to disrupt soldiers' intercultural liaisons. AEF programs were designed to cajole, coerce, or frighten American soldiers away from local women. AEF policies set up disincentives and obstacles when relationships developed and tried to prevent their formation in the first place by minimizing the opportunities for contact. These efforts were a priority for AEF leaders from the beginning. General Pershing issued his first general order on venereal disease just one week after the first American troops arrived, and a major conference on prostitution was held at command headquarters a few weeks later.[30] The AEF's campaign to stigmatize foreign women was centered in the Social Hygiene Division of the CTCA, but it drew support from many other quarters, including military intelligence and the antivenereal program of the Army Medical Department. The motif of American boys as the victims of predatory women ran through all these efforts, though with an emphasis or coloration that could shift and change according to the race and gender contexts. Despite a strong investment of resources in these programs, however, the AEF had highly imperfect success in keeping Americans away from local women.

Leaders of the effort sought to portray intercultural relationships as not only dishonorable but dangerous as well. One approach was a vigorous public awareness campaign among American troops. Using some of the new techniques of public relations and community education pioneered by social reformers in the Progressive Era, the army advertised the threat, both moral and physical, that foreign women posed. The campaign was conceptualized as a form of self-defense: given the tools of knowledge and information, the soldier could learn to protect himself and others. The information was presented with an urgency that must have had some impact. Posters distributed by the CTCA were a graphic reminder of how dangerous women could be. In one, a soldier's "diseased mind," crammed with tiny lewd pictures, is cut open and revealed to the viewer. A flyer created and distributed to the troops by the army intelligence division warned, "There is a great danger for the soldier even from women most innocent in appearance, so that it is no great exaggeration to consider every woman living in the zone of operations worthy of surveillance."[31] Even casual social interaction with foreign women was presented as a high-risk activity.[32]

Some of the most unsettling of these messages, designed through a collaboration of military intelligence and the Medical Department, merged the themes of sexuality, disease, and danger. Foreign women who slept with American soldiers were "dirty" or "dirty whores." Troops were cautioned that "many gonorrheal and syphilitic women are sent among our soldiers for the express purpose of infecting them and rendering them unfit for military service."[33] If the enemy practiced a kind of biological warfare via women, then the individual soldier risked not just his own safety but the security of his country when he pursued his lustful inclinations. The merging of sexuality, disease, and national security was a particularly ominous and powerful message.

The weakness of a health education approach, however, was that it relied on the active choice of soldiers to work: the men had to hear the message, heed its warnings, and act upon it. On some level, AEF policymakers, even those involved in designing the education campaign, must have recognized that abstinence was an unappealing option for most men. By the army's own account, in fact, a full 71 percent of American troops had sexual relations while serving in the AEF—a figure for internal discussion only.[34]

Publicly, the problem that health officials identified was not the soldiers' indifference to the message but their sexual inexperience. The American was an innocent facing the seductive power of professionals. "The American soldier . . . was no namby-pamby individual when he arrived in Europe," Walker hastened to assure (a coded denial, perhaps, of homosexuality, an anxiety about soldiers that would come to prominence in the military during World War II). Even so, the audacity and aggressiveness of the French streetwalker "was not within the range of his experience," and American boys were no match for her. Walker saw the "gravest of dangers" in the simple "propinquity" of American soldiers and French women; allowing them to be in contact would lead almost inescapably to vice. One enlisted man wryly recalled the sexual health lecture that his unit received every time they went on leave, and its startling reversal of gender roles: "According to the lieutenant, we were in much danger of being raped the minute we put foot on French soil."[35]

Posing the doughboy as essentially passive in such interactions, it became difficult to imagine him actively protecting himself. A safer approach to the "propinquity" problem was social separation, and numerous AEF policies were designed to accomplish this. In Brest and Bordeaux, regional commanders issued orders banning AEF soldiers from appearing on the street with any French female, based on the logic that "no decent girl would go out alone with a man."[36] For much of the war, Paris and other major urban centers were closed to enlisted men on leave. To compensate for these restrictions, Pershing ordered the establishment of a leave area program in the summer of 1917. The YMCA was asked to establish a network of nineteen official leave areas, situated in resort hotels and casinos, where American soldiers could take their seven-day leave. The purpose of the program was explicit: to keep men out of unsupervised locales and offer a morally wholesome alternative to the cities. At the AEF leave areas the men were kept busy with social and leisure activities such as dancing, picnicking, sightseeing, and tennis, all in the company of wholesome American girls employed by the YMCA. American women, who staffed the leave centers as well as the "homelike" canteens situated throughout the war zone, were a linchpin of the AEF effort to safeguard the morals and morale of American troops using constructive means. American women were deployed to cheer the men, to remind them of their duty to womenfolk back home, and to direct them away from "loose French shopgirls" and other potentially dangerous foreign women.[37]

The army's "constructive" program, as embodied in the leave area plan, was widely regarded as a success, credited with reducing venereal rates and raising morale. But AEF leaders were not opposed to employing more invasive techniques to keep soldiers away from women when the constructive approach failed. In Base Section 1, commanders were ordered to classify their men by level of moral fitness and to deny all off-base passes to those of "poor" character.[38] The behavior of American officers, who were subjected to many fewer regulations than enlisted men, was another area of concern. For this reason, military intelligence, the secretive G-2 branch of the AEF command structure, launched a covert program to monitor officers' romantic relationships. French intelligence operatives were borrowed by G-2 to tail American officers who were known to be involved with foreign women. The agents were also assigned to gather personal information on the women, their families, livelihoods, social contacts, and political affiliations. The thousands of reports submitted by G-2 operatives trace the mundane comings and goings of intercultural couples out for a night on the town. Though the stated purpose of the program was to identify female spies working on behalf of the Axis powers, G-2 apparently found the program all but useless in this regard. But investigators easily learned to identify women with entangled or promiscuous private lives, and this exculpatory data they readily shared with the women's American boyfriends. Military intelligence officers were pleased, for example, to report on one of their success stories, that of an American lieutenant engaged to a French woman; called in by G-2, the lieutenant was informed that his bride-to-be was probably a prostitute, who had been seen going in and out of hotels with other men, including her French "boyfriend," an alleged cocaine addict. In the face of this rather overwhelming account of misdeeds, the military intelligence agents felt confident that they had succeeded in breaking up this particular affair.[39]

Underlying these efforts at "soldier protection" was a paternalistic or parental attitude toward American troops that was nearly infantilizing. Female welfare workers for the AEF took on this task with particular earnestness, most tellingly through a secretive "rescue" program run by the YMCA in London and Paris after the armistice (presumably kept secret to hide from home front or evangelical audiences the embarrassing fact that American soldiers were frequenting prostitutes). As the capital cities were made more accessible to American troops, army welfare workers worried about the result. In response, several women workers for the YMCA were evidently given permission to institute an off-the-books program. Trained to approach American soldiers cruising the streets, the women were urged to "rescue" them from bad company. The YMCA's rescue workers were hand-picked for their maturity, firmness, and lack of squeamishness. One, a Miss Bain, was said to have "'rescued' about 1,100 men from dangerous companions."[40] The program was a fascinating twist on the U.S. purity movement's "rescue work" with American prostitutes, but here the men, not the women, were the vulnerable victims.

The AEF leadership was particularly persistent in its efforts to prevent the emergence of relationships between African American soldiers and white European women. But in this instance, guided by deeply embedded American racism, the language of danger and impurity was exactly reversed. It was white French women who were regarded as threatened and vulnerable, black American soldiers who embodied sexual danger and corruption, according to the leaders of the AEF. Policies in regard to the social interactions of black soldiers reflected a keen determination to keep them apart from the white French populace. Black enlisted men and officers were subjected to numerous petty and harassing regulations, backed up by the threat of punishment, and sometimes violence. Entering a French home or conversing with a white French woman were both serious offenses for African American troops. Many cafés and public facilities were placed off-limits to black soldiers only, in order to prevent social interaction. When enlisted men of the Ninety-second "Colored" Division took part in a mixed-race celebration for the Fourth of July, at the invitation of nearby village officials, white officers subjected both blacks and whites to a humiliating public lecture on the necessity of racial segregation. Special regulations for the Ninety-second Division at one time limited the movement of African American soldiers to a one-mile radius around the base. What was behind these seemingly endless harassments, according to historians Arthur Barbeau and Florette Henri, was "the neurotic terror of sex relations between black men and white women," and behind that, ultimately, the fear of "black pretensions to equality."[41]

U.S. military leaders worked hard to convince the French that racial intermingling was a dangerous practice but with little impact, according to nearly all observers, who noted French abhorrence for American-style segregation. If the French attitude itself could not be fundamentally altered, however, then American commanders at least expected the French to honor the "racial sensibilities" of white Americans. This was the thrust of an infamous memo that AEF headquarters distributed to French officers and French civilian officials in areas where African American troops were deployed. "Secret Information Concerning Black American Troops" warned the French "not to spoil the Negroes." Attempting to interpret white American racism for the French, the memo warned that Americans were "outraged" by love and physical intimacy between white women and black men, and explained the Americans' fear of the "race mongrelization" of their homeland.[42]

These crude attempts to sow racial prejudice probably had the opposite of their intended effect. The French indignantly refused to practice Jim Crow against African American troops, to the delight of black soldiers and their advocates, who praised the "absence" of prejudice among French whites. This was far from true. White superiority was a central feature of French colonialism, for example, and the French practiced a form of racial segregation against their own black colonial troops. It is also important to note that no widespread pattern of interracial dating or marriage emerged between French women and African American men during World War I, though individual cases of love across the color line did occur. But the U.S. military's heavy-handed attempts to propagandize prejudice generated sympathy rather than fear among the French. To the French, African American soldiers were temporary visitors, who treated French shopkeepers and civilians with great courtesy and earned broad respect, as well as the courteous and friendly attention of many French women.[43]

Though army officials insisted that "most of the soldiers did not resent this interference at all," the high-handed intervention of commanders in their private lives must indeed have sparked resentment among black and white soldiers alike.[44] In fact, soldiers often seemed to subscribe to a more fluid code of social relations and sexual morality than their commanders wished them to. The fascinating case of Private Harlan Jones suggests this was so. In January 1919, Jones and his pregnant French girlfriend made plans to wed at the hospital center where he was posted, but the relationship aroused the suspicion of the center's commanding officer. Under intensive questioning, Jones and the French woman both conceded that he was not the father of her child, but reaffirmed their desire to marry. Undeterred by the couple's wishes, Jones's immediate and chief commanding officers concluded that the marriage was not "in the best interests of the service, nor of society," and pursued what seemed to them the only sensible and decent course of action: finding the woman's French lover who fathered the child and pressuring him to marry his former partner. In the meantime, the judge advocate's office at AEF headquarters was consulted and reluctantly ruled that the marriage of Jones could not be forbidden if the couple remained insistent. A glib note from Jones's commanding officer to army lawyers told the sad and likely conclusion of this standoff: "Your instructions would of course have been cheerfully obeyed but for the fact that Pvt. Jones was evacuated on January 19 to Le Mans."[45] As this story suggests, military officers had many tools at their disposal as they tried to disrupt relationships overseas. Yet despite the army's best efforts, soldiers and their sweethearts persisted in pursuing romantic liaisons.

Marriage and Marriage Policy in the AEF

The marriage of American soldiers to foreign nationals was a natural outcome of intercultural interaction, but it was one that AEF headquarters was strikingly unprepared to handle. Marriage became a significant preoccupation of AEF officials over the course of the war and the postwar demobilization. Reluctantly, AEF leaders found themselves serving as international marriage brokers, a role they relished little more than they had embraced the role of brothel keeper. Within the AEF there was widespread disagreement about what marriage policy the army should practice and about the legal right of soldiers to marry. On one hand, U.S. leaders were ideologically inclined toward marriage; some even saw the individual's freedom to marry as part of the democratic enterprise that the AEF had come overseas to defend. At the same time, many were concerned that allowing marriage could lead to military inefficiency and jeopardize the successful prosecution of the war. Others feared that women would take advantage of marriage access to gain entry to the United States, using

American soldiers for their own grasping purposes. It was quickly apparent too that marriage was not a freestanding issue. Instead, it was tied to a whole series of unsavory and complicated issues that the U.S. military would have preferred to avoid, such as bigamy, desertion, unwed pregnancy, and illegitimate children.

AEF leaders also learned that marriage policy, like marriage itself, could not be unilateral. America's wartime allies had strong opinions on the subject of relationships between their women and American soldiers, and French and British leaders shared these with their American counterparts. Not surprisingly, the families of women connected to American soldiers also attempted to shape the policies and actions of the AEF to make them more responsive to the needs of women. These lobbying efforts had an effect. During the war General Pershing accepted a legal definition and rationale that established a broad right of American soldiers to marry. Ultimately he went further, to endorse an active role for the U.S. government in the formulation and support of "war bride" marriages.

Within six months of the American army's heralded arrival in France, letters of inquiry about marriage had begun to make their way to AEF headquarters. These inquiries indicate the initial confusion surrounding matrimonial policy for members of the AEF. American soldiers who took the initiative to wed on their own often appeared to do so successfully. Yet intercultural couples who requested official permission to marry from the husband's commanding officer were frequently turned down. In frustration or desperation, dozens of French women, their parents, and fiancées turned directly to General Pershing for assistance. A Mademoiselle Laguzan from Pauillac, for example, told Pershing the whole vexing tale of her wedding, canceled by her fiancé's colonel on the very morning it was to occur. "It is exceedingly painful to me to think that my poor parents have spent and sacrificed such a large sum of money only to see their projects fail so utterly," she wrote, seeking Pershing's sympathy as well as his assistance. Sergeant Orley Hill with the Fifteenth Field Artillery, wrote his commander in chief with trepidation but determination, "I have permission to ask the General for permission to marry. Officers of my regiment cannot give me the permission and I am asking you this great favor Sir. The French authorities say I must have permission from you. Sir hoping to get the permission by mail. . . . I hope this is not asking too much of you Sir."[46] As his letter shows, Sergeant Hill faced a classic runaround by both French and American authorities, and his situation was not unique among aspirants to marriage prior to the armistice.

Some of the more sophisticated U.S. servicemen sought legal advice for this problem in the early months of the U.S. deployment. Attorneys for the Paris office of Coudert Brothers contacted the judge advocate general in December 1917 seeking clarification of the soldier's right to marry overseas. "We are receiving daily letters from American soldiers wishing to contract marriage in France," the attorney wrote. Were such marriages permissible, and did the American soldier require the formal permission of his commanding officer in order to wed? [47] The judge advocate's response was clear and, at least initially, seemed uncomplicated. Marriage was a purely private affair, he wrote, not a military one: "The matter of the marriage of an American soldier to a French or other woman in France was a matter that came under French law and subject entirely to French regulation." With no legal ban in place, American service personnel overseas would necessarily be governed by the marriage laws and regulations of the foreign nation in which the ceremony was to take place. The army would neither consent nor decline consent.[48]

The AEF policy of neutrality in regard to marriage was the official position that the judge advocate's office conveyed in response to the small but steady stream of inquiries it received throughout the first winter and spring of the American Expeditionary Force in France. But in fact, this seemingly unambiguous response masked an internal debate on the matter at AEF headquarters. Opinions were so strong and divided that they led the judge advocate's office to revisit the policy in the late spring of 1918. In June, Brigadier General W. A. Bethel, judge advocate of the AEF, penned a long and thoughtful summary of the issue, among the most interesting and revealing of all government documents related to marriage and the military. Although soldiers in the peacetime army married without interference, Bethel made the case against marriage for soldiers in the current conflict. His central argument, a simple one indeed, was that marriage was disruptive of good military order and authority, in the judge advocate's words, "prejudicial to military interests . . . under present conditions." Allowing marriage could presumably get in the way of the AEF's overriding mission, namely, to win the war.[49] Bethel therefore advocated a war zone marriage ban for members of the army for the duration of the conflict. Acknowledging, however, that such a ban would be impossible within the current legal framework, Bethel proposed "action at the highest level"—probably the War Department or White House—to enact a ban.

Bethel's position conformed with the opinion of AEF unit commanders, who exhibited little patience or sympathy for the romantic undertakings of their men. One salty cavalry colonel voiced his disgust to the AEF commander in chief: "When Pvt. W asked permission to marry I refused, as I did in other cases, on the ground that this was no time to be undertaking new responsibilities and obligations; that we were over here to fight when the time came; and to spend the rest of the time getting ready for it and not to marry and raise families." The colonel warned against creating precedents and giving bad ideas to other soldiers: " If Pvt. W. is allowed to marry this girl it will lead to a number of other cases just exactly like this." The colonel concluded darkly, "I have been through the whole thing twice before in Cuba and the Philippines."[50] It is not surprising that many field officers found marriage, and all that preceded and followed it, to be disruptive of discipline and distracting from the war. In their eyes, a marriage ban was also a natural extension of all the other policies they had erected to separate U.S. soldiers from local women. Allowing their men to marry the women they were not supposed to be dating they saw as rewarding insubordinate behavior.

Supporters of a marriage ban pointed out that soldiers had many types of personal liberties taken away in military service—more in this war than in any previous one. These recent abridgments included the right to drink alcohol and, of course, the very fundamental right to choose or refuse military service, taken away by the Selective Service system. Likewise, Bethel pointed out that female family members of soldiers had been barred from the war zone per order of the commander in chief, AEF: no wives were allowed to cross over; even sisters were banned from the AEF, a stringent and costly requirement that ended up wreaking havoc with nursing recruitment. A policy that forbade the taking of new wives in the war zone seemed consistent with the policy of banning wives from home.

There were numerous practical arguments then in favor of a marriage ban. But Bethel was careful to acknowledge that ideology tended to point in the opposite direction, and to his credit, he also provided a detailed review of arguments on the other side. One key consideration was the U.S. government's general bias in favor of marriage. As Bethel pointed out, "The matter of prohibiting marriage is a very delicate one, since it is the policy of our country to encourage matrimony"—an assertion with which historians have concurred.[51] The pro-marriage position was no mere platitude coming from Bethel, who rendered two important decisions in favor of marital rights during the course of the war. Both decisions reflected an official bias in favor of matrimony and a liberal interpretation of the law to favor marriage.[52]

Furthermore, Bethel noted, marriage was a matter of American freedom, an arena in which federal interference in citizens' lives was to be kept to a minimum. This applied to the rights of both states and individuals. In regard to individuals, "the view has always been taken that marriage is a personal privilege with which the government, in general, has no right to interfere"— a startling statement in light of the ban on interracial marriage in so many U.S. states. In regard to the states, the governance of marriage had long been a state prerogative, and the federal government had historically abided by the complex and varied network of state laws regulating matrimony.

By identifying marriage as an American freedom, Bethel was echoing a view of the marital bond that had deep roots in Anglo-American history, law, and culture. Historian Nancy Cott has shown that self-government and mutual consent were intrinsic to the American marriage ideal, marking its connection to the nation's political ideology. Popular culture of the war period echoed this view, celebrating the American way of marriage as free and patriotic. One magazine fiction writer, for example, pointed to the contrast between free and consensual American marriage and the corrupt and autocratic marital bond allegedly practiced in Germany.[53] As an individual right and a democratic institution, American-style marriage could even be regarded as one of the freedoms being fought for in this struggle for democracy.

Finally, Bethel pointed out that a marriage ban might put a strain on Allied relations. Concerned that U.S. actions not be construed as an insult to French women, Bethel cautioned, "I think it is very important to make it clear . . . that there is absolutely no prejudice against matrimonial alliances between the American and French people—that such restrictions that are imposed are a military measure for the purpose of aiding both people in winning the war." He thought it important to reassure the French that the ban applied only for the duration and would be lifted with enthusiasm after the conclusion of the war. And with diplomatic flair, he proposed that the ban might be reconceived as tightening rather than straining the Franco-American alliance as it underscored the common sacred purpose of the two peoples, of transcendent importance over and above the desires of individuals on either side.

Pershing read Bethel's memo with apparent care and interest, but he disagreed with his judge advocate's recommendation in favor of an AEF marriage ban. In his personal response to Bethel, General Pershing affirmed the liberal position, that the right to marry was an important American freedom, one that should not be denied to members of the armed forces. Pershing's willingness to stand for marriage, even in the face of opposition from his officer corps, was a reflection of his biography as well as his political philosophy. Even before his appointment to lead U.S. forces in Europe, John J. Pershing was one of the most popular and admired public figures of his generation, known not only for his military leadership in the Philippine war, but also for the heroically tragic circumstances of his personal life. On 27 August 1915, a fire at the Presidio army base in San Francisco destroyed the Pershings' residence. Home alone with the children at the time, his wife, Frankie, and three young daughters perished, leaving son Warren, then six years of age, as the only survivor. In the loss of his family, Pershing became an almost mythic husband and father figure and an emblem of family devotion. This was the reputation he carried when Wilson appointed him commander in chief of the AEF (an ironic image given his personal taste for nonmarital affairs).[54] There is evidence too that Pershing liked and cultivated his image as the paterfamilias of the American forces in France, frequently using family imagery in his communication with his troops.[55] Pershing's defense of marriage in the AEF was consistent with his iconic public image as a husband and family man.

Perhaps Pershing also recognized something that Bethel did not: that the AEF's laissez-faire marriage policy did a fairly thorough job of suppressing marriage, even while it shielded the army from the controversy that a ban proposal would almost certainly have prompted. Unit commanders found a wide variety of ways to prevent their men from marrying (some of them even suggested by the judge advocate's office in response to officers' inquiries). The simplest, denying the groom his leave requests, was perhaps the most effective, as it would force the soldier to go AWOL if he wished to attend his own wedding—and, indeed, several soldiers faced military imprisonment for this very cause. French marriage law placed an even greater set of obstacles in front of the would-be couple. Two aspects of the law in particular proved difficult for many Americans. Under French law, the partners in a marriage were each required to produce an *état civil*, or civil status certificate, proving their age and identity; such civil registration, however, was not required in the United States, and many American soldiers were unable to produce birth certificates or other legal proof of identity that satisfied the law. The French legal code also required the publication of banns at the soldier's place of residence prior to the wedding; this public declaration of intent, based in the practice of the medieval church, was intended to determine the couple's "competence to marry" by allowing information on prior marriages, if any, to surface in advance. Because there existed no counterpart to this procedure in the United States, American soldiers were usually at a loss when it came to compliance with this feature of the law, though some devised alternatives.[56]

Even as AEF officials debated the pros and cons of a marriage ban, the topic of Franco-American and, to a lesser extent, Anglo-American marriage was gathering steam as a minor diplomatic crisis. For the French government, the problem of American soldiers marrying French women paled alongside their *failure* to do so, or to do so legitimately. The French ambassador in Washington first raised the issue with the U.S. Departments of State and War in December 1917. French government officials had become alarmed that the inability of French women to contract marriage with their American beaux had "produced a very unfortunate state of affairs as regards legitimacy of a child" produced by these relationships. Reports of French women, pregnant and abandoned by American lovers, fed this alarm. They voiced concern, too, that, unscrupulous married men with wives far away in the States would misrepresent themselves as being available. In the French view, young women were being "imposed upon" by American "Sammies," lured into sexual relationships with the promise of marriage and then abandoned.[57] The French reaction was almost certainly shadowed by the earlier, tempestuous social debate over the "bastard" children of the German invaders. Ruth Harris has shown that discourse about "children of the barbarians" was a symbolic way for the French nation to talk about the cultural and political impotence that French men experienced in the early part of the war, as their country was "penetrated" by the enemy. Whether French women had offered themselves to these outsiders or been brutally raped was a matter of much discussion. Either way, French men feared that the French family, the mainstay of the nation, was being undermined by the sexual activities, and especially the pregnancies, of French women.[58]

Naturally, the French public held a far more negative view of the "barbarian children" of "Hun" soldiers than those produced by liaisons with Allied soldiers—but only worse in a matter of degree. Demographics and population decline had long been a political issue for the French, one closely tied to nationalism and ethnic and religious identity. The French worried about the onslaught of a million and more American doughboys and the impact of their presence on French society. The sexual mores of the Americans were also a French concern, as it turned out (even as the American public worried about the sexual mores of the French). In preparing for their negotiations with the U.S. government, the French foreign ministry had researched U.S. marriage law and found much that was disturbing, especially the ease of divorce and the legal recognition of common-law marriage, which in the French view amounted to social sanction for "concubinage." French government officials were anxious to establish some protections for French women as they ventured into relationships with another set of potentially threatening men.

It is interesting that the specter of exploitation that horrified the French was precisely the one described so glibly in "Quand La Guerre Est Fini," probably the most popular of all doughboy songs from the First World War. In each of the versions passed around by American troops, the mademoiselle is left alone at war's end, with a "souvenir" baby to remind her of the Americans:

> Aprés la guerre fini,
> Les Americains partis,
> Mademoiselle seul au lit,
> Bouncing the new baby,

Or in another version,

> Aprés la guerre fini,
> Les Americains partis,
> Laissez les pauvres Françaises
> Un souvenir Bébé.[59]

This scenario might seem amusing to some American soldiers, but it was increasingly a source of anger for the French and British. As allies became vocal about their concerns, the pressure grew for Pershing to respond with a set of policies that would actively facilitate the marriages of French and British women to American soldiers rather than passively watch them flounder. French women and their families were particularly persistent and effective advocates for their rights and needs in the sometimes fragile relationships they had forged with Americans. French civilians succeeded in pressuring the American Red Cross to establish a procedure to help families gather information on the moral reputation of individual American soldiers betrothed to their daughters (the Red Cross refused to investigate a soldier's moral reputation behind his back but agreed with his consent to provide letters of support from his hometown community, pointing out that the man who refused to cooperate might be regarded as suspect).[60] French families also took their stories and concerns directly to AEF headquarters, lodging complaints against individual soldiers and military commanders, calling for justice, and demanding redress. The judge advocate's staff logged dozens of their complaints and pleas: "Says soldier left her sister and failed to marry as promised—left her pregnant. Asks if soldier can be brought to justice"; "Writes that soldier above failed in his promise to marry her and left her alone in the world to care for a child"; "Requests marriage to soldier who is father of child to be born"; "Asks that officer be compelled to support her and her child—or at least her child, soon expected."[61]

These stories were compelling, and also potentially embarrassing to a national army with a reputation for moral rectitude. Wilson administration officials at the highest levels became alarmed, as well, by more general rumors and negative views of American troops that were coming to their attention. From England, U.S. consular officials kept tabs on growing dissatisfaction and complaints about American soldiers deserting wives and children. "These cases of deserted girls are becoming increasingly frequent, and supply a real cause in a large circle of English people for disaffection with the United States," the American consul general in London cautioned the U.S. secretary of state. He pointed out that one case had become something of a cause célèbre in Great Britain, tarnishing opinions of the Americans. An American enlisted man named Dupres had married an English woman he met in the service, but upon his return to the United States he evidently experienced a change of heart. Dupres forbade his wife from joining him in the United States and insisted she file for divorce. The woman's plight had come to public attention in Great Britain, eliciting outrage.[62] The American consul felt the crisis was sufficiently acute that it demanded comprehensive action on the part of the State Department, specifically a campaign to teach American soldiers who wed in Europe the weighty "responsibilities they have assumed," as far too many believed they could marry abroad and then "pursue the matter no further." The secretary of war felt compelled to intervene when the case and others like it came to the attention of the U.S. Senate Committee on Military Affairs.[63]

As the problem of deserted wives threatened to become a public relations fiasco for the United States, efforts to resolve the Allied dispute over marriage intensified. Fourteen months of transatlantic negotiation involving the State Department, War Department, French ambassador, interalliance, and AEF headquarters staff finally yielded an agreement in early 1919. Pershing's new policy on soldier marriage was a historically significant departure. AEF Bulletin 26 introduced procedures to facilitate and streamline marriage and to ensure its legitimacy. American officers would now for the first time be directly involved in the process, by certifying that a soldier under their command was eligible for marriage—that is, not already legally married to someone else. If the American soldier was divorced, the commanding officer must produce legal proof of this. Simultaneously, the French government agreed to accept the sworn affidavit of an American officer in place of the traditional marital requirements for American soldiers with the AEF.[64] The flood of intercultural marriages that followed the armistice was undoubtedly accelerated and even expanded by the new procedures.

The incident taught a number of important lessons. Struggles over marriage brought American servicemen into involvement with French civilians and local communities in entirely new ways. U.S. soldiers learned that they could exercise certain kinds of power in their relations with foreign civilians, but that power also operated under certain constraints. Civilian and military leaders learned that intercultural relationships could strain international relations, and that the behavior of American troops overseas would be closely scrutinized, even interpreted as an indication of what the larger society was about. Though Pershing had been reluctant to take on the issue of marriage during the fighting, a stream of communication from Secretary of War Baker had persuaded him to address it. The concerns of allies and the potential for embarrassment to the AEF's reputation had been the strongest factors in reaching a resolution and designing a more marriage-friendly policy.

The policy, it should be noted, however, had important limitations. Only a small handful of interracial marriage requests emerged during World War I, or at least came to the attention of AEF headquarters, so few that the matter elicited little sustained discussion, internal or external. But the response of military commanders to these few cases suggests the emergence of a racial double standard in soldier marriage. A case that made this clear was that of a Filipino American private who wished to marry a very young German girl with whom he had lived in Coblenz for two years and fathered two children. Not only was his application rejected, but army commanders explored the possibility of charging him with statutory rape—although white soldiers married white European women of the same age without obstacle. The handful of cases involving soldiers of color anticipated what would become a major cause of conflict in the late 1940s. Likewise, the question of marriage to "enemy" German brides was also left to be resolved in the aftermath of World War II.[65]

Relationships between U.S. soldiers and local women were an unavoidable consequence of a foreign war, as AEF leaders came to recognize. Although moral reformers, soldiers' kin, and military commanders would have liked such relationships to be suppressed, government and military leaders came to see that U.S. troops could not be brought overseas in a protected bubble.

The extent and complexity of the problems that these relationships generated took AEF leaders by surprise. In particular, the vexed response of Allied
leaders, who acted to protect their "own" women from harm by American
troops, was a spur to U.S. action. Over the course of the war and demobilization, military leaders were compelled to respond by articulating policies to
facilitate the marriage of American soldiers abroad, creating a crucial precedent for subsequent American wars.

2

"The Worst Kind of Women"

Foreign War Brides in 1920s America

Most of the Franco-American war unions [were] marriages in haste, under impulse of abnormal excitement and of ignorance. . . . The way of the foreign war bride, if one is to judge by periodic reports that have appeared during the last five years, has not been smooth. . . . marriages have not measured up to the average of marital success in America. The brides have not been happy.

John Ellingston, *New York Times Magazine*, 2 August 1925

The arrival of more than 5,000 European war brides in U.S. ports by the early 1920s generated both interest and controversy. Katherine Hardwick, a field representative for the American Red Cross in Boston, was one of the first Americans to meet the newcomers. Delighted by the seven French wives she initially welcomed, Hardwick expressed optimism about the prospects for soldiers' foreign-born brides and for their new country: "We feel that girls like these, strong, honest, and young, with all their fascinating little manners, their charming courtesy and considerations, are real assets for America." Elizabeth Hutchin, another Red Cross worker, was deeply critical instead: "When I say that my personal feeling is that we are all co-operating in making entrance into America extremely easy for a far from desirable class of citizens, I am expressing myself with the utmost restraint!"[1]

"War bride" as a special category of female immigrant was constructed in the postwar period through the efforts of military and civilian agencies to care for and transport soldiers' wives to the United States. "War bride" as a cultural construct was also under development in this era. The intercultural marriages of the First World War embodied some of the most contentious political and social issues of the postwar era. The war brides arrived at a moment when women were on the cusp of enfranchisement in the United States, and feminists sought to clarify and extend the boundaries of female citizenship.[2]

| 39

Simultaneously, the United States was engaged in a sweeping debate over the place of the foreign-born in American society, as Congress pondered unprecedented immigration restrictions. War brides were both immigrants and new female citizens, and as such their presence came under intense scrutiny. The women were closely observed by social workers, military officials, journalists, and immigration agents; their marriages, moral standards, and loyalty were weighed carefully. Americans considered the crucial question of assimilation, asking whether foreign brides, most of whom were French, were capable of becoming good American wives. In the nativist atmosphere of the postwar United States, many Americans shared journalist John Ellingston's conviction that the "fundamental gulf between Latin and Anglo-Saxon society" posed an insoluble barrier to the success of intercultural couples.

Marriages between American soldiers and foreign women gave concrete, physical reality to the question of how World War I had altered the nation and the men who had fought "over there." These marital alliances often stood as a metaphor for the future of international alliances in the postwar era. Americans interpreted intercultural relationships as a story about themselves in relation to foreign others, but what the story meant and how it was told differed across the political spectrum. To a small but important band of liberals and internationalists, the story was a romance that held out the possibility of a happy ending. If French, Russian, British, and even German brides could be embraced by American husbands and their families and communities, then, by extension, the future looked bright for internationalism. To many more Americans, the story of the war brides from overseas was a cautionary tale, suggesting that "getting into bed" with people of other countries would weaken the United States and undermine its moral underpinnings. These women were reputed to be "gold diggers," conniving foreigners who exploited innocent, even naïve, American soldiers. This sentiment echoed and reinforced the language of immigration restrictionists, who contended that foreigners had for too long "taken advantage" of American openness and generosity. Like unregulated immigration in general, critics intimated, these alien marriages were likely to lead to sexual immorality, prostitution, crime, venereal disease, and "racial" degradation.

For internationalists and nationalists alike, these wartime marriages carried a message about the United States in relation to that which was foreign. Americans of all political stripes applied preconceived notions about ethnicity, identity, and citizenship to the phenomenon of intercultural marriage. But the international couples of the First World War did not necessarily represent the amalgamation of cultural and ethnic differences that Americans thought they were observing at the time. Visa data long buried in State Department files suggest that many of the "American boys" who brought home foreign brides were themselves foreign-born, or came from closely knit immigrant enclaves in the United States. While most Americans fretted about these reputedly mismatched couples, the partners were often very similar in background, age, and experience. Absorbed into the family and community lives of their husbands, the foreign-born brides of the Great War were hardly the threatening or disruptive element that many Americans had predicted they would be.

War Brides and the American Expeditionary Force

Foreign-born wives of U.S. servicemen, who at this time became U.S. citizens through marriage, presented an unexpected challenge to American Expeditionary Force (AEF) commanders as they planned the demobilization of U.S. forces in the early winter of 1919. The leadership of the AEF's logistics branch, the Services of Supply (SOS), initially stumbled in its attempts to respond to the needs of foreign spouses. By the end of the demobilization process, however, the AEF had gone decisively into the business of housing, feeding, supervising, and shipping war brides home. It was during this supervisory interval that U.S. officials created the immigration category of "war bride." The new structures that the AEF designed represented novel forms of military responsibility for civilian dependents. These structures, which involved both the provision of basic services and new forms of surveillance and control, became the model for the military's work with foreign spouses during World War II. The period of supervision also brought a number of U.S. personnel, both military and civilian, into close contact with foreign war brides for the first time. Their impressions of the women established preconceptions that continued to shape the war bride debate long after 1919.

Fourteen British brides and one baby—William Lewis Jr., born in London—left the port of Brest on board the transport *Plattsburg* in the third week of January 1919. Their journey to the United States attracted attention from newspapers across the nation, which covered the story of the first foreign war brides from shore to shore.[3] A month earlier, the AEF had announced a policy of providing free transport to the United States for military spouses and children; space as available would be allotted to war brides on government-owned or chartered vessels.[4] Some of the earliest recipients of this largesse were officers who had been reassigned to stateside positions after the armistice, many of whom could have afforded first-class accommodations for their wives on commercial ocean liners. In early February, for example, the Irish bride of Dr. Paul Withington, Army Medical Corps, boarded the military transport *Louisville*. Withington, former captain of the Harvard track team and a physician at Boston's prestigious Peter Bent Brigham Hospital, had met Daphne Beckham when her British volunteer aid detachment was assigned to his base hospital in France.[5] Marriages between American and British citizens were not unusual among upper-class families, and but for the war angle, the Withingtons' marriage could have appeared on the society page of a Boston newspaper. This elite couple was very different from those who began to gather in the French ports of embarkation. Army welfare workers worried that growing numbers of war brides arrived "penniless," with soldier-husbands, many already returned to the United States, who could not afford to provide sufficient funds for their wives while the women awaited transportation.

To meet the needs of this expanding group, SOS headquarters turned to the American YWCA in France, whose work with AEF nurses and telephone operators had impressed General Pershing. The YWCA struggled to respond, but the needs were many. Housing was scarce, and rents and restaurant prices were sky-high in the port cities of Le Havre, Saint-Nazaire, Bordeaux, and Brest, crowded with AEF soldiers and civilian personnel waiting to ship out for home. The YWCA converted several of its "hostess houses," which had been established to provide services to the thousands of American women with the AEF, into temporary shelters for foreign wives and made small "emergency" loans to brides and husbands who had exhausted their personal funds.[6] Almost immediately, hostess house staff found themselves overwhelmed. In one two-week period, for example, the YWCA house at Brest hosted ninety "foreign young women, brides, or fiancées"; most were French, but the group included Belgians, Italians, Russians, Greeks, Luxembourgians, and Portuguese, the majority of whom spoke no English. In addition, the house welcomed six young children, one only six weeks old, and a dog traveling with a bride for her soldier-husband. The limited resources of the YWCA facilities were quickly depleted.[7]

The concerns voiced by YWCA staff members were echoed by other welfare workers and army officials in the ports of embarkation. AEF personnel were frustrated by the lack of clear policies and coordination. Some brides awaiting transport were ill, and many were pregnant, yet no medical care was available to them. Supervision at the point of assignment to transportation was lax and the rules confusing. Ships were departing with too few beds for too many brides. Officials reported that some women had been allowed to board without proof of marriage, stoking the concern that fiancées or even more questionable women were taking advantage of a free ride to the United States.[8] Particularly distressing to SOS headquarters staff was the case of a mother-in-law who was carelessly booked onto a U.S. military transport. This mistake brought a stern warning from the G-1 chief of staff: the war brides program was not intended for family reunification, and no one but authorized and duly married wives should be sent.[9] By early summer, the SOS was receiving criticism on multiple fronts, and some of these problems threatened to reach public awareness. Captains of transport vessels complained that brides and their children were difficult to manage; most were simply sick and miserable from the voyage, but others, characterized as "highly undesirable" or "thoroughly disreputable" women, were "disruptive" to the crew. Immigration and welfare officials at New York ports of arrival cabled AEF headquarters in France to complain that women were arriving infected with venereal disease, and therefore inadmissible to the country; that wives unaccompanied by soldier-husbands were often unclaimed at the ports with insufficient information to locate their erstwhile spouses, or had even been given false addresses. U.S. soldiers joined the chorus of complaint. Doughboy husbands insisted that officers and their foreign wives were given special privileges. U.S. soldiers without foreign wives complained that men who had married foreigners received unfair privileges and priority transportation.[10]

The imputation of sexual immorality to war brides caused the greatest alarm at SOS headquarters. A confidential report from the Atlantic division of the National American Red Cross warned sharply that the "moral situation [on the transport ships] would certainly seem serious enough to warrant immediate action by the War and State Departments in order to safeguard the soldiers." The report insinuated, with little or no evidence, that prostitutes had slipped in among the "decent" brides, and many of the women were "of very questionable character." SOS leaders knew that any public impression that the army was undertaking a boatlift of prostitutes with U.S. tax dollars was political poison. If such a rumor circulated, even if it could be disproved, the embarrassment to the AEF could be considerable. In an inept attempt to head off such a perception before it emerged, the SOS commanding general's office issued a new order on 7 June 1919: every foreign bride of an enlisted man must be prepared to furnish a sworn statement from her husband's commanding officer attesting to her "reputable character" before she boarded ship for the United States. At the same time, the SOS issued secret telephonic instructions to the port commanders to detain in Europe all women who tested positive for venereal disease.

Unfortunately for the AEF leadership, these measures only exacerbated the problem. When word reached the press that the army would now require character investigations of soldiers' wives, eyebrows were raised. "Yank Must Prove French Wife Has Good Character," announced one paper sensationally; "New Order Refuses to Take Girls to U.S. Unless They're Ladies." Far from instilling confidence, the order called attention to the problem while exacerbating social class tensions in the army, as doughboys pointed out that wives of officers were assumed to be ladies without proof.[11]

By early summer, AEF officials recognized that the makeshift system for handling foreign spouses was breaking down under the matrimonial onslaught. Not only did they acknowledge that they had failed to treat the matter with sufficient care or seriousness, but they realized that they had no idea how many more women to expect or how to accommodate them. War Department officials in Washington, who had been briefed on the matter, added to the sense of urgency by forwarding their disapproval to AEF headquarters. Anxious to stem the tide of negative publicity, the SOS acted decisively in May and June 1919 to rationalize the system and address the concerns of army welfare workers, the War Department, and the public.[12] First, SOS headquarters at Tours issued a new order requiring that, whenever possible, husbands and foreign wives travel to the United States aboard the same vessels. Next, SOS commanders asked the AEF welfare agencies to provide competent female chaperones on board ships carrying a substantial number of war brides. In an unprecedented move, the army's medical service agreed to admit foreign wives to U.S. army medical facilities for treatment of tuberculosis, influenza, and other illnesses though they insisted that pregnancy per se was not a morbid condition requiring hospitalization, as some military commanders had suggested it should be.[13]

The most notable policy development was the establishment of three military holding camps for war brides, a formative instance of military supervision of civilians on U.S. overseas bases. The first camp, at Saint-Nazaire, was placed in operation on May 17, 1919. The camp at Bordeaux opened at the end of May on the site of a former hospital barracks. The largest of the facilities, Camp Bouguen outside of Brest, was set up to accommodate 500 women at a time. The women at Bouguen were carefully supervised by a large staff hired by the YWCA. The army provided two physicians, one dentist, and three nurses, although the women preferred the YWCA's female physician for the physical examinations they were required to undergo.[14]

The sprawling army camps were an enormous change from the home-like hostess houses previously operated by the YWCA. The camp at Brest was organized around a string of sleeping barracks, each with army cots and brown wool blankets for fifty or more women. One barrack was set aside as a nursery and outfitted with wooden boxes for the babies; another housed women with their older children. Though the staff tried to hang flowered curtains at the windows of all the sleeping quarters, a military atmosphere prevailed. Order was maintained through military-style discipline. Each morning an army officer conducted an inspection of the brides in their barracks. One Red Cross worker at Bouguen remarked on the pitiable contrast between the young brides' "romantic ideals . . . of future happiness" and the "crude and unromantic" conditions at the army facilities. At Bordeaux the YWCA workers had initially planned for genteel dining with table service and linen cloths, but almost immediately they were forced to transform their dining hall into an army mess with cafeteria lines and dish-scraping stations. The heavy load of kitchen work in the mess halls overwhelmed the YWCA's plans, as war bride details proved unable or unwilling to keep up with the heavy labor. Army officials stepped in with a solution, assigning squads of soldier-husbands to "kitchen patrol" (KP). Though the plan seemed equitable to everyone else, some of the men reportedly groused about washing dishes for their wives.[15]

Women were moved through the camps as quickly as possible, sometimes in as few as four days, but the complex logistics of the army transport system meant that some women were "guests" of these army camps for weeks. The war brides waited eagerly for word of their departure. Excitement in the camps "rose to a high pitch just before embarkation days," one YWCA worker recounted, and "everyone rallied around to help those lucky brides who were sailing." The women were sent once again for physical examinations. Under the sway of the Red Scare, then at fever pitch in the United States, the women were required to have their baggage searched and swear to the statement that they carried no bombs or explosives.[16] As they boarded a U.S. military transport, the war brides' journey to a new life in the United States began at last.

"Undesirable Immigrants": The AEF Judges the War Brides

By the late fall of 1919, the majority of wives had been processed, and the deluge of new brides had begun to slow. All work with foreign wives was transferred to the army's embarkation office in Antwerp, where two YWCA workers handled social and civilian support work for the U.S. army of occupation in Coblenz, Germany, from February to the end of August 1921. The Antwerp staff made individual transport arrangements for war brides from numerous countries, including Germany. They also worked with a number of U.S. soldiers who had originally requested demobilization in France in order to stay with their French girlfriends, wives, or children. Some of these soldiers had found it impossible to obtain jobs in economically depressed postwar Europe and, with or without their French families, wished to return to the United States. Evidently these vagrant American soldiers were a source of embarrassment to U.S. army officials, who volunteered to ship them home even though the men had already relinquished their right to assistance.[17]

As the war bride program in Europe wound down, the AEF personnel who oversaw the program reflected on their experiences, both formally and informally. Army medical corps and transport service personnel and the many female auxiliary workers for the AEF welfare agencies had front-row seats from which to observe the new intercultural relationships that the war had wrought, and their initial reactions had a significant influence on later perceptions and policy regarding war brides as newcomers to the United States.[18] Some AEF personnel viewed the foreign wives with considerable sympathy. YWCA workers in Brest prepared a six-point memo for their U.S. headquarters recommending programs that the organization could implement stateside in order to offer the brides personal support: asking local YWCA secretaries in the brides' new hometowns "to immediately find someone who understands the language to act as brides' friend and interpreter," for example, and making "it possible for the girl to receive French literature, either magazines or papers, after reaching America." These suggestions showed awareness of the sense of displacement the newcomers were likely to experience and empathy for their homesickness. They also reflected the broader outlook of the YWCA, which was known for its enlightened internationalism during the interwar period and for its service to foreign-born women, both in the United States and overseas.[19]

More typically, however, AEF personnel expressed various degrees of resentment toward these new Americans, often in nationalistic and even racialized terms. The director of the American Red Cross Home Service Bureau in Paris, who warned her U.S.-based superiors that the brides were a "far from desirable class of citizens," lobbied the army to "cease to furnish transportation" for foreign wives. An AEF welfare worker from Georgia shared her observation that "mixed marriages, unions between girls of other nationalities and American boys, do not, as a rule, bring happiness. The countries are too widely separated in customs, in traditions," adding that "a carefully brought up, well bred girl does not marry a man she has met once or twice." Frequently, social welfare workers argued that many of the brides would not have been admissible to the country on their own standing—an insinuation that they were "immoral." To one civilian working in a busy army office, marriages between American men and French women could only be explained in terms of seduction: "This place is filled with perfectly beautiful French stenographers. . . . They speak beautifully accented English, and give the young men a time." This American woman could not hide her disappointment and even disgust as she observed one romance turn into a marriage. The groom was a handsome American lieutenant, the bride a French stenographer. "Too bad. He's such a nice boy. I'd as soon marry a coon as a French person," she commented, employing a common racial slur and placing French people in the same undesirable category as African Americans.[20]

AEF women's hostility toward European brides may have arisen from the sexual and social competition between them for American soldiers' attention and affections, as some contemporary observers thought to be the case. "Most of the Red Cross and Y.M.C.A. girls are very fine people, but, as a whole, they could not be called good-looking, and they wear their uniforms poorly," one American war worker explained; in contrast, the "French girls" are "chic always." Yet American men in the AEF often expressed similarly judgmental or negative attitudes toward foreign brides and their comrades who had married the women. "An American married *that*?" was the succinct and telling comment that male transport workers made upon seeing some of the brides—a put-down laden with both gender and nationalist biases.[21]

The diary of one army welfare worker assigned to the war bride service during demobilization gives a rich and unfiltered picture of the complex relationships among American men, American women, and foreign brides in the AEF. Ruth Beane, a YWCA secretary from Lewiston, Maine, was assigned to the war bride camps at Bordeaux and Brest and chaperoned a multicultural transport of Russian, German, Belgian, French, Italian, English, and Irish war brides to the United States in November 1919. Beane developed warm personal relationships with individual women, but she describes the group as "the worst kind of women such as I never saw before coming to France." American soldiers, she and the other staff members believed, had too often chosen brides from a "bad class" of women. Beane's diary is rife with descriptions of stealing, hair pulling, smoking, swearing, and fistfights among the brides. She deplores the women's uncleanness and lack of cooperation in matters of hygiene, especially the staffs' efforts to rid them of "cooties" (body lice).

The AEF staff's patronizing sense of duty toward war brides blended easily with their assumption of a right to control them. Beane noted that one

American husband on the ship had lodged a complaint to the colonel about the procedure for morning inspection of the brides' bunks. "He said he did not want an officer going into his wife's cabin" when she was alone. The man's plea for protection of his wife's privacy was dismissed as absurd, rather than insubordinate, because the crew regarded his "cross-eyed . . . and filthy dirty" wife as too unattractive to warrant the husband's concern or their own regard. Another of Beane's stories epitomizes the troubling sense of class and cultural superiority that Americans brought to their work with foreign women. Conducting their evening inspection of the brides' sleeping quarters one night, Beane and her coworker were upset to find a British woman asleep in her clothes. They woke her up and insisted she undress and put on a nightgown while they waited. This humiliating procedure revealed the reason for the woman's reluctance to change; her underwear was foul-smelling. The American workers derided the woman's embarrassed explanation for the odor: "But I have a nasty discharge from me insides." They "scolded her for having such dirty clothes" and made her finish undressing so they could dispose of her offending undergarments. Beane's diary, written for the private reading of family and friends, reveals a deeply unexamined strain of condescension and distrust of foreigners and their alien ways among the staff of a typical U.S. army transport.

AEF personnel reserved their strongest vitriol for marriages between German women and U.S. soldiers. "Enemy" women aroused suspicion and hostility that matrimony and the citizenship it conferred did nothing to dispel. The YWCA's Antwerp staff did not disguise their outrage, even in official reports. "We are sending [German brides] home, . . . at government expense and on the same transports with the bodies of American dead," Maude Cleveland wrote to her U.S. supervisors in an emotionally fraught memo. German brides were women of low morals, she alleged, who had met their American husbands in "cheap cafés" and on street corners. Although Cleveland was the head of war bride work at the Antwerp office, she bridled at the task of caring for these women. Particularly distasteful to Cleveland was the idea of using funds "collected from the American people to 'help America win the war'" to provide succor and support to "enemy brides," which placed the organization in the position of "encouraging the importation of undesirable immigrants, in a majority of cases enemy aliens." Cleveland found support for her views from the highest leadership of the American Forces in Germany (AFG): Major General Henry T. Allen, commander of the AFG, had a deep suspicion of the German populace and believed that "a certain class" of German families purposefully exposed their daughters to pregnancy in order to "secure" American husbands. Allen took repeated action to prevent and disrupt German-American marriage. Army lawyers in Washington tried to set these critics straight; for better or worse, they pointed out, soldiers were permitted to marry, and their "enemy wives" became U.S. citizens, entitled to the same consideration as American-born wives. While U.S. officials working in Germany complied with War Department directives, they broadcast their concern about German-American marriages in terms that reverberated well into the postwar period.[22]

Marriages between foreign women and American soldiers had little validity, Cleveland asserted, for they were based not on love but on opportunism. "Living in Europe is hard, America is rich," she pointed out bluntly but perceptively, and "the plum of free transportation is tempting even to those who are not unscrupulous." Other war bride workers echoed this view, reporting that wives sometimes "admitted to us they had married simply to obtain free passage." Scattered reports of brides who showed no interest in finding their husbands once they arrived in New York reinforced the anxiety that soldiers and their Uncle Sam were being taken for a ride in more than one sense. Other American workers raised concern that brides were exploiting the generosity of the welfare agencies, requesting assistance they did not need or squandering grants on luxuries. The story of one British bride with considerable fund-raising talent made its way into several AEF communications:

> It is said that this girl had eight pounds given her by the Red Cross. . . . When she reached Southampton she put up at the most expensive hotel . . . the girls did not know how she got rid of her money but when she came on board she did not have enough to meet her mess bill. A YMCA man loaned her the money. Whether it was a mess attendant suggested this to her, or whether she suggested it, a collection was taken up for her on the boat and they raised $250 and this the young woman accepted from these enlisted sailors. It is not known whether she paid the YM man back but it is supposed she did not.

Cleveland's alarm resonated for many war bride workers: she urged American "sentimentalists" to wake up and recognize that foreign brides were "preying upon the American army" and the naïve generosity of the American people.[23]

On balance, the AEF personnel who interacted earliest and most closely with war brides held a negative view of their charges. Not just German, but French, Belgian, British, and Irish brides were judged to be inappropriate wives for American soldiers. The views of welfare workers in France, based as they were on firsthand experience, carried weight with journalists, policy-makers, and the public, as well as with their sponsoring agencies back home. They had direct influence, for example, on a conflict that arose between military officials and the American Red Cross (ARC), when that organization insisted on testing foreign brides for venereal disease as a condition of Red Cross assistance—a conflict that was only resolved through War Department intervention.[24] Their negative views of war brides had more diffuse and longer-term effects as well. The issues that surfaced in France were transported to the home front with returning veterans and their foreign wives.

Postwar America and Fear of the Foreign

The foreign brides of the First World War stepped ashore into a nation roiled by controversy over foreign relations and the place of the foreign-born in American life. Warren G. Harding's 1920 inaugural address, remembered for its evocation of a "return to normalcy," also urged the American people to embrace "triumphant nationality" lest they find themselves "submerged" in "internationality." From the Red Scare and the deportation of "radical" and "anarchist" aliens after the 1919 Palmer raids to the debate over U.S. membership in the League of Nations and the clamor for immigration restriction, many native-born citizens of native parentage sought to isolate "outsiders" and assert an American identity purged of "alien" elements. John Higham's depiction of this era's passions is still incisive: the war "called forth the most strenuous nationalism and the most pervasive nativism that the United States had ever known," and this extremism generated "the storm of xenophobia" that shook the nation in the wake of the war.[25]

The policies of exclusion and inward-looking national interest that the U.S. government adopted during the interwar period were contested in the immediate aftermath of the war. "Liberal internationalists" comprised a network of research, business, and reform organizations working toward international cooperation. Groups such as the Carnegie Endowment for International Peace, the League of Nations Non-Partisan Association, the YMCA, and the Institute of Pacific Relations called for tolerance and argued that world harmony "depended on the globalization of the American liberal tenets of private enterprise, the open door, and free flow" of information.[26] Nonetheless, American xenophobia was building to a powerful crescendo as the new decade opened. Traditional opponents of immigration, like the president-general of the Daughters of the American Revolution, renewed their warning that "nothing will save the life of this free Republic if these foreign leeches are not cut and cast out." By the early 1920s, scare talk about "hordes" of immigrants characterized as "criminals," "anarchists," and carriers of "loathsome contagious diseases" came not only from the extreme right wing but also from the editorial pages of the *New York Times*.[27]

Restrictionists frequently spoke of an impending immigration "emergency" precipitated by the war. Barbarous warfare had devastated Europe, they argued, leaving the United States vulnerable to a flood of impoverished immigrants of unprecedented proportions. One prominent spokesperson for this position was George Creel, who served during the war as the high-profile director of the Committee on Public Information, the Wilson administration's propaganda agency. By 1921, Creel was advertising the dangers of the open door: "Gathered thick on the shores of the Old World, swarming like flies at every European port of embarkation, are several millions of immigrants, . . . feverishly awaiting the opportunity to come to America, the 'land of promise.'" In contrast with the "clear-eyed, clean-limbed men and women" of the "old immigration," Creel asserted, the "new immigration" brought "little more than human wreckage" to America. Congressman Harold Knutson, majority whip, cited this sort of "data" to pitch the case for an emergency twelve-month moratorium on newcomers. Fear of veterans' unemployment, an urban housing shortage, and the "dumping" of Bolsheviks and other unwanted radicals by European governments rounded out the restrictionists' arsenal of arguments linking the war with the immigration crisis. In this atmosphere of urgency, the 1921 and then the 1924 Johnson-Reed National Origins Acts to restrict immigration were passed.[28]

Two issues specific to female immigrants—the entry of contract brides and of prostitutes—featured in the discourse and debate surrounding immigration restriction.[29] Both had important though indirect relevance to the public's response to war brides. Prostitution had long been linked to immigration in the minds and campaigns of vice reformers and immigration restrictionists. Open immigration, they insisted, made the United States vulnerable to the danger of the international sex trade. Career prostitutes from overseas could take advantage of liberal immigration laws and corrupt or naïve immigration officials to gain entry to the country. Even more worrisome were international criminal syndicates trading in foreign women, both innocent and experienced—the so-called white slave trade carried out by male procurers and pimps. The U.S. Immigration Commission devoted an entire volume to the "Importation and Harboring of Women for Immoral Purposes," presenting its findings to Congress in 1909.

According to investigators, "the ease and apparent certainty of profit have led thousands of . . . men, usually those of foreign birth or the immediate sons of foreigners, . . . to undertake the most accursed business ever devised by man." French and "Hebrews" were the alien groups most heavily prone to the trade, investigators said, with French women the most likely to be brought in as seasoned prostitutes. Lurid testimony added a sense of urgency and veracity to the government's report. A brothel-keeper in Chicago, for example, disclosed under oath "that $500 is the ordinary price for a French prostitute when delivered in America"; he had recently "purchased" three girls from France and sold a fourth named Lillie. Informers from the underworld described rings of foreign pimps with such outlandish pseudonyms as "Carl le Terreur des Jeunes Filles." As historians have pointed out, the study had many flaws of evidence and methodology; the report itself quietly acknowledged that the sex trade in the United States was primarily a homegrown problem, not a foreign one. But the commission's report was still the basis for 1910 legislation that provided sweeping police powers to arrest and deport alien women and their associates for almost any connection to prostitution or other "immoral acts." The report created a strong impression that immigrants dominated the traffic in women and closely linked prostitution with immigration from France.[30]

The international scope of prostitution resurfaced as a political issue in the aftermath of the war. In the fall of 1920, the Republican National Committee organized a sub-rosa campaign to discredit the League of Nations among new female voters by declaring that the league covenant promoted the "white slave trade." Prominent spokeswomen for the Republican National Committee insisted that the league "recognizes and ratifies and legalizes traffic in the flesh and blood of God's children." This absurd claim was denounced by a wide array of individuals, but the controversy put foreign prostitution back on the national agenda and renewed the association between prostitution and female immigration.[31]

Contract brides, called "picture" brides because betrothals were contracted through the exchange of photographs between spouses on different continents, also became an acute concern in the immediate postwar period. Contract marriage was essentially an overseas extension of arranged marriage; a single immigrant man working in the United States became engaged to a woman through the mail and paid her passage to America. Contract marriage was widely practiced by Japanese immigrants in America, the group with whom the issue became closely identified, but also less frequently by Koreans, Bulgarians, Italians, Czechs, Slovaks, Greeks, Jews, Armenians, and others in which males vastly outnumbered females. Historian Bill Ong Hing describes the practice as a logical response in the Asian American community to antimiscegenation laws and policies that discriminated against independent female immigrants.[32] Immigration restrictionists seized on the issue in their campaign to highlight the immorality and unassimilability of foreigners. Many native-born Americans regarded these arrangements as an affront to American values of individualism, freedom, and consent in marriage.[33] Distaste for contract marriages played an important role as anti-Asian xenophobes built support in Congress for complete exclusion.

The issue of contract marriages fed the wider anti-immigrant campaign as well. An investigative report in *Outlook* magazine focusing on picture brides from Europe explicated the topic as many saw it at the time. Contract marriages, this journalist concluded after spending a week or more at Ellis Island, were "death sentences to individuality and progress." The article begins with the story of a young Armenian woman—a chilling anecdote in historical hindsight. Tagavna had been brought to the United States by an uncle to marry one of his acquaintances. Asked if she was afraid to marry a man she had never seen, Tagavna replied, "It is better to marry a stranger than to be massacred." Journalist Natalie De Bogory found her answer "simple-minded." De Bogory was aware of the economic and political factors that compelled immigration, yet the solution that women like Tagavna chose was alien and troubling to her: "The thought of those hundreds of women pouring into America, submissively accepting unknown husbands without friendship, romance, love, or any of those backgrounds which we have grown to regard as essential to marriage, was depressing."[34] The journalist's comments betray a disturbing insensitivity to the plight of Armenian genocide victims; they also display an attitude of ignorance, common to middle-class feminists of the time, about the struggles of immigrant working-class women.

This article's configuration of foreign women's subservience versus American women's independence is crucial for understanding gender in the immigration restriction debate. Contract brides and foreign prostitutes brought to the surface many of the factors that so disturbed Americans about female immigrants in general, whether as war brides, wives, or workers. Even their economic motives aroused suspicion. Most female immigrants were impoverished people making pragmatic choices to ensure their own survival and that of their kin. But displays of female self-assertion were disturbing to many American conservatives. Similar concerns were voiced about war brides, whose motives were characterized as materialistic, manipulative, or worse. European "gold diggers" taking advantage of American soldiers were in many ways the counterpart of the foreign "scum" taking advantage of the United States. Worse still, these were *women* acting for personal gain or economic benefit, a serious violation of conservative notions of female propriety.

Contract brides, war brides, and prostitutes were also sexual and procreative immigrants, and here their presence opened up a second set of issues. Just beneath the surface of the immigration debate were explosive questions about "breeding" and the "racial" composition of the American population. Well into the interwar period, most Americans understood national difference in racial and biological terms. Fears of "crossbreeding" were propagated across a broad spectrum of American society during the 1920s, from the Ku Klux Klan to the eugenics movement.[35] A leading business group was told in 1923 that "immigration from . . . countries peopled by races with which inter-marriage gives deteriorated," "half-breed," or "unsatisfactory results" should be banned.[36] An ominous image of the United States being swamped by fast-breeding, racially incompatible aliens was painted in a series on the "problem" of immigration run by the *Saturday Evening Post*, the nation's most influential middlebrow publication, in 1920 and 1921. In "Europe Comes Across," Corinne Lowe described Ellis Island "inundated" with families of portly matrons surrounded by their "bambini." Amalgamation—the mixing of nationalities or races, on an individual and a national level—was one of the most vexing matters of all. War brides tapped this fear: intermarriages between American soldiers and foreign women were "ugly, sordid matings" that were "dangerous" to American society.[37]

The issues associated with female immigration after World War I were highly charged with moral, sexual, and political implications. This sensationalized framing of female immigration formed the backdrop for the reception of war brides. Although the connections to war brides were seldom made explicit in the restriction debate, the parallels and implications are apparent. The moralizing mood and defensive posture of postwar society, the desire for a "pure" America undiluted by "alien" influences, must be understood as a consequence of the war; paradoxically, despite the nation's military success, postwar culture was pervaded by a sense that America was not strengthened but weakened by its outing on the international stage. People moved easily in their associations between corruption emerging from individual sexual liaisons and the metaphoric degeneration of society from promiscuous international mingling.[38] War brides were a concrete embodiment of what had happened to the United States when it went to war and of what the U.S. military had brought home. Many Americans were not prepared to greet these women with warm hearts or open minds.

Soldiers' Foreign Marriages in 1920s America

American anxieties about the social implications of foreign war and foreign peoples were played out in the postwar discourse about intercultural marriage. Three key constituencies—the press, the local communities that received war brides, and the brides' new American families—were most vocal in this discussion. Although war brides had their defenders, the majority of media sources presented the marriages as problematic. Across the political spectrum, journalists and social commentators agreed that intercultural couples faced numerous obstacles to happiness. Differences in language and custom, the overly romantic expectations of the brides, and the hard economic realities of the postwar recession were all cited as impediments. One journalist worried in particular about the difficult days "when the penniless husband is scratching around for a job after his war service," but this writer remained optimistic about the future "because the girls love the husbands they have married and because they are succeeding in making of themselves satisfactory and pleasant wives in spite of all the strangeness." A more negative assessment pictured the foreign bride as unable to accept the fact that her seemingly wealthy and glamorous doughboy was really a "two-dollar-a-day elevator boy."[39]

The alleged failure of French-American marriages was one of the most popular themes in the postwar discussion. On Valentine's Day 1920, *Literary Digest*, an arts-and-culture weekly, assessed the results of "Cupid's work" with the American army in France. The article highlighted a widely circulated rumor: scores of French war brides were running home to *maman*, the editors reported with barely concealed satisfaction. It circulated a report first printed in the Paris press that one ship had brought sixty-two "disappointed or divorced" French brides back to their homeland. The problem was dramatized for the American public when three French brides accosted Marshal Foch, France's victorious military commander, on his tour of the American West in 1921 and "tearfully begged to go back to France." It is likely that the women took this unusual step in order to secure funds for transportation, but Americans viewed it as an unseemly and disloyal public outburst, and even an embarrassment to the United States in the eyes of her allies.[40]

Return migration was a contentious issue in the larger immigration debate of the 1920s. Paradoxically, the restrictionists were most vexed by the phenomenon; apparently they viewed a stream of immigrants returning home as a sign of ingratitude or, even worse, as a retort to American "exceptionalism," the ideal of the United States as a golden land of freedom and opportunity.[41] War brides who returned to Europe were guilty of a similar transgression, but they were also showing disloyalty and ingratitude to the American heroes who had saved their country. It should be noted that the American Red Cross Home Service, the agency charged with war bride resettlement in the United States during demobilization, saw no large-scale pattern of return migration among European brides, only some isolated cases, but that information was generally disregarded.[42] Return migration of war brides, even if limited, raised a number of delicious issues for critics to chew upon. To the naysayers it justified their warnings that soldiers' overseas marriages were impulsive and poorly conceived. "Marry in haste, repent in leisure" was the most frequently repeated expression of newspaper columnists writing about war brides in the postwar era. At the same time, the foreign wives who failed to stay in unhappy marriages were exhibiting a streak of female independence that was unbecoming and even un-American in the eyes of these beholders. Here the acute postwar anxiety about "soaring" divorce rates also came into play.[43] To conservatives, the social and cultural radicalism of the late 1910s—women's rights, free love, anarchism, and other "foreign" ideas—had weakened the fabric of American society and the integrity of family life. War brides, whatever the fate of the marriages, were part of this problem. Conservatives expected these overseas marriages to be troubled, but they thought that the women should live with the consequences.[44]

Liberal and conservative commentators differed most starkly as they considered the possibility of assimilating foreign wives. "Americanization" was a prominent theme in the 1920s, and it figured in the war bride debate through articles with such telling titles as "French War Brides Happy in America," "Paths of French War Brides Are Rocky," and "All French War Brides Didn't Make the Mistake of Their Lives." The pessimistic view about assimilation was built on a simple premise: these intercultural marriages were threatened by fundamental differences between continental Europeans and those they called "Anglo-Saxons," a term used to designate the superior group among whites. "Racial differences" between husband and wife "promised incompatibility," and as a result, all these relationships, even the seemingly happy ones, "bore the seeds of failure." Critics insisted that the marriages had an especially poor prognosis because of Europeans' incomprehension of all things American. One magazine caricatured the "anxious French mothers" who were "flooding the mails with letters of inquiry" about the "distant and no doubt barbarous land" where their daughters had been taken. Some mothers allegedly asked if hostile Indians would endanger their loved one, and others were concerned that polygamy laws would allow their sons-in-law to accumulate multiple wives. "It would be impossible to publish anything that would answer all the questions that might present themselves to the minds of people [so] profoundly ignorant regarding America and its ways," sniffed one magazine editor.[45]

In contrast to the conservative vision of racial immutability, liberals believed that the cultural assimilation of immigrants was possible through an intensive program of education. This progressive creed still commanded the loyalty of liberal internationalists after the war. Reformers who focused on "Americanization" readily applied this approach to foreign brides.[46] Numerous articles highlighted the efforts undertaken by American social workers to facilitate the women's adjustment. "Difficulties of language and customs and seemingly impossible readjustment to their new nationality vanished before the kind aid of Y.W.C.A. secretaries," one supervisor reported. English-language learning was emphasized. YWCA workers, with their own ideals of companionate marriage, were genuinely troubled by the wordless love affairs they sometimes observed between American husbands and European wives. Yet language can be readily taught to the willing, and YWCA staff members and other liberals believed that once the cultural and language barriers between them were breached, intercultural couples had a good chance of success.[47]

For the most optimistic observers, intercultural marriage pointed toward a promising international future. *New York Evening Mail* reporter Mary Margaret McBride, who was assigned to examine the adjustment of foreign brides and the status of their marriages, found more happy than unhappy couplings. Where the brides were unhappy, McBride was almost unique among U.S. journalists in suggesting that the American public's hostility toward the women could itself have been a major factor. More often, she observed, the affectionate bond between husband and wife was strong enough to sustain the marriage. Sympathetic writers granted foreign brides a good share of the credit for marital success: "Most of the foreign girls have come to us in the utmost sincerity. They love their American husbands and they are bound to make every effort to work out the marriage on a basis that will be satisfactory to everyone concerned." McBride and other liberals argued that when "love is big and deep enough the differences are settled by everybody making allowances." She was part of an influential minority of opinion makers who were hopeful not only that the marriages could succeed but that they might point the way to a better "international understanding" between the United States and other nations.[48]

McBride's allusion to Americans' hostility raises questions about another realm of response to foreign brides, the way they were received by their husbands' families and communities. One war bride's poignant self-description captures the fear and insecurity that many felt stepping into the alien environment of a new town or family circle: they were "poor little French strangers all alone in a strange country without even knowing enough language to make us understood." But their sense of alienation stemmed from a deeper source than the language barrier. Communities receiving war brides were often unwelcoming. In Boston, the Red Cross chaperone had difficulty locating a hotel where her seven French brides "would be safe from idle curiosity and where we were sure no harm could come to them." The case worker attributed this attitude to the notorious narrow-minded conventionality of Bostonians, as well as the presence in many Boston hotels of large groups of American relatives awaiting homecoming soldiers.[49] Evidently these servicemen's families found the foreign brides an affront.

In army base communities with a large concentration of war brides—Sackets Harbor on Lake Ontario; Watertown, New York; and Newport News, Virginia—sentiment against the brides ran even higher. In Watertown, Edna Wagner, the Red Cross secretary in charge of war brides at Madison Barracks, became embroiled in a controversy over maternity care in December 1919 after the director of the Watertown Hospital refused to admit war brides to his facility. His twisted logic bespeaks the prejudices and rumors that surrounded these women: war brides, he insisted, were likely to have venereal disease, and his hospital lacked a contagious diseases license, thus barring him from accepting any of them. The women were forced to give birth in their underheated barracks with only a visiting nurse in attendance—a strange irony at the Christmas season that no one seemed to notice. Wagner was especially annoyed to find that even Watertown's local Red Cross committee refused to speak up for the war brides.

The community's opposition to the war brides was echoed and even exceeded by the hostility of military officers on the bases. Wagner was shocked when Major McKellway, an army surgeon and medical director of the base hospital at Madison Barracks, declared that "the Red Cross could render the greatest service [to the brides] by poisoning the whole lot." "His attitude is most unkindly as is the attitude of all the officers on the Post," she complained to her Home Service supervisor in Washington. The husbands of foreign brides were also alarmed by this behavior. "Many a soldier said to me that the Major treated his wife like a dog," she explained, and the men did their best to keep their wives away from him. The commanding officer at Camps Hill and Stuart, Virginia, Captain William Lewis, in an official communication to the Red Cross, referred to the French brides as "peasants and camp followers" and insisted that the Red Cross find some other facility for housing and caring for them. Fieldworkers assigned to supervise war brides on the bases were sufficiently concerned about this matter to bring it to the attention of Red Cross national headquarters on several occasions.[50]

Why did military officers stateside express such a high level of hostility toward these foreign brides, especially when their counterparts in the AEF exhibited a more tolerant attitude? Members of the AEF had months of exposure to European people and customs. Officers in command of stateside bases may have been expressing the kind of hypernationalism sometimes seen in those taking part in war from a distance, or even displacing onto the women their own resentment toward men returning from France with more glamorous and glorious war records. This explanation is suggested by a strange yet revealing passage written by Colonel Charles Gandy, another Medical Corps officer at Madison Barracks. In defending the medical staff's refusal to treat war brides and in responding to the charge that he and fellow officers were not "anxious to cooperate in the treatment of foreign wives of soldiers or sympathetic with the policy of moral uplift," Gandy framed his answer with a biblical analogy, the parable of the Prodigal Son. Gandy expressed personal sympathy for the stay-at-home brothers of the wayward lad. When the prodigal returned to his father's house "after having squandered his substance in riotous living in a foreign country, [he] was received with feasting, while they, who had served faithfully all their lives, received no recognition whatever."[51] As his comment suggests, some members of the military may have seen these brides as the forbidden fruit that other soldiers had illicitly sampled, leaving the resentful brothers at home with little inclination to help make it easier for the men to enjoy their spoils.

The new in-laws were also a group that had qualms about the war brides. The husbands' families sometimes offered a chilly reception to the women; a few rejected them entirely. One unhappy mother-in-law in Georgia tried to have her son's Irish wife sent back to Europe immediately. When case workers in New York City wired regarding the young woman's travel plans, the mother wired back, "Do not send Mrs. Witherspoon, son sueing for divorce, persuaded to marry when drunk." With letters in hand attesting to the deep affection between the bride and her sailor husband, the case work staff intervened and insisted that the mother-in-law had no right to disrupt the relationship, urging her to respect the couple's wishes. Yet Red Cross workers sometimes sympathized with the antagonism of in-laws, at least in the case of older brides and those with children. "Less attractive and appealing than the younger girls, [one felt] how difficult it might be for relatives to meet them cordially and with understanding when the men had not yet returned from overseas. Understanding almost no English with different manners and customs, it would not be strange if a real breach arose that even the man's return could not heal." In one case of an overseas marriage ended by the machinations of relatives, a French Desdemona found herself falsely accused of adultery by her new in-laws, who concocted the story to wreck the marriage before their son's return. Fortunately, she defended herself successfully against the charge and was able to clear her name. But this bride ultimately chose to divorce her mistrustful husband.[52] The hostility of family and friends may well have undermined other intercultural marriages as well.

Alien and Improper Women

The initial atmosphere of curiosity and skepticism surrounding these intercultural marriages soon hardened into a more solidly negative consensus. At the core, the critics' objections to overseas marriages of U.S. soldiers were less about the marriages per se and much more about the character of the women themselves. As female immigrants, the war brides were judged not only in terms of their adherence to American norms but also in relation to norms of femininity. Journalists, social workers, military authorities and others constructed a view of war brides as deviant along both of these axes. Emotionally, physically, and especially sexually, European brides were deemed to be largely incompatible with American values.

Most of those who supervised war brides at the ports of arrival or the military bases described them as crude or uncouth, with habits and practices that were decidedly alien to American sensibilities: "The custom[s] of the country from which these women come are at great moral variance from those of this country. It has been observed that these women in nearly all cases display actions on arrival here that are classed as questionable in this country." In emotional terms, they were "more demonstrative" than Americans, given to quick and hysterical tears. Many commented on their immaturity: "They were like children, for most of them were of the simpler type, acting like children in many ways."[53] Their emotionality could also take the form of angry outbursts. American observers noted that the women were prone to fighting, scratching, pushing, and yelling at one another. Their use of foul language was "the worst he had ever heard," one military officer maintained.[54] This violent and crude behavior was decidedly unladylike. Critics attributed it to the women's hot-blooded, south European nature.

In social terms, Americans found the war brides to be excessively friendly and "approachable"—striking up conversations without introduction, interacting with men other than their husbands, distributing their names or addresses far too liberally—all serious violations of the middle-class code of propriety for women. The story of a British woman, engaged to a Canadian officer when she embarked on her journey and to an American when she landed, caused consternation in several nations and reinforced the image of the foreign wife as flighty, sexually loose, or given to social impropriety.[55] The commentators, of course, made their observations through a veil of stereotypes and biases. This was apparent in the South, where white army personnel and white civilians were troubled to see that French women failed to observe southern racial etiquette. "In France there is a very different attitude on the race question; they do not understand our attitude toward colored people," a situation the "colored people" were all too eager to exploit, bemoaned a white Red Cross worker. The French women's informal and egalitarian interactions with African Americans were alien indeed, creating a "rather serious" problem.[56]

Foreign women were congenitally dishonest, American observers complained. War brides were prone to stealing small items, pocketing silverware from the mess hall, or stealing from other brides. Case workers also found them dishonest in their dealings with the welfare organizations dedicated to their assistance. One soldier "overheard some of the women saying that they were 'going to put one over on the Red Cross and get as much as possible out of them.'" Some suspected an even more fundamental dishonesty in the marriages themselves: these critics maintained that the women had only pretended to care for American soldiers in order to attain the benefits of American life and citizenship, benefits to which they were not honestly entitled.[57]

Most disconcertingly of all, French and other European brides used their bodies differently, in ways that American observers found both fascinating and disturbing. "The habits of most of these women were uncleanly," observed Captain Lewis; "they obeyed the calls of nature where ever they happened to be, regardless of the fact that the best facilities were placed at their disposal."[58] (Lewis was likely referring to urinating out of doors, a common practice among rural people the world over). The sheer physicality of the women was simultaneously repellent and arousing to men. A Red Cross worker reporting on marriages between Siberians and Americans believed that the "animal and romantic appeal" of the women overwhelmed the "nervous system and willpower" of American men.[59] Red Cross workers supervising brides in U.S. military camps noted that it drove uncoupled men wild when the French wives and their husbands touched, kissed, or petted in public view. Frances Willison, a case worker, could understand why this happened: although any newly married couple on an army base would excite attention, "under the somewhat extraordinary circumstances of the wives being more or less 'a souvenir of France,' the amount of curiosity and comment was of course exaggerated." Still, Willison blamed the brides when a riot nearly broke out between married and unmarried soldiers. Similarly, the brides were faulted for arousing or tantalizing the soldiers around them, even when the male voyeurism of the press and army public relations encouraged the women to display themselves in beauty contests held on shipboard and reported in the papers.[60]

The women's foreignness was inextricably linked to sexuality and, by extension, to immorality. Social scientists in this period believed that national groups could be "rated" or quantified for personal characteristics such as "moral integrity" and "self-control" that were the springboard of crime and immorality.[61] The particularly strong association in anti-immigrant discourse between French immigration and prostitution was an important reason for the hostility French brides faced. The prevalent image of prostitutes was readily transferred to war brides, making them sexual temptresses who had seduced unknowing American lads in France. This theme was central to the plot of a Broadway stage play of the mid-1920s, *The Scarlet Lily*, which portrayed the life of Marcelle, a French bride living on a Vermont farm with her American soldier-husband. In the dramatic denouement, Marcelle is publicly unmasked by a former lover, who somehow wends his way to far northern New England to denounce her. The show was disappointing to one theater reviewer because its "predictable" story had been so often told before. Indeed, stories like Marcelle's were rife in social commentary as well: almost every postwar report on the "adjustment" of war brides in the United States restated the concern that many were "bad" women whose seamy past would come back to haunt them and their new American families. The implication of this scenario was that doughboys had been tricked or corrupted into marriage by prostitutes who were really looking for an opportunity to ply their trade in the affluent United States. Concerns about war brides merged with themes from the anti-immigration debate, echoing the vigorous restrictionist campaign against the "white slave trade" as a danger of open immigration.

Women could be sexually loose or immoral in a variety of ways besides the sex trade, and a number of immigration cases reported in the press placed war brides under public scrutiny for adultery and "bastard-bearing."

A British fiancée sent for by a U.S. officer, for example, faced deportation charges at Ellis Island because she had taken up with a different officer on route to the United States (although her new lover offered to wed her and repay her fare). Immigration officials were even more perplexed by a convoluted case that involved an unwed British woman, her three-month old infant, and her American lover's family. At Ellis Island, agents initiated what seemed a straightforward deportation process against the woman on the basis of a morals charge; under the strict U.S. "white slavery" laws, being an unwed mother was ample proof of sexual immorality. The American father of the baby, an AEF veteran who had apparently left his pregnant girlfriend in England, was now married to an American woman. But the immigration proceeding was turned on its head when the baby's father and his new American wife asked to adopt the child, a response that generated intense public interest. Then a brother-in-law stepped forward, volunteering to marry the erring young British woman, sight unseen—merging the picture bride and war bride issues in one suspicious case.[62]

All the central elements in popular representations of war brides' character—their alien emotionality, their violence, and their sexual immorality—came together in a sensational murder trial in 1928. The case of Marlyse Maye was a melodramatic tale of passion, adultery, jealousy, and betrayal, with a troubled French war bride at its center. Police reports and trial testimony gave the outlines of the story. On the night of November 12, 1927, New York City police were summoned to Maye's apartment in the Bronx, where they found her bleeding from a single gunshot wound and the dead body of a man, shot four times, in her bedroom. The man was Andrew Devola, aged twenty-two, her husband's closest friend. Questioned in police custody at Fordham Hospital, Maye readily supplied crucial information about the sad and sordid situation. Her husband, Adam Maye, an army veteran, had been in France with her family at the time of the shootings. The Mayes had met and married in France when Marlyse was only seventeen. Since returning from the war, Adam Maye had suffered from debilitating tuberculosis, and he had spent large portions of their eight years together in veterans' hospitals and facilities. Adam Maye had hoped to recover in the south of France, and on departure, he had asked his unmarried friend Devola to watch out for his wife. Marlyse Maye admitted that she and Devola had become lovers during her husband's long absence.

At the trial, Maye initially testified that Devola's death was a suicide; despondent over the prospect of ending the affair, which his parents had urged him to do, Devola wounded her and then killed himself. The prosecution's argument inverted this story: Maye was despondent at the thought of losing Devola, so she shot him and then turned the gun on herself. The case was standard crime-story fare, but the figure of Marlyse Maye fascinated reporters and readers and kept the story in the news. She embodied the imagined characteristics of the French war bride that Americans found so troubling. Maye was a woman ruled by her passions. Press accounts stressed her almost mysteriously uncontrollable emotions. On the first day of the trial she "collapsed in court"; at the summation, she "became hysterical, wept and collapsed"; and at the sentencing, "she fainted and slipped from her chair to the floor." So baffling was her behavior in the courtroom that the judge invited a "mental diseases" specialist from Columbia University to examine her and testify prior to the sentencing. Her unusual condition of paralysis, fainting, and hysteria, he concluded, was a result of her "excitable temperament" as well as the "ordeal she had undergone."

Maye's sexuality was also on open display in the trial. Her adulterous affair with Devola was at the center of the story. The trial opened her bedroom quite literally to public scrutiny. A bizarre twist late in the trial accentuated the mingling of sex and violence that surrounded the figure of Marlyse Maye. Ten days after the proceedings began, Maye told the court that she had been robbed and gang-raped by three men in her apartment almost exactly one year before the murder took place; she now asserted that the murderer was an unknown assailant connected to this earlier incident. Maye's startling attempt to reframe the case elicited a great deal of disbelief, although the police agreed that her rape story was true. Her effort to exculpate herself and her lover reinforced the aura of sordid, uncontrolled sexuality that surrounded the case and her image as impulsive and dishonest.

The Maye trial offered to those who desired one a sorry example of what could become of intercultural love affairs. Even Maye's unfortunate husband, Adam, the war veteran, entered the trial as an object lesson rather than an object of sympathy. Sick, weak, and deluded, he had delivered his wife into the arms of her lover. Adam Maye, who arrived home in time for the sentencing hearing, "reaffirmed his love" for his wife and declared that he would wait for her and take her back, despite her betrayal and the tragic events that followed. Adam Maye figured as one more American doughboy bewitched by a beguiling, if puzzling, French siren. The trial, a sad footnote to the war, was one of the last in the wave of published stories about the foreign brides of World War I.[63]

What the Marriages Were Like: Demographics and Assimilation

The opinion that the foreign brides of AEF servicemen deviated from accepted models of American womanhood was widely shared by the early 1920s. But marriage American-style could also be a powerful force for the socialization of foreigners, and some Americans were willing to withhold judgment and see how these relationships turned out. It is disappointing, then, that the marriages themselves, as they unfolded in the postwar period, remain largely opaque to historical inquiry, at least from a qualitative perspective. No memoirs or autobiographies, correspondence or newsletters tell the war brides' stories, as they do for the abundantly documented "GI" marriages of World War II. Demographic data from State Department visa and army files are available, however, and coupled with the brief reports of case workers and a handful of interviews with war bride daughters, they allow some conclusions to be sketched.[64]

The quantitative information contains several intriguing surprises and suggests that the public debate in many regards missed the point. Across the political spectrum, American observers imagined these marriages as a mating of opposites. Yet the men and women in these marriages were more alike than different. Take age, for example, a readily available demographic fact. Most brides and grooms were close in age, with the men slightly older on average—making them very similar to American newlyweds. The data belie the popular perception of war brides as older, worldly women taking advantage of innocent American boys. The combination of an older bride and a younger groom was quite rare. Welfare workers were inclined to regard the occasional "older woman" with suspicion, or even distaste. Yet sophisticated older brides usually married men of comparable backgrounds, like the attractive London stage performer who married an American officer, a well-established widower aged forty with a teenage son.[65]

Women working with intercultural couples often remarked instead on the women's youthfulness, sometimes with concern. Very young brides came to the agencies' attention, as the girls were in need of special protection.[66] One welfare worker noted that, in a group of seven brides she received in Boston, six "were girls of seventeen, nineteen and twenty" who had "never been out of their home towns in France." The youngest, "a mere pink and white child of seventeen," seemed especially vulnerable, and she was sent to her in-laws in Brooklyn only when Red Cross workers were satisfied that her situation there would be safe and well supervised.[67] The extreme youthfulness of some brides might suggest exploitation running in the opposite direction—that is, American soldiers taking advantage of young foreign women. Based on the evidence at hand, it is impossible to make any generalizations. Individual cases varied widely, with a few situations in which one party obviously took advantage of the other, but with many shades of gray in between. Indeed, war bride workers frequently described both husband and wife as innocent young persons inadequately equipped to handle adult responsibility.

A few cases with marked disparity in age show that other factors were equally or more important in determining the suitability of a marital choice or the possibility for a mutually respectful relationship. Consider the marriage between Lilly, a "short, stocky" English girl of twenty-three, and a thirty-five-year-old American soldier. Lilly was working as a telephone operator in a London hotel when they met, and after just a few weeks he had proposed marriage. It would be difficult to argue that this practical young woman was exploited by an older man. To the Red Cross staff, Lilly confided that she probably would have rejected his proposal had she a family to care for her or some other source of security, but she had been orphaned in childhood. The man seemed kind and generous, and with few other options, she chose to "take a chance" on their future happiness together. Setting out for Columbus, Ohio, to meet her husband, Lilly was two months pregnant and determined to "try everything to make him happy."[68]

One of the most striking findings about marriages made between U.S. soldiers and foreign women is the substantial proportion of grooms who were themselves of foreign birth or parentage. This phenomenon was observed, quietly but consistently, by a number of war bride workers. Reporting for a magazine, a YMCA social worker noted, "As a rule it was not the American boy of American parentage who married abroad, . . . the soldiers who married [foreign women] were for the most part of their own kind."[69] The marriage data I analyzed document the accuracy of this observation: 35 percent of the doughboy husbands in the sample were born outside the United States. The immigrant soldiers who chose foreign brides fit the general profile of immigrants to the United States in the early twentieth century; 12 percent of husbands were from Italy, 8 percent from Great Britain, and 15 percent from other foreign countries. Many of the family names carried by the native-born husbands on the army rosters were obviously foreign, suggesting that the sons of immigrants, first-generation Americans, were also likely to choose foreign brides. Especially strong evidence of the "like-marries-like" phenomenon appears in the German marriage rosters; German Americans were the single largest group among soldiers who married German women during the occupation.[70] Most immigrant grooms did not marry their own countrywomen, however, but ranged widely in their choices, with Italian-born doughboys marrying French women, Syrians marrying British, and Armenians marrying German brides. Common religious faith often united the partners when nationality differed.

This pattern of marriage among American soldiers of foreign birth or parentage reveals an important but little-recognized fact about American participation in the First World War. As historian Nancy Gentile Ford has shown, "The U.S. Army of World War I was an ethnically diverse force with almost one in every five soldiers born in a foreign country."[71] Foreign-born soldiers appear among war bride husbands even beyond their proportion in the armed services; their propensity to marry overseas was almost twice that of their nonethnic comrades-in-arms. What explains their predilection for overseas marriage? It may have been a response to the discrimination and social isolation such men faced as outsiders in American society and the military. Although the War Department worked closely with ethnic-group leaders and progressive reformers to integrate foreign-born soldiers into the armed services, hostility was still common.[72] Discrimination against foreign-born soldiers by their own officers and comrades may have motivated them to seek the company of local women overseas. An alternative explanation relates to the marital patterns of immigrant groups. Going back to Europe to fetch a bride was a long-standing practice for many immigrant communities in the United States. This family formation strategy was especially important for groups with a marked excess of males and a shortage of females of marriageable age, such as Greeks and Italians.[73] Foreign military service made it easier for immigrant men to accomplish the task of bringing a bride over from Europe. Familiarity with local languages and cultural practices may have put immigrant soldiers more naturally into situations where they could meet people, increasing their chances of finding a mate overseas.

Individual cases in the sample give other clues as to how the broader pattern of overseas marriage developed. Biagio Petani was in many ways typical of Italian-born soldiers who took foreign brides. Twenty-nine years old when he joined the American Expeditionary Force, Petani had been working for a number of years in Seattle, Washington, a city of more than 200,000 people with an Italian ethnic community of only 4,500. Socially isolated in small ethnic enclaves and unable to find an American or an Italian immigrant wife, many men like Biagio evidently saw marriage to a young French woman as an appealing option. So too perhaps did Edmund Zschernitz, born in Hamburg, Germany, in 1889 and settled in tiny Neillsville, in Clark County, Wisconsin. In a county of 30,000 people, Germans and the children of Germans constituted just over one-quarter of the population. Still unmarried at thirty when he joined the U.S. Army, Zschernitz returned from the European war a noncommissioned officer with a twenty-two-year-old bride from Roanne, France.[74]

The very notion of the "war bride" as a soldier's acquisition of overseas service is also thrown into question by demographic evidence. Some brides and grooms were already acquainted before the war. Consider Euphemia and Alex Simpson, both born in Leith, Scotland. Alexander Simpson had emigrated to Salt Lake City in November 1917; within a year he was back in Europe with the U.S. Army. He soon married Euphemia in Scotland and applied to bring her to the United States in 1919. One of the most unusual and tantalizing, though fragmentary, records is the story of 167 war brides and children from Czechoslovakia. YWCA workers, who helped the women to arrange visas and board trains to the French ports in October 1919, observed that "about fifty percent of these were married before the war" and were "taking advantage" of U.S. government transportation to reunite with their husbands, now veterans of the AEF. Although little information about these women was recorded, their experience opens intriguing questions. Husbands and wives were frequently separated by the immigration process in the early twentieth century. Might these and other couples have used the war bride program as an opportunity to reunify families, which might have been unaffordable without this generous government program? Is it possible that some wives utilized the war bride label to press claims on husbands who had been reluctant to bring them to the United States? Many of the Czechoslovakian war brides were not war brides at all, but prewar wives of identical background to their husbands who hoped to immigrate. Other women or couples might have pursued similar strategies without attracting notice.[75]

The data raise a significant question: If immigrant soldiers were instrumental in creating the wave of overseas marriage in the AEF, why was this phenomenon so little discussed in the popular discourse about war brides? The predominant narrative of intercultural marriage in the First World War rested on an assumption of *difference*—the marked disparity between the American groom and his foreign bride. It was the assumed impossibility of bridging this disparity that intrigued the American public in the postwar period. That many couples were more culturally similar than different was news that failed to fit this story. Equally important, few Americans in this xenophobic era were prepared to acknowledge the extent to which the "all-American" U.S. Army was full of men of foreign birth and parentage. Many of these soldiers came from the very same nations of southern and eastern Europe that were targeted by the immigration restriction laws. An American nation defended by Italian, Jewish, Greek, Slavic, and even German soldiers was not one that many native-born Americans of native parentage could recognize.

Husbands and wives were probably closely matched in social class as well, though here the data are more scattered. College-educated officers and airmen often married educated wives from bourgeois families. One air corps officer, for example, a graduate of Oberlin, wed a brilliant young woman from Nice, a teacher of French, German, mathematics, and psychology; after the war, they settled near Oberlin, where she found employment at the college.[76] Most war bride husbands, however, like most AEF soldiers, came from the working class. This was true of wives as well. Sympathetic observers described war brides as industrious and hardworking women of modest means who planned to help their husbands get established in life. Extensive anecdotal evidence demonstrates that the vast majority of war brides had worked for pay before and/or during the war doing industrial labor or munitions work, in domestic service, or in small shops or businesses, while rural women had performed agricultural labor. Many were excellent seamstresses and cooks who intended to put those skills to work in the United States. Many couples had limited financial resources to begin their new lives together. A young pair in New York City, for example, told Red Cross workers of their plans soon after settling: he had found employment as a ticket collector in a movie house, and she was working as a hotel chambermaid. Like them, other war bride couples were predominantly working people, used to laboring for small rewards, with modest but hopeful expectations.

Despite fears of their "unassimilability," most war brides appear to have adjusted to their new social environment. Absorbed into their husbands' lives and home communities, they disappear from the historical record almost without a trace. War bride workers received just a trickle of news about them in the months after the women had settled in their American homes. One army veteran marveled at how quickly his French wife and stepdaughters had adapted to life on a Montana ranch, the girls practicing English with him on the long drive back and forth to school, his wife cooking and tending the garden. It is impossible to ascertain whether, as a group, these women felt happy or welcome in their new homes. The shards of evidence are intriguing but inconclusive, pointing to the manifold personal circumstances that make up a life. An English "country girl" who married a soldier from the American South was delighted by her familiar role as a farmer's wife, now on a prosperous Texas farm. A young German woman who was shunned by her family for marrying an American was so despondent and lonely that she twice tried to kill herself with oven gas in the couple's small Manhattan apartment. A homesick French teenager was comforted by her sympathetic husband, who sent money to her family in France to bring her sister over to keep her company. [77] Only this handful of story fragments remains to tell the lives of World War I war brides.

3

GIs and Girls around the Globe

The Geopolitics of Sex and Marriage in World War II

"You've wondered what they look like—the girls our soldiers meet overseas. Here's the answer, from Iceland blondes to sun-kissed Samoans." In 1943 a U.S. popular magazine published a globe-trotting guide for curious Americans. The article introduced an array of international playmates in cheesecake photos, from Ireland's winsome sweater girl Muriel Lahey, to sultry Iranian "lovely" Bahereh Sabet, to Australia's leggy Pat Julie, posed on a beach blanket. Thumbnail sketches described the girls to be found, and dated, in a dozen theaters of this global war, with specific advice on how to approach each type—whether bowling or tennis, cinema or a dinner dance was her favorite venue. Visually, the women were posed with a nod toward their national identity and costumes, but the text revealed the underlying message of the piece: regardless of their nationality, women around the world were united in their attraction to Yanks. The GIs they encountered were "red-blooded" males whose appetites were international, democratic, and clearly heterosexual. Even parents and the public, the article implied, could take pride in the romantic adventures of America's fighting men.[1]

World War II extended the reach of American power around the globe in unprecedented ways, including power over women. Lands previously distant from American awareness were now crucial to Allied success in the war. One dimension of this new international power was access to local women in the war zone, ranging from marriage to prostitution, and a range of relations and interactions in between. The world war of the 1940s, fought around the globe, produced marriages by the scores of thousands, and did so in every region where American soldiers were posted. This marital pattern stood in contrast with that of World War I, when marriage was more limited and concentrated primarily in a single nation, France. The number of GI marriages in World War II, though impossible to determine precisely, was over 125,000, with more than eighteen countries producing a thousand marriages or more.[2]

One dimension of the magazine article, however, was misleading, for it placed "girls" around the world on an equal basis in the competition for the attention and affection of American GIs. This was decidedly not the case. The geo-racial politics of wartime sex and marriage were as striking a feature of soldier relationships during the Second World War as the numbers themselves. U.S. military policies, practices, and preferences, alongside the preferences of U.S. soldiers, shaped the distribution of marriage in a myriad of ways, with race and political status being two of the most salient features. Out of more than 114,000 wives admitted to the United States in the period covered by the War Brides Act of 1945, almost 85,000 were European. White English-speaking Allied women from Britain, Ireland, Canada, Australia, and New Zealand accounted for close to half of all admitted brides. The numbers for Britain alone dwarfed the marriage figures for every other ally or key area of U.S. military engagement, including China, North Africa, the Philippines, Italy, France, Belgium, and the Soviet Union. The largest number of war bride marriages were produced in the Allied nations between white women and white men, places where women had good access to wartime employment and a relatively high degree of social power. In these places, U.S. military commanders encouraged socializing and dating while suppressing prostitution; in other words, the military helped to create an environment friendly to marriage. The fewest marriages emerged or were permitted with women of color, from colonial or vanquished nations, where military commanders discouraged marriage and dating and instead tolerated prostitution as the best way to service American GIs. Thus, a mixture of desire, expectation, and policy created a very uneven playing field as American men and local women engaged in relationships overseas during World War II.

Women around the globe, however, were not passive targets of military policy or soldiers' desire. They too had desires and made choices that shaped the pattern of interaction between soldiers and local women during World War II. Marriage to foreign soldiers, Americans and others, was one important arena in which women could and did act during the war, but marriage was a complex and even paradoxical expression of women's autonomy and desire. On one hand, "going around with American soldiers"—outsider males who were defined by virile masculinity and a sometimes threatening sexuality—was daring for young women. It was in fact a practice that aligned them with the "modern girl" phenomenon, a move toward greater social and sexual autonomy that emerged as an international development of the interwar years. Many young women who dated Americans were exploring a world of modernity, with access to pleasures and dangers that were unacceptable in the traditional moral and social codes of their societies. Often the women who dated and became engaged to American servicemen did so outside of parental control or even in defiance of their parents' wishes, underscoring the independence of their actions. But an essential paradox also defined the women's behavior. Historically, marriage has been one of the defining features of female dependence, and marriage for overseas brides of American servicemen was a uniquely dependent form of marriage, as women placed themselves in the care of both soldier-husbands and the U.S. government. This paradox is at the heart of how war brides reflected on their decision to marry, or not marry, American soldiers. The final segment of the chapter explores women's subjective understanding of their relationships with American soldiers by "reading" women's written and oral narratives of wartime marriage.

Sex and Marriage in World War II

In 1944, the U.S. Army commissioned a report on the "problem" of soldier marriage in the current war. This was an issue of pressing concern among military commanders, as the report carefully documented. To gain an understanding of marriage in its past and current dimensions, the author of the report initially turned to World War I and stressed the many ways that soldier marriage differed in the current and previous wars. A crucial difference was the unprecedented scale of the marriage phenomenon in World War II. Only two years into the war, it was clear that an overseas marriage boom was in the making. The report reviewed the key developments that had contributed to the increase in matrimony. One was the relative youthfulness of the fighting forces in World War II. The minimum age of draftees in World War I was twenty; in World War II it had dropped to eighteen. This meant "that a larger percentage of the military personnel had not yet married or become engaged to young ladies in the United States" at their time of deployment overseas. A second factor was the length and structure of deployment. In World War II, "a larger number of men lived for a longer period of time in a national setting and environment more like their own than was true of the American Expeditionary Forces of 1917–1919." An early postwar study bore this out: 85 percent of GIs who married foreign brides had served overseas for more than two years, 30 percent for four years or more. Improved base pay for overseas service, which put more money in the pockets of American GIs relative to other Allied troops and to World War I doughboys, also served as an advantage to American men in the competition for women overseas.[3]

The historical comparison of the two wars failed to illuminate, however, what it was that military commanders found so very problematic about marriage in this war. Soldier marriage was not especially controversial as a legal matter. The right of service personnel to marry overseas had been well established in the First World War, as had the right of the military to regulate procedures through which soldier marriage took place. The one significant procedural change in World War II was the requirement, laid out by War Department directive, Circular 179, in June 1942, that all military personnel on duty in a foreign country or territory gain approval to marry from the commanding officer. This change placed much greater formal power in the hands of military commanders to determine the parties' eligibility and "fitness" for marriage—though in a number of settings military commanders had already exercised this de facto power in the interwar decades. Military attorneys throughout the war also delineated the limits on a commanding officer's prerogatives in the marriage arena and emphasized the ultimate legality of a marriage contracted by consenting individuals, whether overseas or at home.[4]

For U.S. military commanders overseas, the *problem* of soldier marriage centered around not its legal but its political and social ramifications. High-ranking military leaders voiced concerns about marriage as a divisive force, focusing on the tensions it could generate between married and unmarried U.S. personnel and the ill will and ensuing "bad international relations" that failed marriages or dalliances could cause between allies. Older arguments against soldier marriage also resurfaced, notably the concern that foreign women with bad intentions might take advantage of naïve American troops. But the global character of the problem was a new component of leaders' perplexity. At a conference on marriage convened by the War Department in 1943, participants noted that the issue was one military commanders were now forced to deal with "in every part of the world," demanding their attention to a myriad of differing cultural practices and legal requirements. When military leaders considered marriage in foreign contexts, they saw a minefield of political, racial, and moral sensitivities. Evidently, they believed the "most distressing of all the marriage problems" was that of race: interracial relationships contracted in foreign countries, or "miscegenous unions," were regarded as a special and troubling category, threatening as they did to overturn a strong body of social and sexual taboos to which U.S. military and political leaders adhered.[5]

What the army report was not able to articulate was in fact the most notable contrast in marriage between the First and Second World Wars:

the changing social-sexual context in which relations between American soldiers and local women took shape. As in World War I, marriage per se was only a subset of a wide array of interactions between U.S. soldiers and women. For every relationship that produced a war bride bound for the United States, there were untold numbers of nonmarital relationships that established the boundaries and set the context for overseas marriage. The patterns of interaction in World War II took shape against a considerably different backdrop of sexual practices and popular understandings than those present during World War I. This new sexual ethos—characterized by sexual liberalism[6]—traveled from civilian society to many aspects of U.S. military life and policy during the Second World War—at least in regard to the sexual needs of white heterosexual males. Progressive reformers in charge of soldier morale and morals in the First World War had worked hard at sexual sublimation through soldier athletics, religious ministry, and wholesome entertainment.[7] But a new approach predominated during World War II, one that acknowledged that "most men would seek and find sex during their military tenures."[8] The earlier conception of the American soldier as a "boy" requiring in loco parentis protection had given way to a "red-blooded" American man to be serviced rather than protected—a view that entailed, of course, a highly instrumental conception of female sexuality. This view was embodied in the army's detailed surveys of soldiers' sexual attitudes and practices conducted in selected command areas during World War II. The responses of enlisted men showed that the military's view of male sexuality by and large closely matched that of the men themselves. The army survey's frank questions, intended to guide venereal disease education and prevention, garnered even franker answers, such as, "As for the whorehouses and etc. I feel as long as they intend to keep the average G.I. overseas for so long a period, . . . it's human for a fellow to want to indulge now and then." Another serviceman summarized more succinctly, "I don't give a damn who he is he can't go forever without a piece of ass."[9]

Military policy and practices in World War II recognized sexuality as an integral need of men, white heterosexual men specifically, while denying or attempting to suppress the sexuality of gay, black, and female recruits and their partners.[10] The military's campaign against homosexuality in particular had a key relationship with the revised view of heterosexuality. New screening procedures and policy directives "introduced to the military the idea that homosexuals were unfit to serve in the armed forces because they were mentally ill." Psychological testing, military psychiatrists maintained, could identify "healthy" fighting material for the armed forces and exclude "effeminate," "deviant" personality types that would endanger fighting readiness. All of this established active male heterosexuality as normative and even patriotic.[11]

To this end, heterosexual eroticism was officially sanctioned and publicly displayed throughout the American theaters of operation. "Pinups" were the most visible example, and Hollywood worked closely with the military to distribute millions of these provocative photographs of female stars. Nude or seminude female figures painted onto aircraft, an extension of the pinups, were another well-known feature of military culture and practice during the war. Entertainment for the troops overseas was frequently bawdy and suggestive. United Service Organizations (USO) shows on the "foxhole circuit" featured "sexual titillation and saucy humor"—over the vocal objection of field chaplains who found the material indecent and morally coarsening. The racy cartoons that ran in periodical for soldiers, *Stars and Stripes*, *Yank*, and their British counterparts, gave new meaning to the expression cartoon "strip."[12]

The military's most forthright and significant accommodation to the new sexual ethos can be seen in the venereal disease program for the Second World War. The management of venereal disease during World War I was built upon education, prevention, and suppression, a formula that generally remained in place during World War II, despite the development of penicillin treatment.[13] What was new in World War II, however, was a "major program of prophylaxis." The condom became the new cornerstone of venereal disease prevention. The mass distribution of condoms—a staggering 50 million per month sold or distributed for free by the armed services during the war—signaled the military's recognition that "the sex act cannot be made unpopular." Coin dispensers were installed at post exchange stores and soldiers' clubs to increase accessibility. Service personnel and civilians alike often remarked on the ubiquity of condoms overseas. One British teenager who volunteered as a hostess for the American Red Cross, a woman who later married a GI, recalled her surprise at seeing signs for prophylactics everywhere at the ARC club, even in the ladies' bathroom.[14] This last observation is somewhat surprising, given that the women's military service corps promoted sexual abstinence for women and barred their access to contraceptives and even contraceptive information—an indication again that it was a narrowly defined male heterosexuality that was tolerated, not a more equitable notion of sexual freedom.[15]

The Geo-racial Politics of Prostitution

The military's revised approach to sexuality and its gender and racialized double standards for sexual behavior were also apparent in wartime policies surrounding prostitution. The story of prostitution during World War II has previously been related as a victory for vice control. The federal May Act, a wartime measure passed in 1942, gave broadly expanded powers to police and federal authorities to prosecute prostitution. Government reports claimed that vice districts were eliminated in more than 600 U.S. cities and towns during the war.[16] Beyond the national and territorial borders of the United States, however, the story of wartime prostitution appears to be far murkier. A study of wartime Hawaii shows that the "Bust the Brothel" policies that applied on the mainland had little impact on Hawaii's booming sex trade, for example. The May Act, as federal legislation, technically applied in Hawaii as much as it did in New York, California, and every military site and installation in between; by the end of the war, a new Hawaiian business class, seeking legitimacy, had succeeded in closing the brothels in Hawaii, and driving many of the prostitutes out of business. But for most of the war, "the brothels were a regulated enterprise supervised by the municipal, territorial and federal authorities."[17]

Of course prostitution, legal or not, existed in every country where U.S. troops were posted. But the policies and practices of U.S. military commanders, their beliefs and their blind spots, had an enormous impact on the economics and demographics of the organized sex trade in the various locales of the war. In essence, area commanders tolerated and sometimes even abetted the establishment of military-regulated brothels for U.S. troops in nonwhite, colonial societies like Hawaii, whereas in white, advanced-industrial, and Allied countries, they committed resources and personnel to the suppression of brothels and the elimination of commercialized sex between U.S. servicemen and local women.

Scattered through scores of military health and medical reports is a surprisingly candid picture of the geo-racial dynamics of prostitution policy during the war years. Army medical staff outlined a taxonomy of sex and prostitution around the world that relied heavily on predetermined assumptions about gender, race, culture, and morality and drew broad conclusions about the essential "nature" of foreign societies based on distorted observation. In Britain, for example, U.S. military reports insisted that the public "frowned upon brothels, so very few were known to exist," and outside of

London, "there was relatively little commercialized prostitution" (an assertion clearly at odds with historical evidence). Moving southward, they claimed, prostitution was "accepted as part of the social structure" in Italy, and "women of all classes" engaged in the trade. In North Africa, prostitution was "huge"; in Iran, "widespread and universal"; and in India, particularly Calcutta, where the population practiced "far eastern vices of all kinds," prostitution was "flagrant."[18]

The moral capacity of civilian populations also followed a diminishing arc from north to south, from west to east, according to these reports. Most disturbing to the sensibilities of military personnel were the sexual habits of West and Central Africans. Here the "native population" was "illiterate and primitive in dress, manners and customs," and sexual promiscuity was "more or less universal."[19] The military's concern with promiscuity and prostitution was, as always, intertwined with its alarm about the venereal disease exposure of American troops. But even the Medical Department's supposedly scientific analysis of disease rates was indistinguishable from its ideological biases and moral judgments. So, for example, in the summary evaluation of comparative infection rates among U.S. troops overseas produced at the end of the war, physicians praised the numbers for the European theater as "commendable," and as remarkable evidence of success for the Medical Department's wartime efforts, but presented those in China-Burma-India as "a special problem." The rates of infection in both theaters were in fact only minimally different.[20]

The cultural, racial, and gender biases of military planners translated directly into prostitution policies on the ground. The U.S. military's preferred and overarching approach to prostitution was suppression, and where it was deemed possible, in Britain, Australia, and Ireland, for example, suppression was practiced. But regional commanders were given wide latitude to determine policies appropriate to their own areas of operation, and in selected areas of the Mediterranean, the Middle East, North and Central Africa, and Asia, suppression was not always considered feasible. Here, as in Hawaii, the U.S. military practiced toleration and at times even sponsorship of prostitution—almost always providing neatly separated facilities for officers and enlisted men and for black and white service personnel. "Tolerated" houses of prostitution were policed by American MPs and inspected by U.S. medical officers, who examined the women for evidence of disease. Often these efforts were reluctant and expedient, applied on an experimental basis and abandoned almost as often as they were started. In Casablanca, for example, 1,500 prostitutes practiced their trade in four city blocks surrounded by thick high walls topped with ground glass. In December 1942, the U.S. Army opened this famed district to U.S. troops, only to close it to Americans three days later when security proved too difficult to maintain. The most extreme program of sponsored prostitution was the one developed by the commanders of U.S. Army Forces in Liberia, where the bulk of American forces were African Americans. At the behest of U.S. Army officials, the Liberian government created two sex camps, or "tolerated women's villages," for the use of U.S. soldiers, fenced encampments adjacent to the main U.S. military reservation near Monrovia. Women who wished to work here were inspected by American army doctors, "tagged," and photographed. A woman purchased a "cottage" from the government and lived in the village. Her tag was removed and she was expelled if she became diseased. The women's villages, founded in 1942, reportedly operated for the duration of the mission, through 1945.[21]

Largely an untold history, prostitution policy across the global theaters of war had an enormous impact on every other kind of relationship between soldiers and local women, including marriage. U.S. military policies regarding prostitution and marriage in World War II existed in a balance. In weighing the need for a disciplined, undistracted fighting force (i.e., an army without romantic entanglements or dependent wives and children) against the need for a fighting force unhampered by rampant venereal disease (i.e., troops that do not engage in commercial, casual, or promiscuous sexual relations), the U.S. military held the two modes of relationship, marriage and prostitution, in tension. In assessing the social and military utility of various types of relations with local women, military officials considered a variety of factors, from public health assessments and police enforcement to Allied and U.S. public opinion. Regional military policies and practices that favored marriage downplayed prostitution, and vice versa.

Deeper beneath the surface, however, the two modes of policy shared a common core, the intention to preserve and extend male control over women. This intention was overt in regard to prostitution. The image of a military red-light district, guarded by American MPs, surrounded by a wall topped with broken glass, and staffed by army-"inspected" prostitutes, is an apotheosis of female disempowerment. But crucial features of overseas marriage policy during World War II also created a wall of male control around the foreign brides of American servicemen. The procedures for wives to enter the United States and the establishment of paternity claims were both areas in which the alien spouse was denied standing to act independently and on her own behalf. In the matter of paternity, an alien woman, married or unmarried, who had given birth to the child of a U.S. serviceman had no access to child support, nor the child, access to citizenship, unless the American father formally agreed to recognize the child.[22] Similarly, though a GI dependent was, theoretically, eligible for transportation to the United States, only the American serviceman could file a transportation request. A husband who had second thoughts about his marriage could simply fail to send for his war bride, leaving her behind in her own country, abandoned and without recourse. In a classic catch-22 that Red Cross case workers encountered on several occasions, the husband in the United States could then file for divorce in a U.S. court; the wife's failure to appear before the court meant in legal terms that she had chosen not to contest.[23] As these examples indicate, structural features of U.S. policy sought to minimize the "messy" problems that marriage between GIs and foreign women often entailed, but time and again they did so at the expense of women.

Solders' Intercultural Marriages: Regional Case Studies

In World War II the U.S. military promoted "healthy," vigorous heterosexuality in order to maintain morale, create a suitable fighting force, and suppress homosexuality. This tolerance could take a wide variety of forms, ranging from American-style dating and military-approved marriage to military-regulated brothels and sex camps. The geopolitics of race, sex, and power on a regional, national, and local basis set the outlines for military policy and soldier behavior in the various theaters of the war. Patterns of soldier marriage must be understood in this wider context of male-female and interstate relations. The sections that follow trace the development of wartime intermarriage in four specific locales of U.S. operation overseas. All were areas of intensive troop deployment for the United States and extensive interaction with local women.[24] All were areas as well that produced substantial numbers of intermarriages—though patterns of marriage differed in striking ways. Significantly, the most desperate circumstances for women and civilians did not produce the greatest number of marriages; in fact, the opposite is true.

Great Britain, Australia, Italy, and the Philippines represent a range of strategic, geopolitical, and racial/cultural relations with the United States during World War II. In Britain, cooperation was the cornerstone of the legendary Anglo-American alliance. This "special relationship" was the incubator for an unparalleled wave of intercultural marriage, the largest from any nation. Similarly, in Australia a sense of mutual dependence in the war effort and cultural and racial affinity contributed to an early and prolonged wartime marriage wave, yielding a GI marriage rate relative to troop deployment at least as high as that in Britain. In both these places, U.S. officials viewed white local women as suitable partners for white GIs (but vigorously discouraged interracial relationships).

Italian and Filipina women, in contrast, were viewed through a different lens, as sexual partners rather than marital ones. In the geopolitical map of sex and marriage during World War II, Italy occupied a midway point between the advanced industrial powers to the north and the colonial societies to the south. Command policy sought to limit the social interaction between American troops and Italian women. These policies had an impact, for the rate of marriage per thousand American men fighting in theater was two and three times higher, respectively, in Britain and Australia than it was in Italy.[25] Marriage suppression characterized policy in the Philippines even more fully. There marriage between American troops and local women was constrained by a legacy of racial and colonial relationships that made it distinct from Allied nations like Britain, France, and Australia. In both Italy and the Philippines, tolerated prostitution was a central component of U.S. policy guiding relations between soldiers and local women. The result of all these factors was a relative paucity of war bride marriage in Italy and the Philippines. As the following case studies will show, then, a comparison of marriage policy and patterns in all four countries reveals the disparate concerns and attitudes of U.S. military commanders against the backdrop of local and regional conditions.

Britain

Cooperation and cultural affinity were the centerpiece of Anglo-American relations during World War II. Like other aspects of Anglo-American cooperation during the war, the marriage wave caused friction on the ground. U.S. and British officials worked diligently to manage civil-military interaction and create a positive climate for intercultural relationships.

The enormous buildup of U.S. forces in Britain was launched modestly at the beginning of 1942. Over Christmas, Prime Minister Churchill had traveled to Washington, where a series of crucial discussions produced a master plan for the prosecution of the war. Britain—densely populated and already stretched for resources—was to serve as the Americans' staging base for a massive invasion of the Continent through northern France, at a date to be determined. General Dwight D. Eisenhower, appointed commanding general of the European theater of operations, U.S. Army (ETOUSA), wryly referred to the massing of more than a million and a half American troops as "our friendly invasion" of Britain. Though publicly the British welcomed the Americans as heroes in 1942, Eisenhower was well aware of the intensive disruption that the American presence could cause in British daily life over the long term. Throughout the war, he and other top officials were sensitive to the concerns of this most crucial ally and aware of the need to work in tandem to court a favorable reputation among the British.[26]

Cooperation extended to moral matters as well. Venereal disease emerged almost immediately as an area of concern in the U.S. deployment. According to army civil affairs officials, "No other public health problem threatened . . . Anglo-American relations more"; yet with satisfaction they noted that "no other problem received closer cooperation and collaboration between the two countries." The problem of venereal infection for U.S. troops in Britain, they concluded, was a product of affinity rather than immorality: men and women from the two countries were drawn together because of their unusually close "cultural similarities"; this sense of familiarity naturally led to high levels of "troop-civilian fraternization," and this in turn to elevated disease rates. In the face of this troubling health development, officials in the ETOUSA were pleased by the vigorous and constructive response of the British. "Excellent cooperative relationships were established" with British health officials, and "many effective measures began to take shape" under the joint auspices of the U.S. Army chief surgeon and the British Ministry of Health.[27] This successful administrative and diplomatic relationship was highly gratifying to ETO leaders—even if venereal disease remained a serious problem in the United Kingdom for the duration of the war.

Ordinary Britons were more uneasy about relations between American soldiers and British women. The famous aphorism that Britons used to describe American GIs—overpaid, oversexed, and over here—captured several aspects of concern. To British adults, Americans seemed impetuous, boastful, and materialistic, and much too intent upon getting acquainted with British girls.[28] Yet young British women were by and large drawn to the newcomers. "The success of the GIs with British women is now part of English folklore," notes a British war veteran and historian. "Suddenly, they were everywhere. . . . They strutted into pubs, cafes and local dance halls looking straight off the silver screen in their well-cut uniforms, . . . so glamorous compared to the British boys in their thick clumsy battledress," recalls one war bride, later a journalist. "A Sunday walk took on new significance as the girls flocked out to look over the Yanks."[29] American troops arrived in massive numbers just as British men were shipping out of the country en masse, awakening jealous rivalry and wartime fears of sexual betrayal.[30] As early news of hasty marriages, "indecent" relations, and infidelity began to circulate, the archbishop of Canterbury himself wrote to the commander of American forces in England to voice concern about these male-female relationships that were causing so much "anxiety to some observers on the English side."[31]

The British public's anxieties in the early 1940s were as much about the behavior of the women as the soldiers. The war years produced rapid and sometimes disorienting change in the lives of British women. Bombing "blitzes," the destruction of homes, evacuation of children, scarcity of consumer goods, and government rationing were all wartime burdens that landed disproportionately on women's shoulders. Britain's "manpower" needs demanded the participation of female workers. The British government went further than any other during World War II to conscript female labor, and conscription fell most heavily on the young—women who were single and in their early twenties. Women were employed in essential industries and sectors and in the women's service corps. By 1945, almost half a million British women were in uniform.[32]

Work away from home was perhaps the biggest change for young British women during the war.[33] Living outside of parent-headed households, in dormitories, hostels, barracks, or billeted with strangers, posed many challenges, but it gave women unprecedented opportunity to manage their own social lives. The most visible expression of this change, for many Britons, was young women's "invasion" of the pubs—often in the company of soldiers. One war worker recalled that "the G. I. s would send yellow cabs to the factory to pick us up when we finished work. We'd all pile in and up to Burtonwood. . . . We'd have a dance and a laugh." "There was nothing more to it," she concluded, though her father was unconvinced of that. "My father used to batter me with shoes, always the shoes, when I got in, not that it stopped me going again!"[34] Going out in public with Allied soldiers, Americans in particular, was an expression of women's newfound independence—one that prompted widespread unease in the British public.

The response of British and U.S. authorities to public anxiety about soldiers and women was a binational campaign to "manage" opinion while trying to steer British-American relations into positive and acceptable channels. As Cyril Radcliffe, head of Britain's Ministry of Information, stated, "There is no limit to the harm that is capable of being done if relations between the American soldiers and the local inhabitants go awry." Britain's Ministry of Information undertook an energetic publicity campaign on behalf of Americans, aided by British magazines and newspapers. Though other foreign troops were also based in England, Canadians and Poles in particular, the Americans were singled out for special treatment. "Meet the Americans," a pamphlet produced by the British government, urged a receptive attitude and encouraged social contact. The Ministry of Information created a "home hospitality" program that was responsible, reportedly, for more than a million GI visits to British homes, a program touted in the U.S. Army newspaper *Stars and Stripes*. Historian Barbara Friedman's summary of these efforts is astute: "familiarizing" British civilians with American service personnel "was an important measure of wartime diplomacy. But it also encouraged Anglo-American romances by privileging the Americans over other allies and equating fraternization with British women's important war work."[35]

The key element of the campaign was the management of male-female relations through the official entertaining of American soldiers. This too was a binational effort, carried out under the auspices of the American Red Cross and financially subsidized by the British government. An extensive network of well-supplied Red Cross clubs crisscrossed the British Isles; like military brothels, these too were racially segregated for black and white troops. Young women were urged to volunteer at these facilities as an important aspect of their patriotic service; and thousands responded—13,000 British volunteers and almost 10,000 British employees worked for the American Red Cross during the war. One of these, barely eighteen when she jitterbugged with the redheaded sailor she would later marry, described the hierarchy of volunteer positions for women. In "voluminous white overalls," she and her friend were first assigned to the basement canteen of a Red Cross club in London; given a choice between ladling food and clearing tables, they were "quick to see the advantage of mixing with the men" and volunteered to be waitresses. But the young women soon learned "there was a more preferable job to be had" for British "Cinderellas" who wanted to shine with Americans—"a dance hostess!"[36] Numerous British war brides met their GI husbands while volunteering at ARC clubs, proving the value of the clubs as a vehicle for Anglo-American understanding and cordiality.

The United States introduced its own propaganda weapon in 1943, in the form of renowned anthropologist Margaret Mead. Mead herself was a partner in a British-American relationship, married at the time to British anthropologist Gregory Bateson. In the summer of 1943, the U.S. Office of War Information sent her on a lecture tour of Britain to help interpret American manners to the British public. The outcome of her investigation was a work of popular anthropology, a booklet entitled "The American Troops and the British Community." The work offered a cross-cultural analysis of "courtship rituals" on both sides of the Atlantic. Mead observed that leisure time was primarily homosocial for British men. American men, in contrast, "enjoy the company of girls and women more than the British do," one reason that British women found American men so attractive. Mead took special pains to interpret American-style "dating," a foreign and puzzling concept to the British on almost every level, and one ripe for misunderstanding. "A 'date' is quite a different sort of thing from an evening spent with someone whom one hopes to marry," she explained.

Mead's observations were both perceptive and entertaining, but they masked a harsher reality. Dating was a ritual well adapted to wartime conditions: extravagant but emotionally casual; lacking in long-term commitment or fidelity; and exploratory in terms of physical intimacy. But the social-sexual choreography she described was a high-wire act for women, and many fell off. By the end of 1943, it was clear from Health Ministry data that the illegitimate birthrate in Britain was undergoing a surge, and at the end of the war, the annual number of illegitimate births to British women had more than doubled over prewar levels, many attributed to American fathers. The illegitimacy rate among married women, that is, pregnancies by men not their husbands, also shot up during the war, reinforcing anxiety about women's infidelity to British men posted abroad.[37]

In the context of the war that Britons experienced, with its social turmoil and displacement and its new freedoms for women, marriage to Americans seemed more like a solution than a problem. Britons may have been surprised by the dimensions of the matrimonial phenomenon, but few objected in any sustained way. Infidelity, divorce, and the illegitimate birthrate were all matters of greater concern. Young people who chose to marry, even interculturally, were engaging in a behavior that was reassuringly conservative beside the behavior of many peers. The patterns of war bride marriage may also have allayed public concern. Most British brides were in their early twenties, with GI husbands just a few years older. In ethnic and social background, brides and grooms were closely matched, according to the best available evidence; American husbands were predominantly native-born, of northern European ancestry and, like their wives, "overwhelmingly Protestant." Critics on both sides voiced a fear of "hasty" wartime marriage, but in actuality, British-American couples engaged in relatively long courtships—much longer than the waiting period the U.S. military required.[38]

Marriage as a personal antidote to Britain's wartime upheaval is illustrated in the life story of one war bride. Doris Bailey was living with her family in a working-class neighborhood of London on the first night of the German blitz, 7 September 1940, when a bomb destroyed their home. The family was scattered, and Doris moved with her company, British Oil and Cake Mills, to Kent. Conscripted for national service, she chose the Women's Land Army and went to work on a farm in Essex. The Land Army girls worked hard, seven days in a row with one day off. But the farm was close to an American air base, and they were frequently invited to dances, where "there were many more men than girls" and the women "had quite a choice." At one dance she met her husband, Roy, an air corpsman from Indiana. They were married five months later, but Doris stayed at work on the farm until she became pregnant. After the war, the couple settled in California. They were married for forty-nine years, until her husband's death—stability indeed.[39]

Doris and Roy's story illustrates further features of British-American marriage during World War II. Although war brides came from across the social spectrum, most observers agreed that they clustered in the working and middle classes, a contention supported by patterns of work and education in the group.[40] British brides were almost universally at work during the war; in one recent study, a striking 96 percent of brides held employment at or around their time of marriage. War service was a prominent factor in the group, as it was for this bride, with one-quarter of the war brides in uniform, and many others in munitions, public sector employment, or factories; a smaller number were nurses, teachers, or other professionals.

There were no doubt marriages that were heedless or hasty. But the wartime earning power of British women meant that marriage was probably a genuine choice for most brides, not a dire necessity; and many seemed to make the choice with care and deliberation. A British war bride's letter, sent to the ETO headquarters in April 1944, captured the deliberate and mature character of such a marriage as well as its emotional roots: "We are not entering into this important phase of life blindly. I realize the importance of choosing the right mate and the years I must spend with him. . . . From the beginning I liked Murray very much and our continued courtship grew to a resolve to become married. I find him steady, conservative and considerate." The relationship was not without romance, however, as the writer readily admitted: "There is really only one main reason for our marriage, a sincere love for each other."[41]

As D-Day approached, support for marriage mounted on both sides of the Atlantic. Members of the U.S. Army chaplain corps, responsible for examining marriage applications in the ETO, showed a consistent pattern of acceptance toward intercultural marriage, even in cases where opposition might have been anticipated, cases of religious intermarriage, for example, or underage brides. The British press reflected a favorable view of marriage with Americans, toward the latter part of the war in particular.[42]

The U.S. military approved and processed an unprecedented number of marriage applications from the United Kingdom, the greatest number in the months before D-Day.[43] British-American intercultural marriage was a consequence of the "special relationship" of the United States and Britain—the legendary Anglo-American alliance of World War II. It emerged as well from a profound sense of common racial and cultural heritage. The racial basis of wartime marriage can be seen most clearly in the ETO's discouragement of racial intermarriages in the United Kingdom, even as white intercultural marriage surged (a topic explored in depth in chapter 5). The consequence of all these factors was an unparalleled wave of intercultural marriage, the largest from any nation. Between 1946 and 1950, records indicate, 36,390 UK women entered the United States under the terms of the War Brides Act (34,944 British, 1,446 Northern Ireland); 35,189 entered prior to the act, for a documented total of more than 70,000 wives.[44]

Australia

As in Britain, intercultural marriages burgeoned in Australia. Commanders of American forces in the Pacific viewed Australia as an oasis of familiarity, with its wholesome moral environment, educated white populace, and low civilian incidence of venereal disease. Military commanders there gave approval to Australian-American dating and marriage. Australians, more socially conservative and insular than their British counterparts and more protective of young women, vigorously debated the issue of intercultural relations during the war, but ultimately they embraced Australian-American marriage within carefully defined moral parameters.

For the Americans, Australia served as primary base of operations for the war in the southwest Pacific region. General Douglas MacArthur, ordered out of the Philippines by President Roosevelt in February 1942, established his first headquarters in Melbourne, later settling in Brisbane. By June 1942, 88,000 American GIs were stationed in the country, a number that topped 100,000 in the fall of 1943 and then declined as troops were redeployed around the Pacific.[45] Australians and Americans shared a common resolve to defeat the Japanese enemy, and for Australians, American troops were a bulwark of security against a Japanese invasion of their homeland—an anxiety that had deep roots in Australian history. Prime Minister John Curtin's famous assertion in December 1942, "Australia looks to America" now, signaled a historic shift away from the nation's traditional protector, Britain.[46]

As U.S. military commanders viewed the situation in Australia, they saw an unusually sanguine one. In all the areas that mattered most to civil affairs and Allied relations, Australia and Australians received high marks from the leadership of the U.S. Armed Forces in Australia (USAFIA). "There were none of the squalid or poverty-stricken slums found in many other countries," military officials observed, and "the general standards of morals and living conditions in Australia were among the highest of any nation of the world"—a fortunate situation that stemmed at least in part from the fact that "the population consisted mainly of white people." American military leaders also praised the "vice situation" in theater, with minimal prostitution and "rather tranquil rates" of venereal disease infection. To some extent, this assessment was based on careful blinders and a series of selective fact interpretations. Medical officers did acknowledge that the venereal incidence among U.S. troops skyrocketed on their initial arrival, briefly reaching the rather high rate of sixty per thousand; but in Australia, U.S. officials did not regard these numbers as a crisis or as a reflection on the character of local women. Public health measures were able to bring rates down steadily over the next two years to the extremely low reported incidence of seven per thousand, an improvement they attributed to the "full cooperation of Australian health and police authorities" and their willingness to adopt disease control measures modeled exactly on those employed in the United States. Army reports also glossed over the fact of legalized prostitution in several of Australia's states, some of which was clearly available to U.S. troops.[47] The bottom line of U.S. military policy was that Australian women were "nice girls" given the benefit of the doubt in their interactions with American troops. Even the army chaplain corps, which generally took a dim view of intimate relations between U.S. troops and foreign women, warmed to the idea of such relations in the setting of Australia. As one American chaplain told the Australian press, there was no moral objection to "sweethearting in a decent way."[48]

The Australian response to intercultural relations, especially those between soldiers and women, was more ambivalent. American troops, though many fewer than in Britain, were concentrated in a few places, amplifying their impact. Christian conservatives, guardians of traditional morality and a potent force in Australian social and political life, blamed American troops for a range of wartime ills, including gambling, drinking, and even the desecration of the Sabbath. American enlisted men, with a rate of pay roughly double that of their Australian counterparts, were a special irritant to Australian troops. Brawling, stabbings, and other instances of violence between "Diggers" and "Yanks" were reported throughout the country. Most famous was the so-called Battle of Brisbane, a night of violence that led to numerous injuries following the shooting death of an Australian soldier by American MPs on Thanksgiving Day 1942. Lesser-known incidents had an equally strong impact on a local level: in Perth more than a thousand servicemen, American and Australian, took part in a riot that riveted the city in January 1944.[49]

Fighting was sometimes incited by jealous competition over women. To calm the situation, USAFIA headquarters issued guidelines for soldiers going out with Australian girls: public displays of affection such as an arm around her shoulder, holding her hand, or sitting close in the park at night irritated local sensitivities and could make the soldier a target for hostility.[50] Despite these warnings, Australian-American couples were a commonplace sight in 1942 and 1943, on the beaches and streets and in the parks of Australian cities and in American clubs and military facilities. Workplace dating was also ubiquitous, with 9,000 Australian women employed directly by the U.S. armed forces, and others in Australia's female service corps, the WRANS, AWAS, and WAAAFs, assigned to duties alongside American troops. Numerous war brides from Australia ascribed their ultimate marriage to its origin in a workplace acquaintance.[51] As in Britain, the American Red Cross maintained an active program in Australia and New Zealand during the American troop deployment, aided by thousands of Australian women who volunteered their services.[52]

The question of Australian women's relations with foreign soldiers led to a contentious debate in Australian society. Conservatives, led by Brisbane's outspoken Archbishop James Duhig, took a strikingly nationalist approach to the matter. In repeated pronouncements on the subject, he urged American soldiers to stay "true to the girls in their own land" and reminded Australian girls of their chief duty, to "build up our sparsely populated country and to make a great nation."[53] Duhig pressed for government action to ban intercultural marriage throughout the war. What better bogeyman could critics hold up as a caution against taking foreign troops into the heart of their society than Private Edward Leonski, an American soldier and serial killer arrested for three gruesome murders of Melbourne women during the month of May 1942. Leonski was convicted by a U.S. court-martial and executed in November, but the atmosphere of fear and danger linked to the case lingered for some time.[54]

By and large, however, Australian people accepted relationships between GIs and Australian women as a by-product of the war, provided they fell within the range of respectability and ended in marriage. Patriotic voluntarism for women was expanded to include care for American boys, who had come so far from their homes to help Australians secure their own. Home and family became an important locus of courtship. Australian support for courtship and marriage to Americans was one aspect of a larger historical and ideological orientation toward family formation among white Australians. Natalism, the imperative for white Australians to "procreate or perish," had been a social preoccupation and a feature of government policy since the beginning of colonization, and natalism continued to dominate women's experience, defining their role as "married mother of the race."[55] In several aspects of wartime behavior, Australians demonstrated their ongoing enthusiasm for marriage, including the in-migration of thousands of war brides *to* Australia, wives of Australian servicemen stationed in foreign lands. Notable as well was the decline of extramarital births to Australian women during the war, a striking contrast with the pattern in Britain, where the illegitimate birthrate increased. When Australian women gave birth, they were more, not less, likely to be married during the war than before it.[56]

The matrimonial orientation of Australian society, reinforced by war, and the tacit approval of Australian-American dating and marriage by U.S. military commanders created the conditions for an intercultural marriage boom during the peak years of U.S. troop deployment to Australia. These marriage patterns to some degree paralleled those in Great Britain, but they also bore the unique features of their "down under" setting and context. Many observers of Australian-American marriage, including American Red Cross officials charged with responsibility for the welfare of war brides, noted the relatively sheltered background of Australian brides, who had received extended "protection" at home by parents. These parents now played a strong role in guarding the marriage prospects of their daughters, sometimes insisting that a marriage take place to protect a young woman's reputation, at other times preventing or disrupting a marriage they deemed undesirable. Australian war brides were also given "protection" by women's organizations. These groups put the U.S. government on notice that they were monitoring war bride marriage policy to ensure decent treatment of Australian wives of American servicemen and a foundation of equality for Australian women as new Americans.

Typical of Australian marriage applicants and their middle-class stability was a Miss C., a twenty-three-year-old telephone switchboard operator. Miss C. met her American sergeant when he came to her office on army business. The couple soon fell in love and dated steadily for the next year, often seeing one another four or five times per week, including frequent visits to her family home. Red Cross workers liked everything about Miss C. and her circumstances, from her "cheery" six-room home, "furnished in a middle-class Australian style" in one of the "nicer suburbs of Brisbane," to her supportive and involved parents. Miss C. herself was an "attractive, well-poised young woman" with a strong interest in "home-making and domestic duties." The couple had good prospects for achieving a similarly stable middle-class lifestyle in the United States, as the husband planned to "earn his livelihood" in his "vocation as an accountant."[57] Though Red Cross workers were not authorized by the army to pass judgment on the suitability of war bride applicants, clearly they regarded this woman as a good match for an American husband.

The story of Miss C. and her American accountant captures several key themes of war bride marriage in Australia. As in Great Britain, these marriages straddled the middle and working classes. In a cluster of six marriage applicants from Brisbane whose detailed case files were preserved in Red Cross files, three were from comfortably middle-class families, one marginally middle-class, and two were the families of "workingmen." Like Miss C. and the vast majority of young single women in wartime Australia, war brides held paid employment, though women's employment was constrained by limitations. Typical of Australian women, who generally completed their schooling at the young age of fourteen, war bride applicants found low-skilled and low-paid employment in the public and private sector—as clerks in shops and offices, waitresses in restaurants, ushers in movie theaters, or employees of a small family business. Some volunteered for the women's auxiliary corps. Wartime employment was part of the patriotic imperative for single women, but work was also a frequent source of conflict between fathers and daughters in the group interviewed by Red Cross workers. Half the fathers in the group objected to their daughters taking employment outside the home; several women curtailed employment, at least temporarily, in deference to their father's wishes. As one father explained, he "did not want his daughter to be working in Brisbane when there were so many strangers and soldiers billeted in the town." Evidently the desire for control over daughters and the reach for respectability sometimes trumped the call for patriotic service.

Many Australian war brides described themselves, and were described by others, as overly protected by their families, and by conservative social mores. "I had led a very sheltered life, and I didn't know too many . . . young men," an Australian war bride looked back on herself at the time she met her husband. Unmarried women in Australia were generally expected to live at home.[58] Of the six case studies of Australian marriage applicants, five lived at home with one or two parents at the time of application, even though their median age was twenty-three—a stability of family relations very different from the disrupted family life seen among British war brides. Parents took advantage of this physical proximity and economic dependence of daughters to monitor their moral and social experiences. When Red Cross workers asked the mandatory question of whether her daughter was pregnant, one Australian mother "emphasized" that her daughter had been "very carefully supervised at home" and "would not be involved in that type of situation."[59] In some cases of unwed pregnancy, parents put pressure on the soldier and his superiors to make a marriage happen. Conversely, parents in Australia were able to prevent some marriages using age-of-marriage laws. In Australia, the family wielded greater legal control over marital choice than in the United States: marriage before the age of twenty-one required permission of the parents or of a judge (the comparable age of marriage independence in the United States varied from state to state but was generally in the late teenage years).[60] Parents could make use of this power to control their daughters and end their relationships with Americans if they thought them adverse.

Some young Australian women, determined to marry GIs, did go to judges and gain their permission despite their parents' disapproval. Strong parental protection also no doubt prevented some potentially unstable, hasty, or risky marriages. One mother, a widow interviewed by the Red Cross, stoutly refused to grant permission for her teenage daughter to wed her American boyfriend because she disapproved of their "morals"; she distrusted the American soldier-boyfriend because he and her daughter were "sneaking" behind her back to see one another and had twice stayed out together until the early morning. Across the distance of time it is impossible to say whether this mother was being overbearing or appropriately cautious. What is clear is that conflict over marriage was inevitable in a society where war had changed the lives of young people even as traditional family structures and values remained strong.

Australian war brides, collectively, received protection from another quarter—the Australian women's movement. The United Associations of Women, the nation's leading advocate for women's rights, took up the cause of war brides soon after the first Australian-American marriages took place. Leaders of the organization did not object to intercultural marriage per se. On the contrary, prominent feminist Jessie Street, the organization's leader for many years, criticized "the ostrich-like policy" of Australian conservatives who refused to face the fact that "where attractive young people are thrown together they are bound to marry."[61] Street's concern was to protect the legal rights of Australian wives vis-à-vis their American husbands. In a letter to Eleanor Roosevelt in June 1942, Street asked for clarification on several key issues, including the lack of guarantee that Australian wives could enter the United States under strict numerical quotas for immigration, and the lack of clarity related to their allotment allowances as military wives. Mrs. Roosevelt sent a personal reply in September, reassuring Street on both points. Street continued to hold military feet to the fire for the duration of the war, meeting with the prime minister and the attorney general to advocate the cause of war brides, objecting, for example, to the USAFIA's marriage application form, which asked women to indicate whether they or their family could support them financially—an illegal requirement, she pointed out, and one that U.S. officials quickly repudiated. Street was joined in her campaign by other prominent women leaders, including the head of the Australian Red Cross and Senator Dorothy Tangney, an outspoken legislator with a strong interest in women's rights. Senator Tangney worked to address divorce laws that placed Australian brides at a disadvantage in conflicts with American husbands and succeeded in adding a six-month waiting period to the marriage requirements for war couples.[62]

When Prime Minister Curtin and his wife traveled to Washington, D.C., in April 1944, they hoped to cement the wartime bond between the two nations and lay out a future of increasingly close alliance between Australia and the United States. It did not escape the notice of the press in either country that three score Australian war brides shared their journey on the USS *Lurline*.[63] As in Britain, a sense of racial and cultural identification and a shared sense of purpose in wartime goals led to an early and prolonged wartime marriage wave between Americans and Australians. Political advocacy from the left and right in Australia also translated into special consideration for Australian war brides. The wartime transport of Australian wives and children to the United States, well before the passage of the War Brides Act and the mass transport of wives from Europe, was the most important indicator of this consideration. Australian war wives became the vanguard of the wider migration of foreign-born spouses and children. One thousand seventy-five Australian women traveled to the United States at government expense during the duration of the fighting. After 1945, the Immigration and Naturalization Service (INS) recorded the arrival of 7,678 brides and 574 fiancées from Australia and New Zealand under the terms of the War Brides Act itself.[64]

Italy

The relative paucity of intercultural marriage in Italy was a consequence of Italy's unique geopolitical position. Historically, Italians in the United States held a lower social status than immigrants from northern Europe, their racial status as "white" less secure than that of northern neighbors. Politically, too, the Italians in World War II had a borderline status, neither formal enemies nor trusted allies. As an occupied people, Italians were subject to different policies than those in the Allied countries. This status was apparent in the treatment of local women, who were stigmatized by U.S. officials as prostitutes and venereal risks. Prostitution flourished in Italy, but intercultural marriage did not.

The Allied assault on the Italian mainland commenced in early September 1943, following the successful drive on Sicily in July. In January of that same year, Churchill and Roosevelt, meeting in Casablanca, had agreed to a southern strategy, attacking the Axis through the "soft underbelly" of North Africa and southern Europe. The collapse of Italy's fascist government just prior to the mainland invasion was an encouraging development for the Allies, but politically, the Italians retained a quasi-occupied status. The campaign in Italy "was always secondary to the western invasion of Europe," and it proved to be one of the most protracted and difficult of the war. The Fifth and Eighth Allied armies inched their way up the spine of Italy, meeting a determined German defense all the way. Rome finally fell to the Allies just two days before the Normandy invasion. German forces in Italy did not surrender until May 2, 1945.[65]

The prolonged military conflict created a desperate situation for civilians. Loss of life was high, with an estimate of 64,000 civilian deaths by Allied air raids alone.[66] Bombing by both sides produced swaths of physical devastation in many cities and towns. When the Allied forces entered Naples, they found conditions appalling. "In no area previously occupied had there been such a complete collapse of all civilian functions," army officials reported. Monetary inflation was out of control, food and clean water in short supply, and transportation unobtainable. Typhus epidemics broke out and were difficult to suppress.[67] Civilian police authority was weak, and local government, in many places, nonfunctional. As they retreated, German forces left mines and booby traps everywhere in their wake, complicating reconstruction efforts. In one town in a heavily contested region of the Abruzzi, nearly one person per day was killed by exploding land mines in the final year of fighting.[68]

Despite the obvious suffering and poverty of ordinary people, Americans tended to view Italians with ambivalence. Many were suspicious of Italy's rapid conversion to democratic ally. Legendary newspaperman Ernie Pyle, traveling with American combat units in early 1944, observed that "our soldiers were slightly contemptuous of Italians and didn't fully trust them. . . . They seemed to us a pathetic people, not very strong in character." The language difference played into these judgments to some extent, but even Italian American GIs expressed hostility at times. "I won't have anything to do with them [Italians]. The minute they find out I speak Italian they start giving me a sob story about how poor and starved they are. . . . They started this fight and they've killed plenty of our soldiers, and now that they're whipped they expect us to take care of them. . . . I tell them to go to hell. I don't like em." Yet Pyle also found that the "typically tenderhearted" American troops "felt sorry" for the Italians and "little by little . . . became sort of fond of them" on a one-to-one basis.[69]

Leaders of U.S. civil affairs in Italy shared the ambivalence of the enlisted men interviewed by Pyle. While the suffering might awaken their compassion, many army officers viewed Italian society as intrinsically immoral and corrupt, Italian people as incompetent and childish. These views, in part, were an extension of the negative stereotypes that surrounded Italian immigrant communities in the United States, but they also grew out of conditions on the ground under the Allied occupation. For civil affairs personnel, no social phenomenon more clearly reflected the moral deficiencies of Italian society than rampant venereal disease spread by an "army" of Italian prostitutes. Prostitution was an entrenched social practice, they argued, rooted in "the moral standards of the Italian people." While civil affairs leaders conceded that unemployment and economic deprivation might be contributing factors, they insisted nonetheless that sexual immorality was "almost universal" in certain regions of Italy and that it cut across all social classes. Military leaders viewed the moral and sexual climate of Italy as radically inferior to that in Britain and Australia.[70]

One indication of the army's concern about sexual immorality in Italy was an extensive sexuality survey ordered by the Mediterranean theater of operations, U.S. Army (MTOUSA) and administered to troops throughout Italy in the summer of 1945.[71] Research studies such as this one were conducted at the request of military leaders to inform key policy decisions, and their parameters themselves speak volumes about the underlying biases of U.S. military leadership. For example, venereal disease studies were undertaken in Italy in 1945 and China-Burma-India in 1944. No comparable studies were ever considered for the ETO as a whole, or for U.S. troops in Great Britain, Australia, or even postwar Germany, where venereal disease rates reached alarming levels. A racialized perspective was built into the research itself, as the primary question in both studies was a comparison of knowledge, attitudes, and behavior for white versus black enlisted men. (It is worth pointing out as well that the research design gave no voice to Italian women as the sexual partners of American soldiers—a contrast with the pioneering sex research undertaken by the Medical Department of the AEF during World War I.) In some important ways the findings of the study confirmed the MTO's anxieties and affirmed its aggressive tactics to fight venereal disease in Italy. Asked, "Have you ever had intercourse in Italy?" 74 percent of white enlisted men and 96 percent of black enlisted men said yes, the largest portion of each race reporting a frequency of about once per month. A majority of soldiers in the study, similar for both groups, 70 percent of white men and 76 percent of black men, stated that they usually paid cash for sexual relations.

Yet in other ways, the results of the study stand as a trenchant and illuminating critique of the MTO's policies on male-female relations from the enlisted men's viewpoint. One area of sharp criticism was the approach to prostitution, which seemed to the men inconsistent at best, hypocritical at worst. In the early months of the Italian campaign, the MTO's approach was one of regulation—to identify certain "better" brothels, and inspect and protect them for the servicing of U.S. troops. This system, established in Sicily, initially prevailed throughout the zone of Allied control. Intense lobbying from the Medical Department of the MTO led to a reversal, and on the last day of December 1943, all brothels in Italy were, theoretically, placed off-limits to American troops.[72] But ample evidence suggests that official and actual practices could differ markedly. When attorney Robert Hill reported to Naples as a newly trained civil affairs officer for the Allied Military Government in January 1944, one of his first official duties was to find housing in suitable hotels and billets for up to a thousand local prostitutes, an order he evidently took in stride.[73] Many enlisted men were certain that officers got away with visiting women of ill repute while enlisted men who did so were subject to punishment, sometimes by the same officers—a form of hypocrisy that enlisted men found demoralizing. Since prostitution was widely available to American troops, enlisted men believed overwhelmingly that the army should provide "clean" inspected houses to help them keep themselves disease-free.

In the free comment section at the end of the survey, black and white soldiers also unleashed a torrent of frustration with the management of their social lives. Many expressed the belief that a more fundamental solution to the problem of sexually transmitted diseases in Italy was increased social autonomy—"not treating us like children." One GI put it crudely but directly: "If a fellow had a chance to have a girl companion to go out with and take to the movies he wouldn't think about getting ass all the time. After all a guy is used to going out with girls when he wants to. But here you can't do nothing about it. . . . So as a result he goes out and tries to find something to f——k." As the men pointed out, regulations imposed in Italy severely limited opportunities for black and white enlisted men to spend time with and get to know "decent" women. The GIs in one outfit wished to take their Italian girls to the beach—pointing out constructively that you cannot "carry on intercourse" in a crowded public venue; but because enlisted men were barred from driving women in military vehicles, the men were forced to rely on the local "seniorina casa [sic]" instead. Short passes, no overnight leave, no transportation, and confinement to base were all used to regulate social life. One black GI reported that "the city near my camp is off-limits to us. To have a decent time we have to hitch hike fifty or sixty miles." Black enlisted men perceived that "Jim Crowism" and the racial biases of white officers intensified the social regulation directed against them as a group: "Normal companionship with Italian white women is not condoned by white officials, not because of the danger of VD but because of their own race hate!"[74]

Men in the MTO were frustrated that organized social life for soldiers was far less developed than in other parts of Europe, an astute observation. The American Red Cross operated clubs and rest areas for the MTO, but the club programs for Britain and Australia dwarfed that in Italy. At the peak of the program in Britain, for example, the ARC ran 265 facilities for American soldiers with the assistance of 23,000 British club workers, paid and volunteer. In Italy, ninety-three facilities were staffed by only 2,500 Italian employees.[75] An important factor in the army's promotion of social recreation in other zones was pressure from Allied governments who wished, to whatever extent possible, to shelter "their women" from unmediated or unsupervised relationships with foreign troops. Largely indifferent to public or government opinion in Italy, U.S. military leaders felt little pressure to promote legitimate or respectable social interaction between American troops and local women.

Underlying the MTO's policies for social interaction in Italy was an assumption that almost all male-female relationships would take place in the realm of commercialized sex. But the testimony of Italian war brides and American soldiers places a different frame around intercultural interaction, one embedded in family and community. Many soldiers who responded to the survey wrote about women they cared about and their efforts to be close to them—although these were matters about which they were not explicitly questioned. One soldier reported, "I met a girl and fell in love so I went with her for a year. Then after checking on her and meeting her folks I asked permission to get married." As in Britain and Australia, visits to the home were crucial to marriage formation. This was in keeping as well with Italian cultural patterns. Italian women of the World War II generation believed "that identity is rooted in membership within a community of others. . . . One's internal state . . . is constrained by the social nature of being a self among other selves," anthropologist Donna Budani has shown, and this worldview was essential to their ability to survive the war. The oral history of one Italian war bride confirms this assertion; her story of courtship and the decision to marry an American is told as an elaborate, labyrinthine tale involving her widowed mother, six siblings, cousins, neighbors, and close female friends, as well as her husband's friends and coworkers. Much intercultural dating took place in the woman's home under the eyes of extended family, a long-standing feature of Italian social and familial structure. Luisa Solomito's Italian American husband, lonesome so far from home, first wooed her family with visits and gifts of food before he turned his attention to her.[76] The lived experiences and preferences of GIs and women in wartime Italy differed little from those in Britain and Australia, but army policy treated their relationships very differently.

No issue better illuminates the divergent understandings of military leaders, American soldiers, and Italian women than that of so-called clandestine prostitution. In the view of civil affairs leaders this was the most fundamental vice problem in Italy—the practice of women who engaged in sex for personal gain outside the structure of the brothels. This informal and decentralized prostitution certainly made legal suppression far more difficult. But the very notion of "clandestine prostitution" moved the issue into a realm of great social and legal ambiguity. What about the Italian woman who took gifts of money or PX food for her family from her GI boyfriend—was she practicing prostitution? And out on the streets, how were allied "vice squads"—teams composed of an Italian civil police officer to arrest the woman and American MPs to subdue or if necessary arrest the American soldier—to distinguish a streetwalker and her customer from an intercultural couple on a date? The frequently violent response of American GIs when police stopped and questioned their female partners suggests that vice squads were often mistaken.

The military's focus on "clandestine prostitution" had the effect of putting many more Italian women at risk of harassment and surveillance. It also placed under suspicion the behavior of all young Italian women. Almost every war bride recollection from Italy spoke to varying degrees about the collapse in category between "prostitute" and "Italian girl"—a pattern distinctive from the American view of women in northern Europe and Australia. Cesira Slawson felt stigmatized on account of her relationship with a GI, in the eyes of Americans and Italians alike; out with her husband, she remembers being called "a bad name" with some frequency, and her husband's violent defense of her reputation.[77] The stigmatization of Italian women who dated or married Americans speaks to the underlying patterns of gender, racial, and cultural bias. This phenomenon of stigmatization, which surfaced in Italy, would be far more pronounced in Asian countries at the end of World War II and beyond, where nonwhite and occupied women interacted with American military personnel.

Intercultural romances in Italy took shape in a tense atmosphere and sometimes faltered because of it. Many soldiers in Italy complained of the obstacles that the army placed in front of their marriage aspirations. "I would like to see the big shots let up on the red tape for fellows wanting to get married over here," one man declared. "There are lots of GIs like I. That came overseas leaving a girl behind and after being over here a short while they get married . . . over here girls can be found that want a good home like I do." After dating his wife for more than a year, and winning her parents' consent, another soldier found his request to marry summarily dismissed: "I had my papers filled out and they refused to send them in. They think if I marry this girl I will ruin my life. I can't get married now but would like to find out how to go about it after the war." One is left to imagine what happened to this man and his partner to produce this heartfelt rant: "I think that the marriage laws that the army has aren't any good at all. They are the cause of more heart breaks and AWOLs than one could possibly imagine."

Despite the stigma attached to intercultural relationships, and the obstacles placed before them, many couples still managed to marry in Italy. What were the distinguishing features of these marriages? The story of Peter and Marie suggests several themes. Peter met his wife, Marie, when she was waiting tables in a Red Cross club for servicemen. Marie was an orphan from northern Italy who had fled the chaos of her wartime community and found work in a larger town already liberated by the Americans. Marie was highly distrustful of American soldiers in general, who only wanted an "overnight friend" to "fool around with." But Peter's ability to speak with her in Italian gave him the chance to woo her, and he eventually gained her confidence and consent.[78] As in the marriage of this couple, Italian American ethnicity was a major component in Italian-American overseas marriage. American Red Cross staff in Italy, responsible for processing brides for their departure to the United States, estimated that up to 40 percent of husbands were Italian Americans; another study found that more than half the brides on a shipping list from Naples had Italian surnames.[79] Italian American and Italian-born service personnel were widely employed by the Allied forces in Italy, where their cultural and linguistic knowledge was invaluable. They took to the country "like ducks to water," Ernie Pyle noted, and their cultural background gave them unique access to Italian women. Many Italian American soldiers were told by their families "to find a nice Italian girl to marry," and many complied. One obedient son, born in Chicago, managed to find his way to his parents' home village during a week's furlough and engaged himself to a hometown girl.[80] Across the theaters of war, military commanders generally had a high level of comfort with intra-ethnic romances, and their approval may help to explain why Italian Americans constituted a large portion of the American soldier-husbands in Italy.

But other aspects of Italian-American marriage suggest that something else was going on under the surface, and perhaps below the radar of U.S. government officials. Case reports from American Red Cross workers in Italy speak to the complexity of Italian immigration patterns at midcentury and their transnational character. One war bride, Mrs. Z., was married to an Italian man who emigrated to the United States during the 1930s, leaving her in Formia with the couple's two children and her parents. The war years were devastating for this family. Their home was destroyed by bombing, the family suffered from chronic hunger, and Mrs. Z's sister died of malnourishment. As an economic refugee from an occupied country, Mrs. Z would have had almost no chance to obtain a visa for the United States. But since her husband had served in the armed forces overseas, he was able to claim her as a "war bride," and in 1946 she and her children boarded an army transport for America. As in this story, an unknown number of "war bride" marriages between American soldiers and Italian women were in fact prewar marriages or engagements—couples separated by poverty or by the politics of the war itself.[81] Government-sponsored transport and liberalized entrance policies for GI wives were a boon to couples such as these.

Italian wives or fiancées of Americans were also more vulnerable to community censure than their British or American counterparts. Italian women recounted numerous incidents of verbal and even physical intimidation when they appeared in public with their American partners.[82] Such incidents of harassment were variously ascribed to jealous Italian boyfriends, their vengeful families, or gangs of pro-fascist youth. In some oral histories and interviews, Italian brides refer to "head shaving" as a form of retribution practiced against Italian war wives with American husbands.[83] The shaving of hair was a misogynistic ritual meant to demean and punish women in public for their involvement with "enemy" men—it was practiced, for example, in postliberation France against French women believed to have "consorted" with the Nazis.[84] Stories about head shaving from Italy are based on hearsay rather than direct testimony, stories the narrator heard about other women and not experiences of her own. Given the limited sources for the topic, it is impossible to determine whether head shaving took place with some frequency or existed primarily in the rich realm of wartime rumor.[85] Whether the stories are rumor or reality, their telling reflected a measure of fear and insecurity on the part of Italian brides—significantly, the only war brides to relate incidents of shorning during or after World War II.

There is, finally, evidence that marriages to GIs in Italy reflected more economic desperation than those in Britain or Australia. One war bride made this observation, for example: "During the war we had many of the girls, you know, that were going with the soldiers just to get some food. Really, [we] didn't have too much [food] over there. . . . So many of the girls would get acquainted with the soldiers just to get some food from them." American Red Cross personnel pointed to generally greater poverty in this group of brides than those from northern Europe, Australia, and New Zealand.[86] Red Cross workers also noticed a strong presence of very young women among Italian brides.[87] One of these brides was Anna, a Neapolitan teenager sixteen years old from a family scraping to survive. Economic desperation was certainly a strong factor in this marriage. Reluctantly, and at the strong urging of her parents, who hoped to provide protection for at least one of their eighteen children, Anna married an American soldier of thirty-five, a man almost exactly twice her age. Although Anna grew to love her husband (and lived with him in California until his death), she has acknowledged that her original decision was not a romantic choice.[88] This is not to suggest that romantic love played no role, or a limited one, in such relationships; it is useful to remember that motives for marriage are multilayered in most marriages, in most times and places. It is worthy of note, however, that Italian brides were the only group of war brides in which women were inclined to acknowledge that their own decision to marry involved a dimension of survival or betterment for themselves and their families.[89]

Intercultural marriage in Italy reflected the political weakness of the country vis-à-vis the Allied powers and its borderline status between north and south. U.S. officials discouraged legitimate socializing between Italian women and American soldiers. Prostitution was penalized in the Italian theater but common nonetheless, placing women in a vulnerable position. Young Italian women had fewer opportunities for voluntarism or paid employment than did women in Britain or Australia. Economic and physical survival was a daily struggle for many women and their families. Going out with American soldiers was, for some, a means to survive, even if it meant they faced hostility from some of their compatriots. Intercultural marriage did occur in Italy, with Italian American soldiers making a major contribution. But the relative paucity of marriage was a reflection of the low status that Italians had in American eyes and the poor matrimonial environment in the Italian theater of war. Under the provisions of the War Brides Act of 1945, a total of 9,046 Italian women emigrated to the United States as wives of American military personnel—a low rate of marriage given the large numbers of U.S. troops deployed to Italy and their lengthy campaign in that country.[90]

The Philippines

The legacy of colonialism in the Philippines shaped relations between soldiers and women and U.S. military policies governing those relations, with prostitution playing a major and marriage a minor role. Marriages formed despite restrictions, yet married couples also faced hostility and exclusion. As Asian immigrants, often married to Filipino American soldiers, Filipina war brides had a highly ambiguous status and identity. Relations between the Philippine Red Cross, the National American Red Cross, and the U.S. military were rife with misunderstanding and mutual suspicion in regard to the brides and their treatment.

American forces returned to the Philippines in October 1944, fulfilling General MacArthur's famous pledge. The massive assault on the island of Leyte, intended to sever Japanese control of the archipelago at its midsection, was a striking success. U.S. forces faced little resistance to the initial landing.[91] What they did meet there was a devastated civilian population with thousands of refugees, dislodged by Japanese atrocities, Allied bombing, and renewed fighting. Many Filipinos were camped on the beaches and on the edge of starvation; in a few months, a civil affairs feeding program was distributing food to 400,000 refugees, as well as food and supplies to almost 200,000 needy local people. Shoes and clothing were the greatest need after rice, requested especially for women and children.[92]

The hunger and poverty of civilians captured the sympathetic attention of the army's First Filipino Regiment, Filipino American soldiers who were among the early landing forces on Leyte. One army corporal noticed a young woman with her feet wrapped in banana leaves and began to bring food to her family; she later became his wife.[93] In and around Manila as well, years of fighting and occupation had created hunger and misery for civilians, now exacerbated by the Japanese retreat. Civil affairs officers were theoretically prepared for the worst as they entered the city, but the unburied corpses of people and animals, the refuse and damage were staggering. The high number of civilian combat casualties also took army medical staff by surprise.[94]

In the short term, the civil affairs division's economic plan for the Philippines focused on resettling refugees, reconstituting households, and putting able-bodied "breadwinners" to work on reconstruction and relief. Women were in large part marginalized in this scenario, which failed to account for the legions of wartime households missing male breadwinners to death, injury, or military service. But Filipina women had long supported families in the absence of men who sojourned for work.[95] The infusion of American troops presented many women with an opportunity for survival. Small-scale enterprises sprang up in the vicinity of American camps, even the temporary ones. Women sold candy and snack foods to American soldiers; they also picked up and washed their laundry for pay. Some engaged in black marketeering, buying surplus cigarettes and other supplies from soldiers and reselling them to Filipino civilians. The selling of sexual services was also, no doubt, among the cash-earning opportunities for women, important in an economy that offered them limited options.

U.S. military officials evinced little interest in the problems that Filipina women faced, but they took enormous interest in the problem that women allegedly *posed*. In the aftermath of the invasion, venereal disease was the leading medical conundrum for the U.S. military, according to medical reports. Prostitutes were seen plying their trade everywhere—"in any wrecked vehicle, behind any stone wall, and even in frontline gun implacements and foxholes." Medical officers estimated that 8,000 women were practicing prostitution in Manila alone. Prostitution was, theoretically, illegal under the laws of the Philippine Commonwealth, but judges and police routinely failed to practice enforcement. An occasional report from venereal disease control officers acknowledged that the behavior of American troops also contributed to the soaring figures for disease exposure; many of the troops had been isolated in jungle combat for almost two years, for example, and the pent-up demand for sexual relations was enormous. But publicly army officials blamed local prostitutes, both professional and "casual," for the VD "crisis" on Leyte and Luzon[96]—a scenario much like the one that prevailed in Italy.

Army officials designed an approach to prostitution in the Philippine Islands that followed the pattern earlier established in VD trouble spots in North Africa, Sicily, and the Middle East—unable or unwilling to suppress the commercial sex trade, the military did its best to regulate and control it. The system of segregation, inspection, and treatment of prostitutes also paralleled the practice of the Japanese Imperial Army in its own occupation of the Philippines, a parallel that army health officials pointed to without evident embarrassment. The story of prostitution control in Tacloban, the principal town on Leyte, illustrates how policy evolved under the leadership of area commanders. Army officials sponsored a "red-light district" near the business district in Tacloban, where forty carefully inspected women serviced as many as 500 "army visitors" daily. The case of Tacloban also reveals the conflict that prostitution control could provoke among Filipino locals. Local people raised a variety of objections to the U.S. Army's plan. Tacloban's municipal council eventually repealed the VD ordinance pushed through by U.S. Army commanders and refused to confine suspected prostitutes in the local jail or force them into treatment. Army officials found the city's response frustrating and "unenlightened." It seems likely that local officials acted not from public health ignorance but from a deep resentment of imperious outsiders extending unwelcome control over local women.[97]

Prostitution was the dominant filter through which U.S. military officials viewed Filipinas. In actuality, interactions between American soldiers and Filipinas entailed a much wider range of relationships than those documented by army sources. The substantial presence of Filipino Americans among the U.S. troops was an important factor in facilitating communication and exchange—much as Italian Americans had played the same role in Italy. One young woman who helped deliver laundry to an American temporary base was initially surprised to see so many Filipino men in American uniforms lounging outside their tents; by their second visit, she and her outgoing cousin were engaged in friendly banter with the men. It was here that she met her Filipino American husband. Dating also occurred in higher social classes. Among Filipino native elites, contact with Americans had been commonplace over the half century of colonial relations, and many had learned English from American-born schoolteachers. The family of a Filipino dentist in Manila had several American friends before and after the war. Their daughter Lydia met her future husband, George, an American colonel, through one of these friends. Lydia's family liked him, especially his sense of family, but they still insisted on a cautious approach and sent Lydia's sister along on all of the couple's early dates.[98]

The preponderance of war couples in the Philippines almost certainly comprised Filipino American GIs and Filipina women. Men from the Philippines had migrated to the United States in ever-growing numbers during the 1920s and early 1930s; there they lived on the Pacific Coast in "bachelor societies," Filipino immigrant ghettos with a paucity of Asian immigrant women to court.[99] War service in the Pacific presented such men with an unexpected opportunity to wed and bring a wife to the United States. One GI husband, Felipe Dumlao, was thirty-five and a noncommissioned officer in the U.S. Army when he attended a liberation fiesta in the town of Villava, Leyte, and asked his future wife for a date. This act changed his life, as overseas marriage transformed the life of Filipino immigrant communities up and down America's West Coast. Dumlao had migrated to Seattle, Washington, in 1930, finding work as a houseboy and later as a migrant in the strawberry fields. His social life in the United States revolved around the rough world of pool halls, gambling houses, and taxi dances. On two occasions, when out with white women, he had been picked up by Seattle police; another time, for the same offense, he was beaten by white men. It was safer, he learned, to date Native American or Mexican women, but his life in the United States was, essentially, a lonely existence. Military service in the Pacific war was a turning point for Dumlao no less than for his wife. She was only twenty when they met, a small-town girl from a large extended family. The couple wed in December 1945. They settled in Seattle, where Dumlao, now a war veteran, found better postwar employment at Boeing Aircraft. He and his Filipina bride raised a family of five children in the United States.[100]

Though most GI husbands were Filipino American, the racial and cultural configuration of war bride marriage in the Philippines was almost certainly more complex and varied than army and Red Cross officials chose to emphasize. An unknown number of white GIs dated and sometimes married Filipinas, as did African American GIs, but their stories are hard to document.[101] It was "love at first glance" for one Filipina who met her American husband, a black army sergeant, when she waited on his table at the Happyland Restaurant in Manila. A widow whose Filipino husband had been killed during the war, she worked in the restaurant to support two children from her first marriage. The couple came to the United States in 1947, living in a predominantly African American neighborhood of Pittsburgh. It took nearly four years for the woman to bring her Filipino son and daughter, now teenagers, to join her in the United States. This marriage came to light not through military records but rather by its coverage in the African American press.[102]

Whether bureaucrats approved or not, the processing of brides brought Filipina women into contact with American Red Cross and army officials. By 1946, the American Red Cross field office in Manila had begun to prepare groups of brides for transport to the United States. To American Red Cross staff in the Philippines, most of them white and middle-class, Filipina brides were exotic and different in the extreme. One case worker, assigned to transport duty, described the brides with anthropological absorption in a report for her ARC supervisor: "At the outset [of the trip] they abandon shoes; they let down masses of long black hair; made hammocks for the babies out of the woven clothes racks in the berths; sat cross-legged singing native lullabies; and nearly froze in their lightweight cotton multicolored dresses." But the women were not incapable or unteachable. Their method of housekeeping was "efficient and tidy," and they seemed to comprehend the "instructions" they were given "regarding tipping and other train 'manners.'" The Red Cross worker also found the women, many of them probably quite young, to be deferential and polite. "I'm in a family way, Mum, and please could I have a lower berth," was the pleasingly respectful way that they asked for her assistance.[103]

American Red Cross staff in the Manila headquarters were much less tolerant when Filipina war brides and their husbands asked for money. The reality was that the majority of Filipina brides were from poor families, far needier as a group than any brides the Red Cross had previously encountered during the war. The men they married were often close to destitution themselves and could provide their wives with little financial assistance. Addressing their subsistence needs during the interval prior to their emigration was a task that fell to the Red Cross. When one group of Filipina brides, for example, was detained for an extra three days in Yokohama en route to the West Coast, Red Cross workers in the port community had to bring them food so the brides and their children would not go hungry. The women's mess funds had covered them for a journey of sixteen days, not nineteen, and they had no personal resources for a contingency.[104]

For the American Red Cross staff in the Philippines, race and poverty combined to place Filipina brides and their Filipino American husbands under special suspicion. Though at times sympathetic to individuals and their circumstances, Red Cross workers saw Filipino people in the aggregate as grasping and wily, prepared to take what they could get from their generous American liberators. They described the main office as "besieged" by "throngs of Filipinos seeking assistance," most the dependents of servicemen.[105] The root of the problem, Red Cross personnel believed, was a War Department policy that gave the ARC responsibility for the care of GI dependents as they waited for government transport. Though this policy was in force in every theater of U.S. military operation, Red Cross officials insisted that Filipinos had stretched the interpretation of the requirement beyond a reasonable point. Husbands, wives, and extended families were all implicated in the complaints of Red Cross staff. It was "not unusual" for servicemen, for example, "particularly colored," to provide false statements of their pay rate or cash on hand to Red Cross case workers in order to obtain funds for their wives. In other instances, the "soldier-husbands will send in the wife alone," pleading poverty, when the husband was in fact in the vicinity and capable of providing assistance. Only "clever questioning" could catch these subterfuges. In still other cases, "extortionists" and greedy family members gravitated to the women when they came into possession of dollars, and some American soldiers eschewed sending funds lest their wives be "victimized" in this way.

For the Red Cross to finance the transport of Filipina brides was uncommonly burdensome, ARC officials insisted. They felt fully justified, therefore, in creating a financial requirement for war brides seeking exit from the Philippines, a qualification unique to this locale. Every GI husband with a Filipina bride would have to bond US$100 before his wife would be cleared or processed for transport to the United States. An initial review by the War Department in December 1946 judged the policy reasonable. But complaints from several veterans brought War Department lawyers onto the case, and they soon rejected the ARC's actions as arbitrary and clearly unfair to servicemen simply on the basis of where they had served. Yet even in the face of definitive government opposition, American Red Cross officials in the Philippines continued to lobby for a financial requirement until the close of the war bride program.[106]

The antagonism that U.S. officials in the Philippines displayed toward Filipina war brides created tensions with their Filipino allies as well. This tension came to a head through an unusual incident late in the summer of 1948. On August 11, the *Manila Times* ran what proved to be a patently false story about Filipina war brides stranded at the Angel Island detention center in San Francisco Bay (a site the INS had ceased to use at the start of the decade). The article's sole named source was a Major Eulogio Balao of the Philippine military, on his way home from a visit to Fort Leavenworth, who claimed to have seen 800 Filipina war wives jailed at the site because their husbands, U.S. army veterans, did not want them. This improbable tale might never have come to the attention of U.S. officials, but it was placed in their sights by Aurora Quezon, chair of the newly independent Philippine National Red Cross, who demanded an investigation into this "alarming" allegation. The U.S. State Department and the Immigration and Naturalization Service were called upon to refute the charges, and the American consulate in Manila was asked to handle the diplomatic aftermath.

Like most wartime rumors, this one blended the purely fantastic with elements of distorted truth and a strong measure of social and cultural anxiety—elements that make it a fitting coda to the history of war bride marriage in the Philippines. The INS was a hostile bureaucracy that Filipino migrants had faced for decades in their well-known struggle to establish themselves on the West Coast, so its role in the story was hardly surprising. Filipina war brides represented an important new wave of immigrants, the first major wave of female immigrants from the Philippines to the United States. The Philippine nation's concern for these young women, the fear for their neglect and humiliation expressed in the rumor, also emerged from the historical context. To many Filipino citizens, Filipina women who dated American soldiers were *hanggang pier* women (literally women abandoned at the pier)— wanted by their soldiers only up to the point of their departure.

In a larger sense, the rumor speaks to the colonial legacy of the Philippines and its insecure status as a newly free nation, resentful of U.S. power yet fearful of American abandonment and neglect.[107] The U.S. military's wartime policies governing relations between Filipinas and American GIs served to heighten these fears. This neocolonial relationship also limited the scope of marriage between American GIs and Filipinas. The Justice Department reported that 2,215 Filipino wives entered the United States under the provisions of the War Brides Act.[108] Scholars of Asian American history have correctly emphasized the crucial importance of these Filipina war brides to the establishment of Filipino immigrant communities in the United States—

a view echoed in the memories of Filipino/a oral history informants.[109] In the broader spectrum of overseas marriage during World War II, however, it is important to note what a relatively small community of brides this was and how embattled was their experience. Altogether, the treatment of Filipina brides was a premonition of things to come for Asian service wives during the Cold War decades.

From Modern Girl to American Wife: Women's Memories of Wartime Relationships

For the U.S. military in every theater of World War II, local women were a "problem"—a public health problem, a morale problem, a diplomatic problem. Pragmatically and expediently, regional military commanders formulated solutions to this problem based on local conditions. Their calculus was cold but practical—it involved STD rates, the level of desperation and poverty among civilians, the degree of cooperation from local law enforcement, the temper of community and local press opinion, the reputation and attitudes of American troops in a given area command, the probability of interracial unions, and so forth. In historical hindsight one can see how deeply all these policies and practices were larded with racial, cultural, and gender biases. Though the policies differed from place to place, they shared an instrumental attitude toward women—women were useful to the military in a variety of ways, as girlfriends, dates, or wives, boosting the morale of American men, or as prostitutes or sexual partners, serving men's sexual needs and demanding little in return.

But women did not see or describe their relationships with soldiers in the same terms of discourse that the U.S. military employed. Feminist scholars in recent years have turned to women's personal narratives to reenvision the history of war, seeking to disrupt the predominant war narratives, which are characterized by their nationalist or militarist interpretations.[110] In the same vein, war bride narratives uncover the remembered experience of women in regard to their relationships with American men.[111] Personal narratives, it must be acknowledged, are a difficult and sometimes problematic source to use. Some narrators (the more educated, affluent, and urban, for example) are more likely to be "heard," because they are more articulate than their peers or have better access to the means of cultural production, and therefore their memories of war stand a better chance of being preserved. As well, each war bride's story is unique, reflecting her individuality and the specific circumstances of her life. My approach to these texts focuses on patterning—repeated words, phrases, and narrative devices that convey under-lying cultural and historical meanings. This group of texts is dominated by Anglo-American perspectives, yet where they are available, war bride nar-ratives from a range of national settings share many of the same tropes and patterns.

War brides' stories are complex and at core contradictory. Frequently, women who dated or "went around" with foreign soldiers were challenging the boundaries of feminine behavior in their own cultural setting—a search for personal independence that the narratives often reflect upon with great self-awareness. Consider the testimony of this Italian war bride who was asked if she felt she had benefited by coming to the United States. The wom-an's response highlighted freedom as the primary gift her marriage had given her: "Marrying my husband and coming over here, I was feeling myself. I was not under my father's thumb at all. And I started to feel a little independent, and my husband was not a dominating person." Reflecting further, she drew a connection between her personal situation and the political context: "I would think it was because, you feel this—you came in a country which was a free country. It was not dominated by anybody. So you kind of feel good to belong to something like that."[112] For many young women of the war years, drawn to a certain version of modernity, a relationship with an American soldier was an outlet for asserting personal freedom, intellectual indepen-dence, sexual or familial independence, or all of the preceding. In the inter-war period, the "modern girl" had emerged as a worldwide phenomenon, disseminated through cinema, advertising, journalism, and the consumer ethos of urban centers across the globe.[113] The American soldier held out the allure of an American lifestyle and the promise of personal freedom (a sharp irony, since few social roles are more restrictive of individual freedom than military service). At the same time, going out with soldiers as a prelude to marriage represented something very different; for although war brides might experiment with independence, their stories ultimately end with mar-riage and dependence. In their narratives, women situate themselves in the role of GI wife, privileging themes of romance, wedding, and family. Lois Battle, Australian-born daughter of a GI bride, was not alone in recogniz-ing the duality of their role: war brides "were so gutsy, and they were also so dependent."[114] Their stories are a reminder of how much women's lives were still bounded by marriage and family in the mid-twentieth century despite the profound disruptions of war and modernization.

Jill Newman, a British war bride, was one woman whose life was thrown open to change by war and the relationships made possible by war. Newman's published memoir, *Rain, Rain, Go Away*, is highly distinctive, yet it also captures the patterns of war bride narratives as a group. The early chapters are dominated by themes of independence for women. Newman describes her child self as unconventional and independent. She also describes her emerging sense of sexuality in her early teenage years: "I was starting to use make-up now and make the most of myself . . . , and the boys starting noticing me." The beginning of the war was marked by well-paid munitions work for Newman; for the first time she had surplus money of her own and took pleasure in spending it. The war also initiated for her a very active social life. For a time she dated a British serviceman, but he was soon sent to fight in North Africa. The arrival of American troops in her town, close to Sherwood Forest, seemed less than dramatic because the town had already hosted an influx of British and Polish troops. At first Jill avoided Americans, who came to town in packs, were "rowdy," "childish," and "chasing after girls." Her growing openness to Americans paved the way for her encounter with John, the American sergeant who would become her husband, in a pub one evening. In a manner both playful and confessional, she describes her attraction to GIs: "A lot of girls at work were going out with Americans. . . . [They] found them refreshing and eager to please, and the uniform didn't hurt either! I must admit, I also succumbed to their charms and, after a while, began to find anything American irresistible."

Women from many cultures shared Newman's perception of these brash but appealing newcomers. In many texts the attraction to Americans is palpable—what historian Marilyn Lake calls the "desire for a Yank." "I wanted to fall in love with a Yank, badly," an Australian woman wrote, something "all the other girls" were already doing, "the sort of love I had always associated with Americans—tender, thrilling, tempestuous."[115] Part of the enthusiasm for American soldiers related to their crucial role in the war, their heroic standing as outsiders come to aid the embattled Allies. Yet gratitude alone cannot explain desire. The GIs were also charming, informal, and "great fun." "I thought it was a lark, an adventure," to date an American, a French war bride confessed.[116] American soldiers and American popular culture were inextricably and irresistibly bound in war bride accounts. To be enchanted with Americans was to be enchanted with things American—jitterbugging, jazz, and the exuberant youth culture that Americans exported so successfully through mass communication in the 1940s. Not all women liked the Americans, it is true, or their brash, bold, materialistic style. But many of the women, teenagers in particular, tried to mold an identity for themselves that absorbed these modern elements.

Above all, it was Hollywood and the irrepressible American film industry that both disseminated and defined the images and desires that war brides cultivated. "Our idea of America largely came from the movies, that international educator," an Algerian war bride explained, an observation on the global reach of Hollywood in the 1930s and 1940s that film history scholarship affirms.[117] The trope of the American GI as Hollywood film star was ubiquitous in women's narratives, as teenage girls from Brisbane to Naples to London compared their soldiers to favorite actors—the heavenly dancer who was Fred Astaire, the sergeant who looked like Clark Gable. These glamorous icons were most popular with women, but others admitted they were drawn to the Hollywood tough guys or "cowboy types" among the Americans they met. Furthermore, women drawn to American soldiers fashioned themselves into their favorite looks and images from Hollywood. Two friends outside of London sewed wide pleated skirts in preparation for their first Red Cross dance, then "practiced in front of the mirror, twirling around to achieve the quick flash of panties that we had seen in the movies." One war bride copied a pair of pants for her trip to the United States, "narrow-legged cuffed trousers" she had seen Greta Garbo modeling in a magazine photo, though she was quite sure "no woman had ever sported men's style pants before in Algiers." Women's efforts to emulate Hollywood style sometimes put them in conflict with their elders, who gave these would-be "bloody film stars" a chilly reception.[118]

Women's interactions with Americans, as framed in war bride narratives, were an extension of the heterosocial, consumer-driven youth culture that American modernity encompassed. Women described meeting their American soldiers at the cinema, in dance clubs, at roller-skating rinks, at the beach, and on the street. Red Cross and government-sponsored recreation and socialization figure in their stories as well, though not precisely in the way that the sponsors hoped they would. These institutions tried to establish strict ground rules for respectable interaction between soldiers and local women, with chaperones, curfews, drink and dance limits, and the vetting of female guests. But young people often pushed the boundaries here as well, turning Red Cross dances into key sites of amorous encounter.[119]

Women's relations with American soldiers were also mediated through gifts and commodities. The "things" that Americans brought to women are an important trope of their wartime narratives. "My sisters and I welcomed the presence of these handsome Americans with open arms. . . . If Mother would only give her permission for us to date just one of these Americans, we confided to one another, wouldn't there be cigarettes, cosmetics, and stockings that looked like silk rather than sackcloth?" "We were obsessed by the lack of such items," she continued, and indeed, in a wartime environment of rationing and deprivation, such longings were all but universal. Wartime critics attacked the "greed" or venality of women who took gifts from American boyfriends, and even questioned their patriotism, but in women's narratives, such gifts appear in a far more nuanced light. In some situations the gifts of American soldiers played a demonstrable economic role in a woman's personal or family survival; this was especially the case for Italian and later German women who wrote or spoke about their wartime experience. More often, in women's accounts, American commodities were a sign or prefiguration of the "good life," the more prosperous future that marriage to an American partner seemed to promise. The things that Americans brought—flowers, chocolate, stockings—became associated with the romance, prestige, and sexual potency attached to American men. "Hollywood had constructed American men as sexual, and their constant identification with the symbols of romance . . . created the Yank as a generic lover," Lake astutely observes. One British war bride wrote with particular insight about the meaning of GI gifts for her younger self: standing eagerly but insecurely on the brink of adulthood, she understood such items as "essential . . . to the unfamiliar world of sophistication where our dreams and schemes were leading us."[120]

Families could present an obstacle or a conduit to women's "schemes" of independence. Almost universally, war brides present their lives as deeply embedded in family, and often as family drama first and foremost. In an important subset of accounts, the war bride's relationship with an American is either initiated or nurtured in the context of family. One British bride wrote, "My mother liked Don very much from the start. Both my brothers were away in the Royal Engineers, and he was like a son to her."[121] As we have seen, parents who extended hospitality to American servicemen for patriotic or personal reasons often paved the way to a marriage, whether intentionally or not. In some cases, families pressured women to marry, for financial reasons or due to pregnancy. Much more often, however, women described their parents as resistant to their involvement with an American—because they were distrustful of American GIs and their intentions, because they believed their girls were too young to make such an important decision, or because they were unwilling to risk the loss of a daughter to a distant land. "The Yanks had a reputation of being very fast with the girls," another British war bride recounted, and her parents were not pleased about her falling in love with a soldier she met at a local dance in Wales, but in time "Bob won my folks over." For other women, parental opposition was far more difficult, if not impossible, to overcome. As one recalled, "My father was very strict and when he found out I was dating a Yank he went up like a balloon. . . . He was angry and said many unkind things. . . . I married against his wishes and he was never reconciled to my marriage." Yet the alteration in social and family dynamics brought on by the war limited the control of fathers and mothers and often emboldened young women to act upon their feelings with heightened self-confidence. "My father didn't want me to go out with a Yank or bring one home. One day I bravely said, 'Wouldn't you rather I brought him home than stay out with him?'" Recognizing that his leverage over his independent daughter was essentially hollow, this father relented.[122]

As these stories suggest, many of the daughter-parent conflicts over American boyfriends were an indirect family dialogue about the sexual autonomy of young women. Parents were understandably concerned with the sexual "reputation" and well-being of their daughters (a concern that many daughters in fact shared). But women's narratives also display a great deal of interest in sexuality—curiosity about sexual experience, interest in sexual experimentation, or unabashed desire. This is an area where one might expect women's narratives to be less open, and yet often they are surprisingly so. In Monette Goetinck's memoir, she and the other French Algerian war brides enjoyed talking about sex and developed a lusty, humorous mode of communication about their American husbands and about Yank men in general. Quoting a shipmate, Goetinck wrote, "'God, look at him eat,' she marvelled. 'I wonder if he screws with the same enthusiasm.'" Goetinck herself frequently daydreamed about her "new American staff sergeant husband," in terms that made the basis of the attraction very clear: "My handsome Bill, muscular and virile, . . . his broad chest . . . his strong arms . . . his manly voice."[123]

In their narratives, women portray themselves as shaping their own romantic and amorous encounters. A significant trope is that of the "choice," a scenario in which the woman must make a romantic decision about a soldier. Many women described making choices between several suitors or, like one vivacious French war bride, having difficulty choosing and therefore trying to keep several men on the line at once. The choice was often one between a local boyfriend and an American GI. War brides, by their very status, eschewed the safe course of waiting loyally for the hometown boy in favor of the much riskier intercultural and international marriage.[124]

Significantly, women also expressed a great deal of ambivalence about their own agency. In their narratives, women reflect on themselves as adventuresome and sometimes even "wild" ("though we were saints compared to the girls today!"). But women mitigate themes of autonomy and choice by simultaneously portraying their younger selves as acting and acted *upon*. There is good reason for this self-presentation: with women called "predatory" in almost every country for pursuing relationships with foreign soldiers,[125] war brides had strong incentive to reframe these affairs as something beyond their control, or even guided by a higher power. This is where the trope of "the romance" emerges in women's narratives. Romance is a convention of storytelling strongly associated with women as readers and writers. "Falling in love," the center of the romance plot, is the central touchstone in almost every war bride's story. It suggests a kind of helplessness—an experience over which one has little control. Not infrequently, women's narratives give "falling in love" a physical, literal dimension, like the war bride who toppled onto her husband at the skating rink, or the one who fell in love when her future husband fell from the sky—his plane forced to land in a field beside her rural village. In some narratives, the American pursues the female protagonist. "I had no intention of getting involved with a GI," wrote one war bride; it took great patience and persistence, she demonstrates, to win her love. Versions of "I said yes just to get rid of him" are a common refrain—one that signals both a choice for women and a lack of choice at the same time. Love also happened spontaneously and mutually in many accounts: in a classic convention of the romance, women describe "love at first sight," love in an instant, a glance exchanged across a crowded room à la Romeo and Juliet.

Falling in love, in the war bride narrative, is necessarily followed by marriage—the transforming event that alters the status of the woman, conveying social status and respectability, and turning a reputation-risking flirtation into the socially legitimate role of "war bride." Once again, Jill Newman's compelling memoir captures this dimension of war bride narrative. The pull of marriage is the theme of her life story's second stage, as strong in its own way as the earlier pull of independence. Newman explicitly contrasts her wedding plans with the situation of those "other" women, the girls at the factory whose relationships were just "wartime flings," women who ended up "pregnant and alone" after their Yanks departed. If that was the risk of "going around with soldiers," marriage was the reward, a public assurance that her GI's love and attentions were sincere. This was important, for in a modern social milieu where casual dating felt romantic, amorous, and sexually charged, male intentions were hard to read. The wedding was concrete and public proof of his love, and war bride narrators reveled in the details of this celebration. A gown made from parachute silk or borrowed from a stranger; a cake made from hoarded ration tickets, a honeymoon only eight hours long—these are the humorous and human touches that convey the longing for normalcy in the very abnormal setting of war. But they are also the essential and universally recognizable features of the wedding ritual, the wedding qua wedding.

The wedding was also a threshold in the woman's personal identity, marking her transition from independent, modern girl into dependent wife. Newman summarized this sense of transformation on the eve of her departure for the United States. Gathering with her girlhood friends to say farewell, she reflected, "They were all starting to marry and settle down, and like me, growing out of their wild ways." Though she looked back on the war years with a bittersweet sense of loss, Newman was ready to embrace the adult woman's life of marriage and family, enhanced by the adventure of travel to a new country. This passage in Newman's text also describes a second transformation, from British woman into American military spouse. For Newman, as for other British brides, this transitional moment was identified in women's stories with a unique stage of their journey, the period of waiting for transport at Tidworth Camp, the U.S. military's enormous processing center in Southwark. For brides from every nation and region, the journey to America on board a U.S. military transport played a crucial role in her story. In this phase of her experience, the woman adopted her first American identity, that of "army spouse."[126]

The central paradox of war bride identity, the tension between dependence and independence, was also captured in a related but quite different body of evidence: the political language and public protest of war brides in England and Australia late in 1945. Frustrated by long separation from their husbands and by indefinite plans for their emigration, the overseas wives of American servicemen took their grievances to the streets. Several thousand wives picketed the U.S. embassy in London near the end of October. Shouting, "We want our husbands!" they demanded immediate family reunification and insisted on a meeting with John Winant, U.S. ambassador, and State Department officials. In Australia, GI brides stormed the offices of the state transportation company, making similar demands. For some months the Australian women had been gathering in local "GI Bride Clubs" with varying degrees of formal organization, for mutual support. The American Red Cross had sponsored and aided these groups, believing that they were an important preparation for the acculturation that the women would soon face, but they almost certainly never imagined that the clubs would become a vehicle for public protest.[127]

War brides were protesting a U.S. government policy with a clear rationale and strong public support in the United States: that all available shipping would be prioritized for the redeployment of American troops, many of whom awaited reunion with wives and children of their own. But these arguments did not dissuade foreign brides awaiting transport. Their minor social movement, the only instance of collective action by war brides, once again reflects the fascinating two-sidedness of their identity. While the women were acting, effectively and publicly, on their own behalf, they were also insisting on the right to be cared for by their husbands and, in absentia, by the U.S. government. Unfortunately, none of the war bride narratives written or collected to date speaks to this rebellion, and none of the participants or organizers has reflected on the event. But the women's signs and slogans, their body language and self-presentation, preserved through photos and news reports, are themselves a form of interpretable speech. With a political framework that might well be described as "maternalist,"[128] the women asserted their right to their husbands and demanded expedited transport to the United States. The women brought babies and small children to help demonstrate their plight (in a smaller protest in Bristol, England, in fact, GI babies *were* the demonstration, placed on display to prick the conscience of public officials). A young British woman, captured by an AP photographer, became the face of this action for American readers: with an infant in one arm and a toddler in the other, she posed before an enormous placard asking, "WHO'LL FEED GI BABIES?"[129]

This was well-staged political theater, and briefly, the women's actions made news on three continents. They also led quickly but quietly to an intergovernmental response. At a meeting between U.S. and British officials during the days following the protest, a deal was struck to begin the transport of brides and their children from Britain in January.[130] But in the open, both the British and the American press dismissed the women's actions as futile, slightly foolish, a little unseemly, and too shrill to be properly feminine. That the women would agitate to secure their rights was certainly not what the U.S. military was expecting when it constructed a carefully delineated role for GI dependents overseas; this was not, after all, the part that foreign women were supposed to play in the drama of the Second World War. A number of commentators wondered aloud if the brides were in fact entitled to special privileges by virtue of marriage, or even if their unruly behavior had proved them unworthy of ultimate American citizenship. What conservative critics failed to see was that the women were in fact acquiescing in their own acceptance of dependency, making their claim on the state solely as wives, and specifically as wives of American servicemen. In many ways, the women's actions foreshadowed their role in postwar America. The paradox of female dependence and independence is crucial to understanding the postwar positioning of war brides in U.S. society as avatars of traditional female gender identity.

Five French war brides dock in Boston, April 1919. One woman, a widow, was accompanied by her French daughter. American Red Cross photograph. (Library of Congress Prints and Photographs Division).

Czechoslovakian women and children arrive on the U.S.S. Chicago, October 1919. The majority of the women had married much earlier; their husbands emigrated to the United States before World War I and later served in the U.S. military. The husbands' service rendered the families eligible for free government transport. American Red Cross photograph. (Library of Congress Prints and Photographs Division).

An iconic image from World War II—an American sailor and his British bride are reunited at the Seventh Regiment Armory in New York City, February 1945. She still wears her identification tags. Photographs like this one streamed from the press at the end of the war. (copyright Bettmann/CORBIS).

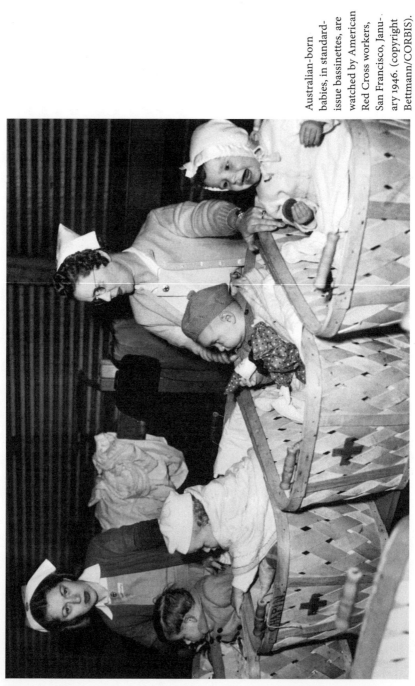

Australian-born babies, in standard-issue bassinettes, are watched by American Red Cross workers, San Francisco, January 1946. (copyright Bettmann/CORBIS).

German war brides and fiancées deplane at Idlewild Airport, December 1948. As the Cold War emerged, German wives were welcomed as NATO "partners" of American servicemen. (copyright Bettmann/ CORBIS).

An army sergeant and his bride-to-be present their application to American consular officials in Tokyo, February 1951. Public Law 717 and others were written with strict limitations to prevent widespread marriage between Japanese women and American GIs. The image was taken by a later-renowned Japanese photographer. (copyright Takamasa Inamura/CORBIS).

Honeymoon: U.S.A.
by William H. Robinson

I WAS meeting my wife. My pretty, blue-eyed French wife. I was standing at the southern dock landing while hundreds of war brides spilled happily down the gangplank of the troopship to their waiting husbands down below.

One of those women would be Annette—my wife. I could see her now. She would hurry down the gangplank, then when she reached the landing she'd look excitedly for me, and when she'd spy me, she'd come walking at first and then running into my waiting arms.

Oh, gosh, it seemed so lovely when I outlined what we would do when I was over in France. I'd look down into her eyes as our eyes would explain the anguish that three years apart can bring. I'd reach out and embrace her and then kiss her long and hard. Maybe I'd even whisper through a choked throat, "Welcome home, Annette."

Yes, there I stood waiting for my wife. I should have been tickled pink. I should have been just as happy and excited about meeting my wife as those fellows were about meeting theirs. But instead I was standing almost huddled behind some big packing boxes on the dock, peering out now and then across the heads of the GIs, seeing if I could glimpse her. And I wasn't a bit happy.

You wouldn't have been either if you were I, awaiting your wife at a Southern dock. No, you'd have done the same thing I was doing, smoking cigarettes, chain fashion, not because you wanted to, but because you were scared stiff.

You cast a hateful glance at the throng of ex-GIs; you'd see some of them sight their wives and clasp them tightly and then you'd ask yourself why. Why couldn't you be standing out there, right next to the gangplank, instead of cowering behind boxes because you were you?

I cursed to myself because the ship was docking in this Southern port instead of New York, where I could have met her with

Coming Next Week . . .

The Courier's talented staff writer, George F. Brown gives us a spot of clever fiction next week . . . which runs along the line of his favorite stint . . . that of theatricals. It's one of the most surprising yarns of the year. Don't miss it .

"WHAT A CHARACTER!"
By George F. Brown

In Alabama, how I had told my mother to leave the garage unfinished as I wanted to finish it when I returned from overseas. I told Annette about the flowers that grew almost up to our front window, and how I would take her picture as she stood among them. I showed her the picture of my home.

"Oh, Johnee, these flowers I must see when I arrive in your America, no?" she asked kissing the picture.

"Sure, sure," I retorted, still kidding myself about all these lies I had told her about how wonderful America was. How we'd have a real honeymoon. In America we'd make up for all the lost time over here. "Don't worry about a thing once you're over there, honey, not a thing . . ." I heard myself saying. I remembered I left her quickly then, for she was crying because I had to leave her and I hated to hear her cry. I left her with her choked voice in my ears and I could hear it even in the many letters which she wrote me weekly—for three years.

ever married her in the first place, that I was nothing more than a liar! Liar! Liar! America isn't what I said it was!

. I don't know how I managed to start walking toward the colored cabbie's taxi I had waiting. I could feel my heart beat in my temples, my eyes watered with sweat and my arm pits were slick with perspiration. I was scared!

Poor Annette! She followed half-wondering and not knowing what this was all about. And how could I tell her? How?

As we walked past the gathering

wouldn't create a spectacle.

I just wanted to get my wife away from this dock, from the men and their glaring, hating eyes.

Suddenly, and in hearing range of the men, Annette, with one foot on the cab's step, tugged at my sleeve and looked up at me, smiling. "I know, Johnee, you play the game, n'est-ce pas? You play, how you say, hard 'to get, eh, Johnee?"

I forced a half convincing smile and shoved her gently inside the cab. The cabbie shoved the gear into second and the car shot away like a rocket!

I squirmed around in the seat, tried not to look into Annette's puzzled eyes and looked through

nostle with trembling lips and for a moment when she asked, "Johnee, we will see the white painted church? and the place where you work?"

I felt myself tighter all over, feeling rotten. I had forgotten that I had told her about the cute white painted church, the town and all, but how could I tell her that we couldn't ride through the city where the church was, without being hanged almost immediately?

I turned my head away from her and gazed out of the window. No white painted church, no Main Street, no bungalow with flowers growing in front, no nothing except fleeting shrubbery.

I held her hand tighter as she looked at me, sensing that I was writing letters and praying. Three years. And now here, in America, I was sneaking out of my city to go North.

Suddenly the tears came; I couldn't help it. I cried ... ashamedly. Honeymoon! Yeah, this was going to be some honeymoon, all right.

An African American veteran and his French war bride are watched by hostile white Americans. This graphic accompanied William H. Robinson's short story for The Pittsburgh Courier, 11 June 1949. (Pittsburgh Courier archives/copyright New Pittsburgh Courier).

This Vietnamese-American couple had themselves photographed on a date at the Saigon Zoo, circa 1969. The soldier broke orders to come to the city and take her out. Almost forty years later, the photo is a treasured memento of their long marriage. (Courtesy J. McDonald).

4

"Good Mothers"

GI Brides after World War II

Welcome War Brides! We have liked your faces as we have seen them in newspapers, magazines and newsreels. You look capable, alert and happy. Your babies are bright faced and sturdy and we know it has not been easy to keep them that way on your meager food rations. Hence, we realize that you are above all, good mothers. . . . We want to help you learn to love America because it needs the best you and your children can give it. . . . You and ourselves must make a special effort to get along because in our dealings with each other we are a test of whether the peoples of the world . . . can live together in peace.

Malvina Lindsay, *Washington Post*, 1946

Writing in *Reader's Digest* just weeks after the atomic bombing of Japan had ended World War II and begun a new era of intense insecurity in global relations, journalist George Kent sounded a hopeful note as he considered America's future role on the international stage. Kent's theme was war brides: the thousands upon thousands of foreign-born wives that GIs were expected to bring home to the United States. Although "a few complaints about these marriages have come from parents and from American girls," he said, "anyone interested in international good will favors them enthusiastically." Kent elaborated his vision of person-to-person diplomacy through the medium of matrimony: "A British girl settled in a small town becomes . . . a force for understanding the British. On her visits to her homeland she becomes a respected spokesman for the United States." In Kent's view, the war bride could also serve as a model for postwar American womanhood: "These girls should make a pleasant addition to any community. They come from middle-class homes. . . . Their eagerness to do the right thing by their new country and by their husbands is a good sign." Loyal, patriotic, and family oriented, the war bride not only had the makings of the ideal wife but also could serve as an exemplar of women's duty to the nation and its homecoming soldiers for her American-born sisters.[1]

The period following World War II was the heyday of the war bride in the twentieth century. From the halls of Congress to Hollywood movie studios, in trial court proceedings, fiction, and the press, the white Allied war brides whom GIs brought to the United States after the Second World War were celebrated—a striking contrast with their reception after the First World War. More than 100,000 women arrived from overseas during the protracted period of demobilization and occupation. As diplomats courted international alliances around the globe, war brides were represented in ways that reassured Americans of their nation's ability to woo and win the admiration of foreigners. Brides (and the occasional groom) from England and Ireland, France and Italy, Australia and New Zealand, and eventually even from Germany and Japan, were perceived as compatible with the new security arrangements that the United States sought to erect as a bulwark against international communism. Columnist Malvina Lindsay's pledge to the GI brides showed the weighty responsibilities resting on their slender shoulders: "We welcome you with the hope that together we may be able to push a little further along the trail toward an harmonious world and a secure planet."[2] That this new international order would take shape under the hegemonic leadership of the United States was increasingly clear as the Cold War political consensus hardened in the late 1940s.

The search for stability in postwar international relations was paralleled by a drive to stabilize domestic gender relations. Changes initiated or accelerated by the war—the separation of families, the employment of wives and mothers, and the growing independence of women—left American men and women in search of a new equilibrium of power, resources, and expectations. The outcome of that historical process is well known: the postwar "embrace" of family-centered domesticity described by Elaine Tyler May, a regime that offered a privatized form of security to many middle-class Americans, sometimes at the cost of personal fulfillment or individual aspirations.[3] Although the outcome is clear in retrospect, it did not appear assured to American women and men in the immediate postwar years. The process of renegotiating gender arrangements was difficult, contentious, and sometimes bitter. GI war brides figured in this debate as exemplars of wifely devotion and good mothering. The valorization of these intercultural marriages was part of a broader effort to affirm heterosexual and marital relationships as the normative experience for young Americans in the wake of the war. The return of

GIs with wives and children in tow was a welcome indication that American soldiers had marriage on their minds. These foreign brides symbolized and personalized what had happened to a generation of young Americans who had fought a long war around the globe. As families, employers, and policymakers pondered the problems of veterans' "readjustment" to civilian life in the postwar moment, they pointed to war brides as a model solution: ideal wives for homecoming soldiers who could be a bridge between the spheres of war and home, both foreign and familiar at the same time. Ultimately, the nation's ability to absorb and accept these "GI brides" appeared to denote its readiness to understand and assimilate the meaning of the war for the men and women who had fought it and to step forward into a new and more "mature" relationship with the world beyond the United States.

The Coming "Crisis" of the Postwar Family

The public discourse about foreign war brides took shape against a backdrop of grave concern over the state of American marriage at the end of the war. "On every side we hear that the family is in danger," anthropologist Margaret Mead observed in 1945. "Conferences are held, committees convene, and professional workers meet together to worry and plan for the family." Although America's first lady of social science dismissed these worries—"the family itself is a very tough institution," she said reassuringly, and still the best option for raising human offspring—even Mead had to acknowledge the "feverish" sense of crisis that surrounded the subject of relationships between women and men, especially returning soldiers. These concerns were widely shared by academics and social critics as well as ordinary citizens during the war years. Juvenile delinquency, adultery, marital discord, and divorce were all cited as the harvest of poorly conceived wartime marriages.[4] Doubts about wartime marriages were expressed in a spate of articles in popular and professional journals, with titles such as "Are They Too Young to Marry?" "Should Soldiers Marry?" and "Will War Marriages Work?"[5]

As the war neared a close, "family readjustment" became the focus of concern. Like "veterans' readjustment," which had economic, social, and emotional dimensions, the repair of families was believed to be crucial for the health of postwar society. The demands placed on women would be great because the needs of veterans were so profound. Writers, both academic and popular, warned of the danger that combat veterans could pose to the good order of American society, a belief with deep roots in America's past.[6] *Newsweek* derided the hysteria of the "women's magazines and Sunday supplements" with their provocative headlines like "Will Your Boy Be a Killer When He Returns?" and "Taught to Kill—the Coming Veteran Crime Wave." But *Newsweek* itself linked veterans to such "rambunctious" behavior as "auto thefts, drunkenness, disturbing the peace, disorderly conduct, and assault and battery."[7] Fortunately, the experts maintained, these men could be tamed, their energy and anger redirected into constructive pursuits. The Servicemen's Readjustment Act of 1944, dubbed the "GI Bill," with its unprecedented education and training benefits, home mortgages, and business loans, was designed to reintegrate America's fighting men into the framework of postwar society.[8] Yet the veteran's wife was an equally, or even more, important force in taming these potentially "dangerous men." The government provided access to economic opportunity; women were charged with the burden of meeting soldiers' social and emotional needs. As a prominent family researcher observed, "The wife must be strong; again and again it has been shown the wife must make the major contribution to marital adjustment. With a soldier-husband, her contribution must be greater than ever before."[9] The GI Bill privileged marriage based on male "breadwinning" and female dependency, codifying the centrality of family in the process of postwar readjustment.[10]

But what if veterans were marriage "slackers"? Given the subsequent marriage boom, it is difficult to comprehend the level of anxiety that this possibility aroused late in the war. Many American women feared that they might never marry. Indeed, the "man shortage" in 1945 was almost as acute a concern as the "manpower shortage" had been in 1943. A journalist captured the fear of many single women "that postwar competition for husbands will be keen and that if she does not capture her man now she may wait out her life without marriage or children." Their anxiety was exacerbated by authoritative warnings that "no matter what happens, two to five million marriageable women in America are doomed to remain spinsters because of the male-female disproportion."[11] Paradoxically, when social commentators considered the U.S. economy, they viewed the demobilizing army as a horde of homecoming job seekers, sweeping women out of work and destabilizing the job market. Yet when they wrote of marriage, the same pool of veterans appeared to be a pathetic trickle of prospective husbands, with so many lost in combat, disabled, or married overseas.

Many Americans initially blamed "foreign women" for stealing American husbands. "Single girls and their marriage-minded mamas . . . are very much aware that a man shortage exists," wrote one woman to the *New York Times*. For these American singles, "every British bride coming to our shores means just one less male for the native American. We have nothing against British brides, but," she concluded with an apt political-economic metaphor, "we cannot help feeling a little disconcerted when so sizable our portion of dwindling stock is consigned over to lend-lease."[12] A Rhode Island woman complained vehemently to her senator about marital competition from "the dregs of Europe and Asia," women "who hi-jack our boys in a weak moment."[13] African American women also complained that "foreign wives" were "stealing" their men, a situation one described as "sickening."[14] The matrimonial nationalism that American women expressed during the war years shows the insecurity that many felt about their future. Fear of hostility from American women was a "number one concern" of the foreign wives of American soldiers as they contemplated emigration.[15]

At the close of the war, Americans at home waited impatiently and with trepidation for the GIs' return. Social anxieties common to all postwar transitions focused especially acutely on family concerns at the close of World War II. In the wake of the profound disruptions caused by depression and war, many Americans regarded a stable home and family life as the best antidote to social upheaval, both domestic and international. But the predicted dearth of marriage-ready men made this goal seem unattainable for many women. Soldiers' overseas marriages only deepened the sense of insecurity about the postwar prospects for the formation of stable families. Columnist Malvina Lindsay sympathized with these concerns and acknowledged that "criticism and resentment" would almost surely greet the foreign brides, but she counseled patience: "Give us a little time to get over the first strangeness . . . and we will reach out a warm and open hand to you." War brides generally shared Lindsay's confidence that "eventually American women will understand and accept them"; after all, one asked, "can anyone blame us for falling in love with an American?"[16] This war bride's comment was insightful for intercultural marriage initially found acceptance in postwar American society as an affirmation of American manhood.

Congress and War Brides

Congress took important action in the immediate postwar era to affirm the overseas marriages of U.S. military personnel. Between 1945 and 1952, Congress passed five bills to address the status of alien spouses and children and to facilitate their entry into the United States: Public Law 271 (the War Brides Act, popularly known as the GI Brides Act), December 28, 1945; Public Law 471 (the Fiancées Act), June 29, 1946; Public Law 450 (an extension of the

Fiancées Act), March 24, 1948; and Public Law 213, July 22, 1947, and Public Law 717, August 19, 1950, allowing entrance of "racially inadmissible" Asian brides on a short-term basis.[17] War bride legislation appeared to go against the grain of postwar immigration policy, for restriction and the national origins quota system were still the law of the land, extended by the McCarran Walter Act of 1952.[18] The GI brides bills were temporary legislation of limited scope, and they were not intended to reshape the outlines of U.S. immigration policy. The rights that they endowed were framed by Congress as rights for veterans, and only incidentally for their spouses and children. In taking this stance, Congress continued a tradition of "martial citizenship," a privileged category of citizenship, earned through military service, that had deep roots in American history. The legislation accepted only *white* brides from overseas; in the initial bills, Asian women were categorically excluded as "racially non-admissible aliens," reinscribing in immigration policy the racist immigration laws in effect since the end of the nineteenth century. Later, with the rise of the Cold War and new threats in Asia, Congress attempted to address the inequity, but in a bill so flawed that it seemed almost a cruel joke to the thousands of couples who were denied permission to wed in Japan.[19]

War bride legislation ultimately highlighted the plight of servicemen's alien spouses and affirmed their status as a special and privileged category of foreigners. The congressional debates that surrounded these bills reveal official attitudes toward intercultural marriage at the close of the war and their complex interaction with issues of gender, race, and national identity. The first War Brides Act, introduced into the House early in 1945, was proposed to ease the entry of alien spouses and children as non-quota immigrants. It applied to the spouses of U.S. citizens serving in or honorably discharged from the nation's armed services, and it covered marriages resulting from the war—those contracted during the hostilities or up to three years following passage of the act. Congressional action was prompted by pressure from servicemen, spouses, and their increasingly impatient families both in the United States and abroad.[20] Though the War Department initially resisted any policy changes that might interfere with priority transport for demobilized troops, the State Department endorsed the legislation. By this time, overseas consular offices faced an onslaught of paperwork from couples struggling to comply with the complex rules for non-quota immigration applications. Officials in Washington were also concerned with the burden and expense of providing medical examinations for war brides and children in numerous overseas ports.

The House Committee on Immigration and Naturalization commenced hearings on May 16, 1945, on a set of "war bride" bills. This was the first time that the issue had been debated in a congressional forum, so the discussion was wide-ranging. The committee's favorable inclination toward the legislation came first and most strongly from a sense of duty to those who had served their country honorably in the war, the sentiment that "nothing is too good for our boys." The opening discussion had little to do with the brides at all. Edward Shaughnessy, representing the Immigration and Naturalization Bureau, assured committee members that "these bills are strictly 100 percent veterans matters." Representative George Sadowski (D-MI), who authored two of the bills, stressed the "entitlement" of veterans: "I do not want to put any additional burdens . . . upon these men who have been fighting overseas. . . . I think they are entitled to have these wives brought in here as citizens and with the least amount of red tape and difficulty" (28–30). Sadowski also raised the banner of "rehabilitation," reminding his colleagues of their responsibility to lighten the burdens faced by vulnerable veterans and ease their readjustment (30). Committee members took careful note of the American Legion's support for the legislation. This large and politically influential veterans' group took a severely restrictionist position on almost every immigration issue of the 1940s. Yet the Legion's 1945 national convention backed the entry of foreign-born spouses.[21]

The fact that the bill was meant primarily to benefit GIs was responsible for a little-noticed but problematic detail of the legislation: the bill admitted alien spouses married to citizens in the armed services, but it made no allowance for the admission of soldiers' widows or orphans. A considerable number of foreign women who had married U.S. soldiers lost their husbands to combat, disease, lingering wounds, or accidents. Some had children who were automatically U.S. citizens. Were these widows entitled to enter the United States and raise their American children there? Evidently not. This feature of the law came dramatically to the attention of the public in October 1946, when the press reported that three GIs' widows were being detained at Ellis Island and awaiting deportation. The Justice Department hastened to explain that the women were not entitled to entry as non-quota aliens because their citizen-spouses were dead. Questioning by reporters revealed additional absurdities: if a foreign wife legally boarded a U.S. transport overseas, but her husband died while she was on the water, she would be sent back on arrival. Even the heartfelt pleas of American in-laws, who wanted the wives and children of their dead sons to join them in the United States, failed to alter the policy.[22]

The "man shortage" did play a role in the committee's deliberations, as some members expressed concern that doing right by veterans might wrong

American women. Sadowski acknowledged this objection. "I know girls generally, including my wife, when I got this bill up, said 'I am not in favor of it.' She said 'We don't want these boys marrying over there; they should marry American girls.'" Representative Noah Mason (R-IL) extended the principle of matrimonial nationalism to servicewomen and their foreign husbands. "With all due respect for the WAVES and the WACS," he intoned, "the bachelors in this country should have consideration, and I do not see why any WAC or WAVE should marry an outside man." While the committee agreed that "marrying American" was preferable, the overseas marriages that had already occurred were indisputable facts, and in the end the committee saw no sense in acting punitively against them.

Gender considerations came into play at another point in the committee's deliberations. A stated purpose of the legislation was to correct a glaring gender inequity in immigration law as it applied to armed services personnel. Although the alien wives of male U.S. citizens were already admissible into the country as non-quota immigrants, Edward Shaughnessy pointed out, the alien husbands of female U.S. citizens were not. As he explained, the bill "would give our American citizen girls in the Armed Forces the same breaks that the law gives to American boys taking on alien wives" (9). Correcting this feature of the law received the resounding support of the committee.

The two serious divisions among committee members involved the question of citizenship and the status of Asian spouses. Representative Sadowski, whose district included the racially and ethnically diverse city of Detroit, advocated legislation that would automatically extend U.S. citizenship to alien spouses following their marriage. As he reminded his colleagues, citizenship by virtue of marriage was the legal principle that had applied to foreign brides in the First World War. This measure would extend important rights and protections to foreign-born spouses, Sadowski explained. It would allow soldiers' widows and their citizen-children to enter the United States. It would protect foreign-born spouses who were currently barred from obtaining a visa because of a criminal conviction for a minor infraction. Sadowski shared an anecdote that had been brought to his attention. One of his constituents had married in Australia. The night before the wedding, he, his wife, and another couple were drinking, and the soldier's bride ended up in court, accused of stealing cash from the pocket of their companions. Though the woman denied she did it, she was persuaded to plead guilty—permanently barring her entrance into the United States (31–32).[23]

Sadowski's proposal for automatic citizenship was a substantial departure from contemporary immigration policy. But Sadowski assured his colleagues: "There is no question in my mind that the wife of a soldier, a veteran, who has fought for the country, is going to make a good citizen, and I think the children are going to make good citizens" (29). For the majority of the committee members, however, Sadowski's proposal "just went too far." Congressmen Mason and Allen (D-LA) were disturbed by the idea that an individual could attain U.S. citizenship without ever stepping foot on U.S. soil (19–20, 30–32). Allen feared that automatic citizenship would encourage "marriages of convenience." The citizenship proposal was rejected.

No issue generated sharper ideological divisions in the committee than the issue of race. At the start, the GI bride legislation reproduced the racial exclusion feature of the U.S. immigrant quota system. The euphemistic language of "admissible" and "inadmissible" aliens was readily recognizable to Americans in the 1940s as referring specifically to Asians, who had been barred from entry into the United States by one legal structure or another since the late nineteenth century. The ban on Chinese immigration had come under fire during the war as an insult to an ally in the struggle against Japan. In a small but symbolically significant shift, Congress voted to repeal the ban and include China in the quota system, with the minimum annual quota of 105 slots. For some, this change revealed the hypocrisy of the remaining edifice of Asian exclusion. Two moderates on the committee, Joseph Farrington (R-HI) and Samuel Dickstein (D-NY), were ready to plead the case for a second group of "worthy" Asian immigrants, the spouses of service personnel. The issue was raised at the first hearing on May 16 (51, 35–36). Ed Lee Gossett (D-TX), a renowned anti-Semite and racist in the House, asked Robert Alexander of the Visa Division, State Department, what might happen to an American soldier who married a woman in India or the South Pacific. A "very cogent problem," Alexander acknowledged, although he hastened to assure the committee that "there are not very many of them." Making his own racial biases quite apparent, he continued: "There are some very pathetic cases where the soldier has married a woman who is not eligible for citizenship, although they look white from their photographs, and we certainly do not blame the boys for being attracted by them" (51). The State Department evidently regarded this as an irresolvable tragedy and was prepared to throw up its hands and lament the plight of these modern Misses Butterfly. But the Hawaiian representative thought otherwise: Why not make exceptions for Asian brides as well? Farrington, whose district included large Chinese

American and Japanese American constituencies, proposed an amendment to allow non-quota visas to otherwise inadmissible spouses on the same basis as those racially admissible.[24]

As Farrington pushed for change, the committee's racial conservatives resisted and pushed back. Congressman Asa Allen asked Alexander of the Visa Division what he knew about reports "that there have been a good many marriages abroad between white persons and colored persons." Alexander replied, again, that the number was negligible, but it had happened. He spoke of the problems these marriages had created for the State Department because antimiscegenation laws in many southern states continued to make such marriages a criminal offense, though under questioning Alexander admitted that if the couple headed to a state where they could "cohabit legally," no action could be taken by his division (16 May 1945, 53). Allen also spoke against Farrington's proposal for suspending Asian exclusion even on a limited basis.[25] At the second hearing later in the month, Farrington proposed a compromise he hoped the committee's solid conservative majority might accept: let Asian spouses into the United States without allowing them to apply for citizenship. This proposal would facilitate family reunification without altering the ban on naturalization. Committee chairman Dickstein approved of the plan: "If the soldier is willing to marry that type of a lady, that is his business, and I do not think we have the right to interfere, and there ought to be some provision made to cover such situations." (23 May [a.m.] hearing, 21 and 23) But the racial moderates were clearly outnumbered, and the Asian inclusion amendment was ultimately dropped.

In late December 1945, the War Department announced that transport of alien spouses would begin after the first of the year, putting pressure on Congress to resolve the remaining issues and ease the entry of GI brides. A wartime measure with a built-in expiration date, Public Law 271 conferred exceptional benefits on a unique class of citizens, World War II veterans, and only by extension on their families. By limiting these benefits to "racially admissible"—that is, non-Asian—spouses, the bill reaffirmed the racial underpinnings of the quota system. The GI Brides Act, coupled with the Fiancées Act passed six months later, showed the importance that Congress attached to marriage in the reintegration of veterans. The new laws secured the rapid entry of thousands of alien spouses and fiancées, the largest influx of foreigners in a generation. Putting "GI brides" and "GI sweethearts" in the spotlight, the legislation not only admitted foreign wives but provided government endorsement of their presence.

"Operation War Bride": The Allied Brides of 1946

Public approval of GI brides gathered force in 1946. The U.S. military's giant boatlift of wives and children from Europe, named "Operation War Bride," was inaugurated on January 26 when the SS *Argentina*, a former army troopship, left England with 451 women and 175 children. When the ship arrived in New York Harbor nine days later, 200 newspaper reporters, photographers, and radio journalists were there to greet them.[26] Magazines and newspapers had an insatiable appetite for photographs and stories about the women. *Life* magazine paid one English-American couple to return to Britain with a photographer and reenact the intimate moments of their courtship. These were displayed for *Life's* readers in a "you were there" format that had great appeal, if questionable journalistic integrity.[27] The arrival of these women and their children was a "feel-good" story, a happy ending to the hard and bitter years of war for tens of thousands of GIs. The boatlift cast the U.S. government in a generous role, as the benevolent caretaker of veterans and their loved ones. The war brides fit the mood of 1946, harbingers of the postwar marriage and baby boom. At the height of their migration, a Gallup poll found the American public resoundingly approved of British brides by a two-to-one margin.[28]

Not far below the surface, the saturation reporting of 1946 contained a strong set of ideological messages about gender, race, and national identity. Although the brides who arrived in 1946 came from many countries, the media highlighted British women, sometimes to the exclusion of any other group. *G.I. War Brides*, Hollywood's first attempt to bring the topic of intercultural marriage to the screen, followed the tribulations of a boatload of British brides. A reviewer for *Kine Weekly*, a film industry magazine, predicted strong sales for this "topical trifle" of a romantic comedy, given the widespread popular interest in "the current invasion of America by GIs' English brides."[29]

Americans of British ancestry or affiliation stepped forward to embrace the brides, underscoring their prestigious ethnic identity. British brides in Chicago were invited to a well-publicized luncheon—featuring roast beef and Yorkshire pudding, of course—by Joseph Kennedy, former ambassador to England. The Anglican bishop of New York emphasized the commonalities between British Americans and British brides. "Most of these young women belong to the Church of England and have a natural claim on us," he remarked, urging parishioners to do "all in their power" to "minister to the needs" of the war brides and their families. The bishop called upon the chaplains and social workers of the Episcopal City Mission Society to provide assistance and praised the work of "worthwhile organizations" such as the Daughters of the British Empire and the English-Speaking Union (ESU).[30] These groups offered services to the new arrivals in many communities and later supported war bride clubs across the country. The ESU was second only to the American Red Cross in its comprehensive programming for these new immigrants. ESU headquarters in New York City opened its facilities to all GI brides; but the "high teas," with child care provided, were especially popular with British brides, who flocked to them by the hundreds.[31] All these efforts placed in public view the idea of a natural affinity between English-speaking brides and their American sponsors.

U.S. observers of British brides emphasized their quintessentially American qualities. To one high-ranking official in the Red Cross's Home Service Department, these women were "pioneering types—coming with the same spirit which many years ago, prompted the women of early America to set off across the unknown continent in covered wagons." They too, like the earlier pioneers, "had Indians to shoot at—the Indians of possible prejudice, coldness, and differences of custom."[32] The British brides' likeness to Americans seemed as much physical and racial as cultural or linguistic. Observers repeatedly singled out their fair complexions, impeccable grooming, and aquiline features as pleasing marks of whiteness.[33] WAC captain Rita Longanecker, the liaison officer aboard a war bride transport, declared to reporters that she had "never seen so many smiling, blue-eyed, curly-haired, blonde little babies" before. Others commented on the brides' "inherent likeness, both in temperament and appearance, to ourselves." A Red Cross worker conjectured that "if an equal number of American girls of the same age had been scrambled in among them and the whole lot had kept quiet, no one could have told the British from the Americans."[34]

Australians, the second-largest group of "Anglo" brides, also captured the sympathy and interest of the American press and public. Women from "down under" seemed more exotic than the British, but they were white, Christian, and English-speaking. The responses to a boatlift of Australian brides, which arrived a year and a half before the better-known British flotilla, set the pattern for the representation of all women of British descent. Reporters emphasized how much the Australian and New Zealand women were "like us." *Newsweek* posited that "Americans and Australians generally like one another" because they are so similar. *Time* reassuringly depicted these brides as familiar "girls next door": "News pictures told the U.S. that its soldiers and sailors had gone for the same sort of friendly, healthy good looks that they had learned to look for at home." Australian and New Zealand brides usually entered the country through West Coast ports, and journalists took the opportunity to highlight the frontier heritage shared by white Americans and white Australians. The outdoorsy, athletic Aussies seemed perfectly suited to life in the Great American West.

Readers were reminded that friendly relations between American soldiers and "ANZAC" brides had important geopolitical implications. Diplomats, on hand to greet the brides, emphasized the growing importance of this strategic alliance. The New Zealand consul in New York declared it "a jolly good thing" to bring "us all closer together. . . . There's nothing like a baby or two to break down international barriers."[35] A report on the landing of "90 Aussie Girls" in San Francisco began as a war bride story but abruptly veered off into a report on Pacific relations, as the reporter quoted Australian prime minister John Curtin's extravagant praise of America's "gallant fighting men," "skillful" commanders," and "magnificent contribution to Australia." Curtin pledged unwavering Australian commitment to the Allied war plan for the Pacific—a significant comment in the spring of 1944 with brutal battles looming for the Pacific theater. But Curtin's hope for "uninterrupted American-Australian friendship" had postwar resonance as well. Americans' acute interest in Australian brides registered a growing sense of the importance of the ANZAC alliance for the future of the United States in the Pacific region.[36]

War brides from the tiny, unfamiliar nation of Iceland were also presented as attractive partners in the postwar world, a striking parallel to their nation's emergence as a junior partner of NATO.[37] A profile of an Icelandic bride published in a monthly magazine was part human interest story, part popular foreign policy lesson. Readers learned that the government of Iceland was a parliamentary democracy, that the dominant religion was Lutheran, and that the capital, Reykjavik, had a population comparable to that of Niagara Falls, New York—where this particular couple hoped to take a quintessentially American honeymoon when they were finally reunited. A lesson in racial categorization accompanied these stories. Although their American in-laws expected the brides to "look like Eskimos"—in other words, to be dark and racially "other"—reporters remarked upon the women's blonde good looks. One enthusiastically declared a group of Icelandic war brides "photogenic enough to be Hollywood bound," offering a photo of three long-legged beauties with Veronica Lake hair to prove the point.[38] Iceland soon became the site of a major U.S. air base, and Icelandic brides served to introduce this new Cold War ally to a broad American audience.

Coverage of the war bride boatlift of 1946 offered readers a dual message: introducing Americans to the more international family to which they would now belong in Europe and the Pacific, it simultaneously showed how familiar and familial a realm it really was. Indeed, war brides were sometimes presented as more "American" than their American husbands and their families. *Yank* magazine told the story of "one English girl" who wed an Italian American serviceman, only to find herself "stuck" in Brooklyn's Little Italy; in less than two months, the strange food, Catholic customs, and Italian language of her husband's family had driven her to find her own apartment in the city, a move that the writer found understandable. "More Americanized" still was Joan Kane, formerly of Sherwood Forest, Nottingham, home of the vaguely Bolshevik folk hero Robin Hood. Yet this British war bride had proved her American credentials. "Mrs. Kane has been working in a war plant, talks 'American,' and roots for the Brooklyn Dodgers," wrote the *Yank* correspondent with obvious approval. GI brides like her would be an asset to their new country, their assimilation nearly complete upon arrival.

Model Wives, Mothers, and Consumers: Domestic Reconversion

GI brides, as presented in the cultural discourse of the mid-1940s, embodied the key characteristics of the ideal postwar housewife: devoted wives, dedicated mothers, and eager consumers. To a large degree these concerns also permeated the reflections and recollections of war brides themselves. As Americans waited with trepidation for the return of the nation's fighting men to civilian life, overseas marriages were scrutinized for the future they might portend. Most observers drew optimistic conclusions. America's veterans looked like the "marrying type" after all, their overseas marriages now regarded as an American success story. Many were reassured to see the men settling down, talking about jobs, and starting a family. The foreign brides had shown extremely good taste in cherishing American men; and they were held up as exemplars to American would-be-wives of the "womanly" behavior that would strengthen the family and American society in the postwar period. Many war brides were willing to adopt this role in their new homes, provided that stability and respect were proffered them in return.

In the language of 1946, it was the "bride" in war bride that commanded respect, a woman who willingly defined her life through her relationship with her husband. The most pleasing characteristic of the GI bride was her devotion to her American soldier. Even in his absence, she worked hard to keep her husband's love and interest, like the British brides assiduously doing calisthenics on board the transport ships to "stay trim for him." Devotion was displayed in the war bride's most fundamental decision, to leave her home and family in order to be with the man she loved. In war bride narratives, connections sacrificed were the most common measure of a woman's love. A British bride recalled, "It was extremely difficult leaving my mother, a widow. My eldest brother had been killed a few days after the D-Day landings, and now I was going to live overseas. It was hard. . . . [But] I was anxious to get going."[39] For American readers, touching stories of personal sacrifice—an only daughter leaving her aging parents, or an entrepreneur giving up her flourishing family shop—heightened the romance surrounding these relationships.

Like their soldier-husbands, the GI brides had seen the reality of war at close range. Commentators stressed the resilience and mutual understanding of marriages forged in the furnace of war, although the "feel-good" tone of most magazine accounts precluded all but the most superficial discussion of wartime tragedy. "An ex-paratrooper and a girl who lived in London during the blitz and the buzz bombings know better than most the ways in which a word like [forever] can be shattered," explained the *Ladies' Home Journal*. The theme of resilience in war bride marriage was also expressed in a flurry of social science research produced in the early postwar years. The most ambitious study, by a team of social workers at Western Reserve University, found a high degree of "marital success" among war bride couples, with maturity gained through life experience as the key ingredient that made for well-adjusted couples.[40]

War brides sometimes voiced a similar perception of their relationships. One British woman described her feelings of alienation from her husband's American family, who, though kind, seemed willfully uninterested in her wartime experiences or those of her husband: "The louder his family chatted about local things and Easter bonnets, the quieter I became. . . . No one talked about what had just happened in Europe; beating the Nazis, something I had grown up with." A bride like this could empathize with her husband's war trauma, and her story implied that the sheltered or shallow American girl would need to work much harder to do so.[41]

American women, praised during the war for their civic and economic participation, were compared negatively with British brides in postwar discourse. The American woman, it was feared, having tasted wartime independence, might not need or appreciate the American man. "Many an American boy told me he was marrying an English girl, rather than an American girl, because 'American women demand so much more.' 'I don't know whether I'm going to have a job when I get back. I don't know how things will be with me. Maybe I couldn't make an American girl happy with what I'd have to offer her'"—these concerns were allegedly voiced by many a GI. Foreign brides, in contrast, were openly appreciative of their "Yank" husbands, building up their egos with attention and praise rather than knocking them down with complaints and criticism. American women could have seen this virtuous behavior as a threat to their own prospects as mates, but the American Red Cross urged them to view these relationships as a valuable lesson in how to treat homecoming veterans: "English girls are simpler in their ambitions; they expect less of marriage and of their husbands than our girls do."[42]

The theme of war brides' simplicity, contentment, and gratitude was so ubiquitous that it came in for gentle parody in the *Saturday Evening Post*. Lovely young Enid Dale is the envy of every middle-aged American husband in her new neighborhood, as she pampers and pleases her youthful veteran-husband. He is hopelessly devoted to his adoring and adorable British wife. No task is too humble for Enid to perform, from shining his shoes to emptying the rubbish, always while clad in form-fitting sweaters. When the American wives see Enid beginning to disrupt the domestic tranquillity of Seaview Terrace by setting an unrealistically high standard for domestic labor, they conspire to set the young couple straight. But the American wives do not teach her a lesson in gender equality. Instead, Enid learns the subterfuge of the disempowered; claiming exhaustion, she soon has her husband performing "her" domestic tasks, gaining control over her house and spouse without appearing to do so. The story satirized the British wife's over-the-top perfection, but it took seriously the domestic arrangements regarded as the underpinning of stable marriage.[43]

GI brides fulfilled the reproductive imperatives of 1950s womanhood as well. Six months into the boatlift, the Justice Department reported that 12,000 GI offspring had entered the country along with 46,000 GI spouses.[44] The giant *Queen Mary*, largest of the transports, sailed from England with 688 children and 404 expectant mothers out of a pool of 1,666 soldiers' dependents in February 1946. War babies had been relatively uncommon among the alien dependents of servicemen in World War I, most likely because of the brief interval between marriage and immigration for the majority of couples. During World War II, many soldiers had been in Britain with their wives for two years or more and had started families there. War brides' testimony speaks to the centrality of childbearing and child rearing in their early years of marriage in the United States. Data samples suggest too that the childbearing pattern of intercultural war couples was comparable to that in the postwar baby boom, with its notable spike in family size.[45]

In the European boatlift of 1946, war babies took center stage. Military bands, which customarily greeted military transports at the pier, played a swing version of "Rock-a-Bye Baby" to welcome the ships. Seventy-six strollers were lined up at the San Francisco pier to meet one boat and its "tiny inhabitants." An army officer "described the whole trip . . . in one word, 'Diapers.'" Army nurses shipping out for home were assigned to nursery duty. On one ship, several army engineers were employed to rig up a baby incubator. Another transport was accompanied into New York Harbor by two coast guard seaplanes and a helicopter, all deployed to assist in the rescue of a premature baby boy.[46] The lavish photo spreads that accompanied news of "Operation War Bride" featured babies: fat, adorable, and proudly held by their beaming parents. The fecundity of these young couples signaled the welcome advent of a postwar baby boom. It was not lost on anyone that the babies, unlike their mothers, were American citizens from birth.[47] This formulation, though a by-product of the law, stressed the generative power of soldier-fathers in making American citizens. The foreign-born mothers of these American babies were portrayed as joyous madonnas and garnered praise for being "good mothers."[48]

Not all war bride mothers were deemed equally worthy of praise, however. A tragic outbreak of infectious diarrhea (a form of cholera) on ships leaving European ports in May and June 1946 took the lives of eleven infants, nine from the army transport *Zebulon B. Vance*. Scores of other babies had to be transferred to New York area hospitals on arrival. The infant deaths generated a controversy. Whose fault were they? Should young children have been allowed to sail? Were medical facilities on board the ships adequate? And what danger, if any, did the sick children pose to Americans in the New York region? A commission of inquiry, promptly appointed by New York City's mayor, turned the sad story into a dark morality play. The military was utterly blameless; care and facilities on the transport ships had been excellent, according to the investigators. The commission placed the blame squarely on the deficient care provided by the alien mothers during the journey: "Health authorities testified that . . . the brides' living quarters were 'filthy' and that spread of the infection was probably due to the improper hygiene practiced by the mothers despite the advice of attending nurses." The commission of inquiry pointedly noted that none of the dead babies had sailed from Southampton, England; the dead infants were all on ships sailing from Le Havre, with mothers of "French, Dutch, Belgian and Polish origin."[49]

Less prejudiced investigators could have pointed out that the awful conditions on shipboard—the overcrowding, the sharing of communal sinks, the lack of a separate facility for rinsing diapers—were not the mothers' fault. Several of the women complained to reporters that physicians on the ship had neglected their babies or dismissed their concerns about them. Decades later, a British war bride's daughter who had survived a trip on the *Zebulon Vance* as an infant recounted the terrible conditions that her mother had described: "There were far too few toilets for the number of passengers . . . so they were constantly overflowing and the women had to walk through the waste to get to one of the 4 showers . . . for water or to wash. So many were seasick that they could not move and so vomit too floated on the floors and was constantly having to be wiped up off the bunks." This woman believed that the mothers who lost babies were "not at fault" and condemned "the horrible and unfair public indictment of their most terrible losses." But Colonel Edward Marsh, director of preventive medicine for the Office of the Surgeon General, insisted that the diarrhea had spread "largely because of the type of individuals concerned and the unhygienic manner of living in their countries of origin." In a neat ethnic logic, wives from continental Europe, so seldom mentioned in press reports of the boatlift, were displayed in the inquiry's final report as inferior mothers whose carelessness had led to the deaths of American children.[50]

Yet these dirty and neglectful foreign mothers were seen as an aberration. British brides, who were more similar to native-born white Americans, were never accused of poor mothering or causing harm to children. Indeed, the dedicated mothering of these war brides was a strong motif in the stories of 1946. The reverence for GI brides as mothers was illustrated by the sad and surprising tale of a young British bride who confessed to the murder of her American husband. The most striking feature of this dramatic incident was the outpouring of sympathy and support for twenty-one-year-old Peggy Poland, who was purportedly driven to kill by maternal devotion. The Poland case was one of several postwar trials in which the war bride's commitment to her child was regarded as an important mitigating circumstance for her crime.[51]

Irene, or "Peggy," a native of the Isle of Man, met Sergeant Graydon Poland at an air base near Warrington, England, where she worked as a civilian employee. Married at nineteen, she spent most of the next two years separated from her American husband. Early in 1947 she journeyed to the United States with her infant son, Calvin, and the family was reunited, first in her husband's childhood home in Kentucky and then on the Fort Walton army base in the Florida panhandle. Conflict between the couple began almost immediately and escalated over the next four months. Graydon accused his wife of adultery, sued for divorce, and sent their baby to his parents in Kentucky. Peggy claimed that her husband beat her regularly. She moved out of their shared army home, found a job as a waitress, and took a room with a friend.

On the night of the murder, a Thursday in late July, Graydon was drinking at the Hi-Hat Tavern in Fort Walton when he summoned Peggy to the bar with a note. The couple argued, and when Graydon left, Peggy followed him to the parking lot. There she shot him once in the chest with a .38 revolver she had concealed in her purse. Mrs. Poland was arrested soon after in a second bar by Marshal Ben Stevens, who claimed to find her distraught and tearful. She readily confessed to the killing.

What distinguishes the Polands' story from an ordinary case of spousal homicide is the response of the townspeople: almost immediately, the citizens of Fort Walton embraced the young newcomer as one of their own. Over the weekend, "Fort Walton men," including the town constable, raised a $3,000 bond for her release. The local press reported the story with great sympathy for the young woman: a front-page photo shows Peggy, looking almost childlike, seated knee to knee with Deputy Sheriff Billy Marsh, as if posed at a father-daughter dance. Communication between her old hometown in England and her newly adopted Florida community underscored their shared commitment to helping the young woman. Mayor Cook of Fort Walton assured his British counterpart that Peggy's defense was provided for, with state senator Philip Beall of Pensacola retained to represent her and prominent citizens of Fort Walton paying the fees. Most extraordinary of all was the decision of the Okaloosa County grand jury, one month later, to drop all charges in the case, a striking example of "jury nullification."[52]

Why did the town embrace Peggy Poland, and why did the jury refuse to bring charges? In the absence of the grand jury transcripts, it is only possible to conjecture. Yet a telling picture emerges from local press accounts and wire service stories and from contemporary interviews. Graydon Poland was an American and a World War II veteran, but he was as much an outsider to the community as Peggy was, and townspeople demonstrated no loyalty toward this hard-drinking troublemaker. The Fort Walton army base, with its row of bars and cheap nightclubs servicing soldiers, and the Eglin Air Force Base, established in 1942, were an alien presence in the county, in 1947 still a rural agricultural community of small towns with local businesses. The men who served on the grand jury were likely to have been white southern farmers and small businessmen imbued with conservative Christian family values. A sense of chivalry was at play as well; male officials, from the mayor to the sheriff, spoke of themselves extending protection to a weak and helpless female. Peggy Poland emerges from local accounts as young, demure, and somewhat helpless, but a fiercely dedicated mother. The young bride from rural England was someone they could understand.

Only one motive for the murder was ever treated with any seriousness: the theory that she killed her husband in order to reclaim her child. Her estranged husband's sending their child away was almost certainly the powerfully extenuating circumstance that the grand jury recognized, as it was the theme that dominated all accounts of her story. When the court announced that no charges would be filed against her, the *Okaloosa News-Journal* reported, "Following a few minutes of stunned silence, her first words were, 'Maybe I'll be able to get my baby back now. . . . The most important thing in the world is to get my baby back.'" Similarly, in a homicide case from Las Vegas, Irish-born war bride Bridget Waters claimed that she "killed her husband . . . to save her baby." Waters fetched a pistol from her bedroom during a domestic dispute and shot Frank Waters because the "dangerous look on his face" made her fear he would harm their eighteen-month-old son, Frank Jr., who was playing on the floor. "My heart goes out to the defendant and her child," said the judge in sentencing her to a short prison term. The presentation of these GI brides in the 1940s contrasts markedly with the sensational 1920s homicide trial that presented the actions of a young French woman as a crime of uncontrollable sexual passion. Peggy Poland is a figure of ultimate maternalism, committed to her child at all costs. Through an act of ideological alchemy, a confessed killer could be transformed into a good mother.[53]

As devoted wives of homecoming American servicemen and as fertile, dedicated young mothers, GI war brides were a perfect fit for the national preoccupations of 1946. They were also eager consumers, according to press accounts, interviews, and memoirs. After years of rationing and shortages, war brides marveled at the array of clothing and household goods in American stores. "It's absolutely heaven to shop here," one newcomer to Chicago declared. "You never have to bother about coupons or long waiting lines." "American stores display their goods so attractively . . . it's hard not to buy everything you see," said another. A pair of British brides missed their train connections to California and Tennessee when they lingered too long while window-shopping in Manhattan—a lapse that their Red Cross hosts appeared to find entirely understandable despite the expense and inconvenience it caused.[54] Red Cross workers routinely took brides shopping in New York City to "cheer them up" when their husbands failed to collect them as scheduled. Several magazines presented the women's stories in a fashion-spread format or photographed them trying on American clothing and cosmetics. British war bride Norma Domina, with her "ideal American model's build," posed in an upscale shoe shop in Los Angeles. "A shapely ankle and red, high-heeled shoes look well, provided you're in America," she declared.[55]

The credo of consumerism was at the heart of the postwar American dream and closely tied to America's foreign policy aims. In the wake of World War I, the "consumer-civilian" ideal had been utilized to integrate veterans safely back into American society, but the parameters of this ideal were confined to the U.S. domestic economy.[56] After World War II, Lizabeth Cohen has shown, government, business, labor, and civic leaders had a "shared commitment . . . to put mass consumption at the center of their plans for a prosperous postwar America."[57] American-style consumerism was an economic and political tool of the Cold War as national leaders mobilized to extend the U.S. sphere of influence in international relations. Freedom of choice for consumers and free enterprise for business were indissolubly linked to political freedom in Cold War ideology. U.S. agencies and trade representatives sought to convert the citizens of other countries into consumers and to turn those countries into consumers of American products, with the rationale that mass consumption would win their hearts and minds for the "free world" and the anticommunist struggle. Military civil affairs officers promoted consumerism to women in occupied countries as a domestic antidote to communism.[58] War brides were the perfect test case for this effort: as foreign shoppers in the American marketplace, they were a kind of focus group for "Brand America."

Foreign women's praise for American consumer goods validated the promise of capitalist democracy that was at the core of the Cold War ideology. As a women's magazine put it, "The biggest attraction for the foreign war brides, aside from their husbands of course, is the American 'gadget' . . . which makes housekeeping infinitely easier." Household appliances such as the electric washing machine, refrigerator, gas range, and vacuum sweeper were "taken for granted in American homes but not in foreign countries." "Housework in England is hard," one war bride told a sympathetic female reporter. "We had one day set aside for washin', another for ironin', another for cleanin' the bedrooms. . . . Here I do all my housework in two hours. It's wonderful." Many war brides listened to daytime radio while they cooked and cleaned, enjoying the virtual "company" it offered and improving their English. Any marketing executive would have been delighted to hear a war bride say that she enjoyed the "singing commercials" with their "catchy jingles" so much that she learned to sing them herself.[59]

Americans reveled in the enthusiastic consumerism of foreign brides because it reflected their nation back to them as a land of plenty. European brides frequently drew a stark contrast between the deprivation of their native countries and the abundance of their new homeland. In order of importance, one sampling of brides listed "(1) the self-service supermarkets; (2) the abundance and variety of food and clothes—'back home we never had such variety even before the war'; and (3) American entertainment" as their new nation's greatest assets. One GI bride, wife of a sociology graduate student at Columbia, observed that the shops were "more luxurious" than those back home and the people "better dressed." Although "the displays of merchandise overwhelmed" her, she managed to navigate her first American shopping trip, purchasing seven dresses in a single day.[60]

Even the case of the war bride turned "luxury thief"—aberrant consumer though she was—reinforced the association between GI brides and consumerism. Early in 1947, a twenty-three-year-old English war bride was picked up by New York City police for a string of hotel thefts through which she amassed $25,000 worth of luxury goods. "Blonde, stylishly dressed and soft-spoken," Betty Margaret Pitt was charged with burglary, possession of burglar's tools, and grand larceny. Pitt's larger-than-life story captivated metropolitan readers. Reportedly the daughter of a former Scotland Yard detective, Pitt was married to a U.S. Army Air Force lieutenant when she arrived in February 1946. Her husband greeted her with the news that his parents disapproved of the marriage and insisted on an annulment. Single again and alone in the United States, Pitt made her way to New York City, where she set herself up at the Hotel Bristol and went into the robbery business. On New Year's Eve she hit the Essex House, taking a Persian lamb coat and evening gown, and a few days later robbed Mrs. Irene Van Buren's room at the Barbizon Plaza, carrying off three diamond rings and a bracelet. Pitt's modus operandi was simple: she asked hotel desk clerks for room keys, winning their cooperation with her "unusual poise," "affluent manner," and attractive appearance. Police detectives were "hardly prepared for the stunning sight she presented as she strolled along the crowded avenue . . . wearing a modish hat . . . [and] a three-quarter length silver fox coat." New Yorkers followed her booking and sentencing with interest, and even a modicum of sympathy, particularly when it was revealed that her baby from a first marriage had been killed in a German bombing raid. Pitt acknowledged her crimes, though she was unable to recount them all, and everyone seemed satisfied with her simply stated motive: a desire for "fine things."[61]

The portrait of war brides as eager consumers was tempered by descriptions of their wise frugality. Anglo war brides were praised for the modesty of their aspirations almost as often as they were lauded for their interest in consuming, especially in the first year of peacetime reconversion when shortages of goods abounded. American women were invited to learn from them how to be proper helpmeets to the nation's homecoming veterans. As one GI husband put it, "these girls . . . don't want so many *things*. You get married to a girl [in the States] and pretty soon she's got to have a fur coat and a washing machine and your car's got to be better-looking than the one next door." British women were different, he believed; they demanded less and appreciated more.[62] British brides wanted only what all middle-class Americans were expected to want in the wake of the war: a home, family, and security. So basic were these to the structure of postwar society that desire for them could be seen as patriotic. This message was the gist of a story from the Bronx about veterans' families facing the severe housing shortage. A British war bride was one of the first residents of a new "Quonset hut" community of small, prefabricated homes offered by the New York and federal public housing authorities. In a different climate, New York housing officials might have wished to hide the fact that a foreigner was the recipient of public generosity at a time when so many native-born families were in desperate need of housing. But evidently the Quonset huts had elicited little interest from the American house-hunters who had come to see them, and the housing authority was happy to have the testimonial of a foreign-born bride. The British woman pronounced this modest four-room home just right for her, her husband, and their two infant children. "The young woman loyally declared that she was not disappointed but well pleased with this country," the housing authority reported, in a mild rebuke to discontented American couples.[63]

In contrast with the representation of French brides after World War I as moved by strange, uncontrollable passions and animal desires, the British brides of World War II were presented as utterly reasonable and comprehensible, their desires familiar and laudable, even patriotic. By consuming appropriately, war brides could demonstrate that they "greet[ed] the American Way of Life with enthusiasm."[64] Accepting substandard living conditions was as improper as demanding too much, suggested another war bride tale reported in the national press. A sixteen-year-old British bride was said to have "fled" from her husband in North Carolina when she realized that her home-to-be was a two-room cabin. "I didn't expect a palace but I didn't expect a shack either," she told reporters, announcing her plan to seek a divorce. The husband's unreasonableness was evident in his expectation that his young wife would raise his two younger siblings, aged three and eleven. This British teenager with middle-class aspirations had married into a white, rural extended family, and their house's lack of electricity and indoor plumbing was typical of poor farmers' homes in large swaths of the country. The story might have been told with an "I told you so" message, emphasizing the naïveté of a teenager marrying a man ten years older, or the negligence of her family for asking so few questions. But this bride was shown as perfectly sensible. She wanted the postwar American dream of a private home, modern appliances, and a nuclear family, and the article seemed to say she should not be expected to settle for anything less.[65]

As 1946 drew to a close, the *New York Times Magazine* summed up the Year of the War Bride in terms that accentuated the ideological frame in which this migration was widely understood. War brides were characterized as loyal, grateful, and deeply in love with their husbands. But the article was minimally concerned with war brides themselves. Instead, the author was interested in how these newcomers could help Americans understand themselves. The article considers the state of the union as seen through the eyes of foreigners, offering a popular explication of American liberalism at home and abroad. What the war brides love best about the United States, the author claims, are its equal opportunity educational system, its meritocratic, classless society, its freedom of expression, and its "efficiency." Several brides criticize racial prejudice and the postwar housing shortage as factors that might make foreigners look askance at American claims of superiority for their social and economic system. This writer was one of many American observers who found war brides a useful vehicle to capture the hopes and anxieties of the postwar moment.[66] Like him, many Americans used war brides as a mirror to explore their own social preoccupations on the domestic and international fronts.

From "Fraternazis" to "Nice German Girls": The International Dimension

As the Cold War emerged, war brides became an increasingly important mirror for international concerns. Brides from enemy nations seemed objectionable at first to most Americans. Wartime hatred toward the people of Axis nations did not dissipate immediately at the close of the fighting. The position of German and Japanese women as "occupation brides" complicated their representation, blurring the clean boundaries between wartime and peacetime. Yet for these very reasons, the ultimate acceptance of German and Japanese wives shows that the decision to "embrace" war brides was an extension of American foreign policy in the postwar period. Nothing makes the geopolitical dimensions of war bride policy and the discourse of intercultural marriages more apparent than the rehabilitation of German and, later, Japanese brides during the early Cold War. The American response to the two groups was quite different, however, since German women were white and Japanese women were not. Japanese brides were barred from the United States in the aftermath of World War II because of their race and were not rehabilitated until the Korean War, when their newly independent nation became strategically important to the United States (a subject treated in chapter 5). White women from enemy European nations, by contrast, were deemed assimilable and acceptable. In the late 1940s, as the Cold War forced the reconfiguration of strategic alliances, German brides of American soldiers were "rehabilitated" and allowed entry to the United States. By 1950, West Germany was second only to Britain as the country of origin for the largest number of soldier wives admitted under the War Brides Act, and German women were the largest group by far of GI fiancées.[67]

Americans' perceptions of German war brides paralleled U.S. military and foreign policy objectives in postwar Europe. Policy and attitudes both changed rapidly in the five years under the Office of Military Government for Germany–United States (OMGUS) following the trajectory of U.S. policy from the pacification and chastening of Western-occupied Germany to the active courtship of a democratic West Germany as the new cornerstone of Cold War defense strategy in Europe. Similarly, German women underwent a rehabilitation process in American popular culture, starting out as suspect subjects—"fraternazis"—but emerging as tame, acceptable, and even appealing. The "whiteness" of German women, who were indisputably Aryan, since women of "inferior races" had been exterminated, was a key factor in their favor. Marriages between American soldiers and German women served as an important object lesson about the prospects for a friendly, even intimate relationship between the two countries. Intimate relations between Germans and Americans, in turn, helped to soften American perceptions of the German state, historian Petra Goedde has shown; American officials came to see their role as masculine protectors of a "feminized" Germany.[68] Care for German brides was an extension of this role.

Furthermore, a policy that permitted soldiers to marry local women and welcomed them to the United States created a pointed and useful contrast with the behavior of the Soviet Union, which refused to grant exit visas to the Soviet wives of British, American, and Canadian men. Although the domestic public's views of German brides consistently lagged behind those of soldiers and commanders in the American zone in Germany, Americans at home eventually learned to accept the "rehabilitated" German war bride as the Cold War took shape.

At the Potsdam conference of July and August 1945, the Allied powers set a course for the governance of vanquished Germany. Germany was divided into four zones independently administered by Great Britain, the United States, France, and the Soviet Union. OMGUS administered the U.S. zone of occupation and the U.S. sector of Berlin until the establishment of the Federal Republic of Germany (West Germany) in May 1949. Large numbers of American troops were posted in the U.S. zone to enforce the occupation.[69] Central to the U.S. articulation of policy in postwar Germany was the effort to "reorient" the German people as a nation-state through the famous "Ds" of de-Nazification, demilitarization, de-cartelization, and democratization.[70] Initially, U.S. troops were strictly forbidden to "fraternize" with the enemy, especially by forming sexual liaisons with local women. Though it proved nearly impossible to enforce, nonfraternization was meant to dramatize the censure and isolation of German people in order to inculcate a sense of shame about their past behavior. By instilling awareness of Germans' collective responsibility for Nazi atrocities, American occupying forces hoped to lay the groundwork for the reeducation and rehabilitation of German people as democratic citizens.[71]

The nonfraternization policy was accompanied by an explicit ban on marriage between Germans and Americans in the U.S. occupation zone. Major General J. M. Bevans, assistant chief of staff for personnel, explained that "the policy of non-marriage with Germans is necessary to emphasize the relationship between the occupying forces and the defeated Germans." Bevans reminded American GIs that their nation should not "confer the benefits which come to the wife of a United States soldier upon an enemy of the United States."[72] Military policies that framed German women as enemies had an impact on domestic perceptions of German war brides. In debate of the GI Fiancées Act, several members of Congress voiced opposition to allowing "Nazi" women into the country. Some in Congress were concerned with the situation of displaced persons, contending that it was unfair to take pro-Nazi women out of line and facilitate their entry to the United States ahead of the victims of Nazi terror, who languished in displaced persons camps.[73] The sexual availability of German women to occupation soldiers was the primary source of disparagement. Many Americans viewed young German women as "prostitutes and seductresses." One U.S. senator asserted that German women were "sabotaging" the occupation's policy of separating American troops from the populace "by wearing as few clothes as possible." The stigmatization of German women was expressed through the use of contemptuous names for those who consorted with Americans: "fraternazis," "Amiwhores," "Veronicas," and "Veronika-Dankeschons." The last, a pun on venereal disease, was made famous by a song with that title and a cartoon character in the army's *Stars and Stripes* newspaper.[74]

The theme of German women as deceitful seductresses was echoed in popular culture, most famously in the character of Erika Von Schluetow, a Berlin singer portrayed by Marlene Dietrich in Billy Wilder's comedy-drama *A Foreign Affair* (1948). Erika has a Nazi past and an American officer for a lover—a combination that instigates a U.S. government inquiry and places the male protagonist between two female love interests, one German and one American. Quentin Reynolds's short story "War Bride," published in *Collier's*, applied similar themes to the figure of a German GI spouse. Reynolds's is a hair-raising cautionary tale, warning against premature forgiveness of the German people. The story is built around the motif of American innocence betrayed by European cynicism and political manipulation, though Reynolds takes the old plot to new and improbable extremes. The evil protagonist of his tale is Anna, rich, thirty-four, and vastly experienced, the gorgeous former mistress to a string of Nazi SS commandants and German army generals. Described as "sleek" and "darkly beautiful," Anna is practiced in the art of using sexuality to align herself with powerful men who offer her not just survival but luxury and protection.

Like the many kindhearted and naïve Americans in the story, the reader meets her as Anna Gerhart, shy, chaste, and supposedly twenty-one, a delicate and trembling beauty. "She looked just as sweet as sugar" to her American companions, but, the writer reminds us, "so does cyanide." Anna, a former Berlin stage actress, has created a false identity for herself in order to capture a wealthy American husband and escape the chaos of postwar Germany. The story opens aboard a U.S. army transport carrying Anna and other German fiancées to meet their betrotheds in the port of New York. Reynolds cleverly unsettles the reader's complacency about "good Germans," showing again and again how Anna hoodwinks everyone she meets, from reporters and ministers to her own fiancé. Two seasoned American newspapermen fall for her story. "Bill Kirk [of the *Times*] said, 'Poor kid, she's really had it. I don't like Krauts but this kid is different.' 'Yeah,' Benny Rose from the *Tribune* said, 'I'll buy that. No one hates Germans more than me, but this kid was—let's see—she's twenty-one now, so she was thirteen when the war began. Besides, she's the first real good-looking war bride we've run into.'" As seductive as Anna's physical appearance is her fabricated life story, used to establish her "good German," anti-Nazi pedigree. Her father, she claims, was a Lutheran minister, an opponent of the regime, who was dragged from his church by stormtroopers and placed in a German concentration camp.

The story reaches for an even higher level of irony when Anna is welcomed in New York City by her ardent fiancé and his wealthy and affectionate family—who just happen to be Jewish! Seated for an intimate family supper and celebration in a well-appointed hotel room, Anna's future father-in-law blesses the bread with a Hebrew prayer. Though Jewish, the appropriately named Ernest and his parents are ready to love and accept this German Christian bride with all their hearts. In the horrifying denouement of the tale, Anna presents her future mother-in-law with a beautiful pair of solid gold earrings, taken, the reader learns, from a concentration camp victim. Ernest's mother "uttered little cries of pleasure. . . . 'Look, Papa—they remind me so much of a pair of earrings my mother once had. She gave them to my sister. I cried because she didn't give them to me.' 'Is your sister still in Hungary,' Anna asked, smiling. Ernest's father said gently, . . . 'Mama's sister was sent to Auschwitz.'"[75]

Anti-German material was meant to keep hostilities from the war years alive and to warn that Nazi inclinations would not be easily expunged from the German character. Still, hatred of German civilians was a hard sell to American troops, despite the horrors of the Nazi genocide. Polls conducted as early as September 1945 showed a surprisingly positive attitude toward Germans among American servicemen. One-quarter of enlisted men had a "very favorable" or "fairly favorable" opinion of the German people. Nearly as many believed that the Nazis had had "good reasons for persecuting Jews," a latent anti-Semitism that must have diluted the lesson of the extermination camps.[76] Even during the war, American public opinion had distinguished between Nazi leaders and the German populace, though it failed to do so in regard to the Japanese. Troops who had fought against Germany were replaced with new recruits who had no combat experience and "little bitterness against Germans." To American soldiers in the army of occupation, Germans were culturally familiar and racially acceptable. A diplomat paraphrased the American view: "Here were no small, dark people, talkative, unreliable folk, with inadequate sanitation and strange messy food. Here were fine-looking, blond, blue-eyed people, just like the Americans in Wisconsin, people who worked full-out from morning to night, . . . and whose girls admired an upstanding he-man."[77] So much had GIs warmed to German people that American occupation leaders found it necessary to remind American troops that "they're still our enemies." As early as June 1945, U.S. congressmen, on a tour of the occupation zone, had made inquiries on behalf of their constituents about when marriage might be allowed.[78]

The fraternization ban proved to be embarrassing, as illicit contacts between Germans and GIs flourished, especially black marketeering and sexual commerce. When the army lifted the fraternization ban in October 1945—allowing social contact that included dating, but preserving the marriage ban—leaders were admitting the failure of their initial policy. But social and moral conditions remained adverse. Sexual relations between Germans and GIs were rampant and a source of great tension with German civilians and local officials. The venereal disease rate for troops in the U.S. occupation zone was the highest for any U.S. military unit during the war and postwar periods. "The apparently unrestrained sexual activity of the American GI" constituted a genuine crisis for the military command, as historian John Willoughby has shown; "normalizing" this "cross-national intimacy was central to the stabilization of the Army's presence in Germany." One part of "normalization" was bringing American wives and children of service personnel to live in occupied Germany, a plan to "domesticate" the American forces instituted in the spring of 1946. The other part was allowing marriage between Germans and American soldiers.[79] This reformulation led to a reversal of policy: on December 11, 1946, the European theatre commander General Joseph T. McNarney pronounced that marriage between Germans and Americans would now be permitted, provided that the German sweetheart passed a vigorous investigation for any evidence of Nazi sympathies and that the marriage occurred just prior to the American service member's rotation home. As with other foreign brides, the U.S. military would provide free transport of German wives as part of its obligation to American troops.

German brides remained anathema to many Americans at home. The lifting of the ban created a small storm of protest. "What will the Government bring into this promised land next?" one woman asked in the *Washington Post*. "A shipload of Hottentots or headhunters would be more welcome to most of us than the proposed shipment of German frauleins which is about to invade our shores." General McNarney had to explain and defend his decision. Even Eleanor Roosevelt was pulled into the fray. In her "My Day" column Mrs. Roosevelt tried to make peace between the sides, but her comments were far from helpful for the army's position. "My correspondents fear that we are building up 'a strong nucleus' of Nazi spies in this country and are 'strengthening the Nazi cause'" by welcoming Germans—a concern she concluded "should not be taken lightly." Roosevelt's perception of these German-American marriages was an updated version of the long-standing view of war front relationships: the "boys" were too young and inexperienced to know better, in this case, too young to have fought in the war and understand the menace of Nazi Germany. And the "girls" were opportunists, much too "ready to be friendly," seducing young Americans who were easily "carried away" by them. Roosevelt proposed her own policy solution: "a rule requiring a boy to be home for at least four months before he could bring over the girl he wished to marry."[80]

Occupation authorities soon mounted a counteroffensive in this war of words. "German Girls Make Good GI Wives," announced an AP story originated through army headquarters in Berlin. After interviewing sixty-five couples in a two-week period under the new marriage rules, the head chaplain of the U.S. occupation in Berlin concluded that German brides were likely to make fine wives for American veterans. In fact, he argued, these were better marriages than those between soldiers and British and French women, because the long waiting period set by occupation rules and the continuous proximity of husband and wife tested their compatibility and commitment. The chaplain's office was "remarkably pleased" with the "quality of German girls brought in by Americans." Most "were well educated . . . with professional training in medicine, dentistry, music or dramatics." The majority spoke "very good English" and, perhaps the best prognosticator of all, had been in correspondence with their future mothers-in-law.[81] U.S. military authorities in Germany made several of these newlyweds available to American reporters, though there was a dispute over who had the first officially approved German American marriage, a claim made by several couples.[82]

"Nice German girls" began to make their way into the home news as well. An early example was the story of twenty-two-year-old veteran Russell Horton and his bride, Trudy. In a news conference in upstate New York, Horton's mother revealed that the couple had wed secretly and against army orders when the marriage ban was still in place; their appeals for help, including one to President Truman, had been fruitless, so Horton's "gray-haired mother" went to the press to ask that the government sanction the marriage and allow Trudy to come "home" to the United States. In reality, the couple had made a risky end run around army regulations. What was most striking about the story was its homey and sympathetic portrayal of a German bride and the community's receptiveness to her. Horton loved his wife for her "virtues" of devotion, patience, and loyalty. Wholesome and sensible Trudy was a far cry from the underdressed German seductresses conjured by American spokesmen and observers. Demonstrating her maternal nurturing qualities, Trudy had won her soldier's heart by putting him to bed when he fell ill, wrapped in her own sweater, and nursing him back to health. These were virtues the gray-haired American mother could appreciate. The hometown postmaster interviewed by the *Newsweek* reporter, as good a barometer of middle-American opinion as any, wished the couple success in their pursuit of love and happiness. Horton insisted, sensibly enough, that it was "nature," not ideology, that drove romances such as theirs; and defending his own choice as well as those of other would-be grooms, he reminded the military that "you can't put love on a political basis."[83]

Or perhaps you can. Domestic sympathy for German war brides warmed slowly throughout 1947, though interest was tepid when compared with the mania for Allied brides in 1946. The takeoff year for the peak immigration of German GI spouses, 1948 was a crucial period of transition for U.S. policy in Germany. With Marshall Plan aid from the United States, the Western powers undertook an ambitious campaign to revitalize the German economy, an embrace of postwar Germany that was unimaginable two years earlier. In 1948, a distinct change was also apparent in the representation of German women as American wives. Newspapers began to cover the story of German brides in ways that clearly "normalized" their experience. In the women's pages, German war brides became "new neighbors" alongside brides from Allied nations. "A small town tradition of neighborliness is flourishing in the big city bustle of Chicago," the *Tribune* noted, as women's clubs from Chicago's northwest side came together to welcome thirteen "foreign war brides" with a luncheon and novelty hat show. The new American neighbors included wives from England, France, Germany, Austria, and Belgium. As "Mrs. West and Mrs. Grimes," these former "enemies" disappeared into the American linguistic melting pot; as generic wives of American soldiers, they blended into their new community without attracting special attention.[84]

The case of a German war bride suggests how far public opinion had evolved by the close of the decade. Neighbors in Kankakee County, Illinois, embraced a "pretty red haired German war bride," Viola Smith, and showed a faith and confidence in her marriage that husband and wife seemed to lack. The Smiths' tale was brief and tumultuous. Private Donald Smith, aged twenty, brought his German wife and her two-year old daughter (from a different father) to the home of relatives just after Christmas in 1948. He quarreled with her and, according to Viola, refused to provide food for herself or the child. A few days later Smith drove his wife to the county courthouse and asked that she be deported, claiming he had "grown tired of her." But Viola, an astute student of American democracy, demanded due process. "Remembering what she had been told in Germany" about the impartiality and fairness of the U.S. legal system, she "fled" to the county judge's courtroom and enjoined him to arrest her husband for nonsupport. Donald Smith was arrested, and Viola and the child, now homeless, were placed in the care of the county juvenile officer. Kankakee citizens were evidently impressed by this resourceful young woman, viewing her with great sympathy despite her background and the strange disruption her arrival had caused. Resolving the Smiths' problems became a civic project. With town leaders, local Red Cross, and military officials all taking part, a marital accord was produced in this miniature international crisis. "I will go back to my husband if he be a good man and beg me a little," Mrs. Smith declared. "I love my wife," Mr. Smith told the judge "tearfully." "Reconciled" was the satisfied headline above the couple's photograph the following day—though it seems doubtful that this fragile marriage could last.[85]

The final impetus for the rehabilitation of German war brides was the mounting tension with the Soviet Union, which centrally involved events in Germany. In June 1948, the Soviet Union protested Anglo-American consolidation in the western zones by imposing a blockade on the city of Berlin. With new enemies looming, the Germans began to look like ever more appealing allies. So, too, German wives began to appear as appealing partners. Malvina Lindsay stated the case bluntly in a column during the summer of 1948: "One thing that should work to the advantage of both German and Japanese brides is the widespread fear of Russia. This channels off much of the aggressive feeling that might have been visited upon natives of former enemy countries." Americans rallied behind German-American marriage when communists in Berlin tried to wield the controversial issue as a wedge against the occupying Americans. As the *Washington Post* reported, "A full-scale [communist] propaganda campaign is under way to convince Germans that their daughters are not safe on the same streets with American soldiers, that death itself awaits German girls who become GI war brides."[86] In the emergent illogic of Cold War politics, Americans had to regard German-American marriage as a compelling good if communists labeled it a dangerous evil.

With the Cold War to bolster their claims to American identity, German wives of U.S. soldiers were refigured as "loyal" American wives and boosters for the American way. One German bride, a "Bavarian brunette," came to public attention when her husband, a career army officer, was captured by "the Red Koreans" in July 1950. Korean communists claimed the American officer, her husband, had "denounced" U.S. intervention in Korea as a "barbarous, aggressive action" and in a radio broadcast had urged American soldiers to desert. The "loyal German war bride" declared in response that "her husband must have been subjected to cruel, oriental torture if he made such a broadcast."[87] As historian Susan Carruthers shows, the "captive" and the "escapee" became potent Cold War symbols of Eastern bloc oppression in U.S. political discourse and popular culture.[88] German brides soon appeared in U.S. news reports in the guise of "escapees"—plucky or fortunate refugees from lands behind the "iron curtain." Edith Baliday, just eighteen years old, had "escaped from East to West Germany" and then met and married Corporal Wilson Baliday in the American zone. Kind Americans had even restored her faith in Santa Claus (eroded perhaps by her stint under godless communism), as they stepped forward and paid her airfare from New York to Hawaii, enabling her to reunite with her husband on Christmas Eve. Another bride from the American occupation zone had outstanding Cold War credentials as a double escapee. Nadja Posey, a Ukrainian-born singer and dancer, was captured by the Germans during the war, but she had managed to escape their slave labor camp. In marrying an American she met in postwar Berlin and immigrating to Los Angeles, she had also managed to escape the life of a Soviet woman. Posey told the press, "American women do not know how lucky they are. . . . In Russia, the women work, work, work. Here it is—what you say—terrific?"[89]

Embracing former enemy wives, the American nation placed its largesse, flexibility, and openness on display in a form that proved politically useful in the international politics of the late 1940s. The State Department was eager to promote the liberalism of American marriage policy when a controversy emerged about Soviet brides of Western husbands. In a front-page story, the *New York Times* reported in December 1947 that the Soviet government had recently confirmed what had long been suspected, that it had banned, and would continue to ban, the emigration of Soviet citizens married to Americans.[90] By 1950, the State Department was reporting that more than 350 Soviet citizens had applied for visas to join American spouses, 95 of whom were U.S. military veterans. An American journalist who had lived and worked in the USSR condemned this "grotesque attempt to legislate affairs of the heart." To these wives, "the Iron Curtain is no abstract Churchillian metaphor, but something very hard and impenetrable."[91] The Soviet Union's ban was a topic of frequent denunciation in the fledgling United Nations. In

April 1949, the General Assembly condemned the Soviet policy as a violation of the UN charter. The Soviet wives were even the subject of their own "kitchen debate"; when a Russian delegate remarked in committee that the Soviet Union was obliged to protect its women "at home" because in other countries "they could be subject to . . . exploitation as kitchen slaves," U.S. ambassador Eleanor Roosevelt shot back, "We might ask, by the way, who does the housework in the Soviet Union?"

In popular discussions of the Soviet marriage controversy, the emphasis was on freedom of choice to love and marry as a human right that was supposedly cherished in the "free world." This stance dovetailed neatly with the efforts of U.S. information agencies to spread the American liberal creed abroad. It was deeply embarrassing when the Soviets pointed out that American "open" marriage law still condemned interracial unions and forbade nonwhite spouses from entry into the United States. Still, in the wake of World War II, Americans came to see the German-born wives of American servicemen as a useful resource in an increasingly unstable world. By the end of the decade, the Immigration and Naturalization Service reported that 14,175 German wives had been admitted to the United States under the War Brides Act. This figure was modest when compared with the vast number of intimate relationships between German women and American soldiers in the zone of occupation—a number very roughly suggested by the 94,000 "occupation babies" of Allied fathers recorded by West German officials at decade's end.[92] Still, it is notable that German women, former enemy women, became the second-largest group of war brides in the wake of World War II.

War Bride Marriage in a Hollywood Drama

"International obligation," symbolically expressed through family ties, was a preoccupation of American cultural texts in the early Cold War.[93] Would Americans shoulder their responsibility as pater familias of the free world? The war bride, a vulnerable foreigner whose life and well-being depended on an American man, was an ideal vehicle for exploring this theme. No postwar text did this more fully than Fred Zinnemann's *Teresa* (1951), a Hollywood film with an intercultural marriage at its center.[94] On many levels, *Teresa* captures the lessons about war brides and foreign relations that Americans had come to take seriously by the end of the 1940s.

Zinnemann's film tells the story of a young army veteran, Philip (John Ericson), who must adjust to postwar life by accepting his obligations to his war bride wife and infant son. In doing so the character is refashioned as a man and an American. The film takes the form of a psychological case study, beginning, quite literally, in the cramped office of a psychiatric counselor at the Veterans Administration of New York City, where a voice-over introduces the patient: "His name is Philip Cass. His occupation is running away." In a lengthy flashback, Philip recounts his war experiences to the counselor, and they are simultaneously uncovered for the viewer—his arrival in Italy, untested and fearful, his first and only combat experience, his subsequent hospitalization as a psychiatric case. The crucial fact about Philip's character is revealed in this sequence: he is a "coward," unable to fight during the war, and his running away under fire was directly responsible for heavy casualties in his platoon.

In the course of the flashback sequence, the viewer meets Teresa. Delicately beautiful and childlike, but also wise beyond her years, Teresa is appealingly played by Italian actress Pier Angeli in her first American film role. Zinnemann was known for using local people and settings to create naturalistic and compelling screen portraits of war and its social impact. The viewer first encounters Teresa in a crowd of children and teens who are begging or bartering for food from the American soldiers in their village. Later Philip protects her from a leering GI who seems poised to assault her. As Teresa and Philip's romance begins, she is presented as someone who needs to be cared for. The haunting image of the couple's wedding ceremony in a half-destroyed village church was undoubtedly meant to elicit sympathy and remind Americans of the suffering of European civilians—a counterpart to government efforts in the late 1940s to build public support for the Marshall Plan.

If Teresa needs Philip for safety and physical survival, Philip needs her to recover from his emotional trauma. Waiting for Teresa back home in New York City, he has fallen into a pattern of idleness, self-loathing, and dependency on his troubled family. Here apparently is the key to his psychological maiming, as in so many Hollywood dramas of the 1950s: the inappropriate personality formation of his two parents—his weak, emasculated father and his dominant, infantilizing mother who prevents him from taking a job. Teresa arrives from Naples and is forced to endure the daily hostility of her mother-in-law. Tension soon grows between the newlyweds. She cannot accept his passivity and helplessness, nor his irritability toward her. When Teresa reveals that she is pregnant, he rejects her and the baby ("You can't do this. It will kill mother"), and Teresa moves out.

Here Philip arrives at the psychological low point where the film began. But the crisis of his wife's departure soon precipitates his recovery, as he finally "learns to grow up." Philip returns to his VA counselor, who helps guide his self-discovery. Philip recognizes that he has been a "jellyfish" like his passive father, "paralyzed" and unable to act at every crucial moment of his life, on the battlefield and in his marriage—"and mom helped make me that way. She wants me to stay a baby, 'cause she knows that's the only way she can keep me." Armed with this insight about his unmanly dependency, Philip is finally able to defy his mother, move out of his parents' apartment, and take a job. He searches for Teresa and finds her, with his father's help, on the public maternity ward at Bellevue Hospital.

In the final frames of the film, Philip brings Teresa home, and they stand together in a tight embrace, alone in their own bare apartment, their baby asleep beside them, ready to start their life together. They have at last become a successful American family in postwar terms, living on their own and headed by a male protector. Philip was a failure during the war because of his inability to commit himself to the fight (read isolationism). The success of his adjustment hinged on his ability to accept his obligation to foreign others. He now has a second chance to shoulder his responsibility to his wife and, by extension, his obligation to his country and its leadership in the new family of "free nations." Teresa, as war bride, has given him the opportunity to mature and redeem himself. Like the social science studies of war bride marriage produced in the same period, the film equates the successful adjustment of this intercultural family with the health and healing of the nation at large.

In the postwar moment, the arrival of thousands of GI brides came to stand for the hope of repairing the wrenching disruptions of the war years. These intercultural relationships appeared to embody what those in power defined as the most vital tasks of postwar society: revitalizing American marriage under the leadership of men, bridging the chasm between home front and war front, and integrating former enemies into the new, American-dominated global order. Like the Hollywood director who conceived of the film *G.I. War Brides* as an effervescent romance with a happy ending, Americans were able to see war brides as an uplifting coda to the war. War brides too embraced this message. In the years that followed, many of the GI war brides continued to affiliate themselves with the "greatest generation" identity of their husbands and with their veteran status.[95] For a historical cohort of Americans, the union of GIs and foreign brides made the world seem safe and familiar in gender, racial, and international terms.

5

Interracialism,

Pluralism, and Civil Rights

War Bride Marriage in the 1940s and 1950s

In 1947, an African American army sergeant serving in the postwar occupation of Germany typed a letter to General Dwight D. Eisenhower, then U.S. Army chief of staff. "Knowing you as a General, and a Soldier, Sir," he wrote to expose "a great injustice . . . being directed towards me." Just weeks before, Sergeant Robert Bennett, an army medic, had filed the requisite paperwork to marry Elfrieda, his German girlfriend and mother of their infant son, Duane. The couple had been dating for two full years and were now certain that they belonged together. Almost immediately after applying, Bennett found himself in a nightmarish situation: accused of an unrelated and serious crime—malicious tampering with medications—and subject to court-martial. "In my eye-sight and in the eye-sight of God, I am no more guilty of this offense than you are," he assured Eisenhower. "All I ask for," Bennett concluded, "is justice." On a different continent, another couple faced a similarly painful dilemma. A white American serving in the army medical corps and a young Japanese woman named Kyo fell in love in Japan just before the outbreak of the Korean War. Because army regulations barred them from marriage, they wed without permission in a ceremony unrecognized by American authorities. Furious when he learned of this, the soldier's commanding officer threatened in retaliation to send the man to fight in Korea. Intermarried couples like Kyo and her husband faced a further and equally daunting obstacle: as a national of an Asian nation other than China, Kyo was barred at the time from entering the United States even if she had been recognized as the spouse of an American citizen. Kyo's recollection of the events, "Army pretty tough to marry," seemed an understatement under the circumstances.[1]

From the perspective of the U.S. government, interracial marriages were an "unintended consequence," and an unwelcome one, of the Second World

War as a global conflict.[2] They were a consequence as well of the military's own liberal policies in regard to soldier marriage during the Second World War. Though the military had tried to draw boundaries around marriages it deemed "inadvisable," the compulsion toward matrimony proved contagious. American servicemen of every racial background met and married women of foreign birth while serving overseas; a subset of these marriages united partners across boundaries of race as well as nation. Falling in love, such couples flew in the face of a long-standing and still powerful proscription against racial intermarriage, or "miscegenation," in the United States. Interracial couples who married overseas did not set out to challenge the legal and social structure of marriage discrimination. But sooner or later, the personal became political for war brides and American soldiers as they confronted the machinery of discrimination in the military and at home. Out of this experience, some individuals or families came to embrace the cause of civil rights. For most the struggle to marry and become an American interracial family in the late 1940s and 1950s remained a largely private crusade.

War bride couples who were also interracial couples, moreover, entered American society at a pivotal moment in the history of U.S. race relations. Ideologically, America's war for freedom and democracy had thrown into high relief the system of racial inequality that prevailed in the United States and its armed services. Soldiers of color had served bravely and in large numbers in a military that segregated and discriminated against them. Race liberals and reformers saw the postwar moment as an unprecedented opportunity to overthrow the Jim Crow system and press equality claims on the state. The equality revolution would not coalesce for another decade and a half, but a nascent civil rights movement gathered momentum in the wake of the war. Voices of resistance to racism were heard in the press, among scholars, artists, and writers, and among activists and reformers. For some groups and individuals, the interracial war couples of World War II were an important touchstone, a symbol of racial transformation. Their struggles were meaningful to many advocates of racial and ethnic equality as they searched for ways to apply the racial and foreign policy flux of the war years to greater social and racial justice in the postwar world. Once again the war bride served an important postwar purpose—in this case to challenge rather than restore a conservative vision of ethnic and race relations for postwar America.

Homecoming GIs with marriages across the color line brought the issue of marriage equality into the open as never before. The interracial couples who returned from overseas in the 1940s were the most visible and dramatic influx of interracial marriages in American history. The soldier-husbands in these marriages, veterans of the war for democracy, had a unique claim on the state. For Americans prepared to challenge racial orthodoxies, such families were bracing evidence that change in the racial status quo was indeed possible, a harbinger of a new racial future for the United States.[3] Most Americans, however, even those willing to consider various kinds of racial "cooperation," were not ready to embrace biracial intimacy. Ultimately the discourse about interracial "war bride" marriage shows the profound ambivalence surrounding race and race relations in the United States on the cusp of the civil rights movement.

Marriage and Race Relations in the Postwar United States

Racial intermarriage was and remained an extremely rare occurrence in the postwar United States. In the 1960 census, the first one to record interracial unions, a fraction of a percent of American marriages involved racial mixing of any combination, 157,000 marriages in total. Black-white intermarriage was the least common, with only 51,000 couples residing in the United States, constituting 0.126 percent of American marriages.[4] Relative to these numbers, the interracial marriages of American GIs, black, white, and others, certainly constituted one of the largest discrete infusions of interracial marriage in U.S. history. Their presence was bound to draw attention as well as controversy in the years following World War II.

In marrying or attempting to marry across the color line, American GIs and their spouses came face-to-face with the long-standing social and legal edifice barring such relationships. The years after 1948 are often described as a period of nascent liberalization in U.S. race relations. Yet this characterization would have been a surprise to the British woman and her African American fiancée, each of whom was sentenced to six months in jail for "unlawful co-habitation" in Virginia; the Japanese bride and her white air force husband who learned their legal marriage was no longer recognized when they were posted to Biloxi, Mississippi; and the British war bride in Washington State who was fired from her job as a department store clerk when her bosses learned that her husband was a black veteran.[5] The almost total taboo against intermarriage dated back to the close of the Civil War, Martha Hodes has shown, with the invention of the term "miscegenation" to proscribe and demean marriage across the color line. "Marriage was the most criminalized form of racially-related conduct" in American life well into the twentieth century.[6] In the 1920s and early 1930s, nativism and a resurgent racism, propelled by the far-reaching political influence of the Ku Klux Klan, extended marriage bans to new states and new populations.

In the western states in particular, anti-Asian racism fueled much of the legislation. States with long-standing black-white marriage bans expanded the scope of their restrictions. As late as 1939, for example, Utah's marriage statute was amended to prohibit marriage between "a Mongolian, member of the Malay race or a mulatto, quadroon, or octoroon, and a white person." When the California Supreme Court ruled that the state's ban on "Mongolian" marriage to whites would not bar a Filipino man from wedding his white fiancée, the legislature quickly altered the law. As historian Peter Wallenstein has argued, the hectic activity of state legislatures in the first four decades of the century—north, south, and west—shows the lengths to which many whites would go to "keep white women from marrying non-white men."[7]

Returning from the war for freedom and democracy, intermarried veterans and their wives found their unions illegal in thirty states. State laws discriminating against marriage on a racial basis were not struck down by the Supreme Court until 1967 in the *Loving v. Virginia* case—one of the last formal, legal structures of Jim Crow to fall. Social norms also reinforced legal restriction in the postwar period. As late as 1958 a Gallup poll recorded a 96 percent disapproval of marriage between blacks and whites among white respondents, "a disapproval that cut across class, educational and regional lines." Individuals involved in racial relationships were widely considered deviant, pathological, or tragic. "Experts from the period generally agreed that marrying across the color line was a neurotic symptom of an underlying psychological disorder," and whites who "married interracially were disturbed individuals," either exhibitionists or self-punishing martyrs, their marriages and children "tragic." Young people who tried to date interracially found parents, judges, and law enforcement officials arrayed against them. A white teenage girl with a black boyfriend could find herself committed to a mental hospital in both the pre- and postwar periods.[8]

Through the middle years of the twentieth century, the marriage taboo remained one of the key ideological and psychological underpinnings of Jim Crow, the American system of racial apartheid that prevailed across the South. Fear of interracial sex was a bludgeon that white racists used to beat back any loosening of racial codes or practices—school desegregation, housing or neighborhood integration, and access to public accommodations or facilities such as libraries, parks, beaches, or swimming pools were all condemned as entry points to sexual intimacy. But the antimiscegenation laws, like segregation laws, were not just a southern phenomenon; they were instead a tool of white supremacism and social control in many regions of the United States, directed at Asians, Native Americans, and Latinos as well as African Americans. Military leaders at every level subscribed to this negative view of intermarriage and worked to oppose the marital requests of interracial couples.

Interracial war couples who hoped to make a life for themselves in the postwar United States found that immigration policies were hostile to their interests as well. Racial inequity remained a structural feature of U.S. immigration law through the mid-1960s, despite efforts at reform; here too norms of segregation and exclusion had a negative effect on interracial couples. Asian nationals were still excluded from immigration and naturalization on the basis of race through 1952, a period that encompassed almost entirely the U.S. occupation of Japan. The edifice of the Asian immigration ban, in place since the late nineteenth century, had begun to crack in 1943 with the admittance of China, a wartime ally, to the national origins system. The Immigration and Nationality Act of 1952, also known as the McCarran Walter Act, encompassed some key reforms, including Asian eligibility for naturalization and end of the outright exclusion of Asians. But it left in place the national origins system, granting only a token of around a hundred quota slots annually from each of the Asian and other former colonial nations.[9] The limitations on Asian immigration barred many Japanese brides from entry to the United States and handed the military an important tool in its attempt to limit GI marriage to Asian women.

Change in the dynamics of U.S. race relations was palpable at the close of the war, but change also led to backlash, with steps both forward and back. New employment and military opportunities during the war were followed by vicious attacks on African American veterans upon their return to the United States. President Truman's executive order of July 1948 ending racial segregation in the armed services was followed by years of wrangling between the military service heads and the implementation of strategies meant to forestall change.[10] Racial intermarriage was part of this dance. As World War II came to a close, Peter Wallenstein points out, no state had repealed a racial marriage ban since 1887; this began to change after 1948, when the California Supreme Court struck down the state's interracial marriage ban in the *Perez* decision, transforming the legal landscape of marriage law and opening "a new phase of repeal."[11] Still, in many parts of the country, statewide bans on racial intermarriage and hostility toward such marriages remained a profound feature of the Jim Crow system in the postwar era, and intermarriage, a criminalized activity. If the war stimulated change in race relations, it also uncovered how much remained unaltered.

European Brides and Interracial Marriage
in the Postwar Black Community

In December 1948, Mr. and Mrs. Milton Alberts mailed a short but sincere "our thanks" in a Christmas card to the National Association for the Advancement of Colored People (NAACP), along with their money order for membership in the civil rights organization. Staff members of the NAACP had worked over many months to help the African American serviceman and his white French bride resolve a dispute with the air force. Milton planned a postwar career in the military, but the couple was initially assigned to an air base in Florida, then to Arizona, both states where it was illegal for interracial couples to marry or cohabit. The NAACP had helped the appropriate military officials to understand that the couple required assignment to a state where their marriage was legal, and the Albertses were grateful. The most intriguing feature of this communication was not the brief note itself but the photograph the Albertses forwarded inside the card. It shows a couple dressed to go out for an elegant occasion; they could be on their way to another couple's wedding, or perhaps they have planned a celebratory evening for themselves. The image is a public portrait, one expressing both intimacy and pride. As the Albertses face the camera together with confident smiles, their upper bodies fill the frame, pressed companionably close together. This self-portrait of a marriage speaks eloquently of emotional satisfaction, marital stability, and middle-class success. Whether their lived behavior followed this intention or not, the partners chose to picture themselves as unafraid of displaying their affection to the outside world. Their bodies, in relation to one another, were a message about interracial love and racial equality.[12]

The Albertses almost certainly never intended to turn their marriage into a political cause. They simply did what thousands upon thousands of other young people did and fell in love during the war. On the other hand, it seems likely that racial difference, given such weight in the United States, influenced their relationship from the start. They were surely aware, for example, that love stories such as theirs were almost never narrated in mainstream American culture. During the war, photographs of black and white couples, GIs posed with white European women, had been banned from domestic publication by the War Department as too abhorrent to white sensibilities. In the years following the war, portraits of successful and fulfilling black-white intermarriage were all but nonexistent in American cultural production.[13] Black men with white wives still tapped an especially deep root of social and cultural anxiety. White fear of intermarriage was expressed on a morale survey of white soldiers conducted during the war. "We are not opposed to the negro 'getting ahead in the world' if he goes about it in the right way," an airforce corporal wrote. "We do object, however, to negro men sexing with white women. . . . We're not fighting for that kind of 'democracy.'" The question of black men's postwar expectations—whether the "liberties enjoyed by the black GI in Britain," including "the freedom to associate with white women," had "whetted his appetite" for further social freedom—was a preoccupation in the military during World War II.[14]

Interracial couples like the Albertses who chose to pursue marriage during the war almost invariably found themselves the object of harassment and discrimination. It was confronting the mechanisms of racial repression that often changed the individuals involved. Black soldiers and veterans in particular saw new possibilities for racial change in the mid-1940s, and many felt entitled to demand justice as a result of their record of service to the nation at war. This sense of entitlement extended to the right to marry wives of their own choosing. More than any other group of servicemen, African Americans viewed their personal fight to marry through a civil rights lens, and many passed this perspective on to the women they married. In search of assistance, they frequently turned to institutions that had gained an enhanced reputation for civil rights advocacy during the war, the NAACP and the African American press, offering to them their stories of struggle and love. Examining the response of these institutions to the plight of interracial couples in the late 1940s shows the possibilities and the limits of change in the racial status quo.

Around 1944, black servicemen began to send scores of documents and letters to the NAACP outlining their individual struggles to marry European wives. As their letters made clear, interracial couples faced an unacknowledged obstacle course of racial exclusion that was all the more difficult to navigate for its invisibility. Technically, soldiers of color and white European women were treated no differently than white couples in overseas military commands. But marriage policy, which left approval to the sole discretion of unit commanders, was manifestly and systematically biased against interracial couples in practice.[15] Black servicemen documented the demeaning racial comments that greeted their marriage aspirations. They told of repeated denials of their applications, with no explanation or with demonstrably false ones. When they submitted applications, men were attacked, transferred, or sometimes accused of crimes and jailed. When they did manage to marry, African American soldiers complained that their foreign wives experienced harassment by military police. Men who planned to make a career in the postwar military also reported problems with army housing and army base assignments when they were transferred back home because, in many states, interracial couples were legally forbidden from residing. For all these problems, they sought assistance from the NAACP.

That race and sexuality were the crux of the matter was abundantly clear in the testimony that African American soldiers provided. When Sergeant Robert Bennett directly confronted his commanding officer, one Colonel Glass, in an ongoing controversy over Bennett's marriage request—a controversy that had already enmeshed Bennett in a court-martial trial—the colonel exploded. "Your girl is a hoare [*sic*] and your baby a bastered [*sic*]," Bennett recalled him saying, and revealingly the colonel asked, "Who gave you the right to lay up with her?" Black men's access to white women violated fundamental aspects of the system of racial hierarchy within the U.S. military. Incidents like this one in many ways reflected the pervasive and daily abuse that African Americans faced in the armed services—incidents of differential and inferior treatment in medical care, physical and verbal assault, and others that are so chillingly detailed in the NAACP Veterans Bureau files. But the personal cruelty of preventing two adults who loved each other from choosing a life together was also a fundamental violation of human rights. The indignity of their treatment was captured well by the case of William Malone, a noncommissioned officer who had waged a years-long battle to wed his German fiancée. Demobilized and demoralized, living in White Plains, New York, Malone lamented the "red tape" and "prejudice" of his commanding officers, who had prevented him from accomplishing his goal during almost three years of overseas service. There was nothing out of the ordinary about Malone's situation, except perhaps for the meticulous string of briefs and requests that this black soldier had prepared, and finally forwarded to the NAACP. The army's final, stated reason for rejecting his marriage bid was particularly galling in the face of his calm perseverance and professional behavior: the soldier's "personal immaturity" rendered the marriage "inadvisable."[16]

Black soldiers in interracial love affairs perceived themselves and their partners, quite correctly, as vulnerable to retaliation and violence. The arresting tale of Corporal Cleveland Scott, fragmentary though it is, makes this point clearly. Scott, his French fiancée, and an army colleague were prepared to enjoy Fourth of July festivities in France in 1945. Encountering a group of white soldiers, the interracial couple was set upon. One white man held Corporal Scott "at bay" with a gun while another slapped the woman, who was pregnant, hurling "obscene" invectives at her and calling the men "niggers." Infuriated, the two black servicemen "jumped on the three white soldiers, beating them into submission." In a matter of hours, a contingent of high-ranking officers (two lieutenant colonels and two captains) had come to interrogate the two black men, preparing to charge them for attacking the whites. Corporal Scott's single communication outlining these events, a V-mail letter to the NAACP, is an eerie artifact, an attempt to get word to the outside world as "they intend to make it quite hard for us." Scott's experiences and observations of race in army life—men in his company "beaten unmercifully by white soldiers and Military Police" but "nothing . . . ever done about it"; officers "refusing to discuss the matter" or evading the issue—had led to this conclusion. Though Scott hoped that the NAACP could intervene on his behalf, he concluded pessimistically: "I fear things will more than likely turn out for the worst."[17]

Scott's letter is a stark reminder of the racial gulag that the U.S. military was for many black men. It also uncovers the motives of many complainants in writing to the NAACP. Most basic of these was to gain the sympathetic attention and practical assistance of the association in advocating their case. Couples viewed the NAACP as a powerful and well-connected institution on the American scene and saw it as an effective resource for racial underdogs like themselves. Beyond the motive of assistance was that of protection: if the man were framed, defamed, jailed, or even killed, he wanted his true story to get out and survive him. This was clearly on the mind of an African American army sergeant when he penned his tale of obstructed love, asking his sister to forward it to a constellation of leading black and progressive publications, along with the NAACP. "I am . . . trying to get help for all the [African American] soldiers over here or die trying."[18]

Despite considerable barriers of language, culture, and political status, some white wives and fiancées also became immersed in the struggle to marry. What began as a personal process sometimes became a political awakening. Women frequently sought to defend their love or convince others of its depth or validity. "Please listen to me," a French fiancée began a letter to the NAACP, "what I have to tell you is a romance . . . and maybe you can help us. . . . One day he asked me if I would marry him, . . . I answered him 'yes.'" For this woman, even the physical details of her attraction, evidently an issue in the relationship, were crucial to reveal. "He is not a white as are generally the French men. He is afraid to impose himself to me because of his cream-coffee complexion and his flat nose, but I love him as he is." Women's self-narratives often acknowledged that their choice of partner had been difficult for their own friends or parents, or for their black partner, his parents, and friends. Stating their love, on one level, was a way to affirm it in the face of opposition. When foreign brides had limited English with which to tell their love story in words, they could turn to photographs. An American Red Cross social worker encountered a white French bride and "her 7 month old Negro son" on board an army transport bound for New York. "She seemed fond of her husband and anxious to have a successful marriage," the social worker reported; "she proudly showed us a picture of her husband and mentioned that the baby looks like him."[19] This woman's unabashed pride in her husband's appearance seemed to be surprising to the social worker, for other Red Cross staff reported their suspicion that brides who demurred from participating in a "handsome husband" contest of photo portraits were embarrassed to reveal that their partners were older men or "Negros."

It is difficult on a deeper level to access the private feelings or political sensibilities of white European women in romantic relationships with African American GIs and other GIs of color. Some husbands made a self-conscious effort to shelter their partners from knowledge about U.S. racism, and barriers of language and culture may at times have narrowed the women's awareness of the racial taboo or led the women to blame their beaux, not the army, for marriage delays. Few sources document women's inner perceptions of their own interracial relationships. But those few are intriguing. A German bride, for instance, described falling in love with her GI husband, a Hawaiian of mixed-Asian ancestry. For her the process was a gradual movement from ignorance to familiarity, from friendship to intimacy: "My friend who met Hawaiian boys had been telling me how Hawaiians looked like, how good-natured and friendly they were. But it was the first time I met any Hawaiian" when she was introduced to her husband at a carnival in Munich. "We had not been used to the Orientals. So at first we were not sure of them. But as we got to know them we liked them very much. We liked these Hawaiian boys much better than the Haole G.I.s from America," she explained, using the Hawaiian term for Caucasians. Part of the adjustment for this woman involved learning the codes surrounding interracial relationships in U.S. society, intimate and otherwise. She observed, "Hawaiian boys stick together and did everything together. They didn't like us girls if we went with mainland boys to nightclubs." The bureaucratic process of achieving marriage, in her account, was secondary to the physical details of their growing affection—becoming "good friends" who "did everything together"; eating with her family, learning to cook rice, going to a nightclub, and dancing together were the prelude to their eventual marriage.[20]

For other white European women, the attempt to marry across the color line was the starting point of a profound process of social and political awareness. Wives who wrote advocacy letters to the NAACP belong in this category. Some of the letters manifest an impressive understanding of civil rights and due process, as well as a good deal of moxie. One German woman went to see her fiancé's colonel (either she or the couple together may have decided that her race provided greater clout in their campaign to sway military authorities). Told point-blank that whites could not marry black servicemen, she challenged the colonel's contention, reminding him that African Americans were citizens as much as he was. This woman shared her problems, as well as her perplexity about American racial hypocrisy, with the NAACP. "Americans forget that they want to teach Germany 'Democracy,' a doctrine guaranteeing to all the 'inalienable rights . . . [of] Life, Liberty, and the pursuit of Happiness,'" she noted.[21]

Being in an interracial relationship was itself a political education, often a brutally physical one. White wives and girlfriends of African American soldiers who told their stories recounted being slapped, punched, spit upon, jeered and shouted at, and beaten to the ground. Women out in public with their black sweethearts were routinely called "whores" and often propositioned by other men. The perpetrators of these acts were sometimes her compatriots, but more often they were white American soldiers. For some white brides, the recognition that their love could arouse the hatred of others created a deep moment of reflection, one they felt compelled to speak about. "My faith in humanity . . . touched bottom when a white GI from the South actually beat me to my knees in an attempt to make me deny my love for a Negro soldier. He hit me four times across the face, knocking me dizzy. Then his fist caught me and I fell. 'That's where you belong for runnin' around with niggers,' he yelled. . . . I'm sure he would have hurt me seriously if I hadn't run."[22] The author of these words, Hazel Byrne Simpkins, understood that such violence, alongside the hostility of U.S. Army and State Department officials, was intended to make her "run away" from the relationship, yet she refused to do so. Simpkins's telling of her painful personal story was a stinging indictment of white Americans' racial beliefs and practices.

The painful experiences that interracial couples recounted made a difference to the NAACP over time, pushing some modulation of their policies and perspective. The organization was at first reluctant to engage the issue of soldiers' marriage, seeing it as a private, individual matter and as an area of military prerogative. This approach was consistent with the NAACP legal department's generally dismissive response to marriage challenges through-out the 1940s, based on the argument that antimiscegenation statutes were a "settled matter of constitutional law."[23] Eventually the staff of the NAACP veteran affairs committee and the executive leadership of the organization were swayed to support the couples. They did so, however, through behind-the-scenes, case-by-case action rather than public advocacy.

There were many reasons why opposing racist marriage laws was not on the NAACP's agenda in the 1940s. "Fear of white reprisal" was one, according to historian Paul Spickard. Segregationists had long asserted that black civil rights leaders coveted "social equality" or "social mixing"—a euphemism for access to white women—an assertion that could be used to undermine any and all black demands for political change.[24] If black civil rights activists openly advocated for interracial marriage, they risked a strong white back-lash. More important, black Americans were themselves ambivalent about the issue. Most, it is true, regarded the so-called antimiscegenation laws as a demeaning form of racial exclusion. But intermarriage in practice was con-troversial among African Americans, for whom it raised often painful ques-tions about race loyalty, assimilation, sexual desire and desirability, skin-color prejudice within the black community, and relations between black men and black women. Gunnar Myrdal's famous study found that black Americans in the 1940s viewed reform of marriage law as the lowest-priority item on their equal rights agenda—even as white Americans put it first and feared it most.[25]

The NAACP's own peculiar history with the issue was a further factor. In 1949, NAACP executive secretary Walter White, the most prominent African American leader of the era, divorced his wife of more than twenty-five years, Gladys Powell, a black woman, and married Poppy Cannon, a white woman born in South Africa. White's interracial marriage "ignited controversy in the black community." Some African Americans were personally appalled at White's actions; others feared that the intermarriage would damage the orga-nization's reputation and undermine its effectiveness. The incident placed in "stark relief" the black community's ambivalence about racial intermarriage as a political cause.[26]

In keeping with these attitudes, NAACP staff initially dismissed soldiers' complaints of marriage discrimination, calling them "entirely personal [mat-ters] between the two individuals." Internal staff communications revealed ambivalence on the issue as well as an inclination to trivialize or even ridi-cule the couple's concerns.[27] Yet the accumulated evidence of racial injustice submitted by interracial couples—their stories of discrimination—eventually swayed NAACP officials to become involved, though it was never a topic the organization engaged with sustained energy. By the late 1940s, staff of the veteran affairs committee treated the requests with almost uniform respect, routinely investigated the soldier marriage cases referred to the NAACP instead of dismissing them, and intervened when they could.[28] This involvement, on a case-by-case basis, was an effective form of advocacy on an individual level, but the organization failed to address the issue of marriage discrimination as a broad matter of justice. Walter White's only direct statement of protest was a pair of private but strongly worded letters to the secretaries of war and navy in late 1945, revealing and excoriating marriage discrimination in the European theater of operations. After receiving a patronizing "Dear Walter" reply from the secretary of war, a communication that absurdly insisted that racial discrimination was not practiced in the armed services, in marriage policy or in any other arena, White took no further action.[29]

Ultimately the NAACP came to serve as an important resource for interracial war couples, responding privately to their individual needs. It is ironic, however, that the premier civil rights organization refused to press the matter as a civil rights issue. In contrast, the African American press was more forthcoming about framing soldier marriage as a matter of racial justice. Its outspoken support was not necessarily a reflection of greater militancy, however. In the complicated politics of the midcentury black community, the socially conservative and middle-class black press was more kindly disposed toward black-white marriage than were the activists of the NAACP. Intermarriage had a certain social prestige and acceptance in elite black circles that it lacked in the mainstream. The black press championed the cause of interracial war couples to fit its own agenda of social integration, middle-class values, family structure, and gender roles. Still, interracial war couples found the black press to be an indispensable ally in advocating their cause. Moreover, many black journalists and editors pursued the political and civil rights implications of interracial marriage in a forceful and effective manner.

In the late 1940s and 1950s, the black press printed soldiers' interracial love stories in many forms and places, from photographs and opinion columns, to news stories, fiction, feature articles, and the society pages. *Ebony, Tan,* and *Negro Digest,* the most prominent of the black periodicals, ran multiple features on the interracial marriages of black GIs. There was no parallel in the white-dominated media, where images and stories of black-white war couples were all but absent.[30] At first glance, stories of war bride couples from the black press looked a great deal like the flood of war bride reportage in the white-dominated press just after the war—but with a critical difference: these stories were invariably, and often poignantly, put to service in a critique of American racism. Press coverage also differed in terms of its timing. White-dominated mass-circulation publications carried numerous war bride stories in 1946, and then the stories dwindled. In the black press, interest in soldiers' intermarriages rose through the end of the decade and continued to the mid-1950s. This reflected both the patterns of marriage for black servicemen—the occupation of Germany playing a large role—and the greater emphasis on interracialism in the years leading up to and following *Brown*.

One of the earliest and most prominent feature stories on the theme of soldier intermarriage appeared in the *Chicago Defender*, the nation's most widely read black newspaper. According to the article, this was a "storybook romance." Albert was African American, an army combat veteran of forty months in the European theater. Maud was white, an ammunitions worker from Liverpool. The readers of the *Chicago Defender* met this couple on Easter Sunday 1946, as husband swept British bride into his arms in Chicago's Union Station, a happy denouement. When Maud and Albert met at a British pub, it was love at first sight. However, they had fought their way through a forest of obstacles to reach this reunion in Chicago: the opposition of her mother, separation during the European invasion, and months of lonely waiting with an ocean between them.[31]

Significantly Maud and Albert's tale concluded not with a "happily ever after" but with an implied political moral: How would this couple fare, the writer asked, in a land of Jim Crow, particularly after tasting the relative racial freedom of British society? In publishing such stories, the underlying purpose of black editors was to attack the racialized marriage laws of the United States as one dimension of an absurd and antiquated system of racial segregation. This was precisely the point of another tale of "war romance" from the national edition of the *Chicago Defender*. In 1947 an Italian woman flew to the West Coast of the United States to join her fiancé, formerly a black army sergeant and now a resident of Santa Monica, California. Following their reunion in California, the couple proceeded to the town of Vancouver in northern Washington State, where their nuptials were performed by a local judge. Though the travel plans of this interracial couple did not hold intrinsic fascination for a national black readership, they were in fact highly significant in legal and historical context, for at the time of their marriage, California was one of the many states that barred interracial marriages (this law would be struck down by the California Supreme Court's *Perez* ruling one year later).[32] Readers of the article were reminded that Washington was the only state "west of the Rockies" where racially mixed marriages were legal. This war bride tale, then, depicts a double border-crossing. Not only does the Italian bride have to leave Europe to marry her beloved, but she and her husband must leave California to legalize their union.

Their story, like other war bride tales in the postwar black press, is about "free" and "unfree" zones for people of color within the United States.[33] A piece of short fiction from the *Pittsburgh Courier* was built around the same dichotomy. It described in dramatic terms an interracial couple's narrow escape from an incipient mob in a southern port city. The black veteran in the story and his "pretty blue-eyed French wife" must flee north to safety. His thought process is revealed through first-person narration: "Three long years we had waited. Three long years of writing and writing letters and praying. . . . And now, here in America, I was sneaking out of my city to go North. Suddenly the tears came. . . . Honeymoon! Yeah, this was going to be some honeymoon all right."[34]

A particularly revealing article about black GIs and their white European wives, one that encapsulated the gender and racial norms of the black press, was featured in *Negro Digest* in 1948. The author, Ollie Stewart, was one of the most respected and recognized black journalists of his generation. As a war correspondent in Europe for the Baltimore *Afro-American*, Stewart had reported on the achievements of black troops and the climate of racial hostility in the military.[35] For Stewart, as for other black journalists, writing about soldiers' overseas marriage was a prime opportunity to review the history and status of antimiscegenation laws in the United States and to underscore the racial hypocrisy of the U.S. military. But his underlying purpose was an even broader and more profound one. In this piece, Stewart used interracial marriage to present an alternative vision of black-white relations. "Negro soldiers" and French, Belgian, British, Australian, and Italian "girls"—ordinary young people falling in love—were "only doing what came naturally." In stressing the "normalcy" of these marriages, and their loving origins, he disrupted the historical construction of black-white intimacy as vile and unnatural. Stewart's formulation was echoed in a brief piece on white brides married to black soldiers that appeared in the *Chicago Defender*. The piece was presented though the eyes of a black female social worker who accompanied the white wives on their journey to the United States. These war brides, in her judgment, were "quite free of racial prejudice" and unable to comprehend America's "racial caste system."[36] Stewart and other journalists were laying out a myth of racial innocence—in a natural state, in the absence of racist socialization, white people would be color-blind and tolerant, they suggest.

Paradoxically, Stewart's article presents interracial war couples as both very ordinary and most extraordinary. If they were simply "doing what came naturally" to young people, they were also doing so in the face of massive resistance. The pursuit of an interracial love affair demanded unusual determination, a love larger than ordinary. Stewart wrote, "Most betrothals were made . . . in defiance of established custom and took a great deal of courage on the part of both bride and groom." Confidently, he concluded that these special marriages would be "more than ordinarily successful" because of the difficulties through which they had persisted.

Foreign wives in particular received paradoxical treatment by the black press. Courageous they may have been in confronting U.S. military police, embassy officials, or hostile neighbors in their countries of origin, but as American wives, Stewart shows them to be decidedly subservient and passive—and seemingly uninterested in social issues: "Louise calls her husband 'Baby' and leaves him to make all the major decisions. They like to dance with each other, and pooh-pooh the idea of prejudice interfering with their marriage." Home and motherhood were the highest aspirations of these war brides—a theme that was common to almost all accounts of interracial war marriage in the black press. The "future plans" of one interracial war couple were entirely domestic, for example, and strikingly modest—Maud would just "try being a pretty good housewife" while her husband would focus on being a good provider for his family. As one veteran said of his Italian-born wife: "Since she's been here she hasn't been bothered much by prejudice. She doesn't go out much, with the baby and all she is kept pretty busy."

On one level the unequal gender roles championed by Stewart could simply reflect the wider social phenomenon of postwar marriage regardless of race; the descriptions here are virtually identical to those of white Anglo brides married to white veterans in the same period. But they are significant on another level. If war brides in interracial marriages were going to pose a solution to the American dilemma of race, they were going to have to do so by fitting into the narrative as proper women who could bolster not just the self-esteem of their African American husbands but the patriarchal claims of all American men over women of all races.[37] America's black veterans were manly men, the literature implies, who knew how to lead and command, but tender enough to be proper husbands and responsible fathers. The presentation of their wives as political innocents and naïve immigrant outsiders also dovetails with this construction. These were "normal" male-dominated marriages, not unnatural, egalitarian ones. In recounting tales of interracial love that flourished despite barriers of racism, African American writers like

Stewart were presenting an antidote to the mainstream depiction of black-white intermarriage as pathological or destined for tragedy.[38] Of course black-white intermarriage in 1940s America was far from "normal"—it was in fact illegal in most states. So the assertion of normalcy was an attempt to imagine a future when they might be "normal" to white Americans too. Treating these relationships like any other marriages was a political statement.

If black journalists tended to present interracial war couples as ordinary, apolitical young people, just "doing what comes naturally," this choice emerged from their own brand of cautious and conservative racial politics. Such true tales of love provided the African American press with a kind of political camouflage, allowing it to advance a racial justice argument implicitly without highlighting black racial activism explicitly. But this approach also elided the emergent political awareness that black and white intermarried couples brought home with them to the United States, a hard-learned lesson of their struggle for marriage.

Intermarriage in the Occupation of Japan

The relationship of Don Tennyson and Masa Soto in postwar Tokyo captured on many levels the politics of intercultural marriage in U.S.-occupied Japan and the postwar United States. Tennyson's first-person narration of his long campaign to wed Masa and bring her home to California, "I Dared to Take a Japanese Bride," was published in 1954, the historic year of the Supreme Court's *Brown* decision, reflecting the intense interest in racial integration that the decision generated; but the article described earlier events from Don Tennyson's tour of duty in the U.S. occupation of the late 1940s. Don was a noncommissioned officer in the air force, stationed in Tokyo, where he was introduced to his future wife, Masa. Barred from marriage by occupation regulations, the couple wed in a Shinto ceremony. The large and boldface title of Tennyson's account pointed to a number of themes in the couple's story. The defiant title speaks to one key dimension of the Tennysons' experience. Like many of the American and Japanese couples that formed during the postwar occupation, the Tennysons chose to ignore the military's marriage ban and wed in open defiance of army regulation. Such marriages were "daring" acts of civil and military disobedience. On another level, the title suggests "daring" in the sensational sense, an unspoken reference to the interracial sexual liaison embedded in the story and the racial taboo that their love defied. This theme is developed in particular in the embedded story of Masa's struggle for the approval of her family. The chilling words of her sister—"He will break your heart and ruin your life. Marry one of your own race"—with shades of Madame Butterfly, served to underscore the transgressive character of such a relationship.[39] Yet it is not clear that Tennyson chose the title or intended to highlight this particular reading of the couple's story; his narrative is far more absorbed with the question of social and cultural assimilation of Japanese wives in the U.S. environment and the lingering hatreds of the war years than it is about interracial sexuality. In the end, this narrative is an upbeat tale of growing pluralism and hope for the future. Much of his account stressed the surprising ease of the couple's assimilation and their pleasure at how welcoming their American neighbors proved to be. In this regard the story functioned as an advertisement for the growing racial "enlightenment" of postwar America and its ability to absorb families such as the Tennysons within its ethnic and gender norms. The Tennysons offered their intercultural and interracial marriage to American readers as a "fact on the ground," a portent of future success and the likelihood of positive social change.

In postwar Japan, American GIs and their would-be-wives, like the Tennysons, strove to achieve equitable treatment and legal recognition for their relationships. Their efforts to marry, however, operated in a more complex and racially ambiguous environment than the one facing soldiers and brides in Europe. African American, Asian American, and European American servicemen with Japanese sweethearts were united by the recalcitrance of the military and its open antagonism toward their marital aspirations, but men of different backgrounds positioned themselves differently and employed different strategies in their individual and collective campaigns for the right to wed. Japanese brides added a further complicating dimension to this political dynamic. The racial and cultural "difference" of Japanese women loomed large in the imagination of U.S. military and government officials, inflecting official policies with racial bias; husbands sometimes shared an "Orientalist" view of their wives or sweethearts, even as they asserted the women's democratic rights and equal humanity. Japanese women in committed relationships with American soldiers had to navigate the bumpy terrain of gender, national, and racial bias and exclusion. Their marriage advocacy both reinforced and diverged from that of their husbands.

The lengthy and momentous U.S. occupation of Japan, from 1945 to 1952, under the direction of the supreme commander of the Allied powers, General Douglas MacArthur, and his SCAP headquarters, took nearly 1 million U.S. troops through the country. American soldiers mingled openly with

Japanese women, despite the enmity of the war years and the occupation's restrictions. "For ordinary enlisted men, it goes without saying, the only female companionship available was Japanese," one SCAP official explained, and "international dating became the norm."[40] Yet from the beginning, leaders of the U.S. occupation took a strong and explicit position against marriage between Americans and Japanese nationals, citing the Asian exclusion in U.S. immigration law as the basis for their policy. Congress reinforced and incorporated the ban on Japanese wives in its formulation of the GI Brides Act in December 1945, excluding from its benefits "all persons ineligible for admission"—a phrase readily understood as a reference to the Oriental Exclusion Law.[41] U.S. military leaders in Tokyo and Washington insisted that intermarriage was "unwise" and would lead to "much unhappiness" for both Americans and Japanese. Military antagonism toward Japanese-American marriage emerged as well from a broader set of attitudes about Japanese people as a race, and about Japanese women specifically, an attitude embedded in the culture and leadership of the U.S. occupation. A short-lived but elaborate system of government-sponsored brothels, the Recreation and Amusement Association, for example, was a joint creation of Japanese and occupation officials where Japanese women were recruited to service American troops in racially segregated facilities.[42] The American occupation of Japan was a neo-colonialist affair, John Dower writes, distinct in many ways from the Allied occupation of postwar Germany. Even as German-American marriage was permitted beginning in December 1946 and German wives transported to the United States at government expense, a U.S. Army circular was clarifying the proportions of "Japanese blood" that invalidated an alien applicant's marriage or visa request.[43] This concern with blood rules was a link to the antimiscegenation tradition in American law and reflected the racialized underpinnings of military policy in Japan.

Extensive disregard of the marriage ban by couples and pressure for change from constituents led Congress to enact limited reforms, though these were passed over the objections of the military. In July 1947, the Alien Brides Act, Public Law 213, permitted entrance to the United States of "alien spouses" otherwise "considered inadmissible because of race." The bill, however, granted this waiver only to couples who managed to apply for permission and wed within thirty days of its enactment—for many couples, an impossibility. The waiver was reintroduced three years later, in August 1950, in coordination with the Korean War (Public Law 717), again on a time-limited basis, and ultimately extended through March 1952. In committee and floor discussion of the first waiver, congressmen were specific in stating that their support for these measures was a desire to recognize *intraracial* marriages, that is, proposed marriages between Nisei servicemen and Japanese women, thereby sidestepping the explosive issue of interracial unions (though the majority of husbands, probably three-quarters according to State Department estimates, were white European Americans, not Asian Americans). Military leaders continued to champion the racially based exclusion of Japanese wives through the end of the occupation. The marriage of American soldiers to Asian brides was not normalized until the McCarran Walter Act of 1952 finally established the right of naturalization for Asian immigrants.[44]

The formal ban on GI marriage to Japanese nationals created a different dynamic than the invisible barriers faced by European and African American couples in Europe. The military's open hostility to Japanese-American marriage and its vigorous enforcement of the ban were touchstones that ignited and focused the anger of servicemen, black, white, and Asian, and their Japanese sweethearts. Although Japanese-American couples were unified by their sense of grievance, their strategies for confronting the ban differed considerably across lines of race, nationality, and gender. White GIs and veterans were the most likely to engage in open defiance of military policy. They challenged the marriage ban repeatedly and sometimes forced civilian and military leaders to modify aspects of their policy, though more often they failed to exact change.[45]

Unauthorized marriage was one of the most defiant actions that a couple could take. White servicemen, with some frequency, chose to marry their fiancées in Japanese civil or religious ceremonies that the U.S. authorities refused to recognize but could do little to stop. Alternatively, white service personnel with Japanese sweethearts often found a bureaucratic solution to their problem: many in this interim period took civilian jobs with the occupation forces at the end of their army tours. This enabled them to stay near their Japanese wives and children, and to marry by the less strict requirements placed upon civilians (though there was still no consistent procedure for bringing their wives back to the United States). Once they were legally married in Japan, Japanese-American couples employed a wide range of advocacy strategies—approaching powerful individuals for assistance, consulting lawyers, appealing to congressional representatives through parents and friends back home. A white veteran, for example, convinced his state legislature in Connecticut to legalize the Shinto wedding ceremony that he and his wife had undergone in Japan. Appeal to Congress for "private" immigration legislation, a long-standing tradition in immigration policy, proved successful in enabling many white servicemen to bring their wives into the United States.[46]

Many of these white servicemen appeared to have an underlying sense of confidence, misplaced or not, that justice would ultimately prevail for them, and this attitude emboldened them to seek help from those in authority. The phenomenon was well illustrated by the case of three white veterans who took their problem straight to the top of SCAP headquarters in order to make their plea for equality and acceptance. All three men had come to Japan in the army, fallen in love, and, unable to wed as soldiers, taken civilian employment with the Atomic Bomb Casualty Commission (ABCC) in Hiroshima. All three had received permission to marry in 1949 from the ABCC director. But, they claimed, the racial harassment and exclusion of their Japanese wives had only intensified following their marriages. They described many embarrassing situations: the wives had been thrown off of trains, ordered to leave the base PX while shopping, and stopped and harassed by military police—a pattern of treatment reminiscent of that suffered by African Americans in the Jim Crow South of the 1940s. These families had also been denied housing, a benefit extended to other commission staff, because the wives were Japanese nationals. Writing a formal letter of complaint to occupation headquarters was a risky strategy, but one the men evidently felt driven to take. All they wanted, the three men explained, was for their wives, and the Japanese wives of other Americans with the occupation force, to be treated on an equal basis with other wives and dependents of U.S. personnel. Significantly, following a lengthy legal review at headquarters, SCAP roundly rejected their plea.[47]

White servicemen had confidence in their entitlement, as citizens and soldiers, to marry the women of their own choosing and in their power to protect their wives from racial harassment (an often misplaced confidence, as it turned out). African American GIs did not share this confidence. Access to power and recognition of their citizenship were not taken for granted by black men in the postwar period. African American men served in the occupation forces in substantial numbers. In an army ostensibly deployed to bring democracy to Japan, black GIs were subordinate and often segregated—a positioning that gave many a sense of empathy for the vanquished Japanese people.[48] Black servicemen pointed to the multiple obstacles placed before their marriages, obstacles that blacks were far more likely than whites to see and name racism. Many African American GIs, for example, identified as a racial inequity the differential treatment of Asian and European war brides.

It was "entirely unfair," one African American serviceman pointed out, to "discriminate" against wives and children of "Japanese blood" by excluding them, when white European wives, even former "enemy" Germans, were welcome to the United States. Such a distinction denied the underlying and common "humanity" of the Japanese people. Another black serviceman linked the marriage ban to wider issues of race and tolerance in foreign policy: "Yes, we had a war: for what? My understanding was that it was for peaceful neighborlihood of the world and to attempt to instill Democratic ideas in the heads and hearts of all people, by ridding the world of thoughts of aggression and domination." To this writer, it seemed transparent that banning marriage to Japanese and other Asian women, solely on the basis of race, was a violation of the "neighborly" and nonaggressive values for which the war had been fought.[49]

Black and white servicemen also appeared to differ in their perceptions of their own relationships as racially transgressive. State antimiscegenation laws, as seen earlier, were often explicit in banning marriage between whites and "Orientals" on the same basis as those between blacks and whites; but that does not mean that white GIs necessarily internalized those legal definitions. White servicemen who advocated for marital equality usually spoke about discrimination toward their wives as Japanese, not toward themselves as an interracial couple per se—or at least the latter was a secondary consideration. As white men they may have held a sense of their own entitlement to "take" Asian women as wives. Black service personnel, on the other hand, were more prone to see their status as an interracial couple as a primary or equal cause of discriminatory treatment.

Based perhaps on this analysis, African American soldiers were more likely than whites to conceptualize the problem as a broad matter of principle and to seek collective solutions. Like black GIs in the European theater, they turned for help to civil rights advocates in the United States, and once again their stories of racial discrimination and thwarted love were an effective political tool. Corporal George Brown's carefully crafted letter to the NAACP, for example, functioned on two levels at once, appealing to principle and emotion. Every day in Japan he came in contact with soldiers who were "suffering from broken hearts," and Brown confessed that he himself was one of these men. Corporal Brown had served for three and a half years in the occupation force for Japan; during this tour he had fallen in love, had a child, and applied for permission to marry—permission that had been stubbornly denied. In penning his young family's personal story, Brown was attempting to speak for the "thousands of GI couples in the Far East Command" who shared their situation. Like other black GIs, Brown had hope that the interracial coalition-building that the NAACP was known for might prove effective in opening marriage on an equal footing to GIs serving in Japan.[50]

Corporal Brown's question, "Doesn't our Democracy advocate that all peoples, regardless of race, creed, or color, are equal?" spoke to his own condition as much as that of his Japanese girlfriend. Likewise, this double-layered racism was readily apparent in the largest and best-detailed case of marriage discrimination in the Japanese occupation. The incident involved men from the Twenty-fourth Infantry Regiment, an African American regiment based at Camp Gifu, Japan, halfway between Kobe and Tokyo, and their Japanese sweethearts. The turbulent and clouded history of the regiment in its final years, including accusations of poor combat performance in Korea, has placed the Twenty-fourth under repeated historical scrutiny since the war.[51] But none of these evaluations has considered the role that marriage discrimination played in the rising tensions within the unit. According to contemporary accounts, 400 men (out of a regiment whose maximum strength was fewer than 3,000) had applied for permission to marry Japanese wives by 1950, permission that few if any had been granted. When the regiment received orders for combat deployment to Korea in early July, just weeks after the fighting began, many of these couples became alarmed. They feared that their physical removal from Japan before their paperwork was approved would prevent them from marrying their wives—an outcome that in all probability came about. Tensions related to these unresolved relationships were apparently the main cause of the pandemonium at the troops' departure from Gifu. In the days before the deployment, the regiment's colonel, a white officer, canceled all leaves and confined the men to base. An investigator noted that "when some of the men went AWOL to see their girlfriends and the military police attempted to round them up, at least fifty joined in confrontations that became [in the words of one rifleman] 'Real heavy.'" During the two days of departure from camp, July 11 and 12, eyewitnesses, with little insight into the background story, observed large number of Japanese women on the train platform adjoining Camp Gifu. Another officer reported that "some climbed aboard one of the trains, . . . soldiers were pulling them through the windows, . . . and the police had trouble getting them off." Several white observers of this scene charged that the women were passing the men illegal drugs through the train windows—but given the circumstances, it seems more likely that the wrapped bundles were mementos or personal effects, exchanged between lovers who were at that point quite certain they were parting forever. Fighting broke out between white military police and black soldiers when one MP tried to prevent a man from kissing his Japanese girlfriend on the platform. As in many comparable scenarios in Europe, black soldiers defended with physical resistance their right to love whom they pleased, an action for which they suffered retaliation.[52]

The deployment of the Twenty-fourth Regiment to Korea was not the traceable end of this tale. Among the reduced force of black officers and enlisted men left behind in Camp Gifu, many felt compelled to "set the record straight" on the regiment's interracial relationships. Here the case study reveals the connection between marriage advocacy in occupied Japan and the civil rights agenda of the early 1950s. Lieutenant Colonel Forest Lofton, the highest-ranking black officer appointed to the regiment, and several black chaplains were deeply concerned about the men's situation and frustrated by their own inability to intercede. At this juncture, they called in outside assistance in the form of L. Alex Wilson, a prominent black journalist and overseas correspondent for the *Chicago Defender*. If the interracial love stories of Camp Gifu were brought to light, the men reasoned, it might be more difficult for the SCAP command to end them. What Wilson gleaned from his visit proved to be eye-opening in a number of ways. The "love-sick" men, he learned, were devoted to their partners. In the small towns surrounding the camp, many had already set up households with their girlfriends and waited for the day that they could bring them home to the United States. Wilson spoke to several men with Japanese partners and also traveled off base to interview several of these would-be wives. The Japanese women spoke "proudly" of their African American husbands and showed off their biracial babies, whom Wilson enthusiastically dubbed "worthy Americans" and "beautiful."

The presence of the babies was a potential complication of the narrative. Were they unwanted by their fathers? Or was their illegitimacy a temporary state? Did the fact of their mothers living with the fathers outside of marriage prove the charge that Japanese women who went out with American GIs were sexually promiscuous, or that the men were? Wilson, representing the values of his black middle-class audience, was anxious to assure that the men's most deep-seated desire was to marry the mothers and make the children legitimate. The racially discriminatory policies of the U.S. government were the only obstacle that now stood in the way of that dream, he told his readers. Interestingly, one black serviceman who wrote to the NAACP from Camp Gifu expressed a similar set of concerns about the biracial babies of American GIs in Japan. In his view, GIs wished to be responsible caretakers of their offspring, but far too many factors were stacked against them.[53] Both men felt compelled to refute the narrative about black men and their irresponsible or aggressive sexuality that was repeatedly aired in mainstream sources.

African American servicemen saw the ban on marriage as one expression of a broad pattern of racial discrimination in the Far East Command. Military leaders limited the freedoms of nonwhites, both military and civilian, and nonwhites often challenged these limitations. The little that is known about Nisei soldiers who sought to marry Japanese wives, for example, suggests that some of these men, too, connected the issue of marriage equality to the wider issue of Asian American civil rights. Like other U.S. service personnel, Japanese American GIs were banned from marrying Japanese brides for most of the occupation period, a policy that they vigorously protested. To assist them, they turned to prominent and familiar civil rights organizations. Several Japanese American GIs enlisted the aid of the Japanese-American Citizens League (JACL) Anti-discrimination Committee in the late 1940s to protest the absurdly and punitively short deadlines allowed for marriage completion under Public Law 213. The committee subsequently raised the issue with the office of the secretary of war and received a surprisingly candid response: the temporary law was a compromise that the military had never favored; in their view, the ban on marriage was a positive and successful policy, a safeguard for Japanese and Korean people as well as U.S. soldiers.[54] Once again the U.S. military refused to give ground on racial matters.

Japanese women engaged to American soldiers also encountered American racial discrimination. How did their relationships with Americans shape their social and political awareness, and how did they respond to the marriage ban? In a handful of cases, there is evidence of Japanese women engaging in direct advocacy. Like the German war brides or would-be brides who confronted U.S. military commanders, such Japanese fiancées used the language and principles of democratic equality to protest their situation. One woman, for example, eloquently pleaded her case to General Douglas MacArthur, supreme commander of the Allied powers in Japan. Teruko Murazawa and Hisao Nakashima, a Nisei army sergeant, were deeply in love, according to Teruko's letter. While searching for a way to wed in 1947, the sergeant was called home to make funeral arrangements for his grandfather in Hawaii. When the army delayed his return to Japan until October, the couple found they had missed the deadline for marriage under the Alien Brides Act by several weeks. Teruko's letter to the general laid out their private love story to enlist his help. But as it did for this woman, the personal experience of injustice often led to wider identification with others in the same situation. Teruko wrote her letter, she explained, not just on her own behalf but for the "many persons throughout the nation who were unable to marry while the Japanese Bride Act was in effect for various good reasons." Sadly, her plea for leniency was rejected in a curt letter from SCAP headquarters.[55]

Evidence of Japanese women's views from the war or immediate postwar period is highly fragmentary, but valuable nonetheless. A postwar interview project captured the personal reflections of several dozen Japanese war brides in some depth. These narratives echo the themes of husbands' stories but add other dimensions as well. As was true for American GIs in intercultural relationships, the struggle to marry shaped or sharpened some women's political and social awareness. Japanese women felt compelled to defend their love for an American as something to be proud of, in contradistinction to those who were shaming her, attacking her dignity or that of her husband. For women, however, the opposition of Japanese parents and relatives loomed much larger than that of the U.S. government. Central to one woman's tale of marriage, for instance, was her confrontation with her guardians, an aunt and uncle, who opposed her engagement to a Filipino American GI. Her account combined her expression of need for personal and social independence with an exposition of American civic ideals:

> My uncle insulted my G.I. friend so much that it made me furious. Right there I told my uncle, "You insulted my friend. It is inexcusable. Your idea is outmoded. You have been talking about what my ancestors were. You never mentioned what I am now. . . . Ux is an American. He is to be judged by the American ideals. In America there is democracy. In democracy everybody is equal. Ux is not responsible for what his parents are. As long as we loved each other nothing mattered. It is what we are that is important and not what our parents are. Uncle, you are all wrong. . . . " That very day I ran away from my uncle's house.

Immediately after this confrontation the couple initiated the marriage application process, for this war bride a very real break with the family that had raised her and their values. Another bride felt deeply ashamed that her GI fiancée was insulted by her relatives and friends; fearing for his safety when he came to visit in her neighborhood, she persuaded him to dress in civilian clothes for these visits. Some Japanese war brides saw their own role in the struggle for marriage as one of cultural negotiation, bridging the gaps and reshaping the dynamics in order to make marriage possible.

Japanese war brides' stories suggest that women's analysis or framing of cross-cultural marriage differed from their husbands' in a number of crucial ways. Racial difference was only one factor in their perception of these relationships. Far more significant was the gap between occupier and occupied: crossing over the divide between former wartime enemies required a leap of faith and an enduring love, especially in the face of community and family opposition. One war bride recounted, "All my relatives were furious about my marriage to a G.I. . . . they felt that I disgraced the whole family and kin by my marriage to a GI and would no longer consider me kin." In contrast with husbands who explicitly spoke about the "common humanity" of Japanese and U.S. citizens, Japanese wives often emphasized that Japanese culture was markedly different from that of Americans, even from that of Japanese Americans.

The most politicizing dimension of intercultural interaction for Japanese women combined race and culture with resistance to gender subordination. Women feared being taken advantage of by Americans, and they feared for their own reputations as well. One woman told her interviewer, "GIs' reputation became very bad in Japan because of the bad behavior of bad Japanese girls. Many Japanese thought that all girls marrying GIs were prostitutes." War brides needed to assure themselves that their GI's love was genuine and that she not be seen, by him or others, as a woman who could be "bought." This attitude could be an embracing of national pride or an internalization of the misogynist view of the "pan-pan" girl. In either case, women frequently felt compelled to defend their dignity as women in relation to their American boyfriends. Another woman, asked to go out by two GIs, responded with caution: "I told them it sounded very interesting [at the enlisted men's club] and I would like to go there. But also I told them if those girls there are the so-called 'Pan-pan girls' I wouldn't go because I didn't want to be taken for one of them." Even when her husband proposed marriage, the woman reiterated her concern. "My husband proposed to me very soon after that. I told him I was not a 'Pan-pan girl.' I also told him that I had been married and had a daughter. From the beginning I showed these G.I.s my little baby so that they wouldn't take me for a young girl."[56] For Japanese women, GI husbands, white, black, or Asian American, were different because they were Americans and because they were occupiers. Resisting opposition to marry an American often required a profound leap of faith. As all these narratives suggest, in the U.S. occupation of Japan, military opposition to intercultural marriage was widespread and multidimensional; to the extent that they can be known, the responses of men and women in those relationships were diverse and complex.

Cultural Pluralism and War Bride Marriage: Explorations in Social Science and Film

Intercultural couples in Japan fought for equal access to marriage in the years following World War II, often with limited success. The occupation leadership yielded remarkably little ground on racial equality, even as Congress signaled a new openness to Japanese immigrants and foreign policymakers increasingly looked to Japan as a linchpin of the U.S. strategy in Asia. These changes slowly paved the way for an unprecedented migration of intermarried couples, despite the opposition of the military. By the early 1950s, several hundred Japanese war brides had made their way to the United States and established lives with their veteran-husbands—a population that would swell after the Korean War and the elimination of the Asian naturalization ban. These interracial and intercultural couples captured the attention and imagination of certain race reformers and liberal intellectuals in the early years of the new decade. Japanese war brides emerged as a motif in two realms in particular, popular film and social science research. These cultural producers regarded the intermarriages of Japanese wives and American veteran-husbands as a social laboratory for more positive American race relations, much as African American intellectuals and activists had held up black and white intermarriages from the European theater as an argument against segregation in the early postwar years. Once again war brides were a vehicle for embodying social trends and reformist arguments, here tied to a message of cultural pluralism.

Social scientists with a race-reform agenda looked to Japanese-American marriage as a model for cultural assimilation in postwar society. Academic studies of "war bride" marriage in the late 1940s and 1950s were shaped by two developments in midcentury U.S. social science: the scrutiny of family and the interrogation of race and ethnic relations in American society. In the relatively new field of marriage and family studies, the "adjustment" of these unique postwar families engaged the interest of liberal scholars who embraced intercultural and even interracial relationships as a direction for the future. The successful adjustment of intercultural couples showed their maturity, resilience, and readiness for life in a pluralistic and international postwar world—and, by extension, displayed the pluralism and maturity of American society itself. The research of these social scientists paralleled a larger cultural and political agenda of the early Cold War: calls for international cooperation abroad and greater racial and ethnic tolerance at home as a way to bolster the case for U.S. leadership of democratic nations.

The positive assessment of interracial war marriage in American social science was a new trend, though still a minority perspective. Earlier, social scientists viewed such marriages with almost universal negativity. The systematic study of marriage and family was a relatively new field of social science, and a racially conservative one, as World War II began. Eugenics played an influential though largely forgotten role in its genesis, first by its dedication to prevent "procreation of the unfit" through "scientific" studies and later to promote "the marital and family stability of the white middle class."[57] Though most scholars were not eugenicists per se, they did espouse a conservative status quo in family, race, and social relations during the war. Central to their view was the concept of "homogamy." Marriage and family researchers posited that "homogamous" marriages—those in which the marital partners were most similar—were far more likely to survive than "exogamous" marriages where the partners differed in important social parameters. Ernest W. Burgess of the University of Chicago, a leading proponent of this view, stated that "a union in marriage is likely to be more happy where both members of the couple belong to the same social class, the same economic, educational and cultural groups and are of the same race and religion," though Burgess also asserted that one particular mismatch had a positive effect—the wife should be less intelligent than the husband, or at least "make him think she is."[58] For this reason, this group of scholars was almost universally negative about the prospect for "mismatched" intercultural couples, whose unions threatened to break down carefully erected social and cultural barriers.

A 1946 article in *Mental Hygiene*, the journal of the National Association of Mental Health, illustrates this preoccupation in relation to war brides. The author, a clinician who counseled couples professionally, defined a hierarchy of bad marriage emerging from the war—with interracial marriages the most problematic of all: "The problems of adjustment are serious enough when [the serviceman] marries . . . some one from a different nation (as England, New Zealand, or Australia)." Most disastrous of all were marriages "with girls of *far* different cultural background [emphasis in original]"—servicemen who married "Chinese or Japanese girls in Hawaii, Polynesian girls in Hawaii and the South Pacific Islands, and Latin-American girls in Panama and the West Indies." Many of these interracial marriages "are frankly temporary," he concluded, and intercultural relationships as a whole had unusually "poor predictability." The "only happy future" such couples might contemplate would be in the wife's native land.[59]

Even as conservative leaders were devising ways to shore up the homogamous family as the cornerstone of American domestic life after the war, the field of social science was changing from within. By the early 1950s, interracialism was the overt and predominant concern of certain social scientists who turned their attention to marriages between Japanese women and American veterans. Major projects on Japanese war brides and their "adjustment" to American life and marriage were undertaken during the 1950s at the University of Chicago, the University of Hawaii, the University of California–Berkeley and the University of Southern California—all institutions known for the study of race relations.[60] Historian Ruth Feldstein has described the "diverse and widespread efforts among antiracists [in academe] in the 1940s and 1950s to expose the psychic toll that prejudice exacted" both on people of color as the "victims" of racism and on whites "suffering from" its distorting effects.[61] War bride studies were built around the metaphor of interracial war marriage as a "laboratory" for the study of racial integration, its promises and its limitations, in American society. This research coincided with the moment when American society was beginning to confront "interracialism," domestically in the debate over school integration and the *Brown* decision, and internationally, with rising U.S. involvement in Asia and Africa. The study teams themselves also reflected interracialism, with Japanese American researchers playing an important role, often under the direction of senior white sociologists.[62]

These researchers set their work up implicitly to challenge the concept of homogamy. They challenged too the "much oversimplified notion" that "Oriental-Caucasian marriages" were "doomed to destruction" from the start. This new wave of research had a decidedly optimistic tone when it came to assessing the future of interracial relationships. In a study cosponsored by the race relations and family study centers, Anselm Strauss, a sociologist from the University of Chicago, found that war marriages between Japanese and Americans were "likely to be quite stable, and to involve fewer major stresses than a great many marriages between native Americans." Schnepp and Yui found remarkable felicity or satisfaction in a sample of Japanese-American intermarriages, concluding that they were successful based on the fact that none of the couples were divorced or considering divorce.[63]

The most sustained and sophisticated study of war bride marriage, which involved both Japanese and European women, was conducted at the University of Hawaii. This project, based on lengthy home-based interviews with dozens of war brides, was under the direction of sociologist Yukiko Kimura. For most of her long career, Kimura was on staff at the Romanzo Adams Social Research Laboratory at the University of Hawaii, an institute for the study of race relations in the social, economic, and cultural history of Hawaii. The laboratory was named for Professor Romanzo Adams, founding director of the Department of Sociology at the University of Hawaii and author, in 1937, of *Interracial Marriage in Hawaii*. Kimura was born in Yokohama, Japan, and became a social worker for the YWCA, first in Japan and then in Hawaii. She completed her Ph.D. from the University of Chicago in 1952 with a study of the Issei during the war and then returned to the University of Hawaii to pursue research.[64]

In the rich racial and cultural melting pot of Hawaii, Kimura was able to study couples in four categories: Japanese brides of "Japanese" (presumably Nisei) husbands; Japanese brides of non-Japanese husbands (this group included an eclectic mix of Filipino Americans, African Americans, native Hawaiians, European Americans and mixed-race individuals); European brides of "Japanese" husbands; and European brides of non-Japanese husbands. Kimura skewered the "assumption . . . that peoples of like or similar cultures may establish quick and easy relations, while great differences impede and complicate" relationships. Comparing relationships between war brides and their in-laws in Hawaii, she found, counterintuitively, that war brides of a different cultural heritage got along not worse but better than those who shared the background of their new relatives. Japanese wives of non-Japanese were the "happiest group," and European wives of Japanese husbands were next. Japanese brides of Nisei husbands were much less likely to experience harmonious relations with in-laws (48 percent) than did Japanese wives of non-Japanese (72 percent), European brides of Nisei husbands (60 percent), and European wives of non-Japanese (55 percent). For Kimura this had much to do with racial and cultural preassumptions. The Japanese American mother-in-law, for example, expected her new European daughter-in-law to be standoffish and haughty due to her whiteness but was pleasantly surprised when the war bride needed help navigating the American setting or expressed an interest in the mother's cultural traditions. The Japanese daughter-in-law, on the other hand, was bound to disappoint: "Her American clothes and make-up, her independence in thinking and acting, are not only unexpected and puzzling but offensive and 'American' and completely unbecoming a Japanese daughter-in-law." In summarizing her findings, Kimura conjectured that "sharing the same cultural background tends to restrict relationships . . . to the forms prescribed and to hamper spontaneous interaction. In contrast, where there is no common cultural definition of roles, . . . [the relationship] depends on the ability of each to achieve a sympathetic identification with the other."[65] Here was the value of interracial liaison for couples and society: it demanded that one walk in the other's shoes, bringing with it greater understanding and cooperation

Despite their generally optimistic results about the prospects for inter-marriage, researchers were not blind to the fact of American racism. For some scholars "selectivity" was an important factor in the success of these marriages in overcoming racism. Caucasian men who chose Japanese wives were lone wolves, who lacked family obligations that might have competed with their marital relationships or exposed the relationships to strong nega-tive pressures. Others argued that white spouses in interracial marriages had been raised in tolerant families, lacking in racial prejudice. The partners in successful interracial couples had few if any institutional, familial, or social affiliations that might have served to block the marriage or place it under pressure. Mixed marriages might thrive because they avoided certain strains or tensions that were operative in many endogamous relationships. Kimura had a more complex view of social identity that recognized class, status, and generational differences within racial and ethnic groups, but she too saw the couple's independence from backward-looking structures and traditions as a key factor in success.

The rosy analysis of these interracial war marriages was not necessar-ily fully justified. Later, even just a few years later, a number of researchers found fault with various aspects of these postwar studies. For example, more in-depth probing of the subjective experience of the Japanese war brides revealed less harmony than met the eye in the earlier research. The isolation of the couples was found to have long-term emotional effects as well.[66] Social science research about war brides in the early 1950s reflected the liberal, postwar faith in American progress toward cultural pluralism at a moment when the issue was poised to move to center stage in the *Brown* decision. The studies emerged out of postwar American liberalism, with its confidence in American individualism and freedom, its attachment to equality of oppor-tunity, and its nationalistic sense of superiority. They reflected as well an embrace of Asia and things Asian in the early Cold War.[67] Liberal social sci-entists who studied Japanese war bride marriage used their research to prove that Americans were ready for change in their social mores and immigration policy, especially with regard to race and ethnicity.

Interest in the adjustment of Japanese-American couples was not confined to the realm of social science. While many Hollywood filmmakers explored the postwar adjustment of veterans, some used war brides as a motif to do so spe-cifically. One film, King Vidor's *Japanese War Bride* (1952) took an in-depth view of race relations in the postwar United States by examining an intercul-tural war marriage. The film reflects the intense interest among liberal artists and intellectuals in cultural pluralism and interracialism in the early 1950s and serves as a brief for racial understanding. Vidor was by midcentury a Hollywood powerhouse whose career had spanned the silent and talking eras, known for such popular dramas as *Stella Dallas* (1937) and *Northwest Passage* (1940), but Vidor had also written, produced, or directed films with a progressive social conscience. In *Japanese War Bride*, Vidor tackled head-on the problem of American race prejudice in postwar American society.[68] Like the social scientists who were his contemporaries, Vidor magnified the problems and the promise of one intercultural marriage in order to explore the importance of intercultural relations for the health of postwar society.

On one level, the advertising poster for *Japanese War Bride* could not have made director King Vidor's pluralist agenda any more plain: "THERE WAS NO EAST OR WEST WHEN THEIR LIPS MET. . . . " The advertisement shows an iconic pose from Hollywood romance: the lovers engage in a sweeping embrace, gazing into each other's eyes as he lifts her off the ground. While the poster headline seems to suggest a fairy-tale theme—the magical kiss will erase all conflict and difference—that was hardly the filmmakers' message. The film presents interracialism as a difficult path, but Vidor uses his story to assert the possibility of love across lines of race and culture, extolling the courage of such a couple to persevere despite opposition and hatred. He also intended to excoriate the small-mindedness and distortion of American racial codes. In Vidor's depiction, the interracial/international marriage is an act of conscience and courage—just as making the film for Vidor was an act of political consciousness. His progressive inclinations about race and ethnicity come out with special clarity in the film's unusual and sympathetic treatment of Japanese Americans—almost unheard of in popular culture of the era.[69] The film's subplot revolves around the return from wartime internment of an intergenerational family of Japanese American neighbors, working as truck farmers on their own plot of land. Their presence in the film sets a larger political context for the racial conflict faced by the story's central characters.

Vidor paints a gripping portrait of the tension generated by the homecoming of this couple, white Korean War veteran Jim Sterling (Don Taylor), son of a California farm family, and his Japanese wife, Tae (played by Japanese actress Shirley Yamaguchi). Jim and Tae had met in a military hospital in Japan where Tae, a nurse, helped him to recover from a wound; thus the film draws upon the motif of the war bride as a healer of American wounds. Now settled in California, the couple must initially live under one roof with Jim's parents, brother, and sister-in-law until they can build a home of their own. The film displays a continuum between hostility and tolerance in the family and community: the father accepts his son's Japanese wife whereas the mother is openly hostile and rejecting; some friends and neighbors welcome Tae, but many more snub or insult the young family. Despite his aspirations to break down the prejudice directed toward such a marriage, Vidor cannot avoid invidious race and gender tropes. The physical difference between husband and wife is sharply contrasted throughout the film, gender and race linked inextricably together. Taylor is tall, lanky, and paternal; Yamaguchi is tiny, delicate, and childlike, much like the doll collection she has brought with her from Japan.[70] Yet the tenderness between them is palpable, bridging cultural and physical difference.

When Tae gives birth, racial hatreds spiral out of control. In the eyes of white neighbors and family, the baby looks "too Japanese" to have a white father, raising suspicions about the behavior of Tae. The sister-in-law, who lusts after Jim, secretly initiates a vicious rumor that the baby is the offspring of an extramarital affair between Tae and the young adult son of the Japanese American family that lives nearby. Pained and horrified by this mistrust, Tae flees in the night with her baby. Jim learns about his sister-in-law's betrayal and breaks with his family of origin; he follows Tae and begs her to return to him, to begin a life on their own.

That Vidor's sensibility about race was at odds with the mainstream views of American whites is apparent from critical responses to the film. Reviewers found it "controversial," first and foremost for its sympathetic depiction of an interracial union. The *Los Angeles Times* dubbed it a tale of "miscegenetic love," invoking in negative terms the legal and social taboo at the heart of Vidor's film. Reviewers were also troubled by the film's exposition of American racism—the "distasteful theme of race prejudice" that many felt Vidor had overstated. Interestingly, critics almost universally read the film as a tragedy. This was a love that could find no place in American society, a West Coast version of *Madame Butterfly*, according to reviewers. "The veteran and his bride are desperately unhappy, and know that the future undoubtedly holds more of the slights and deeper wounds than they have already encountered," one writer divined. Another was equally certain that "no person looking at this picture will doubt for more than a moment that things aren't going to turn out right" (a pessimism that perhaps necessitated a triple negative). The critic for the *New York Times* admired the film's "plea" for racial "understanding" but at the same time saw "inherent" conflict in the couple's choice of mate. The filmmaker won praise only for showing "the good sense" not to embellish the final scene "with any nonsensical 'they lived happily ever after' gloss."[71]

But in fact, *Japanese War Bride* ends quite plainly with an optimistic message. Having reconciled, the couple hold each other close. They are alone against the world—but this image is less about their vulnerability and isolation than about their courage and the sustaining strength of their mutual affection. The close of Vidor's film closely mirrors the arguments of the social scientists who studied Japanese-American war marriages in the early 1950s: the interracial couple does better independently when they remove themselves from the narrow-minded traditionalism of parents and peers. At the end they are standing on a hilltop and looking ahead; we are seeing the future through their eyes, a fresh and hopeful perspective, Vidor suggests.

With measured optimism, Vidor wishes us to see this pioneering couple as ahead of their time, leading Americans into a future of greater racial tolerance and mutual appreciation. Vidor and the social scientists who studied Japanese war brides in the 1950s championed a liberal-reformist vision of American society as strengthened by tolerance and intercultural understanding. It was not a radically egalitarian vision—the United States was represented as a white male soldier (never as African American), and foreign others as dependent, childlike females. It was a discourse for the most part that spoke to white Americans about Asians; in calling for racial tolerance it asked majority Americans to live up to their responsibilities and power—extending an earlier vision of national responsibility for white European wives to encompass at last the Japanese brides of American GIs.

Making Lives in Postwar America

Some Americans in the 1940s and 1950s tried to read the racial future of the United States from the intermarriages of American soldiers and foreign wives, imagining what such lives might be like. In many ways the portraits they created say more about the creators than about their subjects. But their efforts direct our attention to an important area of inquiry. Much remains unknown about the partnerships that interracial war couples created in the postwar years. The limited evidence does suggest that racism and segregation were significant and ongoing experiences, important to women in these marriages as well as to men. It also suggests that veterans and their immigrant wives had a wide range of individual responses to these experiences, determined as much by individual character as by the class, race, and social positionings of the individuals involved.

A comparative and biographical view of the later lives of several interracial war bride families begins to sketch in some of the details. Each family in different ways learned to navigate the treacherous terrain of race and ethnicity in postwar America. For some, the experience of living as a postwar intermarried family was a bridge to the civil rights movement. For others, the personal and intimate negotiations of domestic, family, and neighborhood life, in a culture foreign to the wife, were primary. All these stories are reminders that the lived experience of interracial families transcends in many ways the constructed boundaries referred to as race.

Hector and Wanda Garcia, for example, did not identify the fact of being in an interracial marriage as a potent political touchstone, but in many ways it deeply shaped their political and social experiences in postwar Texas, especially for Wanda. Mexican American physician and activist Hector Garcia lived a postwar life committed to the cause of civil rights for his community. Garcia was founder of the GI Forum, the first nationally recognized Chicano civil rights organization. Its political genesis was a turning point in the political consciousness of Garcia and many other postwar Chicanos: in 1949, a Texas funeral home refused to allow the body of a Mexican American combat soldier to be waked in its chapel for fear that this action would offend whites. The Chicano serviceman had been killed in the Philippines in 1945 in the battle for Luzon, and his remains sent home to his parents in Three Rivers. From the sad case of Private Felix Z. Longoria a movement was born. Garcia and his activist colleagues used the incident to defend the war record of Mexican Americans, to denounce their denial of care, benefits, and jobs, and by extension the discrimination against all Mexican Americans.

The Garcias' life history also suggests the complexity of racial and political identities and their evolution across a lifetime. As a young man, Hector's biographer asserts, his primary goal was to prove himself in a white context and by white standards, which he valued more than his own ethnic and racial identity. Garcia worked hard to put himself through college and medical school, joined the military reserves and tried to improve the living standard of his father and siblings. In interviews later in life, Hector specifically denied facing any discrimination in the military—though it seems quite likely that his initial rejection from the medical corps was due to his race. Hector also denied or failed to recall any difficulties gaining approval for his overseas marriage. His courtship of Wanda, an Italian woman from an educated family, may also have been part of a mobility strategy. Hector never spoke with Wanda or her family about his racial identity or the fact that he was born in Mexico; she and her family believed he was a Spaniard from Spain. To Wanda, the main thing that made this intense, intelligent young man "different" was that he was American, not Italian.

Though a loving husband by all accounts, Hector Garcia was deeply absorbed by his political work in the postwar years. Garcia's biographer believes that Hector kept his wife at arm's length from his political campaigns, and that Wanda's work and identity were at home raising the children. But living in Texas in the 1950s and 1960s, Wanda could hardly have been sheltered from racism or the implications of the marriage she had entered into. Like other white war brides in interracial marriages, Wanda recalled a moment when the racial and social status of her family became clear to her on a very personal level. She and her daughters, traveling with friends, a Mexican American couple, were humiliated and denied service at a roadside restaurant. The incident brought together all the borderland ambiguities of Mexican American experience. The family was generally used to passing for white but never knew which racial categorization would be imposed in any given encounter—they were more white than were black people, but not white enough. For Wanda, a woman with dark hair and complexion and a foreign accent, and with mixed-race children, the claim to whiteness was tenuous at best. This form of racial hypocrisy was eye-opening to Wanda, who explained, "In Italy . . . the word 'America' was always associated with liberty, equality and freedom of opportunity. . . . I was dumbfounded at the attitudes displayed towards the Mexican people." As much as her husband might have wanted to keep her both politically and domestically sheltered, this kind of protection was not fully possible. Wanda Garcia also remembers and describes somewhat differently from Hector's biographer the dynamics in the marriage and her involvement with civil rights. In a recent interview, she recalled many details about traveling with her husband to political meetings and her role as his supporter: "We were just married and we wanted to be together. He was going out of town almost every Sunday. . . . We went to all these little towns talking to so many people. . . . I started to help him because I wanted to. . . . I would go to the meeting, I would pass out leaflets. But I cannot claim that I've done that much. He was the one. . . . I loved him so I would go along." At some point, perhaps early on, perhaps later, she came to understand and embrace his work, work on behalf of her own children and the community she had made her own; as she put it many years later, "Freedom is for everybody. Everybody's equal. Everybody is entitled to a good life and to be free . . . you don't find that in any other country I don't think."[72]

Hazel Byrne Simpkins, a white war bride from Britain who married an African American GI, transferred more directly her experience of marriage discrimination into a life of political commitment. Unfortunately, only fragments of her biography are known. Simpkins's love affair and eventual marriage were the crucible of her political consciousness. Growing up in Britain she lived an ordinary and apolitical life as a young teenage girl and described her encounter with her husband as a fortunate accident. Their circumstances changed quickly once they became serious. She and her fiancé were both the victims of harassment when their affair became public. Simpkins was fired from one job. She was also beaten by a white U.S. soldier. After the attack, she joined and became an active member of a "Negro association" in Manchester where black and white members got along without sign of prejudice, and where she befriended several Afro-British women. Simpkins wrote, "I felt I was one of them and often wished that I really were. I had found so much hate and cruelty in my own that I was ashamed of being white." She finally joined her husband, Buford, in the United States in 1947, and they settled in Chicago; though his family had a pleasant middle-class life in Louisiana, where his father was a dental surgeon, they knew that life together as an interracial couple would be impossible in his home state.

Even in Chicago, the couple experienced jeers and disparaging comments when out together in public. Hazel was often assumed to be a prostitute and propositioned even in her husband's company. As a mixed couple, it was also difficult to find housing. But they made many good friends who accepted them on their own terms. In Chicago she became a member of the East Chicago Interracial Council. At an early meeting she was shocked to learn that even these liberal whites harbored prejudice about interracial relationships and "froze" when they learned her husband was a black man. In 1951 she shared her personal story publicly, publishing a first-person account in *Tan* magazine. There she explained her motivation for political work: "I hope the colored people will keep on fighting for their rights"—including the right to "marry without limitations"—and "that soon they will win the goal they so richly deserve. . . . With my husband, I intend to do my share." This British bride and her African American husband were forerunners of the integrationists of the early civil rights movement.[73]

Gloria Baldecano Santiago Clement, a Filipina war bride married to a GI of mixed African American and European American heritage, fought for the dignity and equality of her family in much more private ways. Segregation and discrimination were powerful threads that ran through their married life, but their dedication to one another and their love for their children were strong compensation. Gloria as a young woman was a junior college student and a clerical worker for the U.S. military in Manila; the man she later married was her supervisor. Like the Japanese war brides discussed earlier, Gloria worried about her moral reputation and social standing when she began dating her husband, not because he was a black man but because he was an American: "You know how it was in the Philippines. If you went out with an American you were no good." After they married, she followed her husband, William, to Japan, where, as a military family in 1947, they lived and worked in a segregated army. Gloria's social circle consisted of African American army wives. Clement told an interviewer, "They sort of adopted me, they called me Baby San because I was the youngest bride." A series of U.S. postings followed. "In Virginia, discrimination was terrible. In Georgia too. It was worse. The officers were not allowed to go to the main officers' club. . . . Any officer with black blood, with a drop of black blood, that was the white law at that time."

After the military was integrated, the family tried to keep to the base, for the sake of their children especially. One incident of racism stood out in Gloria's recollections of those years. Their daughter, five years old at the time, was taking a ballet class on the base, but the recital was to be held in an auditorium in the community. Apologetically, the teacher came to the house to explain that the little girl would need to be excluded or the recital would have to be canceled. Clement recalled, "I had made her dress and everything. . . . That night it rained so hard that I told my daughter that you probably don't want to get your tutu wet. . . . She never even asked me why." In her own accounting of her life, recorded in an oral history, Clement presents such personal experiences of racism as a central theme of her years in the United States. The joys of family life—her great affection for her husband and children—enabled her to sublimate such humiliation. Her formulation of gender roles is still traditional: "I don't know if I call it being subservient, but I guess because of my upbringing, my first duty is to my husband—go wherever he is, make a good home for him and my children." Then she corrected herself: "Not subservient. I work side by side with my husband, we respect each other's opinions. . . . I treat my husband like a king, I really do. And he does the same thing with me; he's very thoughtful." As for the children, "I think parents are the same no matter where they are. They have this dream for their children to be educated." Ballet lessons, PTO, the Officers' Wives Club, home (or multiple homes)—these conventions and trappings of middle-class family life gave structure and meaning to their years together. Gloria does not mention political action as a dimension of her experience, but she does reflect upon racial identity. Her own parents and many older Filipinos, she believed, had internalized a sense of their own racial inferiority and an awe of whites. She is glad to know that her own children, and the next generation more broadly, have absorbed instead a deep sense of equality; "I am glad that they don't think that white is the best."[74]

Whether they would have wished it this way or not, the personal became the political for interracial war couples in 1950s America. Their stories also mattered to many American observers at the time. War brides and their veteran-husbands who had wed across racial boundaries were a visible and often contentious sign of social change in the years following World War II. Though the number of marriages was not large, many Americans saw them as significant. In a society that had a slim record of loving, consensual relationships across borders of race, here was a ready-made social experiment—one that spoke of equality and a better future, something that many World War II veterans had imagined they were fighting for.

6

The Demise of the War Bride

Korea, Vietnam, and Beyond

I had a brother at Khe Sanh fighting off the Viet Cong
He had a woman in Saigon
I got a picture of him in her arms

. . .

Born in the U.S.A.

Bruce Springsteen, "Born in the U.S.A."

During the month of April 1975, the U.S. embassy in Saigon had become a "chaotic madhouse." The crushing North Vietnamese Army (NVA) advance, which had toppled provinces "like an avalanche," now threatened the city, creating desperation and panic among those allied with the South Vietnamese government and the multitude of Vietnamese who had worked for and with the Americans. By six o'clock each morning an enormous crowd had gathered outside the embassy doors. U.S. Marines were assigned to keep the crowd in order.[1] Among those importuning for transport out of the country that April were several thousand Vietnamese war brides and fiancées, many accompanied by children, and some by their American husbands. Their anxiety was heightened by rumors that the "round-eyed" children of Vietnamese mothers and American fathers would make their families the object of special political retribution under a communist regime.[2]

Among the couples looking for safe passage in the final weeks of the war were Larry Hearold and his wife, Lua. Lua had been injured while fleeing the NVA advance on Pleiku. Her husband, an army staff sergeant stationed in Fort Jackson, South Carolina, had left Vietnam a year earlier and was saving money to bring Lua to the United States. As the crisis deepened in 1975, he had returned to Vietnam to find his wife and attempt to take her home. His determination was clear from his words: "I'm going to get her out if I have to

| 203

buy an inner tube and stick an American flag and a radio antenna in it. I can paddle like hell."

Significantly, Vietnamese women like Lua, the wives of U.S. servicemen and veterans who struggled to leave Saigon in April 1975, were *not* classified as war brides, nor were they distinguished from other evacuees in policy or by the press. The fortunate ones, generally those with American sponsors or husbands on hand, were given space on a U.S. naval ship or military plane and evacuated to the refugee camp hastily assembled at Camp Pendleton, California. Others who wished to depart were undoubtedly left behind—left to "paddle like hell" on their own if they could, in Vietnam veteran Larry Hearold's prescient evocation of the boat people tragedy that would follow the American withdrawal.[3]

The fall of Saigon in 1975 is an ideal vantage point from which to view the numerous changes in soldier marriage set in motion by the Cold War. The quarter century between the start of the Korean War and the end of the war in Vietnam witnessed the demise of the war bride in both military policy and cultural representation. With the establishment of permanent U.S. military bases throughout Europe, Asia, and the Pacific, the overseas marriage of U.S. military personnel became institutionalized within the armed services. The American Red Cross, after more than four decades of specialized service, retired its war bride program in the early 1960s, replacing it with a generic counseling program for all military families. At overseas postings, intercultural families were similarly absorbed into the "domesticated" army base lifestyle of the 1950s and 1960s, with its close approximation of U.S. suburban family life. Also institutionalized, in a sense, were the squalid "camptowns" on the rim of U.S. bases overseas, particularly those in Asia. Camptowns, staffed by an army of young Asian women, provided sexual and leisure services to U.S. troops, first in South Korea, then in the Philippines, Okinawa, Vietnam, Thailand, and elsewhere. No one perhaps understood their implications as clearly or as early as U.S. senator J. W. Fulbright, who warned in 1966 that "both literally and figuratively, Saigon has become an American brothel."[4] The camptowns became the primary site of interaction between American soldiers and local people. In many countries, they continue today to define U.S. military relations with host communities. Feminist activism in response to the "bases issue"—a political critique that identifies sexually transmitted diseases (STDs), HIV/AIDS, rape and sexual violence, pregnancy, and trafficking as an ongoing legacy of U.S. military bases abroad—has also focused needed attention on the neocolonial and gender domination embedded in the camptown structure.[5]

All these developments have had profound implications for the marriage of foreign women to U.S. servicemen. The camptowns cast a long "shadow" over these marriages beginning with the Korean War and extending well beyond. When Americans tried to interpret soldiers' intercultural relationships after 1950, they reached back to an earlier historical tradition, stigmatizing foreign wives as prostitutes, economic parasites, and breeders of crime and disease, much as they had in the 1910s. This set of attitudes was intensified by race, poverty, and the neocolonial foreign relations intrinsic to Cold War foreign policy. The women were posited as too different, too alien to be absorbed into the American body. As recently as 1989, a reputable military affairs journal could publish an article claiming that GI marriage to "Korean whores" was a "national epidemic" for the United States; that thousands of Korean prostitutes—perhaps as many as half of all Korean wives of U.S. servicemen—had deceived the INS (and sometimes their own husbands) to enter the country; and that "oriental criminals" were the masterminds promoting this flood of "fraudulent marriage."[6] A 1920s xenophobe could have written the same words.

Also important for the demise of the war bride as a cultural construct was the nature of U.S. military conflict during the Cold War. In contrast with Japan and Germany, sovereign nation-states before and after their defeat, places like Korea and Vietnam were dependent half nations and not full international partners, places where "police action" and "counterinsurgency" were waged instead of war.[7] Triumphal internationalism, intercultural marriage as "happy ending," was no longer a salient metaphor for interpreting the morass of foreign relations and imperial aspirations that characterized U.S. foreign policy after Korea. As "stalemate" and "withdrawal" replaced "triumph" in these Cold War conflicts—wars without endings or concluding victories—the political and cultural dynamics of postwar reconstruction necessarily shifted. In the Vietnam War, for example, U.S. leaders and cultural producers had little interest in showcasing Vietnamese-American marriage as closure to the nation's greatest foreign policy debacle up to that time (although, ironically, the actual patterns of marriage in the Vietnam War in many ways paralleled those of earlier wars). The prostitute replaced the war bride in popular journalism, film, and fiction that attempted to give shape or meaning to the American soldier's experience in Vietnam.[8] Prostitution, not marriage, was the interpersonal metaphor that captured Americans' ambivalence about their commitments to former colonial subjects in Cold War foreign relations.

No longer a dramatic "punctuation mark" to signal or signify the successful conclusion of a U.S. military conflict, intercultural military marriages began more clearly to resemble the ordinary ebb and flow of postwar immigration—itself a product of Cold War politics. Immigration "reform" efforts of the past half century, notably the Immigration Reform Act of 1965, have served to normalize the experience of war brides, from Asia and elsewhere. Historians have identified these postwar brides as a crucial vanguard of migration and settlement for Chinese, Filipino, and Japanese immigrant communities; but these war brides were quickly overtaken and absorbed into the larger story of "Third World" immigration from the late 1960s forward. In recent decades, foreign brides of U.S. soldiers have taken their place alongside the swell of immigrants from the same nations and regions. Like them, war brides have applied for citizenship and sponsored parents, siblings, and extended family to join them in the United States. Still, intercultural military marriage remains a unique phenomenon—the women routinely separated or alienated from ethnic immigrant communities in the United States, living often uneasily between two cultures. The nature of U.S. global power in the late twentieth century has continued to shape these relationships in profound ways.

Korea and the Rise of Camptowns

The story of American soldiers and foreign women in the second half of the twentieth century is in many ways the story of the Korean War. America's "forgotten war" was a watershed both in foreign and gender relations and in the interaction between them. In the second half of the twentieth century, the contours of soldier marriage—as military policy and cultural construct—were shaped around the military conflict in Korea. The armistice of July 1953, which signaled the failure of U.S. forces to "roll back" communism on the Korean peninsula, precipitated a "staggering" buildup of U.S. military capacity, historian Mel Leffler has shown; "the limited war in Korea was a time when U.S. officials mobilized the military power, forged the political and military alliances, and established the economic base to make their ideas triumph in the wider Cold War." A permanent ring of U.S. military bases for the "containment" of the Soviet Union and China, established in Europe, Asia, and the Pacific, was a key dimension of the new security structure. The outcome of the war was momentous as well for Korean politics and people. To U.S. policymakers, South Korea came to be seen as a crucial buffer between Communist Asia and Japan and a test of the Americans' capability and will to succeed in "nation-building." U.S. hegemony in South Korea was implemented and upheld by the widespread and permanent basing of U.S. troops and weapons, both conventional and nuclear, in the Republic of Korea (ROK). As historian Thomas Borstelmann has shown, "anti-Asian sentiment" and Western cultural arrogance characterized the attitudes of U.S. foreign policy elites toward their Korean allies in this era, even as American leaders touted the strategic importance of the alliance. Korea, lacking the status that advanced military and industrial development had conferred on Japan, was an easily dominated "little brother" to the United States. This deeply unequal relationship has influenced Korean political, cultural, and economic life for more than half a century, with wide-ranging consequences for the region as a whole.[9]

Recent scholars, informed by postcolonial and feminist theory, have stressed the centrality of sexual commerce to the underlying structure of U.S.–South Korean relations. Sang-Dawn Lee pictures the selling of Korean women to American soldiers as a dimension of Korean "emasculation" and "infantilization" in its relations with the United States.[10] Katherine S. Moon explores the interconnections between the Korean government's subordination to the United States in exchange for national security and Korean women's sexual subordination. Moon presents the important and disturbing finding that the Korean client state "sold" Korean women to the United States in order to maintain good relations; the imperative to preserve U.S. protection against both North Korea and domestic elements critical of the military regime drove the Korean government to advocate a large American troop presence at all costs. "Both governments have viewed such prostitution as a means to advance the 'friendly relation' of both countries and to keep U.S. soldiers, 'who fight so hard for the freedom of the South Korean people,' happy."[11] Thus the sexual exploitation of Korean women's bodies became a state interest and a medium of diplomatic and transnational exchange. As historian Bruce Cumings sums it up, military prostitution evolved into "the most important aspect of the whole relationship" between the United States and South Korea and "the primary memory of Korea for generations of young American men who have served there."[12]

Camptowns were at the center of this dynamic. The camptowns were organized commercial districts for military prostitution, lying on the margins of U.S. military bases, existing in their shadow, and fueled by American dollars and sexual desires. Bruce Cumings was a young Peace Corps volunteer in Korea during the early 1960s when he recorded this description of a typical camptown in his diary. The community of Uijongbu, once a small town, had swelled to 65,000 by its proximity to a large American military base. Uijongbu offered "filthy, backward, shameful" living conditions to its residents. But the "worst aspect," Cumings found, was "the whoring district":

There are clusters of "clubs," catering only to Americans. Rock and roll blares from them, they are raucously painted and titled, and ridiculous-looking painted Korean girls . . . peer from the doors. . . . Several of them hooted at me as I walked by . . . but the most disconcerting of all was a middle-aged woman with two kids hanging on to her who, in the middle of the street, asked me to come and "hop on" in the chimdeh [bed]. . . . Goofy-looking . . . soldiers walk arm-in-arm with whores who are often only young girls—very, very young girls. How do these men (?) justify this to themselves?[13]

There were precedents for the sexual servicing of American troops in Korea going back to 1945 and the first era of U.S. occupation after World War II. One of the earliest identifiable camptowns, Bupyong, sprang up just months after American troops landed in Inchon in 1945 and serviced troops at Inchon's base. But it was the Korean war, with its massive infusion of American troops, and, later, the Military Defense Treaty signed in 1954 that paved the way for the development of camptowns as an organized commercial enterprise delivering sex on a mass scale. Nor did the camptowns evolve at random, Moon has shown. Throughout the history of the ROK, the Korean and U.S. governments have worked together to "sponsor and regulate" this system. In the 1960s the Korean government created a procedure for establishing special prostitution districts, all connected to U.S. military bases—even as it outlawed prostitution in general. By 1964, a total of 145 military prostitution districts were recognized by the government. Ample evidence also shows that from the beginning, the camptown system flourished with either the tacit approval or the active cooperation of U.S. military officials. The military's experience managing red-light districts for soldiers during World War II paved the way for its more extensive and permanent involvement in Korea. A 1965 "Human Factors Research Report" conducted by the U.S. Army in Korea concluded that prostitution was a "constructive force," one that made American troops "more willing to fight for Korea." U.S. official and semiofficial support in recent decades has included U.S. Army medics examining prostitutes for STDs; U.S. MPs patrolling camptown clubs and brothels and checking women's identity cards; U.S. Army publications advising soldiers and marines on where and how to enjoy the safe services of Korean sex partners; and U.S. military transportation taking soldiers to camptown facilities on a daily schedule.[14] This level of institutionalization set apart the post–Korean War camptowns from forms of U.S. military prostitution practiced earlier in the century.

The development of military prostitution in Korea had an even earlier historical precedent—the system of sexual slavery brutally imposed on thousands of Korean women by the Japanese Imperial Army during World War II. Former military "comfort women," unable to earn their living in any other way, were among the first generation to serve American soldiers stationed in Korea in the newly emerging camptowns. Other early camptown workers were war refugees who had lost home or family as a result of the conflict.[15] Despite the circumstances that had brought them to prostitution—uncontrollable forces of poverty, degradation, and war—Korean women who serviced American soldiers in the camptown districts elicited no sympathy or support from their fellow Koreans. Korea's conservative and hierarchical social structure had no place for prostitutes, particularly those who sold themselves to foreigners. They were *yang gongju* (Western princess, a derisive term) or *yang galbo* (Western whore), social outcasts or "nonpersons" who existed outside of Korean society. Even the Korean government's praise for the women's service as "personal ambassadors" to American troops could not alter this fundamental attitude of rejection.[16]

The pariah status of camptown women within Korean society was one factor that drove them toward intercultural marriage. Many women dreamed that their contact with American GIs would eventually lead to marriage, though for the great majority this was not to be the case. The desire for marriage was fueled by many aspects of camptown relations, its structures and conventions. Superficial contact with Americans in the border zone surrounding the bases led many women to think of the United States, represented by the bases, as a fantasyland of plenty.[17] For others, marriage and emigration meant escape from a bleak future in their own country. One woman hesitated to marry her American boyfriend, a man she knew to be a womanizer and heavy drinker, but her mother persuaded her to accept his offer; "my mother said . . . because I had been a *yang gongju* in the past, I had no hope for a future in Korea. So I agreed to marry him."[18]

It is all but impossible to determine what proportion of Korean women who became American military wives had worked in the camptown sex industry prior to marriage. Few individuals would choose to disclose this information to researchers or government officials. Quantitative research to date has relied on data such as visa or marriage applications that are likely to undercount the phenomenon.[19] Korean military wives married in the 1950s through 1970s routinely told scholar Ji-Yeon Yuh that the proportion of former prostitutes was high in the group overall, though almost always the stories were about women other than themselves. One Korean wife of an

American serviceman who did acknowledge a camptown past told a harrow-ing tale of a life seemingly defined by coercion, disempowerment, and abuse. Yet time and again, this informant, Ms. Kim, demonstrated an indomitable will to survive and make her own choices despite severe constraints. Born to deaf-mute parents in Seoul just after the end of World War II, she was sent as a child to live in a convent orphanage when her parents were unable to support her (already in the early 1960s the orphanage was populated primar-ily by biracial children, the offspring of Korean mothers and American sol-diers). When she was nineteen, her parents summoned her home, but when they tried to force her into an arranged marriage, she ran away. Answering a help-wanted ad for a maid, she found herself "sold" to a brothel catering to American troops. Barely twenty, and a "rather unprofitable *yang gongju*," she was passed from brothel to brothel, living a miserable existence and con-stantly in debt to her keepers. It was in this period that she met the American soldier she would marry, an African American and a veteran of the Vietnam War who had subsequent tours of duty in Korea and Okinawa. His sugges-tion that they marry offered escape from a life of coerced prostitution, but she accepted with trepidation, unable to trust him. Later, living in Texas, she would leave her veteran-husband as well, unwilling to endure his violence and hoping to protect their young son.[20]

Whatever proportion of Korean military wives had worked in the sex trade, camptown relations with American troops came to "shadow" or define all other relationships between American soldiers and Korean women—in both Korean and American eyes. Korean women who intermarried were tainted by their association with American soldiers, assumed to be prostitutes by vir-tue of their intimate relationship with an American and "uniformly treated with suspicion and contempt by their community." One woman, a college graduate who became engaged to an American soldier who volunteered to teach English classes, still faced the reproach of her family, who feared the attentions of the man were sexual and dishonorable.[21] Even Korean Ameri-can scholar Katherine Moon was viewed suspiciously by Korean acquain-tances after spending so much time in military camptowns while conducting her fieldwork.[22] There is evidence too that the sexual and racial subordina-tion of Korean women to American men, inherent in the camptowns, shaped the marriages themselves. In Ji-Yeon Yuh's interview cohort, a quarter of the Korean wives recounted severe and prolonged violence by their GI husbands, directed at themselves or their children; Yuh suspected that other women may have experienced family violence but failed to report it. Yuh also found a high incidence of adultery and marital dissolution in the group: half of the women divorced their American husbands. The most frequently stated cause was the husband "taking up with another woman."[23] Another researcher has pointed to similar themes of strife in the marriages of Korean and Japanese military wives, including a concerning incidence of physical violence, neglect, and desertion (though the subjects in this study were referred for casework support, pointing to a potential bias in the information).[24]

From a demographic perspective, the pattern of Korean-American military marriage was also distinctive—a slow and steady buildup in the postwar years, increasing rather than decreasing with distance from the conflict. This trajectory of marriage looked very different from that in any previous war. During the years of fighting and immediately after, when more than half a million Americans served with the armed forces in Korea, war bride marriage was negligible. Following the cease-fire agreement in July, fewer than 100 war brides made their way to the United States in 1953—to the almost complete indifference of the press. The peak year for Korean military brides to enter the United States during the 1950s was 1959, when 488 Korean women were admitted to the United States as the wives of American citizens, the majority American servicemen. The annual rate of entry for Korean wives of Americans first topped 1,000 in 1963 and continued to climb into the 1970s and beyond. As historian Dave Reimers has shown, Korean wives of U.S. servicemen, many of whom later sponsored family members, were a significant source of chain migration during the "gap years" in Asian immigration between the McCarran Walter and Hart Cellar acts.[25] This again stood in contrast to the immigration experience of earlier war bride groups, where the war bride was usually a stand-alone immigrant. The demographic patterns of Korean military marriage reflected the new realities of the Cold War and the bases regime—marriage oriented around the permanent deployment of U.S. troops and their interactions with local women on and around U.S. military bases.

By the 1960s, as U.S. officials touted the "enduring friendship" between the United States and the Republic of Korea, soldier marriage had become an enduring feature of the military presence in the ROK. But in a decade in which as many as 11,000 Korean military wives came to live in the United States, Korean brides were all but invisible in American culture. Only the occasional courtroom drama, featured on U.S. television, rippled the silence—divorce stories that usually centered on marital infidelity in the marriage of an American veteran and a Korean wife.[26] It was instead the Korean military prostitute who drew the attention, albeit muted, of the American public. In 1964, *Time* published a report on the camptown system—at once lurid and surprisingly matter-of-fact. The article was occasioned by a letter sent to 12,000 Lutheran pastors, in which an American chaplain warned that "our young men aren't spiritually and morally ready for Korea." The source of their temptation was Korea's camptown women, dubbed "mooses" by their GI customers (a derisive derivative of *musume*, a Japanese word for "girl"). If American soldiers were vulnerable to Korean girls in "spiked heels"—and, according to *Time*, 90 percent of American soldiers in Korea reported that they "consorted with prostitutes regularly"—camptown women were motivated by the glint of American cash. "Every major U.S. military installation in South Korea is ringed by villages occupied by campfollowers who make their living on GI largesse," the reporter stated. "We benefit much from the G.I.s stationed here," one prostitute explained. The women reputedly valued PX privileges even more than money, but the entrepreneurial spirit so admired in the South Korean business community was evidently unseemly when practiced by female sex workers. The reporter observed that "simply by reporting a readiness to get married, a G.I. can provide his moose with cigarettes, radios and cameras, all of which are resalable on the black market for several times their original cost." Though the article acknowledged the potentially corrupting quality of the camptown phenomenon, it did so without apparent alarm.[27]

Americans were also exposed during the sixties to a controversy surrounding a salacious Korean best seller, the autobiography of a Korean teenage prostitute. Annie Park was the biracial daughter of a Korean mother who earned her living as a camptown prostitute; Annie's father, who abandoned the mother and child, was a white U.S. serviceman. Annie grew up in and around the bars of camptown. By sixteen, she too was working as a prostitute for American soldiers, "who liked her slim Occidental legs and ample breasts." By nineteen, she had had six abortions and "uncounted liaisons with every variety of G.I." Annie Park's narrative, whether purposefully or not, was testimony to the long-term and degrading effect of the U.S. military sex industry across two generations. Yet, improbably enough, *Time* managed to turn its own story *about* the story into a morality tale pitting enlightened and efficient Americans against backward Orientals. Park's story "at last forces Koreans to think about something they would rather forget—the problem of illegitimate half-castes." Narrow-minded "Confucian concepts" shamefully turned such children into "outcasts" in Korean society. Fortunately, generous U.S. groups like the National Catholic Welfare Conference and the redoubtable Pearl S. Buck Foundation had rushed to the aid of these "little lost half-castes," offering American adoption or funds of support.[28] While lecturing

Koreans about their social and moral failings, the reporter carefully avoided calling attention to something that Americans would also rather have forgotten, the American military's contribution to the problem of abandoned children around overseas bases.

The "stain" of prostitution carried over to the military's policy response to Korean-American marriage. By the middle of the 1960s, Korean wives of U.S. military personnel were no longer regarded as a national responsibility for the U.S. to shoulder, a conduit for international understanding, or a reward to American soldiers. These "immature" and "improvident" marriages, the Eighth Army Command reported, were a source of "trouble," a "problem"— and a growing one at that. In 1965 the military reported that almost one out of every forty American servicemen posted in Korea the previous year had taken a local wife. The problem, as explained by an army spokesmen, was that American troops were marrying the girls they had "met in bars"—a barely concealed reference to camptown prostitution. Prostitution, by the army's own analysis, was a "constructive" influence on troop morale—but only if contained in its proper place. "Military prostitute" and "military wife" were rigidly separate categories in military thinking; the possibility of their overlap created an acute sense of discomfort.[29] This troubling connection probably contributed to the erosion of military-sponsored programming and assistance for war brides. While the popular "bride schools" continued to flourish and expand in Japan, Okinawa, and the Philippines through the end of the 1950s, Red Cross and military leaders in the Far East Command explicitly excluded Korea from such efforts. By the mid-1960s the U.S. military and the American Red Cross had abandoned all their programmatic services for war brides—a shift that would have important ramifications for intercultural couples of the Vietnam War.[30]

On many levels the Korean War was a watershed in the history of war brides in the United States. The institutionalization of military marriage in the context of permanent military mobilization on bases abroad is one of the factors over the long run that eroded the unique status of the foreign war bride. Military base agreements in the wake of the Korean War also changed the pattern of soldier marriage, to a long-term gradual migration flow instead of a sudden, climactic postwar exodus. And camptowns altered the image of women who married U.S. servicemen. These shifts were accompanied by the almost complete cultural invisibility of Korean wives in U.S. popular culture and foreign policy discourse. The military stalemate in Korea signaled a new and troubling direction in U.S. foreign relations during the Cold War, and the war's ambiguous outcome almost certainly contributed to the wives' low-profile status. Year after year, Korean wives continued to be an uncomfortable reminder of a conflict that still appears to have no end a half century later.

Vietnam and the War Brides' Demise

In the past fifty years the only U.S. war to produce a substantial number of "war brides"—that is, intercultural marriages as a direct result of war zone rather than peacetime military activity—was the Vietnam War. No official head count of soldier marriages in Vietnam was ever generated, but evidence of the marriages exists nonetheless in data from the Immigration and Naturalization Service, the U.S. embassy in Saigon, and contemporary newspaper reports. These uncover a minimum of 8,000 Vietnamese-American marriages—a rate of marriage relative to American troop strength that is comparable to that in World War I.[31] When examined at the level of individual relationships, there are striking continuities between intercultural war marriages during the Vietnam War and those of previous wars; but military policy in regard to the marriages differed sharply. The hostile climate for soldier marriage during the Vietnam War was in part an evolution from the experience in Korea, where "war bride" as a privileged status for foreign wives had already been undermined. But the unique circumstances of the Vietnam War added further dimensions. Leaders of Military Assistance Command Vietnam (MACV) viewed serious relationships between U.S. servicemen and Vietnamese women as an acute "security threat." Americans' widespread antipathy toward their Vietnamese allies—denigrated as racial "others," incompetent fighters, and deceitful, corrupt partners—bred further distrust of Vietnamese-American relationships. The result was a U.S. government withdrawal of responsibility for intermarried couples that was thrown into high relief at the moment of America's final withdrawal from the country. The Vietnam War completed the war bride's demise, in policy and in cultural terms.

It is difficult in some ways to imagine how intimate intercultural relationships could have taken form during the Vietnam War, a harsh counterinsurgency war for the Americans, a national liberation struggle for the Vietnamese in which the majority regarded U.S. soldiers as an occupying enemy. Numerous factors, structural, bureaucratic, and ideological, worked to suppress friendly interaction between Americans and Vietnamese. As one infantry soldier recounted, "The Army did its best to keep us from associating with them because 'all' civilians were potential VC and could toss a grenade at us at any moment." American soldiers' responses to Vietnamese people, historians have shown, were varied and complex, ranging between fear, resentment, pity, compassion, and disdain, and too often, beneath all of these, an underlying racism.[32] While American leaders publicly touted the good relations between American forces and their Vietnamese allies and the high morale of American troops, internal reports show that as early as 1966 the executive branch, the Joint Chiefs of Staff, and MACV commanders had grown alarmed by the rapid deterioration of both. The huge buildup of American forces in and around Saigon was a particular irritant to the Vietnamese and fueled the increasingly open anti-Americanism in the city. President Lyndon Johnson's order to disperse American forces out of Saigon (Operation MOOSE—Move Out of Saigon Expeditiously—was openly satirized within the military as GOOSE, Get Out of Saigon Eventually) led to the development of a network of large American bases and the further insulation of American forces.[33] The soldiers' sense of isolation and ambivalence is captured in the words of one U.S. veteran of the Vietnam War: "A lot of us didn't try to understand the people or make friends. Some of us hated them: Everybody was a zip, gook, or animal. I think many of us wanted to be friends with the civilian population and get to know them, but you couldn't. You couldn't trust them."[34]

Vietnamese women were constructed as "untrustworthy" in particular and often sexualized ways. One private first class recalled that "your orientation to Vietnam warned about gook whores and Vietnamese women in general. 'The only good gook is a dead gook'" was the attitude the military tried to instill.[35] The standard but dehumanizing assertion that "all Vietnamese look alike" was also used to warn men against intimate or trusting relations, presumably because a man could not be certain which woman he was with.[36] One of the ugliest and most ubiquitous GI rumors about Vietnamese women was based on the fear that they were sexual saboteurs eager to mutilate American men. Vietnamese women were to be avoided, as one soldier explained it, because "the whores might have razor blades in their vaginas, and we would have a hell of a time explaining to our wives why our pecker was split open like a banana."[37] The myth of the prostitute with a booby-trapped vagina, Chris Appy points out, was part of a larger universe of beliefs and anxieties that focused on the deceitfulness and destructiveness of Vietnamese people as the hidden supporters of the Viet Cong—children with explosives strapped to their bodies was another. Collectively these rumors betrayed the profound insecurity of American combat troops in Vietnam.[38] But this interpretation misses a crucial insight, that the myth of the "castrating whore" is deeply rooted in the history of gender and war in general. In his pathbreaking work on misogyny and militarism, Klaus Thewelheit identifies the castration myth as an underpinning of male violence in the German Freikorps after World War I. Such "male fantasies," in his view, fuel antisocial behavior and the practice of atrocities in wartime.[39] Thewelheit's framework helps to interpret, for example, this recollection of an American GI in Vietnam: the man observed an event that disturbed him deeply, the sexual torture to death of three Vietnamese "whores" by a group of American Green Berets and Army of the Republic of Vietnam (ARVN) soldiers; the women were allegedly being punished for the sexual mutilation and death of an American in that area.[40] Male violence was unleashed on women as vengeance for their transgressions against men. Rumors of female sexual violence *against men* were also a classic example of psychological projection in a conflict in which rape of women was sporadically employed by all sides.[41]

The concept of the Vietnamese woman as a sexual saboteur was also an integral aspect of the "Orientalist" archetype of Asian women.[42] The sexually dangerous "Oriental" female—the "dragon lady"—was an essential component of the Asian stereotype in American popular culture, expressed in radio dramas, comic books, and Hollywood cinema. But the image of the Asian woman was decidedly dualistic—on the one hand, she was a threatening seductress, on the other, a delicate and submissive flower. The dualism of the stereotype carried over decisively to Southeast Asia in the era of the American war. The same magazine articles that warned about the dangers that Vietnamese women posed for American GIs also extolled their ineffable and delicate beauty: "There is one subject on which just about every male American in Vietnam . . . is in complete agreement: that the silken, reed-slim women of Vietnam are just about the nicest, prettiest and most nubile maidens they have seen in a long time." "Reedlike," "slender," and "lissome" were words that came up again and again to describe Vietnamese "maidens." Almost every account by American servicemen or male journalists mentions the "graceful" Vietnamese *ao dai*, the long and fitted traditional outfit of the Vietnamese woman, as a component of her exotic beauty. One journalist wrote, "When they first arrive in Vietnam, GIs are impressed by the grace and beauty of the young women, especially those in the city, who glide along the sidewalks in their ao dais." While this writer found sexually alluring the restraint of the traditional costume, he was also quick to describe the "silk pantaloons and brassiere" that a soldier would find underneath her "thin robe"—though other writers noted that, without her costume, the bodies of Vietnamese girls were too "skinny" and childlike to suit American tastes.[43]

216 | *The Demise of the War Bride*

Woven through this discourse as well was an element of infantilism, also common to the Orientalist vision. If the Vietnamese woman could appear at times as a voracious prostitute, she also had the qualities of a child, innocent, subservient, and in need of protection. Clearly American men's desire for Vietnamese women was constructed on a foundation of deep cultural ambivalence.

Against this complicated backdrop of desire, disdain, and fear, relations took place between American soldiers and Vietnamese women, just as they have in every foreign war. In Vietnam, however, security concerns led to a narrower and more constrained range of social relationships than in previous conflicts. There was little "normal" or sanctioned socializing between Americans and Vietnamese civilians in homes or public places; such interaction was deemed dangerous and undesirable on both sides. The Red Cross and USO provided few if any structured opportunities for enlisted men to meet Vietnamese at dances, beach parties, or clubs. As a result, American servicemen met Vietnamese women almost exclusively through the economic and labor exchange, both formal and informal, that was made necessary and possible by the massive U.S. military effort. On U.S. bases, thousands of Vietnamese were hired by the U.S. military to labor as cleaning women or laundry workers in the barracks, cashiers and stockers in the giant PX stores, and waitresses and kitchen workers in the mess halls and clubs. One Vietnamese war bride can still recall the ride by army bus in the semidarkness that took her and hundreds of other Saigon women each morning to a military base more than an hour from the city to work as domestics. There she got to know the man who became her American husband of forty years.[44] Soldiers also took this type of employment into their own hands. A reporter wrote, "A hootch maid was a Vietnamese woman who was paid by the soldiers to clean their rooms or barracks, do their laundry, shine their boots and provide whatever else she was willing to give."[45] Wages were so low that even lower enlisted men could afford these services, which sometimes evolved into personal relationships of an intimate nature. Further up the social scale, the most westernized Vietnamese women, often Catholic, with some knowledge of French or English, met American personnel as they worked for U.S. military or government offices in Saigon. In these settings, American servicemen were also more likely to have received Vietnamese language training, an important lever of social interaction seen in this and previous military conflicts.[46]

As was true for American troops stationed in South Korea, the primary realm where American men and Vietnamese women came together was the "entertainment" sector—the nightclubs, bars, and brothels that supplied American troops with alcohol, sex, and companionship. Wherever American troops were concentrated in Vietnam, even temporarily, such commercial strips mushroomed. "Bar girl" was the catchall phrase that American journalists and military personnel in Vietnam used to describe the female workers in these establishments. In the harshly simplified view of most Americans, bar girls were prostitutes, women whose driving motive was the American soldier's money. "Tens of thousands of young girls have become out-and-out whores"; such women "have made more money out of the war than they would otherwise have made in their lifetimes," a journalist asserted.[47] In reality, commercial operations that catered to the needs of Americans in Vietnam had their own internal hierarchies and structures, although these were largely invisible to their American clients. Le Ly Hayslip, who spent time working the clubs in Danang, described the complicated division of labor that she knew so well: "Although they made their living in the company of men, . . . bar girls usually weren't prostitutes." The bar girl's job was to "entice" the customer to buy her drinks—iced tea for her, but charged to the soldier's tab as alcohol. Hostesses, dancers, and waitresses also worked in the bars and clubs. If a soldier wanted to take one of these working women home, "he would have to ask her for a date, like any other woman, and could always be refused."[48]

Prostitutes had their own hierarchies and work practices, accompanied, of course, by varying degrees of risk and exploitation. Most tragic to Hayslip was the "slave traffic" in women and girls, a flourishing system that deceived young, often rural women and used violence and intimidation to prevent their escape from brothels. "Regular prostitutes, by comparison, had a much better life," Hayslip observed. The "cheapest whorehouses" were "often no more than shacks" located near military installations, where "local girls" could rent a room and sell sex to servicemen. Some women would forgo even this expense, servicing their customers "in bushes, in trucks, in tanks, or in alleys." The "better hookers had a madam (an older woman—often married to a corrupt official), who organized the girls, looked after their health, and maintained the whorehouse where they worked." The demographics underlying this institution were clear and heartbreaking: by war's end there were estimated to be 1 million widows and 200,000 prostitutes in Vietnam.[49]

Another widely disseminated form of social, sexual, and economic relationship during the Vietnam War was the live-in, "contract" girlfriend who formed a long-term and usually exclusive bond with a particular American for a period of time. Arrangements like this were previously observed in Korea, but the practice first became widespread in the Vietnam War. It was so institutionalized by the late 1960s that a mainstream U.S. magazine for middle-class readers offered this matter-of-fact description: "A typical regular relationship in Saigon will earn a girl kept by a GI about $150 a month. For this she takes care of a small house, which the soldier rents for about $100 monthly, does his cooking and laundry, and is a willing bedmate." Many of the women involved in such relationships "move from one American to another," a journalist continued, and might be "passed on by one GI to his buddy" when his tour of duty drew to a close.[50] This American view, no doubt, oversimplified the gradations and complexities of these arrangements when viewed from a Vietnamese perspective. The older sister of Le Ly Hayslip, who worked as a bar girl in Danang, rented her own tiny apartment but took in a series of American boyfriends, each of whom provided financial support until he tired of the arrangement or returned to the United States. Some women preferred to keep the men at arm's length, but many others considered their resident Americans to be "husbands" and still referred to them this way years later.[51] Frequently these unions produced children. Financial support for the couple's child might be a negotiated piece of the arrangement; in other instances the woman had to keep her children's existence a secret from her American lover.

In rural areas, intercultural interaction took somewhat different forms. It was risky, even at a minimal level, for Americans and Vietnamese to interact, since Vietnamese who cooperated in any way with Americans were a target for Viet Cong retaliation. Yet even in the countryside, relationships developed. On patrol in the "boonies," soldiers made contact with civilians through informal trade or the underground economy of the black market. By day, American units in the field attracted "large numbers of small entrepreneurs," as one veteran described it. On patrol "it was like a circus. Walking with us were girls and kids selling soda, beer, cigarettes, lighters, jackets, etc. You name it, they had it. If they didn't have it, and you asked for it, they'd have it the next day."[52] These fluid and informal contacts were also a conduit for negotiations related to sex. But in the murky world of intercultural contact between American soldiers and Vietnamese villagers, interaction sometimes evolved into intimacy and affection. Americans, for example, operated a firebase outside the village of Cam Lo near the demilitarized zone between North and South Vietnam. Whenever they could, American soldiers slipped away to the riverbank, where young women from the village peddled handicrafts and cold orange soda in exchange for dollars and cigarettes. Here Steve and Leenie Menta met and fell in love—a rare tale of romance in the

Vietnam War narrated for American readers of *Redbook*. This couple's story also illustrates the point that love affairs in rural areas faced extra burdens and pressures from many directions. Cam Lo village was strictly off-limits for American troops, due to concerns about Viet Cong activity and the drug trade. Soldiers from Steve's unit visited the village regardless of the restriction. One day in 1971 American MPs carried out a raid, taking away a number of soldiers in handcuffs. Leenie managed to hide Steve, but after that, visits were nearly impossible to arrange. Leenie also imposed strict limits on the couple's intimacy in order to protect her reputation and his safety. As she explained, "You and I can be good friends. But don't sit too close to me. Don't put your arm around me. Even if we don't do anything wrong people will see and think we do." When Leenie finally accepted Steve's proposal, her agreement was contingent upon her brother's consent; without it, Leenie would not have joined Steve in the United States, a submission to family respect and hierarchy that remained strong in traditional and still-intact families.[53]

It would be easy to interpret relationships between American servicemen and Vietnamese women as deeply and intrinsically unequal. For most American men, interaction with local women was a casual interchange that meant and cost very little. "Whenever we were around a village, the women would come out, the whores," one man recalled, adding, "I paid for a little nooky while I was there." In trying to explain this attitude in retrospect, an attitude that later made him uncomfortable, another man noted that "our guys were mostly teenagers and thought the most about whores."[54] This utilitarian attitude toward foreign women in a war zone was supported through peer pressure and military socialization. No Vietnam-era policy better encapsulated the attitude than MACV's expensive and ambitious R & R program for American troops. Military R & R in the Vietnam War was a seven-day leave to a select tourist destination in Asia, round-trip air transport provided gratis, and offered every soldier once during a one-year tour of duty. Then and since, the program has been touted by the military as a highly successful MACV initiative. It was a special favorite of General Westmoreland, who viewed it as a crucial "midrange" goal that aided motivation and morale for combat forces.[55] Official accounts fail to acknowledge that sexual relations were a central, if not the central, component of the R & R itinerary, but journalists wrote about it openly at the time. Vietnam memoirists recall the orientation lecture they invariably received from an officer on the bus taking them to their hotel in Singapore, Taipei, or Bangkok, informing them of where the girls were "checked" and clean and where they were not.[56] The message of the R & R program was that Southeast Asian women were "open for business" from the American military, with no responsibilities or consequences incurred by the men.

For Vietnamese women, relations with American GIs involved higher stakes and greater risks. Often it was a matter of survival. Women who worked in the entertainment sector, Hayslip observed, were frequently rape victims or widows with children—both categories of women with little future chance of marriage in a combat-ravaged country with too few marriageable men and a conservative moral code. Others turned to prostitution or contract arrangements with Americans to support parents, siblings, and themselves. One teenage girl, financially responsible for her mother and siblings after their Vietnamese father abandoned them to live with a woman in Saigon, worked as a prostitute near the American base at Vung Tau. Though she earned more money than her father did as a government employee, she concealed her occupation from her family.[57] Women who took on long-term American "boyfriends" often did so with the hope that the relationship might produce a marriage proposal—though only a small proportion ever did. Dependence on Americans also meant taking the risk of pregnancy or interpersonal violence, or being shunned by family and community.

Yet it is also an oversimplification to say that these relationships were always one-sided, invariably callous and exploitative. In any time and place, intimate relationships are complex, involving a balance of need and power, both material and emotional. This was as true for intercultural couples in Vietnam as elsewhere. Many soldiers who became involved with Vietnamese women grew to feel deep compassion for them and their families and sympathized with the suffering they had endured through decades of war. One veteran was surprised by the similar perceptions he shared with his girlfriend and how much they had in common in regard to temperament and family values.[58] Women too had a range of feelings about the American men with whom they interacted. In a survey conducted in 1992 by the State Department's Office of Resettlement, three-quarters of the Vietnamese women, all of whom had borne children with American fathers, were found to remember the men with fondness and hold them in high regard, even though the men had left the families behind.[59] In the end, American soldiers' relationships with women in Vietnam looked a great deal like soldiers' relationships with women in any war zone.

Vietnamese-American Marriages

Although thousands of Vietnamese-American couples did manage to wed during the war, MACV leaders vigorously and systematically discouraged marriage for American service personnel in Vietnam, placing a wide array of bureaucratic and financial obstacles in front of marriage aspirants. The difficulty of obtaining the army's permission for a marriage was treated as a known fact by journalists and other observers. "The red tape makes marriage all but impossible," one reporter noted. Another, Gloria Emerson, correspondent for the *New York Times*, drew sardonic contrast between the American army's love affair with Vietnamese pets and its antipathy to wives: "Despite the paperwork, which most soldiers loathed, in 1969 GIs took home two hundred and seventy dogs, thirty-three cats, nineteen reptiles, twenty monkeys, . . . one fox and three lizards. In the same year slightly more Americans—four hundred and fifty five of them—received permission to marry Vietnamese women and take them home, which required more paperwork and unending bribes."[60] It was no laughing matter, however, if a man's future was the one being dangled on a string. "The army made it really difficult for us," one veteran recalls. "In my barracks there were about sixty men, maybe a half dozen of them were trying to get Vietnamese girls back to the U.S. . . . I know of no one who got a wife out from that group."[61]

MACV policies tried to steer men away from committed relationships, directing them instead to the kind of fleeting, no-strings-attached interaction that promised easy exit and few complications for the military to worry about. The military's R & R program, for example, was meant to provide just such a structure. Commanders were surprised and displeased, therefore, when their men returned from these surreal, hedonistic holidays with an infatuation or attachment they wished to make permanent. This was decidedly *not* the program's purpose. Tracy Kidder, the renowned nonfiction writer, was in his early twenties a communications intelligence officer in Vietnam in charge of a small intelligence detachment when one of his men returned from Singapore lovesick for a woman he had hired there. Kidder confessed to being puzzled by the affair—"I kept thinking I could understand his feelings if the girl in question weren't a whore, or were at least good-looking"—and he worked assiduously to break up the relationship.[62] As a young officer, Kidder had learned the lesson that the R & R program was meant to sublimate emotional attachment, not facilitate it. The military's bias against marriage was reinforced and echoed by fellow soldiers. "If I married a Vietnamese my old man would kill me," one GI told a journalist. "I like to go with them but

I wouldn't marry one," another added. "They're too damn skinny. . . . They're too different."[63]

In contrast with the situation in previous American wars, soldier marriage left a scant trace in official records from Vietnam; only scattered documents address marriage policy explicitly or grapple with its management.[64] Yet it is clear nonetheless that the MACV devised and utilized a range of tools for the prevention of marriage. One of the most significant restrictions was the denial of transportation to Vietnamese wives. Following the two world wars, the War Department had taken full financial and operative responsibility for the supervision and safe transport to the United States of soldiers' brides and children—perceived as a responsibility owed to the nation's defenders. During the Vietnam War, in contrast, soldiers and their noncitizen spouses were on their own.

As it turned out, the high cost of emigration (private transportation plus fees for the processing of exit visas and passports) was one of the government's most effective tools to suppress Vietnamese-American marriage, a de facto exclusion if not a formal one. A soldier applicant by 1966 was required by MACV to submit an affidavit stating that he had sufficient funds to pay the cost of his spouse's travel to his location of discharge.[65] In 1970 an American serviceman could expect to pay $500 to fly his Vietnamese wife to San Francisco, $2,000 to transport her to New York City. Such prices were well beyond the means of many Vietnam servicemen, who were, disproportionately, lower-income Americans. One army veteran (who had probably married without permission), now unemployed in Watsonville, California, gained local notoriety when he offered to sell his eye to a hospital to raise the airfare for his Vietnamese family to join him.[66] The actual cost for a Vietnamese wife to emigrate to the United States with her husband was almost certainly even higher than the stated cost of airfare and processing, as the notoriously corrupt Republic of Vietnam bureaucracy could exact bribes and payments at every step of the process. When Le Ly Hayslip left Vietnam with her two children in May 1970, the package of approvals, forms, and clearances cost her American husband more than 50,000 dong—a fee intricately negotiated and paid up front to a Vietnamese marriage broker, wife of a well-placed Republican government official. The financial burden of emigration for Vietnamese brides was simply one more social class inequity that low-income U.S. servicemen faced in America's "working-class war."[67]

On the rare occasion that MACV officials made mention of intercultural marriage for U.S. troops, they identified two main motives for their restrictive policies: protecting the "security" of U.S. forces, and preventing young soldiers from making a hasty, "ill-considered" or "immature" decision. The latter concern, that American soldiers were too young to know their own best interests, strongly echoed the paternalistic mind-set of military officials during the First World War. One military chaplain, who had recently dissuaded five American "boys" from marrying their Vietnamese fiancées, revealed his thinking, that the men were "more lonesome than in love over here." With time and maturity they would be grateful for his intervention, he suggested. The U.S. press picked up on and amplified the view of military officials, that young American soldiers could not handle Vietnamese women. An American man was "a pot of gold at the end of the runway" to women such as these. The "average GI" was "a fairly gullible fellow who tends to believe the bar girls' hard-luck stories." When a Vietnamese woman succeeded in capturing an American man—sometimes by "letting herself get pregnant" near the end of his tour—the mismatched marriage that followed had a poor chance of success. One journalist wrote this description: "The majority of Vietnamese brides . . . have gaudy visions of living in comfort and splendor in the States. The GIs they marry are usually young boys from small towns, whose parents are not especially happy about their sons bringing back Vietnamese wives."[68] Once again, the specter of grasping foreign women, "gold diggers" taking advantage of innocent American boys, resurfaced in the discussion of Vietnamese-American marriage.

There was, of course, no stated age requirement for soldier marriage in Vietnam as the military had no legal standing to create one: an American old enough to marry in his state of residence was old enough to marry overseas. Indirect evidence, however, indicates that in practice, commanding officers and chaplains routinely rejected the marriage requests of soldiers on the basis of age. In a random data sample of more than seventy Vietnamese-American couples that MACV had approved for marriage, only one of the soldier-husbands was younger than twenty at the time of application, or less than 2 percent of approved applicants. This disparity in marriage approvals was particularly striking given the extreme youthfulness of the American troops who served in the Vietnam War, on average the youngest U.S. fighting force of the twentieth century, with an average age of nineteen.[69] Given these data, it seems likely that the army maintained an unspoken policy of disapproving marriage for younger GIs.

"Security" was repeatedly cited as the other main motive for limiting marriage, and indeed, when MACV Directive 608-1 was revised in 1966, it added an extensive security and police background check for Vietnamese spouses.

It also introduced a penalty for the American service member should the security investigation reveal "derogatory" information about the Vietnamese partner.[70] In a political context in which few Vietnamese were fully immune from ties, either personal or familial, to the insurgency, this security screening was a very real and intimidating obstacle to many Vietnamese women. As she debated whether to accept a marriage proposal, for example, Le Ly Hayslip, was fearful that her application for a marriage license would uncover her two teenage arrests for Viet Cong activity, even though National Liberation Front (NLF) forces later put her on trial as a traitor and ordered her execution. It is not clear that she ever shared any of her political past with the American man who became her first husband. The MACV's emphasis on security was an expression of the "national security" milieu of U.S. foreign policy, which reached its heyday in the 1950s and 1960s, and a perhaps justified paranoia that had arisen in the context of prolonged counterinsurgency warfare. Though historically characteristic of the Vietnam War, this particular anxiety about soldier marriage also resonated with themes from World War I, when military officials had worried that foreign women on intimate terms with U.S. soldiers served as a natural conduit for German espionage. The "threat" of Vietnamese women was presented as vague, diffuse, but unmistakable; as in World War I, it combined themes of sexuality and military betrayal.

The purposeful stigmatization of Vietnamese women, for a variety of reasons, probably had a limited impact on soldiers' attitudes or actions. By the late 1960s many U.S. soldiers had simply come to mistrust everything that the military told them about Vietnam. A man who had formed an attachment to a particular woman could easily override the army's negative messages about Vietnamese women. Indeed, for some men, whether overtly or unconsciously, choosing an intercultural marriage was an act of resistance to the military's rules and values. To spend time with his fiancée in her community, learning about her values and beliefs, was to embrace a counterculture to the military that some men found liberating.[71]

When marriage data from the Vietnam War are analyzed, they reveal continuities with the historical phenomenon of soldier marriage in earlier wars.[72] As in the past, the demographic patterns of intercultural marriage in Vietnam are most remarkable for how unpatterned they are: in every measurable parameter except age, soldier-husbands represent a cross section of the fighting force in Vietnam. The racial makeup of the group, for example, followed the contours of MACV personnel as a whole. Three-quarters of GI husbands were white, and one-quarter were soldiers of color. At 10 percent,

African American husbands were exactly proportional to their representation among MACV forces. Latinos, Asians, Native Americans, and Pacific Islanders—groups whose service in Vietnam has just begun to draw the attention of historians—constituted the other 15 percent of husbands from minority groups.[73] The geographic and regional distribution of husbands was also reflective of MACV forces in their broad outlines. The draft during the Vietnam War ensured that military service was distributed across the states and regions of the United States, and husbands too were dispersed in their origins, from the small towns of the South and West to the big cities of the northeastern industrial belt. In fact, Chris Appy's composite portrait of American soldiers in Vietnam could just as well describe GI husbands: "They grew up in the white, working-class enclaves of South Boston and Cleveland's West Side; in the black ghettos of Detroit and Birmingham; in the small rural towns of Oklahoma and Iowa; and in the housing developments of working-class suburbs. They came by the thousands from every state and every U.S. territory, but few were from places of wealth and privilege."[74]

If the group of husbands as a whole reflected the character and distribution of military service in the United States in the late 1960s, the wives mirrored the dislocation that war had wrought in Southeast Asia over four decades. Vietnamese women who resided in proximity to the largest concentrations of American troops were far more likely to marry American GIs. More than half the wives in the sample (53 percent) listed Saigon or the greater Saigon area as their place of residence. Another 11 percent were residents of three communities, Da Nang, Cam Ranh, and Bien Hoa, that hosted some of the largest U.S. military bases in the country. The rest of the women were from a range of provincial market towns and hamlets across the South. The brides as a group were younger than the soldier-applicants, but not dramatically so. The most typical age at time of application was twenty-one for women, twenty-two for men. Young teenage brides (under eighteen) were a rarity, only 7 percent of all brides in the sample, and they had a greater tendency to be from small towns or villages than the group of brides as a whole.[75] In any case, the marriage applicants of the Vietnam War looked much like the intercultural couples of other American wars—young men and young women of culturally disparate backgrounds, who were drawn together by the serendipity of wartime.

Official army records and the raw data derived from them raise as many questions about Vietnamese-American marriage as they answer. One soldier-applicant was a Native American from a town of 1,700 in the foothills of the Piedmont, North Carolina. By the age of twenty-three, he had already spent several years in the military. In Saigon, he met his fiancée, one of the youngest brides in the sample group; she had been born just after the French defeat at Dien Bien Phu in 1955. Did he plan to make a career for himself in the army? Did her family flee to the South after the partition of the country mandated by the Geneva Agreements? Were they both Catholic? The sources do not say, and in contrast with World War II, the intercultural marriages of Vietnam have not produced the memoirs, articles, or recollections that enable a historian to tie the pieces together.

Military marriage applications as a source of information about marriage in Vietnam have other limitations as well. For one thing, an unusually high number of marriages took place outside of the army's purview. Many Americans determined to marry their Vietnamese girlfriends were unable to complete the process during the standard one-year tour of duty. Frequently such men sought the opportunity to return to Vietnam as civilian workers, employed by government agencies or U.S. businesses doing contract work for the government. Under these circumstances, the men were free to marry and live with their wives while working and saving toward bringing them home. Other men chose to stay in Vietnam with a wife and family on a longer-term basis. Some of these circulated in the American enclave in Vietnam, but others embraced a more fully integrated Vietnamese lifestyle, and sometimes disappeared from sight altogether. A white American from Honolulu, for example, deserted from the U.S. Army in 1972, rather than "abandon" his Vietnamese wife and children, only reemerging when the Vietnamese communist government expelled him as an unwanted foreigner in the fall of 1975. Similarly, an American deserter and the Vietnamese woman he loves deeply, a former bar girl, are the protagonists of veteran Robert Olen Butler's novel *The Alleys of Eden* (1981). Hiding from U.S. authorities in her tiny home in a back alley of Saigon, the couple creates a secret life that sustains the man and shelters both from the war.[76]

Deserters and expatriates as a group were a source of worry to American officials. Men who lived "off the grid" sometimes slipped into the murky world of drugs, crime, black marketeering, or even espionage for hire. In many ways they were the descendants of U.S. veterans who had "gone native" in earlier colonial interventions in Central America, the Caribbean, or the Philippines.[77] Army psychologist John Talbott, who had served a tour of duty in Vietnam, attempted a psychological characterization of the men who had made the "pathological" choice to remain in country (the "last place on earth where most Americans would want to live and work," according to Talbott). Among those who opted for such a lifestyle, he claimed to observe an alarming incidence of "alcoholism, psychopathic behavior, and frank psychosis." Certain personality types were drawn to the isolated, chaotic, and violent atmosphere that was South Vietnam in the late 1960s, he argued. For these men, Vietnam represented a fantasy landscape where they could reinvent themselves, a place to find "combat exposure, primitive, manly living without rules, regulations, or bossy American women." Some of the men he encountered, those he labeled "extenders," had been in Southeast Asia almost continuously for five or six years, and "they consider it unthinkable to return to a place as constricting as the U.S."[78] Although he never connected the dots in any analytical sense, Talbott's observations of men with a reputedly "pathological" inability to leave Vietnam were deeply intertwined with stories of the women they had met there. Like the army itself, Talbott did not seem able to accept the idea that American men could have meaningful or mutually fulfilling relationships with Vietnamese women, but it seems likely that at least some of the "cases" he purported to describe were simply men who were in committed relationships with Vietnamese women—a decidedly unpathological reason to stay in Vietnam.

In the end it is impossible to know how many of these uncounted expatriate men there were, and how many took up residence in Vietnam primarily because of wives or lovers. As army helicopters prepared to evacuate Americans and their allies from Saigon in 1975, *New York Times* correspondent Fox Butterfield estimated that such intercultural couples living unofficially in Vietnam counted in the thousands. These were many of the families who reemerged at the U.S. embassy that spring, asking for safe passage out of the country. The fall of Saigon momentarily shone a spotlight on intermarried couples, but they were quickly subsumed in the larger and more prominent story of the evacuation crisis. Two days before Saigon fell to NVA forces, Dennis and Lan Phung Thi (along with Lan's two sons from a previous relationship) were placed on a ship and evacuated to Guam. From there they boarded a plane for San Diego and were taken to Camp Pendleton. There they were processed, not as a war bride family but as refugees, and interned at an emergency refugee camp hastily assembled by the U.S. military. It was clear to Dennis, in retrospect, that he had been the family's ticket to safety. As an American citizen and a combat veteran, his safe departure from the country was an urgent responsibility for the State Department—but not that of his Vietnamese dependents. They "wanted me out as badly as I wanted to leave. Lan and the boys were just baggage."[79] The U.S. government had withdrawn its support of intercultural couples in the Vietnam War long before the withdrawal from Vietnam itself.

Leaving Vietnam Behind

In the years following the American withdrawal from Vietnam, thousands of Vietnamese-American couples settled into a life in the United States. Much remains to be learned about these relationships. No national or regional network of Vietnamese war brides has formed since the end of the war, and Vietnamese women have not yet created a platform, in print or on the Internet, for their stories or concerns—a significant contrast with the war brides of the World War II generation. The men and women in these marriages often faced profound trauma during the war years, and it is easy to imagine that difficult war experiences may have left a residue of pain and psychological suffering in later lives. But without a representative data sample or comparison groups, it is impossible to say whether the incidence of family violence, alcoholism, mental instability, or divorce differs in any way from the population as a whole or from the population of Vietnam veterans married to American-born wives.[80] Satisfying intermarriages are also easily found. The tidy and cheerful home of Joe and Dinh McDonald, a Vietnamese-American couple living in southeast Massachusetts, is covered wall to wall with photos of children, grandchildren, and family celebrations—testament to the thirty-plus years of marriage that the couple has enjoyed.[81] One theme that is common to the stories of Vietnamese war brides gathered to date is that of isolation. The Vietnamese wives of U.S. war veterans describe a sense of social and cultural marginalization that characterizes their experience in the United States. They feel themselves apart from and unwelcome by Vietnamese immigrant communities in the United States. But they also find that the mainstream American communities where they have lived their adult lives have been less than fully welcoming due to barriers of race, language, religion, and political history. One couple's closest friends, outside their family, are other intermarried couples they met while in Vietnam, now scattered around the country. The only comprehensive demographic study of Asian war brides in the United States (a data set that merges Vietnamese wives with those from other Asian nations) confirms this view. Compared with Asian immigrants who lived in the United States in 1980 and were not intermarried, Asian war brides had lower levels of education, labor force participation, occupational status, and family income, and higher use of native language in the home—all factors expressive of or contributing to isolation.[82]

The social marginalization of Vietnamese war brides in the United States has been paralleled in cultural representation since the end of the war. In cultural terms, Vietnamese wives or would-be wives were left behind—abandoned like the women still waiting at the U.S. embassy when the last American helicopters departed. This theme is played out most revealingly in John Ketwig's memoir of the Vietnam War, recently reissued to critical praise. *And a Hard Rain Fell* is a tale of damage and healing. It is unusual among published narratives by Vietnam veterans in placing an intercultural love affair at its center. Yet Ketwig unfolds the relationship only to reveal it as a dead end, a self-delusion. John, a car mechanic, was barely nineteen when he was sent to Vietnam. Serving in a combat unit in the central highlands, he feels his sense of morality, even his sense of reality, slipping away. During an R & R leave to Panang, Malaysia, John develops an infatuation with the prostitute he hires for the week. Lin is described as a beautiful and sensual young woman, with special abilities as a "healer" of GIs' souls and bodies: "I like GIs. They are so hurt, so vulnerable. I feel I am like a doctor. . . . Do you understand? I try to do something very nice for very hurt people." Lin becomes the author's only tenuous thread of emotional security. He makes plans to marry her. In his mind, he rescues Lin from her life as a prostitute, bringing her and their imaginary son home to upstate New York. So changed by fighting a war he cannot believe in, and so alienated from his own country, he requires Lin whom he comes to see as his purpose for living.

Back in Buffalo, he is devastated to receive Lin's kind but firm letter of rejection. Satisfied with her work and her life circumstances, Lin had never had an interest in making a new life with John in the United States. She had gone along with his plans only to preserve his sense of hope. Now she fervently urges him to find his own happiness and future. Lin's letter creates a new and terrible emotional wound for John. Ultimately, to get over Lin and heal himself, John must learn to accept and repeat his own father's words: "Forget her. . . . She's just a whore. You'll get over it." In many ways, the message of Ketwig's text is the inverse of that in the film *Teresa*: postwar recovery for Philip, the troubled veteran of World War II, entails his "mature" acceptance of responsibility for his Italian war bride and their newborn baby. The Vietnam veteran, instead, recovers by learning to walk away, making a clean break with the war. John marries the wholesome, hometown American girl who wrote to him in Vietnam; she too is a healer, a labor-and-delivery nurse who longs for children and is willing to be patient during her husband's long struggle back from despair. His failed intercultural love affair, like the war itself, is a painful and lingering illness from which he slowly recovers. The protagonist had wanted to "save" the Southeast Asian woman and give her a better life, but inexplicably, ungratefully, she does not wish to be saved by him. It is difficult to imagine a better metaphor for the Vietnam War.[83]

If the war bride disappeared as a signifier of U.S. foreign policy, the American impulse to understand war through familial relations did not. In the decades following the Vietnam War, it was the Amerasian child—offspring of a GI father and Southeast Asian mother—who filled the void. Considering the "war orphan" as a trope of postwar "recuperation" helps to highlight what was both similar and different about the American recovery from the Vietnam War.[84] The intercultural offspring of American servicemen had made earlier appearances on the American cultural scene, but never with such urgency or persistence.[85] Vietnamese "war orphans" and the effort to airlift them to the United States saturated print and broadcast media in the weeks leading up to and following the collapse of the Saigon government in 1975. "Operation Babylift" was a partnership of private adoption agencies, the State Department, and the U.S. Air Force. President Gerald Ford pledged $2 million to the effort. When a shortage of planes slowed the exodus, millionaire Hugh Hefner volunteered his private jet, and Playboy bunnies "cradled" Vietnamese babies on the long journey from Saigon, or so American readers were told. Emotional and domestic scenes on airport tarmacs were a precise parallel to the greeting of foreign brides at docks and train stations for earlier postwar generations, but here the arrivals were dependent children, not dependent wives. *Newsweek* described the arrival at Kennedy International Airport of two boys from a Saigon orphanage in ecstatic prose, an almost religious conversion to American life: their "new parents immediately renamed them Christian and Adam, bundled them into snowsuits and swept them off to a home in upstate . . . that came complete with seven brothers and sisters, two ponies and a friendly Saint Bernard named McDuff."[86] A wire service photo of President Ford, a sleepy Vietnamese toddler draped across his arms, was widely printed. Some claimed, not unreasonably, that the government was shamelessly exploiting babies for propaganda (a charge reinforced by the leaked statement of a Vietnamese official to the U.S. ambassador in Saigon, expressing his hope that the babies would elicit a strong sympathy factor for Thieu's slipping government). Critics pointed out that the State Department had extemporized for years as adoption agencies and prospective parents had implored it for assistance; orphans during the war had been an unpleasant reminder of the American role in *making* orphans.

Suddenly, however, the children had transformed into a comforting sign of U.S. benevolence. The overwhelming response of American families to the Vietnamese orphans—when the State Department set up a special adoption hotline for Vietnamese evacuated children, it logged more than 1,000 phone calls per minute—suggests that the children hit a deep chord with the American public.[87]

The symbolic meanings of the Vietnamese orphans were not difficult to discern. Unable to save South Vietnam, we could at least "rescue" its children. Supporters of the babylift pointed ominously, though vaguely, to the life of deprivation and danger that orphans would allegedly face under a communist regime, especially the "half-blood" children of Americans. They dismissed the argument that the vast majority of parentless children in Vietnam were taken in and raised by extended kin. No child could expect to have the good life in a Vietnamese communist state that they could have in the United States, with spaghetti, bicycles, and a family dog. Taking in orphans was, most important, a way to feel good about being Americans again, an expiation of guilt from the war. Redeeming the Vietnam fiasco through familial love and adoption was the theme of middlebrow periodicals from *Saturday Review* to *Reader's Digest*.

Critics of the babylift, however, pointed to its utter inadequacy as a gesture of reconciliation. "Babies are a nicer story than the 26 million craters we gave South Vietnam, nicer than the 100,000 amputees in that wretched country, more fun to read about than the 14 million acres of defoliated forest and the 800,000 acres that we bulldozed," Gloria Emerson pointed out in her typically blunt style. She and others viewed the airlift as a cynical distraction from the unmet obligation to provide reparations to the Vietnamese people.[88] The project to recuperate the American soul through adoption soon floundered as the reality of the hasty airlift became apparent. Social workers and immigration officials interviewing the children in U.S. points of entry made the disturbing observation that many of the so-called orphans had at least one living parent in Vietnam. Stories came to light of wealthy Vietnamese, sometimes a relative and sometimes not, making arrangements to "chaperone" a child as their own ticket out of the country. The tragic crash of an American C-5A airplane packed with children killed more than 150 and fueled the controversy.[89]

But the issue of Vietnamese children was the issue that would not die. By the beginning of the 1980s it had morphed into a more specific but also broader concern—what to do about the Amerasian children still living in

Vietnam, but also in Korea, Cambodia, Laos, and elsewhere in Asia. "The Amerasians are our children, and ought to be allowed to come here without restriction," wrote a columnist for the *Chicago Tribune*.[90] The matter of American blood and Western features figured large in this discussion, as did the alleged mistreatment of these racially mixed offspring "sired" by Americans. The Amerasian child was "a half-breed outcast born into poverty and bigotry in Vietnam. . . . In a society proud of its ethnic purity, they are ostracized for their black or Caucasian features, unwelcome reminders that Vietnamese women slept with the enemy." "These are the progeny of our own loins," an adoption advocacy director declared, fuming about State Department inaction. A decade after the American withdrawal, journalists and humanitarian workers from the United States began to make their way to Vietnam, where they reported on the pathetic plight of the *bui doi*, "dust of life," young people of mixed ancestry living on the streets or with criminal gangs.[91] Amerasian children (many were no longer children at all but young adults, some married with families of their own) found champions in Congress, as the public and policymakers called for immigration reform to bring the children of American servicemen "home" to the United States. The most important of these initiatives was the Amerasian Homecoming Act of 1987. For a window of time it allowed the Vietnamese children of Americans to emigrate to the United States even if their father could not be found or identified; in 1990 an amendment enabled spouses and mothers of the Amerasians to accompany them. The legislation also granted refugee benefits to these individuals, including resettlement assistance in the United States. By 1994, more than 69,000 Amerasian men and women had settled in the United States under this program.

Almost universally these young people shared the goal of finding the fathers who had left them behind, but the vast majority found themselves disappointed. Resettlement officials estimate that only 2 percent were successful in locating their fathers, and even fewer were able to establish relationships with them (though this handful of happy endings was the focus of the media).[92] As the numbers suggest, real-life fathers had understandably moved on with their lives, but on many levels the nation had not. In the story of the Amerasian children, Americans had found a narrative that allowed them to reconfigure the war and reconceptualize victims and victimizers. This was one of the central tasks of America's reckoning with the Vietnam War, so adroitly described by cultural critic Susan Jeffords as the "remasculinization of America."[93] In the process of identification that the Amerasian issue allowed, the American soldier merges with the mixed-race child—each is an innocent victim of the war. The American nation becomes father and also, paradoxically, child. Vietnam, the mother, the war bride, is not part of this reconciliation.

The arrival of Vietnamese Amerasians as immigrants in the early 1990s coincided with the arrival of a bicultural import from the London stage. *Miss Saigon*, the much-anticipated musical, came to Broadway in April 1991, offering a forum, once again, for Americans to consider the meaning of relationships between foreign women and American soldiers. *Miss Saigon* is a popular commentary on American foreign relations, written as a doomed and operatic love story. The protagonist is Kim (a role created by Lea Salonga, a teenage singer and television personality from the Philippines), a seventeen-year-old forced by her caretakers into prostitution in Saigon during the waning days of the American-backed regime. She has the briefest of love affairs with Chris, a U.S. Marine, who cares for her but leaves her pregnant when the last of the Americans withdraw from the city. Quite explicitly, the show recycled Puccini's turn-of-the century opera *Madame Butterfly* and absorbed in the process much of its nineteenth-century ethos of cultural essentialism. The production was updated with helicopters and miniskirts, but it retained the opera's central trope, the tragic impossibility of an East-West love affair. The Vietnamese mother kills herself in order to "save" her mixed-race child—that is, save him by compelling Chris and his American wife to take the toddler home to the United States, where he can live the life to which he is entitled, in the play's terms, by his American paternity.

Symbolically, relationships between foreign women and American soldiers were once again in play in a postwar debate over the meaning of a U.S. military intervention. William Safire, the conservative columnist, also perceived that *Miss Saigon* the modernized fable was, intrinsically, a political commentary, one that derided the American war as an impossible, quixotic, and ultimately tragic campaign that hurt much more than it helped. Safire wryly proposed a rival theater production more in keeping with his own political sensibilities. "Miss Ho Chi Minh City" would bring out different themes, "the nobility of trying to save an ally from invasion" or "the indecision that kept us from striking hard early." His hypothetical show has an ending almost as depressing as the original he parodies: Ho Chi Minh's beautiful granddaughter, now "disillusioned and broke" under the flawed communist regime, has fled to Hong Kong, where she works as a bar girl for American customers.[94] For Safire, it was communism, not capitalism or militarism that produced this degraded status for foreign women—but prostitutes they were in both political scenarios.

Military conflicts down to our own time have continued to call up a need for understanding and interpretation that follows the patterns established in the wake of the Korean War. Operation Desert Storm, ordered by President George H. W. Bush, had recently concluded when *Miss Saigon* arrived on Broadway in the spring of 1991. The *New York Times* theater critic Frank Rich noted in his review this odd juxtaposition of timing: the play "insists on revisiting the most calamitous and morally dubious military adventure in America history . . . even as the jingoistic celebrations of a successful American war are going full blast." With the First Persian Gulf War the American state launched a spiral of military intervention and violence in the Middle East that is far from over. Americans have found themselves "embedded" in a part of the world that most know little about, a place that seems radically foreign to many.

To make some sense of this international relationship, Americans have turned once again to *personal* relationships, most recently between American service personnel and Iraqi civilians. Here Americans have fallen back upon the trope of the tragic and impossible love affair to understand our relationship with Iraq. "Even among those couples who fell in love, the abyss of religious and cultural misunderstandings has been hard to cross," *Newsweek* noted. "Every one of them has seen the clash of civilizations up close and personal." The emblematic love story of the Iraq War has surely been the marriage of U.S. Army sergeant Sean Blackwell to an Iraqi physician. Articles, television reports, and blog comments about this relationship were routinely headlined with titles such as "Romeo and Juliet, Baghdad-Style" and "Star-Crossed Courtship"—a strange choice indeed given that the couple was happily married and living in Florida with their young daughter at last report.[95] Yet Americans feel unloved and insecure in the Middle East. As the long history of war brides suggests, the American sense of discomfort in the international arena—our anxiety about "getting into bed" with other countries, has often been projected onto the foreign wives or partners of U.S. military personnel, a cultural practice that has had consequences in both personal lives and public culture.

Notes

NOTES TO INTRODUCTION

1. "Poll Shows View of Iraq War Is Most Negative since Start," *New York Times*, 25 May 2007, A16; "Delay Decision on Major Cuts, Petraeus Says," *New York Times*, 10 September 2007, A1; "The General on the Hill: Some Reviews" (letters to the editor), *New York Times*, 12 September 2007, A20. The announcement in early October of British plans to start a troop drawdown intensified discussion at that time of an American withdrawal; see "Britain to Halve Its Force in Iraq by Spring of '08," *New York Times*, 9 October 2007, A1.

2. Christopher Dickey and Jessica Ramirez, "Married to Iraq: What the War's Few Marriages Tell Us about Culture, Conflict and the Road Ahead," *Newsweek* 150 (22 October 2007), 28–34. It is notable that the authors chose to exclude discussion of marriages between Iraqi American soldiers and Iraqi nationals—relationships that have in fact accounted for the great majority of intercultural marriages during the Iraq war, as the authors concede. The article is concerned instead with the admittedly small number of "love stories between *American* soldiers and Iraqi civilians" (my emphasis)—in other words, those marked by the "chasm" of cultural difference. The unintended implication of their wording, that Iraqi Americans, even those serving in the U.S. Army, are too different to be fully American, underscores the point here.

3. Works from this global women's history discourse that have influenced my thinking include Seungsook Moon, "Transnational (Hetero)sexuality and U.S. Military Empire in Korea," Thirteenth Berkshire Conference on the History of Women, Scripps College, Claremont, California, June 2–5, 2005; Ruth Harris, "The 'Child of the Barbarian': Rape, Race and Nationalism in France during the First World War," *Past and Present* 141 (November 1993), 170–206; Susan Grayzel, "Mothers, Marraines, and Prostitutes: Morale and Morality in First World War France," *International History Review* 19 (February 1997), 66–82; Anja Schuler, "The 'Horror on the Rhine': Rape, Racism and the International Women's Movement," working paper no. 86, John F. Kennedy-Institut fur Nordamerikastudien (Berlin: Freie Universitat, 1996); Maria Hohn, *GIs and Frauleins: The German-American Encounter in 1950s West Germany* (Chapel Hill: University of North Carolina Press, 2002); Fabrice Virgili, *Shorn Women: Gender and Punishment in Liberation France*, trans. John Flower (London: Berg, 2002); Ji-Yeon Yuh, *Beyond the Shadow of Camptown: Korean Military Brides in America* (New York: NYU Press, 2002); and Margaret Randolph Higonnet et al., eds., *Behind the Lines: Gender and the Two World Wars* (New Haven: Yale University Press, 1987).

4. Influential scholarship that has reconfigured the history of U.S. foreign relations through the lens of gender includes Elaine Tyler May, *Homeward Bound: American*

Families in the Cold War Era (New York: Basic Books, 1988); Kristin L. Hoganson, *Fighting for American Manhood: How Gender Politics Provoked the Spanish-American and Philippine-American Wars* (New Haven: Yale University Press, 1998); Christina Klein, "Family Ties and Political Obligation: The Discourse of Adoption and the Cold War Commitment to Asia," in Christian G. Appy, ed., *Cold War Constructions: The Political Culture of United States Imperialism, 1945–1966* (Amherst: University of Massachusetts Press, 2000); Kathleen Kennedy, *Disloyal Mothers and Scurrilous Citizens: Women and Subversion during World War I* (Bloomington: Indiana University Press, 1999); Emily S. Rosenberg, "'Foreign Affairs' after World War II: Connecting Sexual and International Politics," *Diplomatic History* 18 (1994), 59–70; Robert Westbrook, "'I Want a Girl Just Like the Girl Who Married Harry James': American Women and the Problem of Political Obligation in World War II," *American Quarterly* 42 (December 1990), 587–614.

5. John Horne Burns, *The Gallery* (New York: Harper and Brothers, 1947), quoted in Elfrieda Berthiaume Shukert and Barbara Smith Scibetta, *War Brides of World War II* (Novato, CA: Presidio Press, 1988). For background and critical reception of the novel, see Paul Fussell's new introduction, *The Gallery* (New York: New York Review of Books, 2004), vii–xi.

6. Important titles written by war brides or the family members of war brides include Pamela Winfield and Brenda Wilson Hasty, *Sentimental Journey: The Story of the GI Brides* (London: Constable, 1984); Vera A. Cracknell Long, *From Britain with Love: World War II Pilgrim Brides Sail to America* (New Market, VA: Denecroft, 1988); Carol Fallows, *Love and War: Stories of War Brides from the Great War to Vietnam* (Sydney: Random House, 2002); Shukert and Scibetta, *War Brides*. Lois Battle, *War Brides* (New York: Penguin, 1982) is a fictionalized account by a popular novelist whose mother was the Australian-born wife of a GI in World War II.

7. Cynthia Enloe, *Bananas, Beaches and Bases: Making Feminist Sense of International Politics*, updated edition (Berkeley: University of California Press, 2000), 93–95. Also see Enloe, *Maneuvers: The International Politics of Militarizing Women's Lives* (Berkeley: University of California Press, 2000); and Theodore Nadelson, *Trained to Kill: Soldiers at War* (Baltimore: Johns Hopkins University Press, 2005), 144–147.

8. Saundra Pollock Sturdevant and Brenda Stoltzfus, *Let the Good Times Roll: Prostitution and the U.S. Military in Asia* (New York: New Press, 1992); Enloe, *Bananas, Beaches and Bases*, xiii–xiv. The Coalition against Trafficking in Women is a leading organization in the campaign against sexual trafficking (www.catwinternational.org) that is informed by this understanding. For an excellent introduction to ideological and political debates within the campaign, see the webpage authored by Mini Singh, "Debate on Trafficking and Sex-Slavery," sponsored by the Feminist Sexual Ethics Project, Brandeis University (http://www.brandeis.edu.projects/fse/pages/traffickingdebate.html).

9. "American Girl War Bride. Miss Wood Goes to Wed General Huerta's Officer," *New York Times*, 24 May 1914, 11.

10. U.S. Army, Division of Cuba, *Annual Report 1900* (Washington, DC: Government Printing Office, 1900), Chart of Births, Deaths and Marriages, p. 249. Also see *Civil Report of Brigadier General Leonard Wood, Military Governor of Cuba*, 1901, 3, "Report of the Office of Chief Sanitary Officer" (Washington, DC: Government Printing Office, 1901), Chart of Births, Deaths and Marriages, p. 207. The phenomenon of intercultural marriage is universal to foreign war, and such marriages may well have taken place earlier as

a result of the Mexican-American War or the War of 1812, for example; earlier marriages have not been documented to date.

11. "Our Honor Roll of War Brides," *Independent* 96 (30 November 1918), 294–297; "Defending War-Marriages," *Literary Digest* 51 (21 August 1915), 354–355; "Why I Married before Going to War," *American Magazine* 85 (May 1918), 33; "Midnight Wartime Wedding," *Touchstone Magazine* 4 (December 1918), 188–189; "Fascinating Story of an American War Bride as Told by Herself," *Ladies' Home Journal* 36 (May 1919), 7–9.

12. Marion Craig Wentworth, *War Brides: A Play in One-Act* (New York: Dramatists Play Agency, 1928). Wentworth's play took the patriotic iconography of the war bride as a woman who marries a soldier at war and turned it into a feminist antiwar motif—a critique of propagation for the war state. It first appeared as a magazine story and was adapted as serious fare for the vaudeville circuit, where it was apparently a popular success. See reviews and articles in the *Atlanta Constitution*, 22 May 1915, 10; 23 May 1915, B7; 24 May 1915, 5; and 25 May 1915, 14; *Chicago Tribune*, 8 June 1915, 15. An earlier edition of the play, published in 1915, included photographs from the production. Joseph Rumshinsky and B. Thomashefsky, *Milhama Kalot*; music album of the play "Jewish War Brides" (New York: Hebrew Publishing Company, 1917).

13. "French Envoys of Cupid in America," *Literary Digest* 64 (14 February 1920), 57–61.

14. The extraordinarily rich historiography of the post–Civil War Reconstruction has found no echo in the study of twentieth-century postwar eras. The sole comparative study of America's postwar moments was published by a popular historian before the Second World War was over: Dixon Wecter, *When Johnny Comes Marching Home* (Boston: Houghton Mifflin, 1944).

15. I follow here Penny Summerfield's theoretical discussion of the "interplay between discourse and subjectivity" in women's memories of wartime; Penny Summerfield, *Reconstructing Women's Wartime Lives: Discourse and Subjectivity in Oral Histories of the Second World War* (Manchester: Manchester University Press, 1998).

NOTES TO CHAPTER 1

1. A version of this song with multiple verses is found in a collection assembled by three AEF veterans, John J. Niles, Douglas S. Moore, and A. A. Wallgren, *The Songs My Mother Never Taught Me* (New York: Macaulay, 1929), 15–17.

2. *Stars and Stripes* 1 (22 November 1918), 4. See also response *Stars and Stripes* 1 (6 December 1918), 4. Dixon Wecter discusses the exchange and quotes additional letters in *When Johnny Comes Marching Home* (Boston: Houghton Mifflin, 1944), 332–333.

3. Allan M. Brandt, *No Magic Bullet: A Social History of Venereal Disease in the United States since 1880* (New York: Oxford University Press, 1985), 96.

4. The rumor was first reported in "Cupid's Success in A.E.F.," *New York Times*, 30 January 1919, 3, citing as its source a Paris paper. The *Times* later published a follow-up story retracting the rumor: "Doughboys and French Girls—Not Many of Them Are Marrying, and the Soldiers Long for Their Homes," *New York Times*, 11 May 1919, sec. 4, p. 7.

5. Marvin Kreidberg and Merton Henry, *History of Military Mobilization in the United States Army* (Washington, DC: Department of the Army, 1955), 297; Edward M. Coffman, *The War to End All Wars: The American Military Experience in World War I* (New York: Oxford University Press, 1968), 42.

6. Nancy K. Bristow, *Making Men Moral: Social Engineering during the Great War* (New York: NYU Press, 1996); Thomas C. Leonard, *Above the Battle: War-making in America from Appomattox to Versailles* (New York: Oxford University Press, 1978), 35; Edward Frank Allen, *Keeping Our Fighters Fit for War and After* (New York: Century, 1918); Joseph H. Odell, *The New Spirit of the New Army: A Message to "Service Flag Homes"* (New York: Fleming H. Revell, 1918).

7. John Whiteclay Chambers, *To Raise an Army: The Draft Comes to Modern America* (New York: Free Press, 1987). Near the end of the war, September 1918, the age of registration was lowered to eighteen, but only men twenty years of age or older were called into service.

8. Harvey Levenstein, *Seductive Journey: American Tourists in France from Jefferson to the Jazz Age* (Chicago: University of Chicago Press, 1998), chaps. 6, 14, and 15; Jefferson quote p. 5; Brandt, *No Magic Bullet*, 108.

9. Groups that engaged these issues included the Woman's Christian Temperance Union (WCTU), the United Society for Christian Endeavor, and the foreign mission societies. Ian Tyrrell, *Woman's World, Woman's Empire: The Woman's Christian Temperance Union in International Perspective, 1880–1930* (Chapel Hill: University of North Carolina Press, 1991), especially chap. 9. On the Mexican border controversy, see Raymond B. Fosdick, *Chronicle of a Generation* (New York: Harper, 1958), 135–141; Bristow, *Making Men Moral*, 4–6.

10. Mary A. Renda, *Taking Haiti: Military Occupation and the Culture of U.S. Imperialism, 1915–1940* (Chapel Hill: University of North Carolina Press, 2001), 215–216.

11. Frank E. Vandiver, *Black Jack: The Life and Times of John J. Pershing* (College Station: Texas A&M University Press, 1977), 398–407. Resentment toward Pershing within the officers' corps stemmed from his rapid promotion, in violation of what was at that time the long-standing tradition of promotion by seniority. Disgruntled colleagues claimed that his career was advanced through political connections. The scandal was especially high-profile because Congress had to approve Pershing's nomination; Pershing was married to the daughter of a prominent senator. The Filipina woman, Joaquina Ignacio, was located in Manila and swore an affidavit that the accusations were lies, and that she and Pershing had been only "friends." The sex scandal is also discussed in Gene Smith, *Until the Last Trumpet Sounds: The Life of General of the Armies John J. Pershing* (New York: Wiley, 1998), 92–93.

12. Odell, *New Spirit of the Army*.

13. Paul Boyer, *Urban Masses and Moral Order in America, 1820–1920* (Cambridge: Harvard University Press, 1978), 220.

14. Bristow, *Making Men Moral*, chaps.. 1 and 2; Susan Zeiger, *In Uncle Sam's Service: Women Workers with the American Expeditionary Force, 1917–1919* (Ithaca: Cornell University Press, 1999), chap. 3; Jewish Welfare Board, *First Annual Report* (New York: Jewish Welfare Board, 1919). On Baker's high regard for the work of the CTCA, see Newton Baker to Raymond B. Fosdick, 1 July 1919, Raymond Blaine Fosdick papers, Princeton University Special Collections, Princeton, NJ.

15. Draft memo on venereal disease for Chief of Staff, General Staff, GHQ, 6 August 1918, RG 120, Series 29, Box 3786, National Archives and Record Administration, Washington DC (hereafter NARA); Bulletin No. 54, AEF, 7 August 1918, reprinted in George Walker, *Venereal Disease in the American Expeditionary Forces* (Baltimore: Medical Standard Book Company, 1922), 67.

16. Wecter, *When Johnny Comes Marching Home*, 335; "Franco-Yanko Romance," *Literary Digest* (10 November 1917), 46–50. Also see "Overseas Openings, May 1920," unpublished typescript, World War I Files, "Status of Work in Europe," Reel 154, YWCA Archives, YWCA National Board, New York, New York.

17. Margaret H. Darrow, *French Women and the First World War: War Stories of the Home Front* (Oxford: Berg, 2000), 71.

18. "Franco-Yanko Romance."

19. *New York Times*, 7 July 1919, 13; Hilary Kaiser, ed., *French War Brides in America: An Oral History* (Westport, CT: Praeger, 2008), 3–23.

20. Report of the Coblenz Hostess House, June 1919, unpublished typescript, World War I Files, Overseas Committee, "Reports," YWCA Archives; *New York Times*, 17 February 1919, 13.

21. Zeiger, *In Uncle Sam's Service*, 89; *New York Times*, 31 January 1919, 4.

22. Walker, *Venereal Disease*, 226–230.

23. *Stars and Stripes* (4 April 1919), 6.

24. Robert H. Ferrell, ed., *A Soldier in World War I: The Diary of Elmer Sherwood* (Indianapolis: Indiana Historical Society Press, 2004); George Browne, *An American Soldier in World War I*, ed. David L. Snead (Lincoln: University of Nebraska Press, 2006); James H. Hallas, *Doughboy War: The American Expeditionary Force in World War I* (Boulder, CO: Lynne Rienner, 2000).

25. Hallas, *Doughboy War*, 202–205; Ferrell, *A Soldier in World War I*, 142–143. On immigrants in the armed services in World War I, see Nancy Gentile Ford, *Americans All! Foreign-Born Soldiers in World War I* (College Station: Texas A&M University Press, 2001). On immigration as a factor in war bride marriage patterns, see the end of chapter 2.

26. Walker, *Venereal Disease*, 226–230. Walker's investigators were sent to Paris, Bordeaux, Grenoble, Nantes, and Saint-Nazaire and interviewed 237 women he met in public places. Although the investigation was meant to focus on sexual practices, he found much incidental information about women's lives in the war.

27. Susan R. Grayzel, *Women's Identities at War: Gender, Motherhood, and Politics in Britain and France during the First World War* (Chapel Hill: University of North Carolina Press, 1999), chap. 6.

28. Walker, *Venereal Disease*, 230.

29. "Franko-Yanko Romance"; Hallas, *Doughboy War*, 205–208; James F. McMillan, *Housewife or Harlot: The Place of Women in French Society, 1870–1940* (New York: St. Martin's Press, 1981), 125–128. In 1911, the female population exceeded the male by 684,000; in 1921, the female "surplus" had risen to 1,904,000. On the widow as patriotic symbol, see Darrow, *French Women*, 58–64, 66–68.

30. Brandt, *No Magic Bullet*, 101–102.

31. "Venereal Disease and Its Prevention in the Army," draft bulletin prepared by Hugh H. Young, Lt. Col., submitted 2 August 1918 to G-1, GHQ, AEF, RG 120, Series 29, Box 3786, NARA.

32. "Soldiers and Officers of Base Section No. 7," flyer from G-2 Military intelligence, RG 120 Series 1705, G-2 S. O. S. investigations, Box 447, NARA

33. Brandt, *No Magic Bullet*, 101, 118; "Venereal Disease and Its Prevention in the Army."

34. Walker, *Venereal Disease*, 101.

35. Ibid., 224. The perception of male effeminacy as a threat to military fitness is discussed in Susan Zeiger, "She Didn't Raise Her Boy to Be a Slacker: Motherhood, Conscription, and the Culture of the First World War," *Feminist Studies* 22 (Spring 1996), 7–39. The soldier's quote is from Browne, *American Soldier*, 43.

36. Walker, *Venereal Disease*, 68

37. Brandt, *No Magic Bullet*, 108–110; Young Men's Christian Association, *Service with Fighting Men*, vol. 2 (New York: Association Press, 1922), 142–162.

38. Brandt, *No Magic Bullet*, 108 n. 46.

39. Case Files, RG 120, General Headquarters, G-2, Box 5998, NARA.

40. Published YMCA sources make no mention of this work, but unpublished sources do. See Helen King, "Women's Work in the Paris Region," unpublished typescript, January–April 1919, AS 26, YMCA Archives; Susan Zeiger, "In Uncle Sam's Service: American Women Workers with the American Expeditionary Force, 1917–1919," (Ph.D. diss., New York University, 1991), 130 n. 72. Also mentioned in Walker, *Venereal Disease*, 154.

41. Arthur E. Barbeau and Florette Henri, *The Unknown Soldiers: Black American Troops in World War I* (Philadelphia: Temple University Press, 1974), quote p. 143.

42. Barbeua and Henri, *Unknown Soldiers*, 114–115, 142–145.

43. Jennifer D. Keene, *Doughboys, the Great War, and the Remaking of America* (Baltimore: Johns Hopkins University Press, 2001), 126–131.

44. Walker, *Venereal Disease*, 154.

45. Memo from Commanding Officer, Hospital Center, A. P. O. 765, to the Adjutant General, G.H.Q., 11 February 1919, Office of the Judge Advocate General, General Correspondence Files, RG 120, Entry 594, Box 22, NARA.

46. Sgt. Orley R. Hill to General Pershing, 25 February 1918; Mlle. Adele Parriaux to the American Consul, Feb 4, 1918 (trans.); M. Laguzan to General Pershing, 3 April 1918 (trans.); Mme. Vve. Hubert to American Army, 8 March 1919 (trans.); and letter file index of JAG Headquarters Office; all in RG 120, Entry 594, Box 22, NARA.

47. Coudert Brothers to Adjutant General, AEF, 6 December 1917, RG 120, Entry 594, Box 22, NARA.

48. Final report of Judge Advocate, AEF, 19 August 1919, p. 16, RG 120, General Headquarters, C in C reports, Entry 22, Box 42, NARA. For American citizens overseas, marriage was and is governed by the laws of the nation in which the marriage takes place. In the United States, marriage is governed by state law in the various states.

49. W. A. Bethel, Judge Advocate AEF to Commander in Chief, "Marriage of American Soldiers to French Girls" (memo), 18 June 1918, RG 120, entry 594, Box 22, NARA.

50. This and other letters from unit commanders compiled in Lt. Col. Albert B. Kellogg, "Marriages of Soldiers, Report for the Historical Section of the Army War College" (July 1942), p. 5, RG 165, Records of War Department General and Special Staffs, War College Division, Entry 310C, Box 74, NARA.

51. Nancy F. Cott, *Public Vows: A History of Marriage and the Nation* (Cambridge: Harvard University Press, 2000).

52. Kellogg, "Marriages of Soldiers." One decision granted survivor benefits to common-law citizen wives of soldiers. The other allowed a form of "proxy marriage"— marriage from a distance—for army personnel overseas. The question of common-law wives arose in relation to assigning War Risk Insurance beneficiaries; in most states these women were legal wives by reason of cohabitation. The judge advocate general ruled that

they and their children be granted benefits as other spouses would be. "Report on Common Law Marriage in United States," RG 120, JAG papers, Entry 594, Box 22, NARA.

53. Cott, *Public Vows*, chaps. 3 and 10; Marguerite Wilkinson, "A Midnight War-Time Wedding," *Touchstone* 4 (December 1918), 188–189. American marriage and patriotism are also linked in popular film of the war era; see Zeiger, "She Didn't Raise Her Boy to Be a Slacker."

54. Pershing's wife, Frances "Frankie" Warren, was a Wellesley graduate and suffragist, daughter of Senator Francis E. Warren, first governor of the state of Wyoming. The romanticization of John J. Pershing's life and his mythic status as a father can be seen in Harold F. Wheeler, "The Romance of General Pershing," *Ladies' Home Journal* 36 (July 1919), 44; Cullom Holmes Farrell, *Incidents in the Life of General John J. Pershing* (New York: Rand McNally, 1918); and Everett T. Tomlinson, *The Story of General Pershing* (New York: Appleton, 1932), a children's biography. Young readers of the Tomlinson book were told that a framed photograph of "Mrs. Pershing and the four children as the family was before that terrible fire in the Presidio" was the general's most beloved object, and always the first item unpacked by his orderly; the general "often sits in silence before it," and for a moment, "his family again seems complete" (214–215). The William Fox film company also produced a movie entitled *Why America Will Win*, highlighting "historical events in the life of General John J. Pershing." Pershing's relationships with women, including one in Paris during the war, are discussed by his biographer Frank Vandiver, *Black Jack*, 1006–1009.

55. Zeiger, "She Didn't Raise Her Boy to Be a Slacker," 6–39.

56. "Final Report of Judge Advocate," RG 120, NARA; Memo for Undersecretary of State, Central Office of Franco-American Relations: Marriage of Soldiers to French Women, RG 120, E 594, Box 22; Louis Nail, Le Directeur des Affaires Civil to JAG's office, 13 March 1919, E 594, Box 22, NARA. Some men were reported to have arranged resourcefully for their families to "post banns" through their hometown newspapers or have them read at the parish church.

57. Newton D. Baker, Secretary of War, to Senator James Wadsworth, 4 November 1919; Newton D. Baker, Sec'y of War to Sec'y of State, 18 November 1919, RG 165, War College Division, Gen'l Correspondence, E 296, Box 489, NARA.

58. Ruth Harris, "The 'Child of the Barbarian.'" On fears of women's sexuality in wartime Britain and France, see Grayzel, *Women's Identities at War*, chap. 4.

59. Niles, Moore, and Wallgren, *Songs My Mother Never Taught Me*, 15–17. In still other versions, the father might be African American, in which case "Yvonne has a pickaninny," 55–57

60. Compendium Change No. 109, "Character and Family Investigations for Soldiers," 23 June 1919; RG 200, National American Red Cross papers, 1917–1934, NARA.

61. Letter and cable log, Adjutant General's Office, AEF, RG 120, E594, Box 22, NARA.

62. Newton D. Baker, Secretary of War, to Secretary of State, 27 August 1919; Secretary of War to Senator James Wadsworth Jr., Committee on Military Affairs, 4 November 1919; Secretary of War to Secretary of State, 18 November, 1919; RG 165, Records of the War Department, General and Special Staff, General Correspondence, Entry 296, Box 489, NARA.

63. Memo for Chief of Staff, "Subject: Desertion of Wives by American Soldiers," 26 August 1919, RG 165, Office of Chief of Staff, Correspondence, Box 102, NARA.

64. "Cupid Has Had to Print a Set of Rules for the Doughboys in France," *Literary Digest* 62 (12 July 1919), 78–80. War Department and military concern about the bad reputation and negative publicity that bigamy cases could bring to American servicemen overseas was also reflected in a series of cases immediately following the war: when a small number of French, British, and Italian war brides arrived in the United States and learned that their husbands were already married to American women, the War Department volunteered to transport the women back home free of charge on U.S. naval ships. Memo for Assistant Chief of Staff, War Department Transportation Service, RG 165, Office of the Chief of Staff, Box 102, NARA.

65. Memo for Chief of Staff, 18 October 1921, Other Related Expeditionary Forces, General Correspondence, RG 120, Entry 1362, Box 3, NARA; Susan Zeiger, "U.S. Soldiers and French, German, and Siberian Women: Transnationalism and Sexuality in the First World War," Thirteenth Berkshire Conference on the History of Women, Scripps College, Claremont, California, 2–5 June 2005.

NOTES TO CHAPTER 2

1. Katherine Hardwick, American Red Cross Home Service, untitled report, 15 April 1919, and memo to Emmet W. White, Department of Civilian Relief, American Red Cross National Headquarters, Washington, DC, 31 October 1919, RG 200, National American Red Cross papers, 1917–1934 (hereafter ARC papers), NARA. On the estimate of 5,000 war brides, neither the War Department nor the State Department issued an official summary of the number of war brides after World War I, although the figure 5,000 was consistently shared with the press. See *New York Times*, 14 December 1919, 20, and *New York Times*, 4 December 1921, 25. It is almost certainly an underestimate. The YWCA estimated that its staff had processed 4,300 wives at the French ports of embarkation. The American Red Cross Home Service reported that its staff had received more than 5,200 brides off of army transports. These numbers do not include couples who arranged and paid for the wife's transportation themselves. Servicemen and officers of financial means often preferred this option, but even couples with limited resources sometimes opted for private, third-class transportation; see Fred Moran, memo to L. E. Skerin, Director General of Civilian Relief, 29 July 1920, ARC papers; Edna Wakefield to John McCandless, 4 September 1919, ARC papers, NARA.

2. Candace Lewis Bredbenner, *A Nationality of Her Own: Women, Marriage, and the Law of Citizenship* (Berkeley: University of California Press, 1998).

3. *New York Times*, 31 January 1919, 4; *Los Angeles Times*, 31 January 1919, 1; 17 February 1919, 1; 31 March 1919, 12; *Atlanta Constitution*, 28 March 1919, 12; 31 March 1919, 10.

4. Special Regulations no. 71, U.S. Army Transport Service, reproduced in AEF (London) Bulletin 50, 19 December 1918, RG 200, ARC papers, NARA. Cable from Endicott, American Red Cross, London office, to Davison, ARC, Washington, DC, 26 November 1918, ARC papers, also attests to the need for AEF involvement and shows the policy in formation; hundreds of AEF soldiers and officers based in England were asking ARC for assistance to get their wives onto commercial ships, and ARC originally contemplated providing funds for this purpose.

5. *New York Times*, 17 February 1919, 13.

6. Memo for Col. H. H. Tebbetts, 27 May 1919, Headquarters, Services of Supply (S.O.S.), General Staff, Entry 1691, Box 144, RG 120, NARA.

7. "Report of Work, 1917–1920," unpublished typescript, World War I Files, Overseas Committee, "Reports," YWCA Archives; "Report of Hostess House II, Brest, 1919," unpublished typescript, World War I Files, Overseas Committee, "Reports," YWCA Archives; Report of Hostess House I, Brest, 1919," unpublished typescript, World War I Files, Overseas Committee, "Reports," YWCA Archives; "Co-operation with Army in the Transportation of Families of Soldiers to the United States," 15 October 1920, unpublished typescript, ARC papers.

8. "Report of Hostess House II, Brest, 1919," unpublished typescript, World War I Files, Overseas Committee, "Reports," YWCA Archives; E. E. Booth to Commander Fremont, U.S. Navy, Tours, 19 July 1919, RG 120, Entry 1691, Box 144, NARA.

9. *New York Times*, 27 June 1919, 12; Memo from H. H. Tebbetts, Ass't. Chief of Staff, G-1, 30 June 1919, RG 120, Entry 1691, Box 144, NARA.

10. "War Brides—English," unsigned report, 3 February 1919; and Col. Charles M. Gandy, Army Medical Corps, memo, "Hospital Treatment of Soldiers' Families at Madison Barracks, NY," 30 December 1919, ARC papers; *New York Times*, 14 July 1919, 14; *Stars and Stripes*, Paris edition 2 (11 April 1919), 4.

11. Newspaper clipping, no source, no date, in S.O.S. files, RG 120, Entry 1691, NARA; Jane M. Hoey, Atlantic Division, American National Red Cross, to J. Byron Deacon, 26 March 1919, RG 200, ARC papers, NARA; H. H. Tebbetts, Headquarters S.O.S., to Mrs. S. C. Seymour, YWCA, Paris Headquarters, 18 July 1919, and S. C. Seymour to Colonel Tibbetts [*sic*], 9 July 1919; RG 120, Entry 1691, NARA.

12. On pressure from War Department, see E. E. Booth to Commander Fremont, U.S. Navy, Tours, 19 July 1919, RG 120, Entry 1691, Box 144, NARA. See J. H. McCandless, Department of Civilian Relief, the American Red Cross, to Brig. General Frank T. Hines, 16 April 1919; McCandless to Edna T. Wakefield, New York Branch, ARC, 19 May 1919; and Edna Wakefield to McCandless, 22 May 1919; McCandless memo, "English and French War Brides," 19 May 1919; all in RG 200, ARC papers, NARA.

13. E. E. Booth to Commanding Generals, Ports of Embarkation, 22 May 1919; Colonel Daniel Van Voorhis, S.O.S., to Executive Officer, YWCA Paris, 14 May 1919; and Colonel Daniel Van Voorhis, S.O.S., to Colonel H. H. Tebbets, 21 May 1919; RG 120, Entry 1691, Headquarters, Services of Supply, General Staff, Reports and Studies Relating to Various Personnel Matters, Box 144, NARA.

14. Ruth N. Beane, "Impressions in World War I with the Y.W.C.A.: War Brides, June 4 to November 18," unpublished handwritten account, Ruth N. Beane Irving papers, Archives of the Young Women's Christian Association—National Board, New York City, New York (hereafter YWCA Archives); "Report of Work, 1917–1920," unpublished typescript, World War I Files, Overseas Committee, "Reports," YWCA Archives; report of Harriet Taylor, 15 November 1919, unpublished typescript, World War I Files, Overseas Committee, "Misc. Reports and Correspondence," YWCA Archives.

15. Beane, "Impressions in World War I"; "Report, Red Cross Representative who accompanied transport Pocahontas carrying English war brides" (1919), unpublished typescript, ARC papers, NARA.

16. "Report of Work, 1917–1920" (unpublished typescript), World War I Files, Overseas Committee, "Reports," YWCA Archives.

17. "Cooperation with Army," 15 October 1920 (New York: YWCA, 1920), 178.

18. Numerous documents in American Red Cross and YWCA files speak to the influence that the reports sent home by AEF workers had on the thinking of U.S. leadership of these organizations. See, for example, internal memo of R. C. Branion, Director of ARC Civilian Relief, Atlantic Division, to John McCandless, Director Civilian Relief, National Headquarters, American Red Cross, 7 August 1920, ARC papers, NARA.

19. "Report of the Hostess House at Brest, May to June 1919," World War I Files, Overseas Committee, "Reports," YWCA Archives. The internationalism of the YWCA is documented in the reports and correspondence of its Migration Service, also contained in the World War I Files, Reel 154, and in its Department on Work for Foreign-Born Women. The Migration Service established an office to assist would-be immigrants to the United States; their work included tutoring to enable women barred from the United States by the literacy exclusion to pass the test. Also see Nancy Boyd, *Emissaries: The Overseas Work of the American YWCA, 1895–1970* (New York: Woman's Press, 1986).

20. Elizabeth Hutchin, Memo to Emmet W. White, Department of Civilian Relief, American Red Cross, Washington, DC, 31 October 1919, ARC papers, NARA; Jane Dixon, "It's Love's Blue Monday for the Doughboy Now Who Took Himself a War Bride," *Atlanta Constitution*, 14 September 1919, C3; Mary Lee, undated letters to her family, January and February 1918, Folder 21, Arthur and Elizabeth Schlesinger Library on the History of American Women, Harvard University, Cambridge (hereafter SL). On hostility toward foreign wives, also see Jane M. Hoey to J. Byron Deacon, American Red Cross, 26 March 1919, and Mary Glenn to Frederick Keppel, 6 August 1920, ARC papers, NARA.

21. Beane, "Impressions in World War I"; "Doughboys and French Girls," *New York Times*, 11 May 1919, sec. 4, p. 7.

22. Maude Cleveland, YWCA Antwerp, to Mary Willcox Glenn, 1 July 1920; Mary Willcox Glenn to Frederick Paul Keppel, 6 August 1920; and R. C. Branion to John McCandless, 7 August 1920; ARC papers, NARA; Susan Zeiger, "U.S. Soldiers and French, German and Siberian Women," Thirteenth Berkshire Conference on the History of Women, Scripps College, Claremont, California, 2–5 June 2005.

23. Maude Cleveland (YWCA, Antwerp), to Mrs. John M. Glenn (Home Service Section, American Red Cross, New York district), 1 July 1920; "War Brides—English," unsigned report, 3 February 1919; Jane M. Hoey to J. Byron Deacon, ARC Atlantic Division, interoffice memo, 26 March 1919; ARC 1917–1934, Box 604, ARC papers, NARA.

24. R. C. Branion, Director, Civilian Relief Atlantic Division, to John McCandless, Civilian Relief National Headquarters, 7 August 1920; Mary Glenn, New York County Home Service, to Frederick Keppel, Director, Foreign Operations, August 1920; Maude Cleveland to Mary Glenn, 1 July 1920; L. E. Stein, Ass't. Director, to Frederick Moran, Director, Civilian Relief, 20 October 1920; Frederick Moran to L. E. Stein, 29 July 1920; Livingston Farrand, Chair, ARC Executive Committee, to Secretary of War Weeks, 30 June 1921; and Weeks to Farrand, 13 July 1921, ARC papers, NARA.

25. John Higham, *Strangers in the Land: Patterns of American Nativism 1860–1925*, 2nd ed. (New York: Atheneum, 1985), 195, 222.

26. Emily S. Rosenberg, *Spreading the American Dream: American Economic and Cultural Expansion, 1890–1945* (New York: Hill and Wang, 1982), chap. 6; Charles DeBenedetti, *Origins of the Modern American Peace Movement, 1915–1929* (Millwood, NY: KTO

Press, 1978), and *The Peace Reform in American History* (Bloomington: Indiana University Press, 1980). Examples of articles expressing a moderate to liberal position on immigration restriction include Lyman Abbott, "At the Gate," *Outlook* 126 (29 December 1920), 748–749; Elias Tobenkin, "The Immigrant Speaks," *Collier's* 65 (27 March 1920), 20; editorial, "A Truce to Immigration," *New Republic* 25 (22 December 1920), 95–96.

27. Quoted in Higham, *Strangers in the Land*, 227–228; *New York Times*, 27 November 1920, 12.

28. Roy L. Garis, *Immigration Restriction* (New York: Macmillan, 1927), 142–143; Harold Knutson, "The Incomparable Migration," *Outlook* 126 (29 December 1920), 763–765; Higham, *Strangers in the Land*, chap. 11.

29. Nancy F. Cott, *Public Vows: A History of Marriage and the Nation* (Cambridge: Harvard University Press, 2000), chap. 6.

30. Immigration Commission, *Importation and Harboring of Women for Immoral Purposes*, U.S. Senate, 61st Cong., 3rd sess. (Washington, DC: Government Printing Office, 1911), 65, 82, 85; Mark Connelly, *The Response to Prostitution in the Progressive Era* (Chapel Hill: University of North Carolina Press, 1980), chap. 3; Barbara Neil Hobson, *Uneasy Virtue: The Politics of Prostitution and the American Reform Tradition* (New York: Basic Books, 1987), 141–147; Garis, *Immigration Restriction*, 114; and Martha Gardner, *The Qualities of a Citizen: Women, Immigration, and Citizenship, 1870–1965* (Princeton: Princeton University Press, 2005), chaps. 3 and 4. Gardner shows a transition in the early twentieth century, when the concept of "sexual slavery" previously associated with Asian women came to be applied to white Europeans, based on an evolving belief "that prostitution could be linked to racialized ethnic categories." For a critique of the commission's study, see Gardner, *Qualities of a Citizen*, 60, and Ruth Rosen, *The Lost Sisterhood: Prostitution in America, 1900–1918* (Baltimore: John Hopkins University Press, 1982), 118–119.

31. *New York Times*, 1 October 1920, 5, and editorial, 10; 18 October 1920, 6; 21 October 1920, 4. The Republican Committee's sensational claim depended on a willful misreading of Article XXIII, which was intended to suppress international prostitution, not promote it. In December, the League of Nations Assembly established a commission to write a worldwide standard for the prevention of the traffic in women; *New York Times*, 16 December 1920, 12.

32. Bill Ong Hing, *Making and Remaking Asian America through Immigration Policy, 1850–1990* (Stanford, CA: Stanford University Press, 1993), 54–55. For contract marriage in the immigration restriction drive, also see Garis, *Immigration Restriction*, 326.

33. Cott, *Public Vows*, 148–155.

34. Natalie De Bogory, "Adventurers in Marriage," *Outlook* 128 (17 August 1921), 618–620.

35. Daniel J. Kevles, *In the Name of Eugenics: Genetics and the Uses of Human Heredity* (Cambridge: Harvard University Press, 1995); Kathleen Blee, *Women of the Klan: Racism and Gender in the 1920s* (Berkeley: University of California Press, 1991).

36. Higham, *Strangers in the Land*, 317.

37. Corinne Lowe, "Europe Comes Across," *Saturday Evening Post* 193 (25 December 1920), 18; Kenneth L. Roberts, "Plain Remarks on Immigration for Plain Americans," *Saturday Evening Post* 193 (12 February 1921), 21. This was one installment of a series featured by the *Post* and written by Roberts. Dixon, "It's Love's Blue Monday."

38. Higham, *Strangers*, quotes on pp. 270, 385.

39. "Assimilation of War Brides," *New York Times*, 14 December 1919, XX7; John R. Ellingston, "Paths of French War Brides Are Rocky," *New York Times Magazine*, 2 August 1925, 10.

40. "French Envoys of Cupid in America," *Literary Digest* 64 (14 February 1920), 57–61; *New York Times*, 4 December 1921, 25; Ellingston, "Paths of French War Brides," 10. The *Literary Digest* pointed out with concern that Paris and London newspapers "chuckled" over the story of the French brides "who couldn't stand it over here." Dixon Wecter, *When Johnny Come Marching Home* (New York: Houghton Mifflin, 1944), 67.

41. Mark Wyman, *Round-Trip America: The Immigrants Return to Europe, 1880–1930* (Ithaca: Cornell University Press, 1993), 99–105, 118–122.

42. Moran memo, 29 July 1920; Wakefield to McCandless, 4 September 1919, ARC papers.

43. Wecter, *When Johnny Comes Marching Home*, 340–341; Calvin Hall, "The Instability of Post-war Marriages," *Journal of Social Psychology* 5 (1934), 523–530.

44. J. Herbie DiFonzo, *Beneath the Fault Line: The Popular and Legal Culture of Divorce in Twentieth-Century America* (Charlottesville: University Press of Virginia, 1997); Glenda Riley, *Divorce: An American Tradition* (New York: Oxford University Press, 1991).

45. "Assimilation of War Brides," XX7; Ellingston, "Paths of French War Brides," 10.

46. Frank V. Thompson, *Schooling of the Immigrant* (New York: Harper, 1920); *New Republic* 22 (5 May 1920), 314–317; Noah Jedidiah Pickus, *True Faith and Allegiance: Immigration and American Civic Nationalism* (Princeton: Princeton University Press, 2005).

47. Report of Harriet Taylor, 15 November 1919, Misc. Reports and Corr., YWCA; "Overseas Openings, May 1920" (unpublished report), World War I Files, Overseas Committee, "Status of Work in Europe," YWCA Archives.

48. Mary Margaret McBride, "All French War Brides Didn't Make the Mistake of Their Lives," *New York Evening Mail*, c. 1921, news clipping in the Mary Margaret McBride Papers, Motion Picture, Broadcasting, and Recorded Sound Division, Library of Congress, Washington, DC. I am very grateful to Susan Ware for bringing this article to my attention. The career and political outlook of McBride are examined in Susan Ware, *It's One O'Clock and Here Is Mary Margaret McBride: A Radio Biography* (New York: NYU Press, 2005). Other examples of the internationalist point of view in war bride discourse include "At the War Brides' Home," *Independent* 99 (6 September 1919), 328–329, and "French War Brides Happy in America," *New York Times*, 4 December 1921, 25.

49. Hardwick report, 15 April 1919, ARC papers.

50. Edna Wagner, Atlantic Division, American National Red Cross, to Jane Hoey, 10 December 1919; Jane Hoey, Assistant Director, Civilian Relief, Atlantic Division, to Mrs. Donald Wilhelm, ARC, Washington, DC, 26 December, 1919, ARC papers.

51. Col. Charles M. Gandy, Army Medical Corps, to the Field Director, American Red Cross Headquarters Eastern Department, New York, 16 January 1920, ARC papers.

52. Report, Red Cross Representative on the U.S.S. Pocahontas, 1919, ARC papers; Hardwick report, 15 April 1919, ARC papers; "Assimilation of War Brides," *New York Times*, 14 December 1919, XX7.

53. Frances Willison to W. A. Harris, Department of Civilian Relief, Potomac Red Cross, 28 July 1919; Colonel Roger Brooke, memo to Chief Surgeon, Department of the East, Governors Island, NY, 13 January 1920, ARC papers, NARA. Also "Report of Hostess House, Brest, May 1919," unpublished typescript, complete.

54. Jane M. Hoey to J. Byron Deacon, 26 March 1919, ARC papers, NARA.

55. "Changed Fiances," *New York Times*, 22 June 1920, 4.

56. Frances Willison to W. A. Harris, Department of Civilian Relief, Potomac Red Cross, 28 July 1919, ARC papers, NARA.

57. Beane, "Impressions in World War I"; Jane M. Hoey, memo to J. Byron Deacon, Atlantic Division, American National Red Cross, 26 March 1919, ARC papers, NARA.

58. Captain William Lewis to Frances Willison, 29 July 1919, ARC papers, NARA.

59. L. Cody Marsh to Pacific Division, American Red Cross, July 1920, ARC papers, NARA.

60. *New York Times*, July 14, 1919, 14. This reflected as well the growth of the beauty contest as a form of popular and commercial entertainment in the 1920s. Established during the demobilization of the AEF, the shipboard beauty contest for war brides became a standard feature of American Red Cross recreation on war bride transports during and after World War II.

61. Howard Woolston, "Rating the Nations," *American Journal of Sociology* 22 (1916): 381–390. The French were not included in this study. French-Canadians and Italians both ranked close to the bottom in characteristics that were thought to lead to prostitution, while Germans, English, and Scandinavians were at the top.

62. F. P. Keppell, Vice Chair of ARC, to Adjutant Gen. of the Army, 19 August 1920, ARC papers. Review of "Scarlet Lily," *New York Times*, 31 January 1927, 12; 22 June 1920, 4; 18 February 1920, 8. For another illegitimate baby story, see *New York Times*, 31 January 1920, 6.

63. *New York Times*, 1 December 1928, 12; 13 December 1928, 13; 4 December, 12; 11 December, 14; 12 December, 16, 13 December, 22; 14 December, 11; 18 December, 20.

64. Fifty visa applications were randomly sampled (approximately five each from ten boxes) from the World War I War Bride Visa Applications in RG59, State Department papers, NARA, Washington, DC, to create a database. Information from the visa applications was matched with data about locales and birthplaces from *The Thirteenth Census of the United States, 1910: Population, Reports by State* (Washington, DC: Government Printing Office, 1913); *Census of England and Wales, 1910: Summary Tables, Areas, Houses and Population* (London: Her Majesty's Printers, 1903); and *Annuaire Statistique de la France* (Paris: Imprimerie Nationale, 1904). Hilary Kaiser, *French War Brides in America: An Oral History* (Westport, CT: Praeger, 2008), an important addition to the literature, re-creates the life history of three brides from World War I, all from middle-class families, based on interviews with their adult children.

65. Hardwick, untitled report, 15 April 1919, ARC papers, NARA.

66. "War Brides—English," unsigned report, 3 February 1919; and "Chaperoning War Brides," unpublished American Red Cross article, c. 1919, ARC papers.

67. Hardwick, untitled report, 15 April 1919, ARC papers, NARA.

68. "War Brides—English," unsigned report, 3 February 1919.

69. Harriet H. Macdonald, "At the War Brides' Home," *Independent* 99 (6 September 1919), 328–329. "Doughboys and French Girls," *New York Times*, 11 May 1919, sec. 4, p. 7, reported the observation of other soldiers that the grooms were "of foreign birth, either French or Italian." See also "Chaperoning War Brides," unpublished American Red Cross article, c. 1919, and "War Brides—English," unsigned report, 3 February 1919.

70. List of soldiers who received permission to marry, 23 August 1919; Headquarters, American Forces in Germany, RG 120, Office of Civil Affairs, Entry 1367, Box 1121, NARA. I sampled 10 percent of 737 listed surnames and analyzed these for ethnic origin, using a dictionary of surnames, Elsdon C. Smith, *New Dictionary of American Family Names* (New York: Harper and Row, 1973). One-third were distinctly non-Anglo names, with the largest single group being of German derivation.

71. Nancy Gentile Ford, *Americans All! Foreign-Born Soldiers in World War I* (College Station: Texas A&M University Press, 2001), 5–6, 66–67.

72. Ibid., 123–124.

73. Wyman, *Round-Trip America*, 39–41, 78.

74. *Thirteenth Census of the United States, 1910; Census of England and Wales; Annuaire Statistique de la France* (Paris: Imprimerie Nationale, 1901).

75. YWCA, *Report of the Overseas Committee*, 179–180.

76. Kaiser, *French War Brides*, 9–15.

77. "War Brides—English," 3 February 1919, ARC papers; "German Bride, Lonely, Takes Gas, Tries to Die," *New York Times*, 2 July, 1921, 3.

NOTES TO CHAPTER 3

1. "Girls They Write Home About," *American Magazine* 135 (February 1943), 26–29.

2. *Annual Report of the Immigration and Naturalization Service* (Washington, DC, U.S. Department of Justice, 1948, 1949, and 1950). See tables 9A and 9B, "Alien Spouses and Alien Minor Children of Citizen Members of the United States Armed Forces Admitted under the War Brides Act of December 28, 1945 by Country or Region of Birth" and "Alien Fiancees or Fiances of Members of the Armed Forces of the United States under the Act of June 29, 1946, by Country or Region of Birth," for data on the distribution and number of "war bride" marriages. The figure of 125,000 as an estimate of military marriage is almost certainly an undercount to some degree; it may exclude, among others, couples who made their own private arrangements for transportation and immigration processing—couples, perhaps, who were denied permission to wed by the military or who missed the deadlines for filing. It also excludes marriages in which the couple chose to live together outside the United States and those in which the wife did not emigrate to the United States to live with her husband. However, the estimate of 1 million war brides as a result of World War II, from the study by Shukert and Scibetta, is without support in the available data and certainly a substantial overestimate—one that has been widely cited. There was no postwar immigrant influx of that magnitude attributable to military spouses. Elfrieda Berthiaume Shukert and Barbara Smith Scibetta, *War Brides of World War II* (Novato, CA: Presidio Press, 1988), 1–2.

3. "The Problem of Marriages in the European Theater of Operations," report of the Past Affairs Department, History Subsection ETOUSA, April 1944, RG 498, ETO Historical Division, Administrative Files, 1942–1946, Box 129, NARA; Nancy Ashcraft et al., "Here Come the Brides! A Study of the Nature of the Adjustment of Foreign Born War Brides in Greater Cleveland with Reference to Contributing Factors and Implications for the Use of Community Resources" (a joint master's thesis, School of Applied Social Science, Western Reserve University, 1948), 17.

4. Bulletin No. 26, GHQ, AEF France, 29 March, 1919; and "Marriage of Soldiers," typescript report, Records of the War Department General and Special Staffs, RG 165, War College Division, Historical Section, Entry 310C, Box 74, NARA; "Problem of Marriages"; War Department Circular 179, 8 June 1942; and ETO Circular No. 20, 28 July 1942, RG 498, NARA. See, for example, the letter from Lieutenant General Andrews, ETO headquarters: "On the ground of common sense you may consider it advisable to discourage marriage, but you cannot do so officially or prevent them by any official act unless they reflect discredit on the military service"; quoted in "Problem of Marriage," 10. David Reynolds points out that the requirement of commanding officer's permission to wed was to some extent a game of mirrors, as a couple married legally under the requirements of a foreign country would be recognized as legally married in the United States. A soldier who wed without permission could be punished only under military, not civil, law, and military benefits of marriage could be withheld from his spouse. David Reynolds, *Rich Relations: The American Occupation of Britain, 1942–1945* (New York: Random House, 1995), 214–215.

5. "Problem of Marriage," 3, 10; Frederick Hagan, Office of the Chief of Chaplains, to Chaplain Karl Darkey, 14 September 1943, RG 247, Chief of Chaplains Decimal File, Marriages (volume IV), NARA.

6. John D'Emilio and Estelle B. Freedman, *Intimate Matters: A History of Sexuality in America*, rev. ed. (Chicago: University of Chicago Press, 1997), 242; Kevin White, *The First Sexual Revolution: The Emergence of Male Heterosexuality in Modern America* (New York: NYU Press, 1992). For the analogous change in sexual mores in Great Britain, see John Costello, *Love, Sex, and War: Changing Values, 1939–1945* (London: Collins, 1985).

7. Nancy K. Bristow, *Making Men Moral: Social Engineering during the Great War* (New York: NYU Press, 1996).

8. Allan M. Brandt, *No Magic Bullet: A Social History of Venereal Disease in the United States since 1880* (New York: Oxford University Press, 1985), 165.

9. "Mediterranean Theater of Operations, Venereal Disease Survey, June–August 1945," World War II Survey Collection: SO 233, RG 330, Records of the Office of the Secretary of Defense, Research Division, NARA.

10. On the repression of African American, female, and gay sexuality during World War II, see Allan Berube, *Coming Out under Fire: The History of Gay Men and Women in World War Two* (New York: Free Press, 1990); Marilyn Hegarty, *Victory Girls, Khaki-Wackies, and Patriotutes: The Regulation of Female Sexuality during World War II* (New York: NYU Press, 2007); and Graham Smith, *When Jim Crow Met John Bull: Black American Soldiers in World War II Britain* (London: Tauris, 1987), chaps. 8 and 9.

11. Berube, *Coming Out under Fire*, 33.

12. Costello, *Love, Sex and War*, 122, 194.

13. Medical scientists had recognized the remarkable success of penicillin for the treatment of venereal infection, but the drug was not widely available to the military until 1944, and even then the medical department limited its distribution (in part through fear that wider availability would become a spur to sexual license). Brandt, *No Magic Bullet*, 161, 172–174.

14. Brandt, *No Magic Bullet*, 163–165. Also on prophylaxis distribution, see Medical Department, U.S. Army, *Preventive Medicine in World War II*, vol. 9, *Special Fields* (Washington, DC: Office of the Surgeon General, Department of the Army, 1969), 69; Pamela Winfield, *Melancholy Baby: The Unplanned Consequences of the G.I.s' Arrival in Europe for World War II* (Westport, CT: Bergin and Garvey, 2000), 3; Reynold, *Rich Relations*, describes used condoms "littering churchyards, school playgrounds, and other secluded places" (321).

15. Leisa Meyer, *Creating G.I. Jane: Sexuality and Power in the Women's Army Corps during World War II* (New York: Columbia University Press, 1996), chap. 5. On the government's suppression of female sexuality at home, consult Hegarty, *Victory Girls*.

16. Brandt, *No Magic Bullet*, 162, 165–170.

17. Beth L. Bailey and David Farber, *The First Strange Place: The Alchemy of Race and Sex in World War II Hawaii* (New York: Free Press, 1992), chap. 3; quote p. 100.

18. Medical Department, U.S. Army, *Preventive Medicine in World War II*, vol. 5, *Communicable Diseases* (Washington, DC: Office of the Surgeon General, Department of the Army, 1960), chap. 10.

19. Ibid.

20. Ibid., 266; table 30. Between 1942 and 1945, the number of cases per year per thousand troops averaged 47 in Europe and 50 in China-Burma-India. Both rates were markedly lower than those in the Mediterranean region, which averaged 91.

21. Ibid., chap. 10.

22. Pamela Winfield, *Melancholy Baby: The Unplanned Consequences of the G.I.s' Arrival in Europe for World War II* (Westport, CT: Bergin and Garvey, 2000), chaps. 3 and 4; Shukert and Scibetta, *War Brides*, 132–133.

23. Frederick Hagan, Office of the Chief of Chaplains, to Chaplain Karl Darkey, 14 September 1943, RG 247, Chief of Chaplains Decimal File, Marriages (vol. 4), NARA.

24. In all four countries, overseas staff of the American Red Cross (ARC) were integrally involved with work on behalf of foreign war brides, a role assigned to the organization by the U.S. military. The existence of detailed ARC and U.S. military records about war brides in the four countries accommodates a close comparative analysis.

There is a very limited historical literature analyzing the overseas work of the American Red Cross. Patrick F. Gilbo, *The American Red Cross: The First Century* (New York: Harper and Row, 1981), provides an organizational perspective. For an anecdotal view, see George Korson, *At His Side: The Story of the American Red Cross Overseas in World War II* (New York: Coward-McCann, 1945). The papers of the American Red Cross at the National Archive, College Park, Maryland, RG 200, are extensive and detailed on the topic of war brides.

25. War bride marriage per thousand U.S. soldiers in Italy was eighteen, in Great Britain, forty-three, and in Australia, fifty-three. These figures are necessarily a rough estimate, as both troop strength and marriage totals are impossible to establish with exactitude. The concentration of troops in a given theater of war is generally expressed by the military in terms of peak troop strength. For those figures I relied on Michael Clodfelter, *Warfare and Armed Conflicts: A Statistical Reference to Casualty and Other Figures, 1500–2000*, 2nd ed. (Jefferson, NC: McFarland, 2001). He gives an estimate of peak troop strength in Italy in early June 1944 of close to half a million—231,306 in the Fifth Army and 265,371 in the Eighth (the latter figure includes Allied soldiers, but the preponderance were American GIs). Peak troop strength for Americans in Australia is variously

estimated between 150,000 and 200,000; I used the figure in the middle. In Britain, peak strength of 1.65 million was achieved just before the cross-channel invasion.

26. Norman Longmate, *The G.I.'s: The Americans in Britain 1942–1945* (New York: Scribner's, 1975), chap. 3; Dwight D. Eisenhower, *Crusade in Europe* (Garden City, NY: Doubleday, 1948), quoted in Longmate, *G.I.'s*, 32; Reynolds, *Rich Relations*, chaps. 7 and 8.

27. Medical Department, U.S. Army, *Preventive Medicine in World War II*, vol. 8, *Civil Affairs* (Washington, DC: Department of the Army, 1976), 396–401.

28. Jenel Virden, *Good-bye, Piccadilly: British War Brides in America* (Urbana: University of Illinois Press, 1996), 20–21.

29. Longmate, *GI's*, 261; Pamela Winfield and Brenda Wilson Hasty, *Sentimental Journey: The Story of the GI Brides* (London: Constable, 1984), 3–4.

30. Virden, *Good-bye*, 29.

31. The Archbishop of Canterbury to the G.O.C. in Chief, U.S. Forces in England, 18 May 1943, RG 498 European Theater of Operations, Historical Division, Administrative File, 1942–1946, Box 39 , NARA.

32. Penny Summerfield, *Women Workers in the Second World War* (London: Croom Helm, 1984); Pat Ayers, *Women at War: Liverpool Women, 1939–1945* (Merseyside: Liver Press, 1988), chaps. 1 and 2; quote from Virden, *Good-bye*, 13.

33. Reynolds, *Rich Relations*, 268.

34. Ayers, *Women at War*, 46–52; oral interview quoted p. 48. Mass Observation conducted a study of women in pubs, published June 1943. On the interaction between women's sexuality, labor, and leisure during war, see Phil Goodman, "'Patriotic Femininity': Women's Morals and Men's Morale during the Second World War," *Gender and History* 10 (August 1998), 278–293; Penny Summerfield, *Reconstructing Women's Wartime Lives: Discourse and Subjectivity in Oral Histories of the Second World War* (New York: Manchester University Press, 1998).

35. Cyril Radcliffe, quoted in Reynolds, *Rich Relations*, 144; also cited by Barbara G. Friedman, *From the Battlefront to the Bridal Suite: Media Coverage of British War Brides* (Columbia: University of Missouri Press, 2007), 59. For Friedman's summary, see page 58.

36. George Korson, *At His Side: The Story of the American Red Cross Overseas in World War II* (New York: Coward-McCann, 1945), chap. 12; Winfield, *Melancholy Baby*, 2–4.

37. Virden, *Good-bye*, 26–29.

38. On the demographics of partners in British-American marriages, see Virden, *Good-bye*, 47, 117–118, 165 nn. 27, 31. Two studies that posed the question of courtship in British-American marriage had roughly congruent findings that 40 percent of couples went out for one year or more before marriage, and the vast majority, more than three months. Only a handful of couples in either study were acquainted three months or less. The required wait period imposed by the government was two months. Betty Eulalia Street, "The Adjustment of Foreign War Brides" (master's thesis, University of North Carolina, 1948), 23, table 1; Ashcraft et al., "Here Come the Brides," 18.

39. Eileen Orton, ed., *These Are My Sisters: World War II War Bride Memories* (Donald, OR: privately printed for the World War II War Brides Association, 2000), 70.

40. In a 1948 study that examined education and parents' occupation, 40 percent of wives and 45 percent of husbands had occupations that can be classified as "working-class"; 40 percent of each group, middle-class; and 15 percent high professional/managerial

occupations. The wives had lower educational attainment as a group: half of the wives had less than twelve years of education, 25 percent had completed twelve years, and 25 percent had at least some college or higher education; of the husbands, 20 percent had completed less than twelve years of schooling, 45 percent were high school graduates, and 35 percent had done at least some college before the war.

Interestingly, the husbands in this study took strong advantage from the push for veteran's postwar education (almost half the men were back in college or graduate school three years after the end of the war), although these findings are not generalizable, since the study was conducted in a "college town." Betty Eulalia Street, "The Adjustment of Foreign War Brides" (master's thesis, University of North Carolina, Chapel Hill, 1948), table 5, p. 79, and table 3, pp. 42a and b.

41. Miss Kathy Lede to ETOUSA headquarters, 15 April 1944, RG 331, SHAEF Special Staff, Headquarters Command, Decimal Correspondence File, 1944–1945 Entry 100, Box 14, NARA.

42. Friedman, *From the Battlefront*, chaps. 4 and 5.

43. Shukert and Scibetta, *War Brides*, 25.

44. *Annual Report of the Immigration and Naturalization Service*, tables 9A and 9B; Virden, *Good-bye*, 2–3. The actual number is likely to be higher, as a substantial number of British-American couples used private, commercial transportation instead of free government transport—25 percent in Virden's 1989 study cohort.

45. E. Daniel Potts and Annette Potts, *Yanks Down Under, 1941–1945: The American Impact on Australia* (Melbourne: Oxford University Press, 1985), 11–12, 29–30; Michael McKernan, *All In: Australia during the Second World War* (Melbourne: Thomas Nelson, 1983), 187; Reynolds, *Rich Relations*, 432.

46. McKernan, *All In*, chap. 7; Potts and Potts, *Yanks Down Under*.

47. *Preventive Medicine*, vol. 5, pp. 285–290.

48. *Brisbane Courier-Mail*, 23 March 1942, reprinted in Annette Potts and Lucinda Strauss, *For the Love of a Soldier: Australian War Brides and Their GIs* (Crows Nest, Australia: Australian Broadcasting Corporation Enterprises, 1987), 38.

49. McKernan, *All In*, 201–204; Potts and Potts, *Yanks Down Under*, chap. 17.

50. McKernan, *All In*, 201.

51. Potts and Strauss, *Love of a Soldier*, 30–31.

52. Potts and Potts, *Yanks Down Under*, chap. 6; McKernan, *All In*, 187–196; George Korson, *At His Side: The Story of the American Red Cross Overseas in World War II* (New York: Coward McCann, 1945), chap. 3.

53. Potts and Potts, *Yanks Down Under*, 320.

54. Ibid., 233–234; John Hammond Moore, *Over-Sexed, Over-Paid, and Over-Here: Americans in Australia, 1941–1945* (Brisbane: University of Queensland Press, 1981); McKernan, *All In*, 196–197. Hammond overstates the incident as a decisive downturn of U.S.-Australian relations during the war; Potts and Potts argue that "there is no evidence that the incident prejudiced community attitudes against other GIs."

55. Jill Julius Matthews, *Good and Mad Women: Historical Constructions of Femininity in Twentieth Century Australia* (Sydney: Allen and Unwin, 1984), 198–199.

56. Carol Fallows, *Love and War: Stories of War Brides from the Great War to Vietnam* (Sydney: Bantam Books, 2002), chaps. 6–10 on Canadian, British, and other brides of

Australian servicemen. On the extramarital birthrate, see Potts and Strauss, *Love of a Soldier*, 44; Potts and Potts, *Yanks Down Under*, 364. These historians attribute the decline in extramarital births not to a drop in pregnancy but to the phenomenon of pregnant couples choosing to wed at a higher rate.

57. Case histories prepared by American Red Cross field staff, Australia, for Major K., Assistant Adjutant General, U.S. Army, RG 200, National American Red Cross papers, Group 3, 1935–1946, Box 985, NARA.

58. Potts and Strauss, *Love of a Soldier*, 44, 50.

59. ARC case histories, RG 200, ARC papers, Box 985, NARA.

60. Potts and Potts, *Yanks Down Under*, 351.

61. Jessie Mary Grey Street (1889–1970), feminist and internationalist, was the founder of the United Associations (later the United Associations of Women), New South Wales affiliate of the Australian Federation of Women Voters. A woman's right to employment, regardless of marital status, was a central issue for Street throughout her long political career. During World War II, in addition to championing the rights of war brides, she agitated against the violation of women's civil liberties in regard to harsh antivenereal measures. Street served in the Australian delegation to the United Nations founding conference in San Francisco, the only woman credentialed by the Australian government. Heather Radi, "Street, Jessie Mary Grey (1889–1970)," *Australian Dictionary of Biography*, vol. 16 (Melbourne: Melbourne University Press, 2002), 328–332.

62. Letters from Street and Eleanor Roosevelt reprinted in Potts and Strauss, *Love of a Soldier*, 60–63. Potts and Potts, *Yanks Down Under*, chaps. 18 and 21; Shukert and Scibetta, *War Brides*, 22–23.

63. Potts and Potts, *Yanks Down Under*, 334; Potts and Strauss, *Love of a Soldier*, 68.

64. Potts and Potts, *Yanks Down Under*, 372–373; Annual Report of the INS, 1950, tables 9A and 9; B. E. E. Salisbury, "Wives and Fiancees of Members of Our Overseas Forces," *Monthly Review, Department of Justice, Immigration and Naturalization Service* 2 (December 1944), 78–79. The INS report noted that three-fifths of the visa petitions received for wives and fiancées of U.S. service members during 1944 were for Australians.

65. Eric Linklater, *The Campaign in Italy* (London: Unwin Brothers, 1977), 5–6; Robert Wallace, *The Italian Campaign* (Alexandria, VA: Time-Life Books, 1978); "The Italian Campaign, September 1943 to May 1945," A Brief History of the U.S. Army in World War II, U.S. Army Center of Military History (CMH online), http://www.army.mil/cmh-pg/overview.htm; Martin Blumenson, *Mediterranean Theater of Operations: Salerno to Cassino, United States Army in World War Two* (Washington, DC: Government Printing Office, 1988).

66. Clodfelter, *Warfare and Armed Conflicts*, 520.

67. *Preventive Medicine*, vol. 5, p. 213.

68. Robert M. Hill and Elizabeth Craig Hill, *In the Wake of War: Memoirs of an Alabama Military Government Officer in World War II Italy* (University: University of Alabama Press, 1982); Wallace, *Italian Campaign*; Donna M. Budani, *Italian Women's Narratives of Their Experiences during World War II* (Lewiston, NY: Edwin Mellen Press, 2003), 36.

69. Ernie Pyle, *Brave Men*, edited edition (Lincoln: University of Nebraska Press, 2001), 124.

70. *Preventive Medicine*, vol. 5, p. 213

71. "Personal Participation in World War II: 'The American Soldier' Surveys," Reference Information Paper no. 78 (compiled by Benjamin DeWhitt and Heidi Ziemer) (Washington, DC: National Archives and Records Administration, 1977); Survey 233, Mediterranean Theater of Operations, "Venereal Disease," June–August 1945, RG 330, Records of the Office of the Secretary of Defense, Research Division, Entry 92, NARA.

72. *Preventive Medicine in World War II*, vol. 5, pp. 211–220.

73. Hill and Hill, *Wake of War*, 20–21.

74. Survey 233.

75. George Korson, *At His Side: The Story of the American Red Cross Overseas in World War II* (New York: Coward-McCann, 1945), 46, 241, 260.

76. Testimony of Cesira Slawson, Italian war bride, interviewed by Gretchen Morgan, n.d., "Immigrant Journeys" website, http://www.immigrantjourneys.com/stories/slawson_italy.html (accessed 12 April 2007); interview with Anna Della Casa Gonzales, "War Brides Gather to Tell Tales," *San Francisco Examiner*, online edition, 31 July 1999, http://www.examiner.com/990801/0801brides.html (accessed 22 May 2000); Luisa Solomito oral history, interviewed by Michelle McCleary, n.d., The American War Bride Experience: GI Brides of World War II, http://www.geocities.com/us_warbrides/; Budani, *Italian Women's Narratives*, 106.

77. Slawson interview, "Immigrant Journeys." Also see Deborah-Ann Giusti, oral history of Marie Muscato, Lexington, MA, 17 March 2002, in the author's possession. I am very grateful to my former student Deborah Giusti and to Mrs. Muscato for giving me permission to use this excellent oral history.

78. Giusti, oral history of Marie Muscato.

79. "Report of the Transport Service, Naples," War Brides Ship Service, July–December 1946, RG 200, ARC papers, Box 986, NARA; Shukert and Scibetta, *War Brides*, 98.

80. Shukert and Scibetta, *War Brides*, 98.

81. "American Red Cross Report, War Bride Operations, 1946," RG 200, National American Red Cross papers, Group 3, 1935–1946, Box 985, War Brides, Mediterranean Theater, NARA. Also see anecdotes in "American Red Cross Narrative Report, USAT Thomas H. Barry, July 1946," including cases of prewar marriage and a teenage bride born in the United States and raised by relatives in Italy after the death of her Irish American mother; RG 200, Box 985, NARA

82. Slawson interview, "Immigrant Journeys."

83. Interview with Anna Della Casa Gonzales, "War Brides Gather to Tell Tales," *San Francisco Examiner*, online edition, 31 July 1999, http://www.examiner.com/990801/0801brides.html (accessed 22 May 2000). Also see head-shaving stories in Shukert and Scibetta, *War Brides*, 100. Hill and Hill, *In the Wake of War*, 99, refers to a trial of a youth gang in Rome that allegedly practiced head shaving against women.

84. Fabrice Virgili, *Shorn Women: Gender and Punishment in Liberation France*, English edition (New York: Berg Press, 2002).

85. Shukert and Scibetta, *War Brides*, 101.

86. "The Trip Back to America," Naples, June 1946, War Brides, Ship Service, July–December 1946, RG 200, ARC papers, Box 986, NARA; Shukert and Scibetta, *War Brides*, 100.

87. Marcella Olschki, *Oh, America* (Palermo: Sellerio Editore, 1996), 27. Selections from Olschki's memoir were translated from Italian for the author by Daria Lewis.

88. Interview with Anna Della Casa Gonzales, "War Brides Gather to Tell Tales." Also see testimony of the same bride in Shukert and Scibetta, *War Brides*, 96–97.

89. Slawson interview, "Immigrant Journeys."

90. Annual Report of the INS, 1950, table 9A. There were substantially more than twice as many American troops deployed in Italy as in Australia, for instance, but this much larger group of soldiers took home a smaller absolute number of war brides. Troop strength in the Italian campaign and Australia is discussed above; see Clodfelter, *Warfare and Armed Conflicts*, 518–522.

91. "MacArthur in Philippines," *Los Angeles Times*, 20 October 1944, 1.

92. *Preventive Medicine*, vol. 8, pp. 575, 593–599, 602.

93. *San Jose Mercury News*, 20 October 1995; linked as "Filipino-American War Brides—Banana Leaves for Shoes," The American War Bride Experience: GI Brides of World War II, http://www.geocities.com/us_warbrides/.

94. *Preventive Medicine*, vol. 8, pp. 595–608.

95. Maureen C. Pagaduan, "Leaving Home: Filipino Women Surviving Migration," in Sadhna Arya and Anupama Roy, eds., *Poverty, Gender and Migration* (Thousand Oaks, CA: Sage, 2006), chap. 2.

96. *Preventive Medicine*, vol. 8, p. 608; vol. 5, pp. 290–302.

97. *Preventive Medicine*, vol. 8, pp. 584–585. The Southwest Pacific Area command remained dissatisfied with venereal infection rates in the Philippines and called in a team of consultants for the army's surgeon general to assess the situation. Their report, submitted in June 1945, made eleven major recommendations, including the "vigorous" enforcement of laws for the legal suppression of prostitution. It is not clear whether these recommendations were implemented in the postwar period; see vol. 5, pp. 291–299.

98. "Filipino-American War Brides"; Caridad Concepcion Vallangca, *The Second Wave: Pinay and Pinoy (1945–1960)* (San Francisco: Strawberry Hill Press, 1987), oral history of Lydia Pataki, pp. 64–70. Shukert and Scibetta also discuss dating among elite Filipinos and American service personnel; *War Brides*, 200–203.

99. Posada, *Filipino Americans*, 22–24. Filipino immigration to the United States was sharply curtailed in 1934 by the Tydings-McDuffie Act, which pledged independence for the Philippine Islands in ten years but immediately imposed an immigration quota of fifty persons per year. Juanita Tamayo Lott, "Demographic Changes Transforming the Filipino American Community," in Maria P. P. Root, ed., *Filipino Americans: Transformation and Identity* (Thousand Oaks, CA: Sage, 1997), 11–20. In 1940 the Filipino population in the United States was 80,835 males and 17,700 females, according to Lott.

100. Interview with Felipe Dumlao, 22 November 1975, Washington State Oral/Aural History Program, 1974–1977 (microfiche) Washington State Archives, Olympia, WA, 1977. I am grateful to Chris Capozzola for directing me to this valuable collection of oral histories.

101. Shukert and Scibetta, *War Brides*, 200–203. Neither the American Red Cross, the military, nor the Justice or State Department broke down or maintained any figures on the racial/ethnic background of GI husbands, so information is necessarily anecdotal.

102. *Pittsburgh Courier*, 22 December 1951, 2.

103. Train Service report, 4 November 1946, RG 200, ARC papers, Box 986, NARA.

104. Memo "Re: War Brides aboard the General Patrick," 11 February 1948; also on the poverty of Filipina brides, typescript report, "War Bride Program in the Philippines," 27 April 1947, RG 200, ARC papers, Box 985, NARA.

105. Gilbo, *The American Red Cross*, 167.

106. American Red Cross, Military Welfare Service, "Subject: Phillipine [*sic*] War Brides," various correspondence, 21 and 27 December 1946 and 21 July, 6 October, 11 October 1948, RG 200, National American Red Cross papers, Group 4, 1947–1964, Box 985 (Folder: "War Brides, Philippines"), NARA.

107. Vallangca, *Second Wave*, 59–60; Nilda Rimonte, "Colonialism's Legacy: The Inferiorizing of the Filipino," in Root, *Filipino Americans*, 39–61.

108. *Annual Report of the INS*, 1950, table 9A.

109. Ronald Takaki, *Strangers from a Different Shore: A History of Asian Americans* (Boston: Little, Brown, 1989), 417; Barbara M. Posadas, *The Filipino Americans* (Westport, CT: Greenwood Press, 1999), 27; Vallangca, *Second Wave*, 57–76. Takaki calls the entry of Chinese and Filipina war brides as non-quota immigrants "the most important [immigration] loophole" in the wake of World War II to build Asian American communities.

110. Penny Summerfield, *Reconstructing Women's Wartime Lives: Discourse and Subjectivity in Oral Histories of the Second World War* (New York: St. Martin's Press, 1998); Budani, *Italian Women's Narratives*; Sherna Berger Gluck, *Rosie the Riveter Revisited: Women, the War and Social Change* (Boston: Twayne, 1987).

111. My analysis of war brides' narration of intercultural relationships is based on the following texts: Jill Newman, *Rain, Rain, Go Away: Story of a G.I. Bride* (Braunton, Devon: Merlin Books, 1991); Irene Hope Hedrick, *Memories of a Big Sky British War Bride* (Guilford, CT: Globe Pequot Press, 2006); Margaret Wharton *Recollections of a GI War Bride: A Wiltshire Childhood* (Gloucester: Sutton, 1984); Vera A. Cracknell Long, *From Britain with Love: World War II Pilgrim Brides* (New Market, VA: Denecroft, 1999) (collects the first-person accounts of more than thirty-five World War II British brides); Pamela Winfield, *Melancholy Baby: The Unplanned Consequences of the G.I.'s Arrival in Europe for World War II* (Westport, CT: Bergin and Garvey, 2000); Olschki, *Oh, America!*; Monette Goetinck, *Bottled Dreams* (Napa, CA: Abbott/Adele Books, 1998); Mathilde Morris, *Dreams and Nightmares of a German War Bride* (Aurora, CO: Cambridge Writers Press, 1998); Potts and Strauss, *For the Love of a Soldier* (collects the first-person accounts of eighteen World War II Australian brides); and oral histories collected at the World War II War Brides Reunion, Newport, RI, October 2001, by the author, Professor Wendy Lement, and students in our oral history and performance course, Regis College.

112. Testimony of Cesira Slawson, Italian war bride, interviewed by Gretchen Morgan, n.d., "Immigrant Journeys" website, http://www.immigrantjourneys.com/stories/slawson_italy.html (accessed 12 April 2007).

113. Priti Ramamurthy, Alys Eve Weinbaum, Madeleine Yue Dong, Uta G. Poiger, Lynn M. Thomas, and Tani E. Barlow, "The Modern Girl around the World: Six Case Studies," Schlesinger Library Symposium, 16 March 2007, Radcliffe Institute for Advanced Study, Harvard University, Cambridge; "The Modern Girl Project," depts.washington. edu/its/moderngirlmain.htm; Jill Julius Matthews, *Dance Hall and Picture Palace: Sydney's Romance with Modernity* (Sydney: Currency Press, 2005).

114. Potts and Strauss, *Love of a Soldier*, 47.

115. Marilyn Lake, "The Desire for a Yank: Sexual Relations between Australian Women and American Servicemen during World War II," *Journal of the History of Sexuality* 2 (1992): 621–633; Maureen C. Meadows, "I Loved Those Yanks" (Sydney: George M. Dash, 1948), 50; also quoted in Lake, "Desire for a Yank," 627.

116. Personal interview with Jacqueline Xindaris, WWII War Brides Reunion, Newport, RI.

117. Kerry Segrave, *American Films Abroad: Hollywood's Domination of the World's Movie Screens* (Jefferson, NC: McFarland, 1997). Also see Matthews, *Dance Hall*, chap. 5.

118. On Hollywood and overseas perceptions of American soldiers, see Lake, "Desire for a Yank," 629–630; Hedrick, *Big Sky*, 65; Winfield, *Melancholy Baby*, 3; Long, *From Britain with Love*, 67, 131; Goetinck, *Bottled Dreams*, 4, 25; Newman, *Rain, Rain, Go Away*, 27, 45, 57.

119. On Red Cross clubs as a site of romance, see, for example, Muscato interview; Winfield, *Melancholy Baby*, 2–4.

120. Hedrick, *Big Sky*, 63–64; Goetinck, *Bottled Dreams*, 15, 21–22, 29, 49; quote from Lake, "Desire for a Yank," 631. Also see, for commodities, Newman, *Rain, Rain, Go Away*, 51; Long, *From Britain with Love*, 67, 149; many oral histories.

121. Long, *From Britain with Love*, 67.

122. Ibid., 67, 149, 63, 105.

123. Goetinck, *Bottled Dreams*, 5, 19.

124. Long, *From Britain with Love*, 71; Jackie Xindaris interview, WWII War Brides Reunion, Newport, RI.

125. Friedman, *From the Battlefront to the Bridal Suite*, 25; Shukert and Scibetta, *War Brides*, 30–32, 78–82.

126. Newman, *Rain, Rain, Go Away*, 61. Newman's memoir has a second act that sets it apart from the majority of war bride narratives: her American husband turns out to be an abusive alcoholic, and Newman describes her courageous and ultimately successful struggle to free herself from his grip and establish an independent life in the United States. Other war bride narratives I characterize as "survivor's tales" are Morris, *Dreams and Nightmares*, and Goetinck, *Bottled Dreams*. It is fascinating that all three writers fully embrace their adopted identity as Americans, though being American to them means something different than being an American army wife.

127. Potts and Strauss, *Love of a Soldier*, 71–72; Reynolds, *Rich Relations*, 417–418.

128. For an excellent treatment of maternalist politics in historical and contemporary scenarios of female activism, see Alexis Jetter, Annelise Orleck, and Diana Taylor, *The Politics of Motherhood: Activist Voices from the Left to Right* (Hanover, NH: University Press of New England, 1997).

129. "British Brides," *Life*, 19 November 1945, 45–48; "'Ome Is Where the 'Eart Is," *Newsweek*, 22 October 1945, 58; Reynolds, *Rich Relations*, 418; Shukert and Scibetta, *War Brides*, 37–39.

130. Reynolds, *Rich Relations*, 418.

NOTES TO CHAPTER 4

1. George Kent, "Brides from Overseas," *Reader's Digest* 47 (September 1945), 97–98.

2. Malvina Lindsay, "The Gentler Sex," *Washington Post*, 6 February 1946, 14.

3. Elaine Tyler May, *Homeward Bound: American Families in the Cold War Era*, rev. ed. (New York: Basic Books, 1999).

4. Margaret Mead, "What's the Matter with the Family," *Harper's Magazine* 190 (April 1945), 393–399; *War Marriage and Its Problems: Proceedings of the Annual Institute on Marriage and Home Adjustment*, Pennsylvania State College, State College, PA, October

23–25, 1944; Samuel Tenenbaum, "The Fate of Wartime Marriages," *American Mercury* 61 (November 1945), 530–536; William K. Reed, "One Out of Three Breaks Up," *New Republic* 116 (24 March 1947), 17–20; William M. Tuttle, Jr., *Daddy's Gone to War: The Second World War in the Lives of America's Children* (New York: Oxford University Press, 1993), chap. 5.

5. See titles listed in the extensive bibliography, "Conserving Marriage in Wartime," appendix to *War Marriage and Its Problems*, 113–115.

6. Charles G. Bolte, "The Veterans' Runaround," *Harper's* 190 (April 1945), 391–392; Willard Waller, "Why Veterans Are Bitter," *American Mercury* 61 (August 1945), 147–154. Patrick J. Kelly, *Creating a National Home: Building the Veterans' Welfare State, 1860–1900* (Cambridge: Harvard University Press, 1997), 70–71, discusses fear of Civil War veterans as a factor in postwar social policy, though concepts of political entitlement played a stronger role, Kelly contends, in the mobilization of social resources for veterans' care. Kimberly Jensen, *Mobilizing Minerva: American Women in the First World War* (Chicago: University of Illinois Press, 2008), connects postwar anxiety about veterans as discontented radicals to the construction of a new ideal in the 1920s, the "consumer-civilian," married to a contented and dependent consumer-wife; see chap. 8.

7. "Veterans: Better Than Most," *Newsweek* 28(2 December 1946), 34–35.

8. Michael J. Bennett, *When Dreams Came True: The G.I. Bill and the Making of Modern America* (Washington, DC: Brassey's, 1996).

9. "Gangplank Marriages," in *War Marriage and Its Problems*, 83.

10. Nancy F. Cott, *Public Vows: A History of Marriage and the Nation* (Cambridge: Harvard University Press, 2000); Margot Canaday, "Building a Straight State: Sexuality and Social Citizenship under the 1944 G. I. Bill," *Journal of American History* 90 (December 2003), 935–957.

11. Tenenbaum, "Fate of Wartime Marriages."

12. Letter to editor, *New York Times Magazine*, 24 February 1946, 89; Isabelle Mallet, "Marriage Banns across the Sea," *New York Times Magazine*, 26 November 1944, 20.

13. Miss Marilyn Penner to the War Department, 3 July 1942, RG 247, Chief of Chaplains Decimal File 1920–1945, NARA; letter to Senator Theodore F. Green, quoted in Vera A. Cracknell Long, *From Britain with Love: World War II Pilgrim Brides Sail to America* (New Market, VA: Denecroft, 1999), 55.

14. Letters to the editor, *Ebony*, November 1951 and June 1953, quoted in Paul R. Spickard, *Mixed Blood: Intermarriage and Ethnic Identity in Twentieth-Century America* (Madison: University of Wisconsin Press, 1989), 302.

15. See, for example, testimonies of British war brides in Long, *From Britain with Love*, 81, 135; Norma Lee Browning, "They Like It Here," *Chicago Daily Tribune*, 27 October 1946, B8; and Frances Van der Meid, "Those English Brides," *Christian Science Monitor*, 25 May 1946, 5.

16. Lindsay, "Gentler Sex," 14; Browning, "They Like It Here," B8. On Americans' attraction to domesticity to counteract Cold War anxiety, see Elaine Tyler May, *Homeward Bound: American Families in the Cold War Era*, rev. ed. (New York: Basic Books, 1999).

17. Elfrieda Berthiaume Shukert and Barbara Smith Scibetta, *War Brides of World War II* (Novato, CA: Presidio Press, 1988).

18. David Reimers, *Other Immigrants: The Global Origins of the American People* (New York: NYU Press, 2005), 175–177. Historians of Asian American history, Ronald Takaki

and others, have interpreted the McCarran Walter Act more favorably, due to its elimination of the long-standing and racist Asian exclusion feature, but this change was symbolic rather than structural, as each Asian nation was given only 100 immigration slots annually under the discriminatory quota system retained by McCarran Walter. Ronald Takaki, *Strangers from a Different Shore: A History of Asian Americans* (Boston: Little, Brown, 1989), 417.

19. The term "martial citizenship" is defined by Kelly, *Creating a National Home*, 2. See also Theda Skocpol, *Protecting Soldiers and Mothers: The Political Origins of Social Policy in the United States* (Cambridge: Harvard University Press, 1992), 149. On the mechanisms for the exclusion of Asian wives, and later, their entry, see Shukert and Scibetta, *War Brides*, chaps. 13 and 14.

20. Shukert and Scibetta, *War Brides*, chaps. 13 and 14.

21. U.S. Congress, House Committee on Immigration and Naturalization, Subcommittee Hearings, "To Facilitate the Admission to the U.S. of Husbands, Wives and Children of U.S. Citizen Men and Women Who Have Served Honorably in the Armed Forces of the U.S. during the Present World War," 16 May, 23 May, 26 September, 26, 27, and 29 November 1945, 79th Cong., 1st sess., 1945 (House Unpublished Hearings Collection). The American Legion opposed the end of Chinese restriction, adopted by Congress in 1943. The Legion also called for the postwar deportation of all war refugees from the United States, another expression of its anti-immigrant views. *Reports to the Twenty-fifth Annual National Convention of the American Legion, 1943* (n.p., American Legion, 1943), 230, and *Reports to the Twenty-seventh Annual National Convention of the American Legion, 1945* (n.p., American Legion, 1945), 258–259.

22. *New York Times*, 12 October 1946, 8; House Hearings, 32.

23. House Hearings, 31–32; *Biographical Directory of the United States Congress*: George Gregory Sadowski (1903–1961), Democrat, MI; served in Congress 1933–1939 and 1943–1951, http://bioguide.congress.gov (accessed 4 October 2006).

24. *Biographical Directory of U.S. Congress*: Samuel Dickstein (1885–1954), served in Congress 1923–1945 (Dickstein was a Jew, born near Vilna, Russia); Joseph Farrington (1897–1954), served in Congress 1943–1954; Ed Lee Gossett (1902–1990), served 1939–1951, http://bioguide.congress.gov (accessed 5 October 2006). Gossett was a leading figure in the fight against the Displaced Persons Act of 1948 and for the Internal Security Act of 1950, two important causes of the political right. See the finding aid for the Ed Lee Gossett papers, Baylor University, Collections of Political Materials, Congressional papers, www3. Baylor.edu/Library/BCPM/Gossett (accessed 10 October 2006).

25. *Biographical Directory of U.S. Congress*: Asa Leonard Allen (1891–1969), served in Congress 1937–1952, http://bioguide.congress.gov (accessed 10 October 2006).

26. Jenel Virden, *Good-bye, Piccadilly: British War Brides in America* (Urbana: University of Illinois Press, 1996), 81–82 and n. 46. Also Scibetta and Shukert, *War Brides*, chaps. 4 and 5. Barbara G. Friedman, *From the Battlefront to the Bridal Suite: Media Coverage of British War Brides, 1942–1946* (Columbia: University of Missouri Press, 2007), provides a useful media analysis based on several U.S. women's magazines, the *New York Times*, two British daily papers, and several armed services publications. She traces a trajectory from wartime press hostility to postwar acceptance of the relationships. A sampling of this media barrage can be seen in the notes that follow.

27. "Life Records an Anglo-American Romance," *Life* 18 (1 January 1945), 71–74.

28. Cited in David Reynolds, *Rich Relations: The American Occupation of Britain* (New York: Random House, 1995), 417.

29. *Kine Weekly* 67 (6 September 1946), 2. Because almost all war-themed scripts were submitted to the War Department for review, the full script for *GI War Brides* can be found in the National Archives, RG 107, Office of the Secretary of War, Bureau of Public Relations, Motion Picture Scripts, Entry 354, Box 15, NARA.

30. "41 Brides Tour Mart and Have English Lunch," *Chicago Daily Tribune*, 20 February 1946, 19; "Bishop Asks Aid for War Brides," *New York Times*, 23 February 1946, 11.

31. "Weekly Nursery to Aid War Brides," *New York Times*, 3 April 1947, 29.

32. Daniel Green, National American Red Cross, Home Service Department report, quoted in Betty Eulalia Street, "The Adjustment of Foreign War Brides" (master's thesis, University of North Carolina, 1948). Similarly, a reporter for the *Ladies' Home Journal* imagined one British wife in a sunbonnet "walk[ing] beside the covered wagons"; Jessamyn West, "Meet an Overseas War Bride," *Ladies' Home Journal* 63 (August 1946), 127–132.

33. *New York Times*, 31 May 1945, 22; Marjorie Cassels, "GI Schools for Brides," *Christian Science Monitor*, 26 May 1945, 9; West, "Meet an Overseas War Bride," 127–132.

34. *New York Times Magazine*, 10 February 1946, 89; *New York Times*, 11 February 1946, 1.

35. "Homecoming: Australian Wives and Sweethearts of U.S. GI Joes," *Time* 43 (1 May 1944), 19; "Australian Wives," *Life* 17 (10 July 1944), 43–46; "Entangling Alliances," *Newsweek* 19 (6 April 1942), 22; *New York Times*, 16 May 1944, 17; 13 August 1944, 27; 9 March 1946, 15; 10 March 1946, 9.

36. "90 Aussie Girls Wed and to Be Wed, Reach U.S.," *Chicago Daily Tribune*, 20 April 1944, 7; Thomas-Durrell Young, *Australian, New Zealand, and United States Security Relations, 1951–1986* (Boulder, CO: Westview Press, 1992).

37. Albert Jonsson, *Iceland, NATO and the Keflavik Base* (Reykjavík: Icelandic Commission on Security and International Affairs, 1989); Benedikt Grondal, *Iceland: From Neutrality to NATO Membership* (Oslo: Universitetsforlaget, 1971).

38. *New York Times*, 27 August 1945, 21; "I Married a Yank," *American Magazine* 138 (July 1944), 33; "Overseas Brides," *Yank*, 16 November 1945, 6.

39. Long, *From Britain with Love*, 67.

40. Nancy Ashcraft et al., "Here Come the Brides! A Study of the Nature of the Adjustment of Foreign War Brides in Greater Cleveland with Reference to Contributing Factors and Implications for the Use of Community Resources" (a joint master's thesis, School of Applied Social Science, Western Reserve University, 1948). The Western Reserve University study is the most methodologically sound of any war bride research in that the authors did a random selection of more than 100 subjects based on Red Cross and government information on all war brides known to have settled in the Cleveland area after the war. See also Betty Eulalia Street," The Adjustment of Foreign War Brides" (master's thesis, University of North Carolina, Chapel Hill, 1948), as well as social science studies I discuss in chapter 5.

41. Jessamyn West, "Reunion Half a World from London Bridge," *Ladies' Home Journal* 63 (August 1946), 127–132; Long, *From Britain with Love*, 80; other war bride recollections of wartime trauma on pp. 67, 79, 84. Also see "Overseas Brides," *Yank*, 16 November 1945, 6.

42. Frances Van der Meid, "Those English Brides," *Christian Science Monitor*, 25 May 1946, 5; Lee E. Graham, "Yank on a Pedestal," *New York Times*, 13 April 1947, 152; "In Defense of War Brides," letter to the editor, *Chicago Daily Tribune*, 10 March 1946, 20.

43. David Lamson, "Bride from over the Water," *Saturday Evening Post* 219 (9 November 1946), 28.

44. *New York Times*, 8 August 1946, 21.

45. Short autobiographical sketches, written in a reunion-booklet format, were submitted by 180 war brides and published by the World War II War Brides Association: Eileen Orton, ed., *These Are My Sisters: World War II War Bride Memories* (Donald, OR: privately printed for the World War II War Brides Association, 2000). A data sample drawn from these sketches shows an average family size of 2.9 children, similar to but slightly below the 3-plus figure given for childbearing women in the early 1950s. Many of these war brides also list diverse and interesting work histories, a plausible explanation for the slightly lower birth trend in the group. On the propensity toward large families in the postwar years, see May, *Homeward Bound*, 14.

46. *Chicago Daily Tribune*, 19 January 1946, 7; 5 February 1946, 1; 6 February 1946, 8; 12 February 1946, 7; 9 March 1946, 6; *New York Times*, 11 February 1946, 1; 19 March 1946, 13. The baby died after nine hours despite the emergency delivery of oxygen. Also see *New York Times*, 27 January 1946, 31; 17 January 1946, 22; 22 April 1946, 22; *Washington Post*, 11 February 1946, 1.

47. Van der Meid, "Those English Brides"; "I Married a Yank."

48. Lindsay, "Gentler Sex."

49. *New York Times*, 23 May 1946, 23; 24 May 1946, 38; 27 May 1946, 18; 30 May 1946, 24; 6 June 1946, 20; *Chicago Tribune*, 22 May 1946, 1; 8 June 1946, 1; 28 August 1946, 20; 29 August 1946, 34. At the time the report was completed, nine infants had died, all the children of continental European mothers. However, two subsequent deaths were to British mothers whose transport sailed from Southampton, England.

50. Joyce Bryan Vonstrahl, "Horrors on Board the Zebulon B. Vance," The American War Bride Experience: GI Brides of World War II, http://www.geocities.com/us_warbrides/ww2warbrides.html.

51. In addition to the Peggy Poland case, see "Bride Fleeing Hick GI Gets Child Back," *Los Angeles Times*, 10 February 1948, 7, a transatlantic custody case; and the Bridget Waters case, *Los Angeles Times*, 7 November 1946, 6; 8 September 1946, 3; 26 October 1946, 2; 2 November 1946, 4; 31 October 1946, 2.

52. I am indebted to Kathy Abrams, Boalt School of Law, University of California–Berkeley, for her comments on the legal issues in the case.

53. *Okaloosa News-Journal*, 1 August 1947, 1; 29 August 1947, 1; *Washington Post*, 29 July 1947, B8; 29 August 1947, 5; *New York Times*, 29 August 1947, 10; personal correspondence and telephone conversations with Ann Spann, North Okaloosa Historical Association and Baker Block Museum, Baker, Florida, January and February 2004. I am deeply grateful to Ann Spann for locating these news stories from microfilmed newspapers and for speaking with me about the case. Bridget Waters was sentenced to one to five years, with release after ten months for good behavior; *Los Angeles Times*, 7 November 1946, 6.

54. *Chicago Daily Tribune*, 5 May 1946, W5; Norma Lee Browning, "They Like It Here," *Chicago Daily Tribune*, 27 October 1946, B8; *New York Times*, 13 February 1946, 29.

55. West "Reunion Half a World from London Bridge." For clothes, shoes, and shopping sprees, also see "Australian Wives," *Life* 17 (10 July 1944), 43–46; *Chicago Daily Tribune*, 5 March 1946, 13; "They're Bringing Home Japanese Wives," *Saturday Evening Post* 224 (19 January 1952), 26.

56. See Jensen's important discussion, *Mobilizing Minerva*, chap. 8.

57. Lizabeth Cohen, *A Consumers' Republic: The Politics of Mass Consumption in Postwar America* (New York: Knopf, 2003), 11.

58. Yuka Tsuchiya, "Military Occupation as Pedagogy: American Women in the U.S. Occupation of Japan, 1945–1952," Thirteenth Berkshire Conference on the History of Women, Scripps College, Claremont, CA, June 2–5, 2005; May, *Homeward Bound*, chap. 7.

59. Browning, "They Like It Here"; *Chicago Daily Tribune*, 5 May 1946, W5. On the significance of radio in the lives of midcentury homemakers, see Susan Ware, *It's One o'Clock and Here Is Mary Margaret McBride: A Radio Biography* (New York: NYU Press, 2005), chaps. 3–6.

60. Joyce R. Brandt, "A G.I. Bride at Home," *New York Times Magazine*, 17 March 1946, 15. Although the article makes no mention of the woman's life beyond consumerism, the number of dresses, seven, suggests the possibility that she might have had or anticipated having a career, and thus needed a different outfit for each workday; I am grateful to Grey Osterud for this insight. For brides' admiration of American consumer goods, also see Gertrude Samuels, "40,000 GI Brides Appraise Us," *New York Times Magazine*, 1 December 1946, 11; and West, "Reunion Half a World from London Bridge."

61. The story broke on the front page, and the trial was well covered in subsequent months; *New York Times*, 5 January 1947, 1; 6 January 1947, 10; 8 January 1947, 48; 25 March 1947, 35.

62. Van der Meid, "Those English Brides."

63. *New York Times*, 27 December 1946, 21.

64. "British Brides on West Side Greet American Way of Life with Enthusiasm," photo spread, *Chicago Daily Tribune*, 5 May 1946, W5.

65. *New York Times*, 10 April 1946, 27.

66. Samuels, "40,000 GI Brides Appraise Us," 11.

67. *Annual Report of the Immigration and Naturalization Service* (Washington DC: U.S. Department of Justice, 1950), tables 9A and 9B.

68. Petra Goedde, *GIs and Germans: Culture, Gender and Foreign Relations, 1945–1949* (New Haven: Yale University Press, 2003), chap. 3; quote on pp. 80–81.

69. The history of the U.S. occupation of Germany is covered in a substantial literature. Standard works include Daniel J. Nelson, *A History of U.S. Military Forces in Germany* (Boulder, CO: Westview Press, 1987); John Gimbel, *The American Occupation of Germany: Politics and the Military, 1945–1949* (Stanford, CA: Stanford University Press, 1968); Gimbel, *A German Community under American Occupation: Marburg, 1945–1952* (Stanford, CA: Stanford University Press, 1961); and Franklin M. Davis Jr., *Come as a Conqueror: The United States Army's Occupation of Germany, 1945–1949* (New York: Macmillan, 1967). On democracy as the key ingredient in rehabilitation, see Nicholas Pronay and Keith Wilson, eds., *The Political Re-education of Germany and Her Allies after World War II* (London: Croom Helm, 1985). For American opinions of German people based on social-scientific opinion polling, see Richard L. Merritt, *Democracy Imposed: U.S. Occupation Policy and the German Public, 1945–1949* (New Haven: Yale University Press, 1995).

70. The main articulation of U.S. policy was JCS 1067, a directive of the Joint Chiefs of Staff approved by President Truman in May 1945. Historians have pointed out, however, that U.S. policy in practice was broader than this blueprint, as it encompassed goals of economic revitalization and the containment of Soviet power. See Gimbel, *American Occupation of Germany*.

71. For other evidence of psychological reorientation as a goal of the Allied occupation, see Susan L. Carruthers, "Compulsory Viewing: Concentration Camp Film and German Re-education," *Millennium: Journal of International Studies* 30 (2001), 733–759.

72. *New York Times*, 16 March 1946, 8.

73. In congressional debate the issue had two dimensions: First, allowing marriage might project a premature message of forgiveness to the as-yet-unrehabilitated German people. Second, if all the German people were culpable for the disastrous actions of the Third Reich, embracing German brides might reward bad and potentially dangerous people with the gift of American citizenship.

74. *New York Times*, 25 June 1945, 2. These labels for young German women who went out with Americans had equally vicious counterparts among Germans, though for very different reasons; see Maria Hohn, *GIs and Frauleins: The German-American Encounter in 1950s West Germany* (Chapel Hill: University of North Carolina Press, 2002), 128–130. Elizabeth Heineman, "The Hour of the Woman: Memories of Germany's 'Crisis Years' and West German National Identity," *American Historical Review* 101 (April 1996), 354–395, cites the *Stars and Stripes* character; she argues that for Germans, "fraternizers" became "the symbol of Germany's moral decline." See also John Willoughby, "The Sexual Behavior of American GIs during the Early Years of the Occupation of Germany," *Journal of Military History* 62 (January 1998), 155–174.

75. Quentin Reynolds, "War Bride," *Collier's* 120 (September 13, 1947), 12.

76. "GI Poll: Sweetkraut," *Newsweek* 27 (4 February 1946), 58; Merritt, *Democracy Imposed*, 38–40. On democracy as the key ingredient in rehabilitation, see Pronay and Wilson, *The Political Re-education of Germany and Her Allies*.

77. Heineman, "Hour of Women"; Lord Ogmore, "A Journey to Berlin, 1944–45," quoted in Johannes Kleinschmidt, *Do Not Fraternize: Die Schwierigen Anfange deutsch-amerikanischer Freundschaft, 1944–1949* (Trier: Wissenschaftlicher Verlag, 1997), 91. Petra Goedde describes this phenomenon as a "diffuse sense of cultural affinity," in *GIs and Germans*, 67.

78. *New York Times*, 25 June 1945, 2; 16 March 1946, 8.

79. John Willoughby, *Remaking the Conquering Heroes: The Social and Geopolitical Impact of the Post-war American Occupation of Germany* (New York: Palgrave, 2001), chaps. 2 and 6; Willoughby, "Sexual Behavior of American GIs"; "Operation: Homemaking," *Woman's Home Companion* 73 (July 1946), 4.

80. *Washington Post*, 19 December 1946, 8; *New York Times*, 22 December 1946, 32; David Emblidge, ed., Eleanor Roosevelt's *My Day 2, The Post-war Years, 1945–1952* (New York: Pharos Books, 1990), 85–87.

81. *Washington Post*, 23 February 1947, B7.

82. "Ex-GI Weds a German in Occupation Zone," *New York Times*, 28 March 1947, 5, described former U.S. army sergeant Peter Rupeka and his wife, Erika, as the first officially approved American-German marriage. A different couple is described in a journalists' account: Bud Hutton and Andy Rooney, *Conqueror's Peace: Report to the American Stock-*

holders (New York: Doubleday, 1947), 51, cited by Willoughby, "Sexual Behavior of American GIs." Still others appear in war brides' testimony. On intercultural marriage in postwar Germany, see Shukert and Scibetta, *War Brides*, chap. 9. For first German male spouse to join his veteran wife in the United States, see *Washington Post*, 7 November 1947, 4.

83. *Newsweek* 27, 4 February 1946, 57–58. Two other ex-servicemen with unauthorized German brides joined Horton in his plea to President Truman and in a press conference in Frankfurt, Germany.

84. "Foreign War Brides Given U.S. Welcome, Neighbors Want to Be Friends," *Chicago Daily Tribune*, 8 February 1948, NW7. Also see photo and caption of Peggy Johnson, eight months old, *Chicago Daily Tribune*, 18 February 1948, 4.

85. "Tries to Shed His War Bride; GI Is Jailed," *Chicago Daily Tribune*, 5 January 1949, 3; "All Try to Help a Bewildered German Bride," *Chicago Daily Tribune*, 6 January 1949; "Reconciliation," 7 January 1949, 3.

86. Malvina Lindsay, "Marriage Melting-Pot," *Washington Post*, 14 August 1948, 4; "Reds Stress Sex in Drive against U.S.," *Washington Post*, 22 November 1949, 20.

87. "Reds' Prisoner Picture Makes U.S. Wife Happy," *Chicago Daily Tribune*, 22 September 1950, 7.

88. Susan Carruthers, *Cold War Captives: Imprisonment, Escape, and Brainwashing* (Berkeley: University of California Press, 2009). I am grateful to Susan Carruthers for calling this theme to my attention and generously sharing material on the Soviet brides controversy.

89. "Young German Bride Finds Santa Exists," *New York Times*, 24 December 1954, 15; *Los Angeles Times*, 15 December 1947, A1. Other reports of escapee brides are in *New York Times*, 16 December, 1952, 17, and 23 June 1950, 28.

90. *New York Times*, 5 December 1947, 1.

91. Department of State *Bulletin* 20, no. 496, 2 January 1949; Edmund Stevens, *This Is Russia: Uncensored* (New York: Didier, 1950), 83–84.

92. *New York Times*, 12 December 1946, 22; *Chicago Daily Tribune*, 12 December 1946, 15. On the German-American marriage report, see Willoughby, *Remaking the Conquering Heroes*, 173n. 50. On the report about illegitimate births of "occupation babies," see Heide Fehrenbach, *Race after Hitler: Black Occupation Children in Postwar Germany and America* (Princeton: Princeton University Press, 2005), 74.

93. Emily S. Rosenberg, "'Foreign Affairs' after World War II: Connecting Sexual and International Politics," *Diplomatic History* 18, no. 1 (1994), 59–70; Christina Klein, *Cold War Orientalism: Asia in the Middlebrow Imagination, 1945-1961* (Berkeley: University of California Press, 2003).

94. On Zinnemann's career and vision, see Neil Sinyard, *Fred Zinnemann: Films of Character and Conscience* (Jefferson, NC: McFarland, 2003). "Teresa" has received almost no attention by Fred Zinnemann, "A Film Is Born," *New York Times*, 25 March 1951, 80; Bosley Crowther, review of "Teresa," *New York Times*, 6 April 1951, 31.

95. Evidence for this assertion is found in the newsletter of the War Brides of World War II Association, the *Courier*, and the reunion book the association published, Orton, *These Are My Sisters*. Among the 186 short life sketches published in this collection, many of the women mention with great pride the U.S. military service of their own children in the Korean and Vietnam eras, and into the next generation, the military service of their grandchildren (girls as well as boys). Other World War II war brides became long-term military spouses when their husbands took service careers.

1. Robert Bennett Jr. to General Dwight D. Eisenhower, 14 June 1947, copy enclosed in a letter to the soldier's sister, NAACP Papers, Part 9, Series C, Reel 10, Soldiers' Complaints (Folder "B"), Papers of the NAACP (microform), ed. Mark Fox (Frederick, MD: University Publications of America, 1981); Elfrieda Berthiaume Shukert and Barbara Smith Scibetta, *War Brides of World War II* (Novato, CA: Presidio Press, 1988), 206.

2. "Unintended Consequences of War" is the title and theme of the first chapter of Renee C. Romano, *Race Mixing: Black-White Marriage in Postwar America* (Cambridge: Harvard University Press, 2003), about marriages between African Americans and whites during World War II.

3. Some recent scholars of racial "amalgamation" have cautioned against an overdetermined reading of interracial marriage. In a compelling critique, Henry Yu has argued that the historical phenomenon of racial intermarriage has not undermined—and perhaps has served to reinforce—patterns of white supremacy in U.S. society and in our relations with other countries: "A racially 'mixed' individual and the sexual boundary crossing that produced such an individual do not in themselves challenge the existence of the boundaries between categories. Indeed, they can serve to highlight the conceptual stability of the categories being mixed, even as they purport to challenge the effectiveness of boundaries in maintaining a sense of difference." Yet Yu's argument overlooks the subjectivity of the individuals involved in such relationships, and ahistoricizes their practice. While Yu is correct in arguing that intermarriage has no fixed or inherent political meaning, it is the case that intermarried war couples and their supporters in the postwar decade were inclined to view such marriage as a form of resistance given the state of legal and social proscription against interracial marriage. Henry Yu, "Tiger Woods Is Not the End of History: or, Why Sex across the Color Line Won't Save Us All," *American Historical Review* 108 (December 2003), 1406–1414. Yu was critiquing, and perhaps oversimplifying, a large and valuable literature on racial mixing in the American social sciences; see note 10 below.

4. Romano, *Race Mixing*, 3; in 1960, 157,000 marriages, or 0.4 percent, "involved a white, black, Native American, or Asian-American wed to a spouse of a different race."

5. Ollie Stewart, "How War Brides Fare in America," *Negro Digest* 6 (April 1948), 25; "Miss. Segregation Laws Hit Oriental War Brides," *Chicago Defender*, 31 May 1952, 1.

6. Martha Hodes, *White Women, Black Men: Illicit Sex in the Nineteenth-Century South* (New Haven: Yale University Press, 1997); quote from Nancy F. Cott, *Public Vows: A History of Marriage and the Nation* (Cambridge: Harvard University Press, 2000), 164. Other major contributions to the historical literature on interracial marriage include Paul R. Spickard, *Mixed Blood: Intermarriage and Ethnic Identity in Twentieth-Century America* (Madison: University of Wisconsin Press, 1989); Maria P. P. Root, ed., *Racially Mixed People in America* (Newbury Park, CA: Sage, 1992); Martha Hodes, ed., *Sex, Love, Race: Crossing Boundaries in North American History* (New York: NYU, 1999); Romano, *Race Mixing*; Peter Wallenstein, *Tell the Court I Love My Wife: Race, Marriage, and Law—An American History* (New York: Palgrave Macmillan, 2002); Peggy Pascoe, *What Comes Naturally: Miscegenation Law and the Making of Race in America* (New York: Oxford University Press, 2009).

7. Wallenstein, *Tell the Court*, chap. 9; quote p. 145. Wallenstein notes that by the 1930s, fourteen states "expressly restricted marriages between Caucasians and at least some Asians" (280 n. 37). David H. Fowler, *Northern Attitudes towards Interracial Marriage: Legislation and Public Opinion in the Middle Atlantic and the States of the Old Northwest, 1780–1930* (New York: Garland, 1987), chap. 5.

8. Romano, *Race Mixing*, p. 2, and chap. 2, quote on pp. 54–55. On juvenile court and mental hospital admission, p. 67. Also Cynthia L. Takeshima, "An Invisible Monster: The Creation and Denial of Mixed-Racial People in America," in Root, *Racially Mixed People*, 162–178.

9. There has been a vigorous debate over the significance of the McCarran Walter Act and the impact of its liberal and conservative features. Roger Daniels stresses liberal reform elements, arguing that "in practice the act was not as restrictive as it seemed," and that non-quota immigrants came to dominate the flow, circumventing to a large degree the biased national origins quotas; Daniels, *Guarding the Golden Door: American Immigration Policy and Immigrants since 1882* (New York: Hill and Wang 2004), chap. 6. However, Asian immigrants constituted only 7 percent of all immigrants who entered during the life of the bill. For a still trenchant interpretation stressing the restrictive elements and ideology of the bill, see David M. Reimers, *Still the Golden Door: The Third World Comes to America* (New York: Columbia University Press, 1985), chap. 1.

10. "Desegregation in the Armed Forces," Harry S. Truman Presidential Library website, http://www.trumanlibrary.org; Kimberley L. Phillips, *War, What Is It Good For? Black Freedom Struggles and the U.S. Military* (Chapel Hill: University of North Carolina Press, forthcoming).

11. Wallenstein, *Tell the Court*, chap. 13; quote p. 190.

12. Milton Alberts to Franklin Williams, Assistant Special Counsel, NAACP, date obscured 1948, Part 9, Series B: Armed Forces Legal Files, Reel 15.

13. Romano, *Race Mixing*, 21–22, 30–38. Romano notes a growing public fascination with interracial liaisons expressed through popular film and theater in the late 1940s, but all stressed the tragic or impossible outcome of such unions.

14. Graham Smith, *When Jim Crow Met John Bull: Black American Soldiers in World War II Britain* (London: Tauris, 1987), chaps. 8 and 9; quotes on pp. 206, 222.

15. Ibid., 205–206; Shukert and Scibetta, *War Brides*, 28–30.

16. Robert Bennett Jr. to General Dwight D. Eisenhower, 14 June 1947, copy enclosed in a letter to the soldier's sister, NAACP Papers, Part 9, Series C , Reel 10, Soldiers' Complaints; William Malone to Leslie Perry, NAACP Papers, 5 October, 16 November, 18 November 1949; Leslie Perry to William Malone, 13 October, 7 November, 21 December 1949 plus enclosure: "List of decisions in Malone case," a memo prepared by the NAACP; NAACP Papers, Part 9, Series C, Reel 11. In response to the NAACP's repeated request that the marriage rejection be overturned in this case, the secretary of defense stood by the commanding officer's decision to reject the marriage.

17. Corporal Cleveland Scott to Dave Ringten, NAACP, 4 July 1945, NAACP Papers, Part 9, Series C, Reel 11.

18. Sgt. Robert Bennett to "Sis" (Hazel Days), 16 July 1947, NAACP Papers, Part 9 Series C, Reel 10. He asked his sister to forward his letter to the *Pittsburgh Courier*, the *Amsterdam News*, and *PM Magazine*, a left-liberal publication, in addition to the NAACP. Bennett may have been politically active on the left.

19. "War Brides Report, Mediterranean Theater," unpublished typescript, RG 200, American Red Cross Papers, 1935–1946, Box 985, NARA.

20. Interview, 18 January 1954, Romanzo Adams Research Center, War Bride Interview Project Papers, University of Hawaii, Library Archives, Honolulu, HI.

21. Translated copy, name obscure, to Jesse O. Dedmon, NAACP Papers Part 9, Series B: Armed Forces Legal Files, Reel 15, Folder: "Soldier Marriage." Also in folder, Jacqueline Riols to NAACP, 14 August 1947, and Julia Baxter, response to Mme. Marie Pruaux, 14 November 1946.

22. Hazel Byrne Simpkins, "A Negro's British War Bride," in Clotye Murdock Larsson, ed.., *Marriage across the Color Line* (Chicago: Johnson Publishing, 1965). The story was originally published in *Tan* magazine under the title "I Married a Tan Yank," March 1951. This relationship is also discussed by Romano, *Race Mixing*, 25–26. On violence and hostility directed against white wives of black GIs, see Corporal Cleveland Scott to NAACP, 4 July 1945, NAACP Papers, Part 9, Series C, Reel 11; Bennett to "Sis," 16 July 1947, Part 9, Series C, Reel 10; and anecdotes from Stewart, "How War Brides Fare."

23. Legal department correspondence of Thurgood Marshall and others regarding an interracial marriage case from Oklahoma, *Willie Stevens v. U.S.*, 1942–1945, NAACP Papers, Part 18, Series A: Legal Department Files, Reel 3; Benjamin E. Mays to Roy Wilkins, 16 December 1954 and reply 23 December 1954, NAACP Papers, Part 16, Series B: Board of Directors' Correspondence, Reel 10. When Wilkins of the NAACP asserted that antimiscegenation laws were a settled matter of constitutional law, Mays, president of Morehouse College, rejoined that the Supreme Court had last spoken on the issue in the nineteenth century.

24. Spickard, *Mixed Blood*, 297–305.

25. Spickard discusses this finding from Gunnar Myrdal, *An American Dilemma: The Negro Problem and American Democracy*, in *Mixed Blood*, 300.

26. Spickard discusses "fear of reprisal" as a factor in black organizations' reluctance to address the issue (*Mixed Blood*, 298). Born into Atlanta's black elite and very light-skinned, Walter White (1893–1955) was a novelist and social investigator as well as a civil rights leader. Issues of racial identity and skin color were central to his life and writings. On the career of Walter White, see Kenneth Robert Janken, *White: The Biography of Walter White, Mr. NAACP* (New York: New Press, 2003).

27. Jesse O. Dedmon, Secretary, Veterans Affairs Committee, to Pfc. Reginald Calder, 21 August 1945; Robert Carter, NAACP Legal Defense and Educational Fund, to Leslie Perry, NAACP Washington Bureau, 7 July 1945; NAACP Papers, Part 9, Series C, Reel 10. Carter and Perry joke about the "unpronounceable" name of the soldier's Italian fiancée and mock his attachment to her.

28. Walter White to Secretary of Navy and Secretary of Army, 20 December 1945, Sec'y Stimson response, 5 March 1946, NAACP Papers, Part 9, Series B, Reel 15. In private writings of the same period Stimson wrote with disgust that "radical leaders of the colored race" were using the war as a pretext to push for intermarriage. It is possible, given the timing, that Stimson's diary comment was in part a response to White's letter. Richard Dalfiume, "The Forgotten Years of the Negro Revolution," *Journal of American History* 55 (January 1968), 106; also James Patterson, *Grand Expectations: The US, 1945 to 1974* (Oxford: Oxford University Press 1996), 5; Romano, *Race Mixing*, 17.

29. Walter White to Secretary of War and Secretary of Navy, 20 December 1945; Secretary of War to Walter White, 5 March 1946; NAACP Papers, Part 9, Armed Forces Legal Files, Series B, Reel 15, "Soldier Marriage."

30. Romano, *Race Mixing*, 21–22. George H. Roeder Jr., *The Censored War: American Visual Experience during World War II* (New Haven: Yale University Press, 1993), 57. On the absence in mainstream media of war bride stories about black soldiers and white women, I found none among the several hundred newspaper articles I reviewed (*New York Times, Wall Street Journal, Los Angeles Times, Chicago Tribune*). I identified a handful of references to interracial marriages involving black GIs in mass-circulation periodicals, but these were presented as "tragic" aberrations; see, for example, "Homecoming," *Newsweek* 43 (1 May 1944), 19. The only photo I found of an African American husband with a foreign war bride appeared in *Life* magazine, and the bride was Japanese.

31. *Chicago Defender*, 27 April 1946, 12.

32. Romano, *Race Mixing*, 38–43; Cott, *Public Vows*, 184–185.

33. "Flies from Italy to Marry Ex-GI," *Chicago Defender*, 16 August 1947, 5.

34. William H. Robinson, "Honeymoon U.S.A.," *Pittsburgh Courier*, 11 June 1949, 19.

35. Todd Steven Burroughs, "Turn of the Century Births: The Afro-American Newspaper," http://www.blackpressUSA.com/history/Timeline_essay. John D'Emilio places Ollie Stewart in the history of the 1940s civil rights movement in *Lost Prophet: The Life and Times of Bayard Rustin* (New York: Free Press, 2003), 135.

36. *Chicago Defender* 25 January 1947, 12.

37. Ruth Feldstein, *Motherhood in Black and White: Race and Sex in American Liberalism, 1930–1965* (Ithaca: Cornell University Press, 2000), 40–44. Studying the work of scholars and researchers, Feldstein shows that ideas about race and gender in family relations were mutually reinforcing in American postwar liberalism.

38. For another example of African American intellectuals drawing a message of optimism from interracial war marriages, see a book review by Alice C. Browning in the *Pittsburgh Courier*, 22 April 1950, 27. Browning critiques a novel by Loren Wahl, *The Invisible Glass*, that deals with two kinds of "forbidden love" in the overseas war, interracial (a black GI and his Italian fiancée) and homosexual (between two GIs): "The tragedy of this book lies not in the affairs of the people concerned, but in the inability of the author to accept normal happiness between the races. With so many war brides brought back to America by Negro soldiers the author had to find an unusual case like this where permission was denied to bring out the frustration of intermarriage."

39. Don Tennyson with Lloyd Shearer, "I Dared to Take a Japanese Bride," *Washington Post*, 8 August 1954, TA6. For another popular depiction of an intermarriage between a white American and a foreign-born Asian, see Agnes Davis Kim, *I Married a Korean* (New York: John Day, 1953), published one year earlier. Caroline Chung Simpson makes an intriguing argument that stories such as this one were a displaced way to discuss African American racial integration and the *Brown* decision. See *An Absent Present: Japanese Americans in Postwar American Culture, 1945–1960* (Durham, NC: Duke University Press, 2001), chap. 5.

40. Theodore Cohen, who himself married a Japanese woman he met while serving with the occupation, has a detailed discussion of the climate for male-female relationships in his memoir, *Remaking Japan: The American Occupation as New Deal* (New York: Free Press, 1987), chap. 7.

41. Shukert and Scibetta, *War Brides*, chaps. 13 and 14; "Connecticut Validates GI's Shinto Wedding," *New York Times*, 16 February 1951, 25; "6,000 US Servicemen Are Marrying Japanese," *New York Times*, 17 November 1951, 2.

42. John W. Dower, *Embracing Defeat: Japan in the Wake of World War II* (New York: Norton, 1999), 123–139, discusses the origins of the Recreation and Amusement Association. Occupation authorities eliminated government-sponsored prostitution in early 1946 to address a surge in venereal disease. On the disdainful attitude of U.S. officials toward Japanese women, see Debbie Storrs, "Like a Bamboo: Representations of a Japanese War Bride," *Frontiers: A Journal of Women's Studies* 21 (2000), 194–224. Theodore Cohen, an official with the labor department of the occupation headquarters, notes in his memoir that several high-ranking U.S. leaders were "undoubtedly racially prejudiced" against the Japanese, a fact that shaped policy in several regards, though Cohen also contends that "very little of the black-white racial antipathy among so many Americans of the time transferred itself to the 'yellow' Japanese, hence the dimensions of the 'fraternization problem'"; Cohen, *Remaking Japan*, 131–133.

43. Dower, *Embracing Defeat*, 79–80. Scibetta and Shukert have an excellent and detailed discussion of Japanese-American marriage after World War II in its legal and social aspects; *War Brides*, chaps. 12–14. The army circular is quoted on p. 204.

44. Shukert and Scibetta, *War Brides*, chap. 14. U.S. Congress, House Committee on Immigration and Naturalization, Subcommittee Hearings, "To Facilitate the Admission to the U.S. of Husbands, Wives and Children of U.S. Citizen Men and Women Who Have Served Honorably in the Armed Forces of the U.S. during the Present World War," 26 and 27 September and 29 November 1945, 79th Cong., 1st sess., 1945 (House Unpublished Hearings Collection).

45. Correspondence between General Headquarters, Far East Command, G-1 Division, and various couples, RG 331, Adjutant General's Section, Operational Division Decimal File, Box 643, NARA. See cases of Teruko Murazawa, Mikio Uchiyama, Wilbur Hughes Kent, Sumiko Yukinaga, and Sergeant Hoke Garrett.

46. Unclassified memos from Adjutant General's office, SCAP Headquarters, to State Department, one about request submitted by Congressman Sidney Yates, another about four Japanese nationals and their children as beneficiaries of private laws waiving Japanese immigration exclusion; 27 October 1950, RG 331, Adjutant General's Section, Operational Division Decimal File, Box 643, NARA; Congressman Cecil White to Commanding General 8th U.S. Army, 2 March 1949, Box 643, same as above. Tennyson, "I Dared to Take a Japanese Bride," also involved an attempt to get a private bill passed through his congressman.

47. "Status after Marriage to Japanese National," memo of Clinton McClarty, Louis Binick, Jesse Lusk to Commanding General, Eighth Army, 31 January 1950, and extensive correspondence regarding the memo; RG 331, Adjutant General's Section, Operational Division Decimal File, Box 643, NARA. Military lawyers used an ingenious catch-22 argument: only servicemen, not civilians, were entitled to the benefits for their Japanese wives; but of course, as military service personnel the men had been forbidden from marrying the women in the first place.

48. Dower, *Embracing Defeat*, 130, 212. SCAP attention to the details of segregation included GHQ insistence that separate houses of prostitution be maintained for African American troops under the short-lived Recreation and Amusement Association scheme

of 1945. Michael S. Molasky, *The American Occupation of Japan and Okinawa: Literature and Memory* (New York: Routledge, 1999), chap. 3, argues that many Japanese in turn had a "political empathy with the plight of African Americans" even while viewing black soldiers through a highly stereotypical lens; quote p. 71. Japanese views of Africans and people of African descent over a long historical span are presented in Gary P. Leupp, *Interracial Intimacy in Japan: Western Men and Japanese Women, 1543–1900* (London: Continuum, 2003), 92–96.

49. Cpl. George Brown to Legal Committee, NAACP, 28 November 1949, NAACP Papers, Part 9, Series B: Legal Files, Reel 14 ("Foreign Dependents"); Cpl. Theodore Washington to Walter White, 19 July 1949, NAACP Papers, Part 9, Series B, Reel 14 ("Foreign Dependents").

50. Cpl. George Brown to Legal Committee, NAACP, 28 November 1949; NAACP Papers (microfilm), Part 9, Series B, Legal Files, Reel 14 ("Foreign Dependents").

51. William T. Bowers, William M. Hammond, and George L. MacGarrigle, *Black Soldier, White Army: The 24th Infantry Regiment in Korea* (Washington, DC: Center of Military History, United States Army, 1996). Bowers et al., in this important reexamination commissioned by the army in 1989, concluded that "a lack of unit cohesion brought on by racial prejudice and the poor leadership it engendered at all levels" was "mainly at fault" for the regiment's lapses of performance in Korean combat.

52. Ibid.; "400 Infantry GIs Lovesick," *Chicago Defender* (National), 4 November 1950, .

53. L. Alex Wilson, "400 to Wed Tokyo Girls," *Chicago Defender*, 4 November 1950, 1; Cpl. Theodore Washington Jr. to Walter White, NAACP, 19 July 1949, NAACP Papers, Part 9, Series B Legal Files, Reel 14.

54. Shukert and Scibetta, *War Brides*, 209–211.

55. Teruko Murazawa to General MacArthur, 22 June 1948 (translation and digest by Military Intelligence Translator and Interpreter section, 15 July 1948), RG 331, Adjutant General's Section, Operational Division Decimal File, Box 643, NARA. Also see in Box 643, Sumiko Yukinaga to Mrs. Jean MacArthur, 14 August 1948.

56. Interviews August 23, 1954; 4 January 1954; 18 January 1954; Romanzo Adams Research Center, War Bride Interview Project Papers, University of Hawaii, Library Archives, Honolulu, HI. On pan-pan girls and American occupiers, see Dower, *Embracing Defeat*, 132–139. Evelyn Nakano Glenn, *Issei, Nisei, War Bride: Three Generations of Japanese American Women in Domestic Service* (Philadelphia: Temple University Press, 1986), 58–66, concurs with the point that intercultural marriage necessitated "some degree of alienation" from parents, kin, and culture, a painful experience for all the war bride subjects she interviewed.

57. Wendy Kline, *Building a Better Race: Gender, Sexuality, and Eugenics from the Turn of the Century to the Baby Boom* (Berkeley: University of California Press, 2001), chaps. 3–5; quote on p. 125.

58. *War Marriage and Its Problems: Proceedings of the Annual Institute on Marriage and Home Adjustment*, Penn State College, State College, PA, 23–25, October 1944, 29.

59. Edgar W. Gregory, "Help Bolster Those War Marriages," *Mental Hygiene* 30 (October 1946), 624–627. With such a grim view the author took the unusual step of encouraging clergy and other service providers to counsel divorce. Though divorce per se was undesirable, in this instance it might purge the nation of undesirable families and help restore its prewar equilibrium.

60. The research was undertaken through departments of sociology or social work, or through interdisciplinary institutes on the study of race. Study findings were often published in leading journals, a signal of the growing influence of race liberalism in postwar social science. Studies in this group include Anselm Strauss, "Strain and Harmony in American-Japanese War-Bride Marriages," *Journal of Marriage and the Family* 16 (May 1954), 99–106; Gerald J. Schnepp and Agnes Masako Yui, "Cultural and Marital Adjustment of Japanese War Brides," *American Journal of Sociology* 61 (1955), 48–50; Yukiko Kimura, "War Brides in Hawaii and Their In-Laws," *American Journal of Sociology* 63 (July 1957), 70–76; Yoshiko Gloria Yamaji, "The Impact of Communication Difficulties in Family Relations Observed in Eight Japanese War-Bride Marriages" (master's thesis, School of Social Work, University of Southern California, 1961). George DeVos, a prominent scholar of psychology and anthropology with a specialization in Japanese culture and personality, organized a group research project on Japanese war brides at Berkeley using students from the School of Social Welfare in the late 1950s. Several of his papers, both published and unpublished, were cited by other scholars, including several on "personality patterns" of the partners in Japanese-American marriages, and William Caudill and George DeVos, "Achievement, Culture and Personality: The Case of the Japanese Americans," *American Anthropologist* 58 (December 1956), 1102–1126. An excellent literature review of Asian war bride studies is found in Bok-Lim C. Kim, "Asian Wives of U.S. Servicemen: Women in Shadows," *Amerasia Journal* 4 (1977), 91–115.

61. Feldstein, *Motherhood in Black and White*, 40–41.

62. Henry Yu, *Thinking Orientals: Migration, Contact, and Exoticism in Modern America* (Oxford: Oxford University Press, 2001). Yu's fascinating work is a highly nuanced history of the research institutions and intellectual movements in which the "Oriental Problem" was analyzed during the first three-quarters of the twentieth century. Yu writes that the Chinese American and Japanese American researchers within this network "came to know themselves through theories and institutions of 'Orientalism'" (vii)—a problematic or at least highly ambiguous process in Yu's view. Though they were acting on a "stage" set by whites, their academic positions as cultural translators were also an "institutional opportunity" of some significance. Yu's work, however, is not specifically engaged with the history of antiracism as an intellectual and political movement, a dimension of the research tradition that I regard as central to the discourse about war bride marriage.

63. Strauss, "Strain and Harmony"; Schnepp and Yui, "Cultural and Marital Adjustment."

64. Romanzo Adams, *Interracial Marriage in Hawaii* (New York: Macmillan, 1937); "History of the Romanzo Adams Social Research Laboratory," http://libweb.hawaii.edu/libdept/archives/univarch/rasrl/history/htm. Yukiko Kimura (1903–2002) was born in Yokohama, Japan, and became a social worker for the YWCA, first in Japan and later in Hawaii. She completed her master's thesis at the University of Hawaii, "Social Readjustment of Alien Japanese in Hawaii since the War" (1947). Her Ph.D. from the University of Chicago was awarded in 1952 for "A Comparative Study of Collective Adjustment of the Issei in Hawaii and in the Mainland United States since Pearl Harbor." She also authored *Issei: Japanese Immigrants in Hawaii* (Honolulu: University of Hawaii Press, 1988). A brief obituary was published in the *Honolulu Advertiser,* 2 November 2002. I am very grateful to James Cartwright, university archivist at the University of Hawaii, for compiling the biographical material used here. Kimura's life history is also discussed in brief by Yu, *Thinking Orientals,* 155.

65. Yukiko Kimura, "War Brides in Hawaii and Their In-Laws," *Report Number 32,* Romanzo Adams Social Research Laboratory, University of Hawaii, March 1962. An earlier version with the same title was published in the *American Journal of Sociology* 63 (July 1957) and released by the laboratory as *Report Number 22.*

66. Yoshiko Gloria Yamaji, "The Impact of Communication Difficulties in Family Relations Observed in Eight Japanese War-Bride Marriages" (master's thesis, School of Social Work, University of Southern California, 1961); Kim, "Asian Wives of U.S. Servicemen"; John W. Connor, *A Study of the Marital Stability of Japanese War Brides* (San Francisco: R&E Research Associates, 1976); Shizuko Suenaga, "Goodbye to Sayonara: The Reverse Assimilation of Japanese War Brides" (Ph.D. diss., Boston College, 1996); Yasuko Kawarasaki, "Negative Stereotypes of Japanese War Brides: An Outburst of Japanese Frustration" (master's thesis, UCLA, 1994). Note that some of these later studies were written by clinicians who encountered individuals or couples in crisis, so their studies also had a significant built-in bias.

67. Christina Klein, *Cold War Orientalism: Asia in the Middlebrow Imagination, 1945–1961* (Berkeley: University of California Press, 2003).

68. Vidor's film's reflecting a progressive social outlook included *Our Daily Bread* (1934) about the economic struggles of the Great Depression, and, earlier, *The Big Parade* (1925), an indictment of the First World War's inconceivable violence. *Japanese War Bride* has been little recognized in the literature on Japanese Americans in the postwar period. See Gina Marchetti, *Romance and the "Yellow Peril": Race, Sex, and Discursive Strategies in Hollywood Fiction* (Berkeley: University of California Press, 1993); although Marchetti acknowledges that the film condemns racism and unfolds the contradictions that derive from it, her primary purpose is to depict *Japanese War Bride* as a domestic melodrama that ultimately reasserts "the legitimacy of white patriarchal rule" (169).

69. Caroline Chung Simpson, *An Absent Presence: Japanese Americans in Postwar American Culture, 1945–1960* (Durham, NC: Duke University Press, 2001), 3–8.

70. L. Hyun-Yi Kang, "The Desiring of Asian Female Bodies: Interracial Romance and Cinematic Subjection," *Visual Anthropology Review* 9 (Spring 1993), 5–21. Contemporary articles about Yamaguchi also play off the image of the simpering, doll-like, and comical Asian female: Louis Berg, "Yum Yum Yamaguchi!" *Los Angeles Times,* 27 January 1952, G16; "Story of a Japanese War Bride," *New York Times,* 30 January 1952, 22; Ray Falk, "East Meets West with Varying Reactions as American Producers Invade Nippon," *New York Times,* 3 February 1952, X5.

71. "Japanese War Bride Film Has Punch, Pathos," *Chicago Daily Tribune,* 4 February 1952, B6; "'Japanese War Bride' Arrives on Screens," *Los Angeles Times,* 8 February 1952, B7; "War Bride's Story Unique," *Los Angeles Times,* 5 February 1952, B6; "Story of a Japanese War Bride."

72. Ignacio M. Garcia, *Hector P. Garcia: In Relentless Pursuit of Justice* (Houston: Arte Publico Press, 2002); Carl Allsup, *The American G.I. Forum: Origin and Evolution* (Austin: Center for Mexican American Studies, University of Texas at Austin, 1982); "Selected Interview Segments: Wanda F. Garcia," *Justice for My People: The Hector P. Garcia Story* webpage, www.justiceformypeople.org/interview_wgarcia.html; "Dr. Hector P. Garcia," La Voz de Aztlan, vol. 1, no. 4, 14 February 2000, http://atzlan.net.

73. Simpkins, "A Negro's British War Bride."

74. Caridad Concepcion Vallangca, *The Second Wave: Pinay and Pinoy, 1945–1960* (San Francisco: Strawberry Hill Press, 1987), oral history of Gloria Clement, pp. 60–63.

NOTES TO CHAPTER 6

1. James H. Willbanks, *Abandoning Vietnam: How America Left and South Vietnam Lost Its War* (Lawrence: University Press of Kansas, 2004), 257; Olivier Todd, *Cruel April: The Fall of Saigon*, trans. Stephen Becker (New York: Norton, 1987).

2. Albert Sexton, "V.C. or No V.C. . . . I Will Stay," *Chicago Tribune*, 8 July 1972; in this polemical first-person account, the author warns against an American withdrawal, reporting that "the V.C. have vowed to slaughter every half-American child in Viet Nam and its mother." There appears to be no evidence that the Vietnamese government engaged in systematic or severe retribution against Amerasians or their mothers after 1975; the Vietnamese government cooperated with the office of the United Nations High Commissioner for Refugees to allow remaining Americans and their Vietnamese families to leave in the 1970s and, later, worked with the U.S. State Department to enable the departure of Amerasians. The children of American fathers were, however, the victims of social discrimination in postwar Vietnam. Some Amerasians have also maintained that they were disproportionately subjected to relocation. An excellent discussion of all these issues is found in Steven DeBonis, *Children of the Enemy: Oral Histories of Vietnamese Amerasians and Their Mothers* (Jefferson, NC: McFarland, 1995), 8–11.

3. *Los Angeles Times*, 7 April 1975, A1; Le Ly Hayslip with James Hayslip, *Child of War, Woman of Peace* (New York: Doubleday, 1993), 124–134. Estimate of the numbers of Vietnamese wives and fiancées requesting safe passage and other analysis of the evacuee crisis are from an article by Fox Butterfield for the *New York Times*, 18 April 1975, 14.

4. J. W. Fulbright, address to the School of Advanced International Studies at Johns Hopkins University, 5 May 1966, reprinted as a forum with rejoinders, *U.S. News & World Report* 60 (23 May 1966), 113–119.

5. Cynthia Enloe, *Bananas, Beaches and Bases: Making Feminist Sense of International Politics*, updated edition (Berkeley: University of California Press, 2000), chap. 4; Saundra Pollock Sturdevant and Brenda Stoltzfus, *Let the Good Times Roll: Prostitution and the U.S. Military in Asia* (New York: New Press, 1993); Chalmers Johnson, *Blowback: The Costs and Consequences of American Empire* (New York: Metropolitan Books, 2000), especially chap. 2 on Okinawa.

6. William J. Bartman, ""Korean War Brides, Prostitutes and Yellow Slavery," *Minerva* 7 (1989), 30–36. The article, which cites no sources, appears to be based on interviews with a handful of individuals: a senior special agent with the Immigration and Naturalization Service and two to three local law enforcement officials in Houston, Los Angeles, and Washington State.

7. I am deeply grateful to Marilyn Young for her insights about the complex international politics of this period, many of which informed my understanding in this chapter.

8. The Vietnamese woman as the sexual partner of an American war adviser appeared first and perhaps most famously in Graham Greene, *The Quiet American* (New York: Viking Press, 1956); Phuong is the object of a power struggle between two Western men, the novel's protagonists. The novel was adapted to film in 1958 and 2002.

An American novel by a war veteran that presents a rare alternative perspective in American literature of the Vietnam experience is Robert Olen Butler, *The Alleys of Eden* (New York: Horizon Press, 1981). The story centers on the deep and loving connection between an American serviceman and a Vietnamese woman, a former bar girl who is presented as a complex, sympathetic, and fully realized human being. Their relationship in the United States, however, is shown as tragically impossible and unsustainable—a construction of Asian-American intercultural marriage that harks back to *Madame Butterfly*. Thanks to Marilyn Young for directing me to this text.

9. Bruce Cumings, *The Origins of the Korean War* (Princeton: Princeton University Press, 1981); Cumings, ed., *Child of Conflict: The Korean-American Relationship, 1943–1953* (Seattle: University of Washington Press, 1983); Mel Leffler, "American Globalism and the Korean War," The Legacy of Korea: A Fiftieth Anniversary Conference, 25–27 October 2001, Truman Presidential Library and University of Missouri, Kansas City, http://www.trumanlibrary.org/korea/leffler.htm; Sang-Dawn Lee, *Big Brother, Little Brother: The American Influence on Korean Culture in the Lyndon B. Johnson Years* (Lanham, MD: Lexington Books, 2002), 14–16; Thomas Borstelmann, *The Cold War and the Color Line: American Race Relations in the Global Arena* (Cambridge: Harvard University Press, 2001), 48–53, 81–82.

10. Lee, *Big Brother, Little Brother*, 9–13. Lee follows and extends Edward Said's argument in *Orientalism* (New York: Vintage Books, 1979).

11. Katharine H. S. Moon, *Sex among Allies: Military Prostitution in U.S.-Korea Relations* (New York: Columbia University Press, 1997), 2.

12. Bruce Cumings, "Silent But Deadly: Sexual Subordination in the U.S.-Korean Relationship," in Sturdevant and Stoltzfus, *Let the Good Times Roll*, 170.

13. Ibid., 171.

14. Moon, *Sex among Allies*; Eighth U.S. Army, Office of International Relations, "Human Factors Research: Part II. Troop-Community Relations," quoted in Moon, *Sex among Allies*, 84–85; Sturdevant and Stoltzfus, *Let the Good Times Roll*, 308–315.

15. Moon, *Sex among Allies*, 46; Ji-Yeon Yuh, *Beyond the Shadow of Camptown: Korean Military Brides in America* (New York: NYU Press, 2002), 14–20.

16. Lee, *Big Brother*, 103–105; Yuh, *Beyond the Shadow*, 4–5, 36–38; Moon, *Sex among Allies*, 3–4 and chap. 4.

17. Yuh, *Beyond the Shadow*, 39.

18. Ibid., 61.

19. Daniel B. Lee, "Transcultural Marriage and Its Impact on Korean Immigration," in Inn Sook Lee, ed., *Korean-American Women: Toward Self-Realization* (Mansfield, OH: Association of Korean Christian Scholars in North America, 1985), 42–64. Lee favorably cites a study conducted under the auspices of the Office of Eighth U.S. Army Chaplains in Korea; the author of the study reviewed a random sample of 264 marriage applications and concluded that the "Korean girls" were not predominantly engaged in prostitution prior to marriage. The study, however, reported employment data for only 98 of the women (including 59 who said they did not work). Similarly, Lee cites a second study that downplays prostitution, this one based on the applications of Korean wives seeking to emigrate; interestingly, this study did find that the majority of wives with employment history cited work in the service sector—a finding consistent with Yuh's camptown argument.

20. Yuh, *Shadow of Camptown*, 58–62, 225.

21. Bok-Lim C. Kim, "Asian Wives of U.S. Servicemen: Women in the Shadows," *Amerasia Journal* 4 (1977), 91–115.

22. Moon, *Sex among Allies*, 7.

23. Yuh, *Shadow of Camptown*, 223–229.

24. Bok-Lim C. Kim, "Casework with Japanese and Korean Wives of Americans," *Social Casework* 53 (May 1972), 273–279; Kim, "Asian Wives of U.S. Servicemen."

25. "Asian Women Immigrants Admitted to U.S. as Wives of American Citizens by Country of Origin and Year," U.S. Commissioner of Immigration and Naturalization, Annual Reports, 1947–1975, table 6 (Washington, DC), reprinted in Kim, "Asian Wives of U.S. Servicemen," 91–115; David M. Reimers, "The Korean-American Immigrant Experience," The Legacy of Korea: A Fiftieth Anniversary Conference, 25–27 October, 2001, Truman Presidential Library and University of Missouri, Kansas City, http://www.trumanlibrary.org/korea/leffler.htm; Reimers, *Other Immigrants: The Global Origins of the American People* (New York: NYU Press, 2005), 175–177.

26. A search of three newspapers, the *New York Times*, the *Chicago Tribune*, and the *Washington Post*, using the Pro-Quest Historical Newspapers database (accessed 1 August 2007), found one match for "Korean War Brides" in the period 1950–1970; for "Korean Wives," three to four documents for each of the three publications. Two of the matches were announcements for television "divorce court" programs.

27. "A Hooch Is Not a Home," *Time* 84 (16 October 1964), 48. Also discussed in Lee, *Big Brother*, 10–11.

28. "Confucius' Outcasts," *Time* 86 (10 December 1965), 10. The book and review are also discussed in Lee, *Big Brother*, 5. On Asian adoption in Cold War cultural construction and the role of the Pearl Buck Foundation, see Christina Klein, "Family Ties and Political Obligation: The Discourse of Adoption and the Cold War Commitment to Asia," in Christian G. Appy, ed., *Cold War Constructions: The Political Culture of United States Imperialism* (Amherst: University of Massachusetts Press, 2000), 35–66.

29. Eighth Army resistance to Korean-American marriage is evidenced in "Marriage by GI's Problem in Korea," *New York Times*, 24 October 1965, 2. Also see Moon, *Sex among Allies*, 84–85.

30. Various documents in RG 200, ARC papers, Group 4, 1947–1964, evidence the exclusion of Korea from war bride support programs; see, for example, Memo, Subject: Brides' Schools, 4 April 1957, and Memo: Japanese, Philippine-Okinawan Bride Schools, 20 September 1956, which single out Korea for exclusion from the program. In RG 200, ARC papers, Group 5, the decimal number that had previously referred to war brides was reassigned to family counseling and support services.

31. Immigration and Naturalization Service, Annual Reports, 1947–1975, table 6; reprinted in Kim, "Asian Wives of US Servicemen," 99; marriage applications, Personnel Management files, Adjutant General's Office, RG 472, U.S. Forces in Southeast Asia; NARA, College Park, MD; "Increase Seen in US-Viet Marriages," *Los Angeles Times*, 1 January 1970, A12; "GI Marriages on Increase in South Vietnam," *Los Angeles Times*, 6 September 1972, A21.

In World War I, 1.95 million Americans served in the military overseas and approximately 5,000 married, for a rate of 2.5 marriages per thousand U.S. servicemen. In the Vietnam War, 2.7 million served and approximately 8,000 married, for a rate of 3.0 marriages per thousand U. S. servicemen. For service numbers for both wars, I consulted John Whiteclay Chambers II, *The Oxford Companion to U.S. Military History* (New York: Oxford University Press, 1999), 759, 816.

32. Eric M. Bergerud, *Red Thunder, Tropic Lightning: The World of a Combat Division in Vietnam* (Boulder, CO: Westview Press, 1993), 219–220, quote on 224; Christian G. Appy, *Working-Class War: American Combat Soldiers and Vietnam* (Chapel Hill: University of North Carolina Press, 1993), 253–255.

33. RG 472, MACV Command History, p. 147, Box 3, NARA.

34. Bergerud, *Red Thunder*, 223–224.

35. John Ketwig, *And a Hard Rain Fell: A GI's True Story of the War in Vietnam* (New York: Macmillan, 1985), 73.

36. Robert Shaplen, "The Girls They Leave Behind in Saigon," *McCall's* 95 (July 1968), 80+

37. Bergerud, *Red Thunder*, 224–225.

38. Appy, *Working-Class War*, 136.

39. Klaus Theweleit, *Male Fantasies*, trans. Stephen Conway (Minneapolis: University of Minnesota Press, 1987), vol. 1, chap. 1, pp. 70–79 on the "castrating whore."

40. Ketwig, *And a Hard Rain Fell*, 71.

41. Susan Brownmiller, *Against Our Will: Men, Women and Rape* (New York: Simon and Schuster, 1975), 86–113; Theodore Nadelson, *Trained to Kill: Soldiers at War* (Baltimore: Johns Hopkins University Press, 2005), 153–154; Le Ly Hayslip, *When Heaven and Earth Changed Places: A Vietnamese Woman's Journey from War to Peace* (New York: Doubleday, 1989), 88–97.

42. Edward Said identified the gendered typology in Western views of the East in *Orientalism*. Scholars of Asian American and feminist studies have further elucidated this imagery in many aspects of U.S. culture; for an overview, see Aki Uchida, "The Orientalization of Asian Women in America," *Women's Studies International Forum* 21 (March–April 1988), 161–174.

43. "An Honorable Estate," *Newsweek* 67 (8 August 1966), 31; Shaplen, "Girls They Leave Behind," 80+; "Love That Began with a Bullet," *Redbook* 140 (March 1973), 90+; "How U.S. Troops Really Behave in Vietnam," *U.S. News and World Report* 60 (23 May 1966), 57.

44. Personal interview with Joe and Dinh McDonald, Rockland, MA, 14 October 2006.

45. Gloria Emerson, *Winners and Losers: Battles, Retreats, Gain, Losses and Ruins from a Long War* (New York: Random House, 1976), 16; Appy, *Working-Class War*, 290.

46. Carol Fallows, *Love and War: Stories of War Brides from the Great War to Vietnam* (Sydney: Bantam Books, 2002), 217–223. Also on language translators and office romances, see Judy Klemesrud, "Vietnamese War Brides: Happiness Mixed with Pain," *New York Times*, 13 September 1971, 42.

47. Shaplen, "Girls They Leave Behind."

48. Hayslip, *When Heaven and Earth Changed Places*, 223–227, 169–170.

49. Ibid.; Marilyn Blatt Young, *The Vietnam Wars* (New York: HarperCollins, 1991), 302.

50. Shaplen, "Girls They Leave Behind."

51. DeBonis, *Children of the Enemy*, 18.

52. Bergerud, *Red Thunder*, 230; Emerson, *Winners and Losers*, 241.

53. "Love That Began with a Bullet," 90+.

54. Bergerud, *Red Thunder*, 42, 223; Appy, *Working-Class War*, 131–132, 237–238.

55. Erik B. Villard, "From Pat Pong to King's Cross: A Closer Look at the Seven Day Out-of-Country R & R Program during the Vietnam War, 1962–1973," Society of Military History Conference, University of Calgary, May 24–27, 2001; Villard, of the U.S. Army Center of Military History, calls the R & R program "one of the great accomplishments of the Vietnam War" in that it was able to overcome "logistical, financial and diplomatic

challenges"; but he does not address the sexual tourism dimension. RG 472, U.S. MACV Command History, 1966, typescript, pp. 148–173, Box 3, NARA.

56. Appy, *Working-Class War*, 237–238; Ketwig, *And a Hard Rain Fell*, 98–99; Kidder, *My Detachment*, 114–115.

57. Suzan Ruth Travis-Robyns, "What Is Winning Anyway? Redefining Veteran: A Vietnamese American Woman's Experiences in War and Peace," *Frontiers: A Journal of Women's Studies* 18 (1997), 145–167.

58. "Love That Began with a Bullet." Christian Appy relates the powerful story of a love affair between an American soldier from an extremely poor family and a Vietnamese woman in the countryside. The man contemplated proposing to the woman but was intimidated by the application process; years later, when he spoke with Appy, the man was living on the street in Boston. His fondness and sympathy for the woman were still apparent; *Working-Class War*, 290–292.

59. DeBonis, *Children of the Enemy*, 8.

60. "Girls They Leave Behind"; Emerson, *Winners and Losers*, 239. On the difficulty of attaining marriage, also see "Honorable Estate"; "This War's War Brides," *Chicago Tribune*, 6 June 1969, A1; *Los Angeles Times*, 7 April 1975, A1; *New York Times*, 18 April 1975, 14.

61. Author's personal interview with Joe and Dinh McDonald, Rockland, MA, 14 October 2006.

62. Tracy Kidder, *My Detachment: A Memoir* (New York: Random House, 2005), 106–124, 149–153. John Ketwig had a similar attachment for a woman he met during R & R in Malaysia; he too was berated by his officer, his marriage application repeatedly rejected; Ketwig, *And a Hard Rain Fell*.

63. "Girls They Leave Behind."

64. The files of the Adjutant General, Administrative Services Office, MACV, contain boilerplate copies of directives regarding marriage for the command and almost nothing else; RG 472, Directives, Box 43, NARA.

65. "Procedures to Marry," MACV Directive 608-1, 22 June 1966, Adjutant General Administrative Services, Reference Library, RG 472, Box 43, NARA.

66. *Los Angeles Times*, 1 January 1970, A12; *New York Times*, 13 September 1971, 42. The story of the unemployed veteran is from the *Los Angeles Times*, 7 April 1975, A1.

67. Hayslip, *When Heaven and Earth Changed Places*, 345–355; Appy, *Working-Class War*.

68. "Girls They Leave Behind." Also see "Back to the Brothel: Discussion in Senate Foreign Relations Committee Hearings of Conditions in Saigon," *Time* 87 (20 May 1966), 29; Judy Klemesrud, "Vietnamese War Brides," *New York Times*, 13 September 1971, 42.

69. Appy, *Working-Class War*, 27.

70. *Los Angeles Times*, 1 January 1970, A12; "Procedures to Marry," MACV Directive 608-1, 22 June 1966, Adjutant General Administrative Services, Reference Library, RG 472, Box 43, NARA. If the security investigation revealed "derogatory information" about the intended spouse, American military personnel were warned that they could lose their own security clearance and be removed from the country within twenty-four hours. The revised procedures also state that no information on the progress or results of the security investigation will be reported to the parties and added a Vietnamese police certificate of "good conduct" of the intended spouse covering the entire period of her residence in Vietnam. This directive updated that of 2 September 1964, where a much less elaborate process is described.

71. John A. Talbott, "The American Expatriate in South Viet Nam," *American Journal of Psychiatry* 126 (October 1969), 555–560.

72. Marriage applications at the National Archives—thirty-one boxes representing all applications for the year 1971—were randomly sampled to create a database (absent all names and identifying information). Personnel Management files, Adjutant General's Office, RG 472, U.S. Forces in Southeast Asia, NARA, College Park, MD.

73. Charley Trujillo, *Soldados: Chicanos in Vietnam* (San Jose, CA: Chusma House, 1990).

74. Appy, *Working-Class War*, 27–28.

75. In the group of female marriage applicants as a whole, only 36 percent were from rural areas or small towns; the comparable figure for younger teenage brides was 43 percent.

76. *Chicago Tribune*, 10 November 1975, 18. A U.S. Army deserter, in hiding with his Vietnamese lover, is the protagonist of Robert Olen Butler's novel *The Alleys of Eden* (New York: Horizon Press, 1981). A group of forty to fifty Americans remaining in Vietnam, most of whom had stayed for the sake of Vietnamese wives and children, was identified by the House Committee on Missing Persons in South East Asia in the summer of 1976; the Vietnamese government agreed to allow for their departure; *Chicago Tribune*, 22 July 1976, 6.

77. Mary A. Renda discusses the phenomenon of white soldiers "going native" in Haiti, "generally to live with native women"; women were "an important link in the process of going native because they often served as a key to intercultural contact." Renda, *Taking Haiti: Military Occupation and the Culture of U.S. Imperialism, 1915–1940* (Chapel Hill: University of North Carolina Press, 2001), 169–171.

78. Talbott, "American Expatriate in South Viet Nam," 555–560.

79. *Los Angeles Times*, 7 April 1975, A1; Le Ly Hayslip with James Hayslip, *Child of War, Woman of Peace* (New York: Doubleday, 1993), 124–134. Estimate of the numbers of Vietnamese wives and fiancées requesting safe passage is from an article by Fox Butterfield for the *New York Times*, 18 April 1975, 14.

80. A Vietnamese war bride whose personal narrative is richly probed in the women's studies journal *Frontiers*, for example, suffered from the flashbacks and nightmares characteristic of posttraumatic stress disorder and twice attempted suicide; the veteran-husband who brought her to the United States has had a history of violence and unemployment. Travis-Robyns, "What Is Winning Anyway?" 145–167.

81. Interview with Joe and Dinh McDonald.

82. Rogelio Saenz et al., "In Search of Asian War Brides," *Demography* 31 (August 1994), 549–559; Judy Klemesrud, "Vietnamese War Brides: Happiness Mixed with Pain," *New York Times*, 13 September 1971, 42; author's telephone interview with Tuyet "Snow" Pyle, 21 July 2005; interview with Joe and Dinh McDonald.

83. Ketwig, *And a Hard Rain Fell*. Ketwig's narrative has been widely admired by critics for its emotional honesty; it was republished in a twentieth anniversary edition in 2005.

84. Velina Hasu Houston, "To the Colonizer Goes the Spoils: Amerasian Progeny in Vietnam War Films and Owning Up to the Gaze," *Amerasia Journal* 23 (Spring 1997), 69–85. Houston writes, "The representation of Amerasian children in Vietnam War films recuperates victory by reclaiming the children as imperial product, as figures of innocence who can be liberated only by deliverance into Western beneficence" (70).

85. Christina Klein, *Cold War Orientalism: Asia in the Middlebrow Imagination, 1945–1961* (Berkeley: University of California Press, 2003), chap. 4, "Family Ties as Political Obligation," brilliantly analyzes the "discourse of adoption" in the musical *South Pacific* and other U.S. cultural production of the Cold War era. For another fascinating riff on intercultural adoption and its connection to foreign and domestic policy in the Cold War, see Caroline Chung Simpson, *An Absent Presence: Japanese Americans in Postwar American Culture, 1945–1960* (Durham, NC: Duke University Press, 2001), chap. 4 on the Hiroshima Maidens Project.

86. *Newsweek* 85 (21 April 1975), 39.

87. Susan Abrams, "The Vietnam Babylift," *Commonweal* 60 (24 September 1976), 617–621; Jane Cary Peck, "Of Politics and Vietnamese Orphans," *Christian Century* 91 (3 July 1974), 704–705; Gloria Emerson, "Operation Babylift," *New Republic* 172 (26 April 1975), 8–10; "And Now a Domestic Babylift?" *Ebony Magazine* 30 (June 1975), 134–135; "Rescuing Vietnam Orphans: Mixed Motives," *Christian Century* 92 (16 April 1975), 374–375; Nguyen Thi Ngoc Thoa, "The Vietnamese Orphans," *Progressive* 39 (June 1975), 6–7.

88. Quote is from Emerson, "Operation Babylift," 9.

89. *Newsweek* 85 (21 April 1975), 39–40; *Time* 105 (21 April 1975), 10–13 and (28 April 1975), 20; David M. Reimers, *Still the Golden Door: The Third World Comes to America* (New York: Columbia University Press, 1985), 175.

90. Bill Raspberry, "Our Amerasian Children," *Chicago Tribune*, 8 April 1982, 19.

91. The quotes are from Melinda Beck et al., "Where Is My Father? The Legacy of Vietnam," *Newsweek* 105 (15 April 1985), 54–57; Kieu-Linh Caroline Valverde, "From Dust to Gold: The Vietnamese Amerasian Experience," in Maria P. P. Root, ed., *Racially Mixed People in America* (Newbury Park, CA: Sage, 1992), 144–161.

92. DeBonis, *Children of the Enemy*; Thomas A. Bass, *Vietnamerica: The War Comes Home* (New York: Soho Press, 1996); Reimers, *Other Immigrants*, 278–279.

93. Susan Jeffords, *The Remasculinization of America: Gender and the Vietnam War* (Bloomington: Indiana University Press, 1989).

94. Edward Behr and Mark Steyn, *The Story of Miss Saigon* (New York: Arcade, 1991); Frank Rich, "'Miss Saigon' Arrives, from the Old School," *New York Times*, 12 April 1991, A1; William Safire, "Some Enchanted Saigon," *New York Times*, 2 October 1989, A19; Craig Whitney, "America's Vietnam Trauma Is the Stuff of British Musical," 23 September 1989, 12.

95. Rich, "'Miss Saigon' Arrives,", A1; Christopher Dickey and Jessica Ramirez, "Married to Iraq: What the War's Few Marriages Tell Us about Culture, Conflict and the Road Ahead," *Newsweek* 150 (22 October 2007), 28–34. The marriage of Sean and Ehda'a Blackwell has been the emblematic love story of the Iraq War, covered broadly in the media, including a feature on CBS's *60 Minutes*. For a sampling of the "star-crossed lovers" theme in relation to this marriage, see "Romeo and Juliet, Baghdad-style," www.theage.com/au/articles/2003 (accessed 3 November 2005); "Baghdad's Romeo and Juliet Find Love in Iraq War," www.breitbart.com/article (accessed 10 July 2008); and "Star-Crossed Courtship," 25 August 2004, www.cbsnews.com/stories/2004/05/03/60II/main615303.shtml (accessed 10 July 2008).

Index

abandonment/desertion by American soldiers: of children, 35–36, 244n4; fears of, in Philippines, 108; of pregnant women, 33–35; of wives, 35–36, 80

ABCC (Atomic Bomb Casualty Commission), 183

abstinence as a patriotic duty, 16

abstinence policy for servicewomen, 76

Adams, Romanzo, 192–193

adultery, 62–63, 210–211

AEF (American Expeditionary Force), 11–37; abstinence as a patriotic duty, 16; banning of female family members from the war zone, 30; Base Section 1, 24; billeting in French homes, 18; Bulletin 26, 35–36; Bulletin 54, 16; children, desertion of, 35–36; "clean army" campaign, 15–17; dating opportunities, 17–18, 25–26; demobilization of, 4, 41; deployment, length and structure of, 73; doughboys, European women's interest in, 20–21; doughboys' view of French women, 19–20; in England, 35, 244n4; fears about moral dangers of military service, 13–14; female rescue workers for, 25; Fifteenth Field Artillery, 28; foreign-born soldiers in, 67–69; foreign women, campaign against, 22–27; "Franco-Yanko Romance" phenomenon, 17–21; G-2 branch, 24–25; guidebooks to amorous conversation, 19; idealization of the American soldier, 12; intercultural relationships, spying on, 24–25; interracial sex, policies against, 25–26; Jim Crow, attempts to export, 26; leave

area program, 24; marriage policy, 12–13, 27–37, 242n52, 251n4; military draft, 13; moral reformers' concerns about, 14–16; Ninety-second Division, 26; off-base passes, denial of, 24, 32; Office of the Chief Surgeon, 19; officers' romances, monitoring of, 24; overseas personnel, number of, 13; pregnant women, abandonment of, 33–35; prostitution and, 18–19; "proxy marriage" for army personnel overseas, 242n52; reputation of, embarrassment to, 35–36; "Secret Information Concerning Black American Troops" (memo), 26; Selective Service Act (1917), 13–14; sexual relations, percentage of troops having, 23; "social purity" campaign among, 16; SOS (Services of Supply), 41, 42, 43–44; survivor benefits to common-law citizen wives of soldiers, 242n52; transport to U.S. for military spouses and children, 41, 244n4; venereal disease, campaign against, 22–23; war brides, negative view of, 45–50; war brides, number of, 13, 244n1; war brides, rationalization of handling of, 44; wives, desertion of, 35–36; women employees at AEF sites, 18

AFG (American Forces in Germany), 48

Africa, prostitution in, 78

African Americans: ambivalence about interracial marriage, 174; black press, 175–179; French and, 26; French people compared to, 47; French war brides of, 125; husbands of Vietnamese wives, 225–226; Japanese empathy with, 271n48;

African Americans (*continued*): prevented from dating in Italy, 97; prevented from marrying in Japan, 183–187; segregated houses of prostitution for, 78, 181, 271n48

Afro-American (newspaper), 177

Albert, Mr. and Mrs. Milton, 168–169

alcohol: availability in Vietnam, 218, 219; drinking by GIs in Australia, 88; prostitution and, 14–15, 16; in war bride narratives, 259n126

Alexander, Robert, 135–136

Alien Brides Act (Public Law 213, 1947), 132, 181, 187

Allen, A. Leonard, 135

Allen, Asa, 136

Allen, Henry T., 48–49

The Alleys of Eden (Butler), 227, 275n8

Allinger, Richard, 1

amalgamation, fears of, 54

Amerasian children, 203, 231–234, 275n2

Amerasian Homecoming Act (1987), 233

American Expeditionary Force. *See* AEF

American Forces in Germany (AFG), 48

American Legion, 133, 261n21

American men: attraction to, 111–113; as boys/innocents, 12, 75; Europe as moral threat to, 12; foreign-born among American soldier husbands, 20, 41, 66–67; gifts and commodities from, 112; heteronormativity, 75–76; as "red-blooded," 75

American popular culture, 111–112

American Red Cross. *See* Red Cross, American

American Society for Social Hygiene, 16

"The American Troops and the British Community" (Mead), 85

Americanization, 56–57

And a Hard Rain Fell (Ketwig), 230–231

anti-immigrant sentiments: during 1920s, 50–51; amalgamation, fears of, 54; of American Legion, 261n21; anti-Asian sentiments, 53; contract marriages, distaste for, 53; "crossbreeding," fears of, 54; Europe as a moral threat to American men, 12; female immigrants, concerns

about, 53–54; "foreignness" of French war brides, 7

Antwerp, Army embarkation office in, 45–46, 48

Appy, Chris, 215, 226

Argentina (ship), 137

Army Medical Department: foreign women, campaign against, 23; penicillin, limited distribution of, 21n13; sex research by, 96; venereal disease, campaign against, 15, 22, 78

Army War College, 13

Asia, prostitution in, 78

Asian immigration: chain migration, 211; during life of McCarran Walter Act, 268n9; naturalization, right of, 182; racial exclusion of, 132, 135–136, 260n18, 261n21

Asian war brides, 109, 229. *See also* Filipina war brides; Japanese war brides; Vietnamese war brides

Atomic Bomb Casualty Commission (ABCC), 183

Australia in World War II, 87–90; Battle of Brisbane, 89; dating opportunities, 87, 89; female Red Cross volunteers, 89; GIs stationed in, number of, 87, 252n25, 257n90; illegitimate birthrate, 90; intercultural marriage in, 80–81; intercultural relations, response to, 88–90; marriage rate per thousand U.S. soldiers in, 252n25; marriages, military approval of, 87; natalism in, 90; Private Edward Leonski murders, 89; venereal disease infection rate, 88, 96; women employees of U.S. armed forces, 89; women's movement, 92–93

Australian-American marriages, 90–94; brides' wartime paid employment, 91; military approval of, 87; parental protection, 90, 92; rate, 81; social class, 91; transport of wives and children to U.S., 93–94

Australian Red Cross, 93

Australian war brides: babies of, *122*; number of, World War II, 93–94, 257n90; public approval of, 138–139; public protest by, 116–117; stability of family life, 92

Bailey, Doris, 86
Bailey, Roy, 86
Baker, Newton D., 13, 15, 16, 36
Balao, Eulogia, 108
Baliday, Edith and Wilson, 159
"bar girls," 218
Barbeau, Arthur, 26
Battle, Lois, 110
Battle of Brisbane, 89
Beall, Philip, 145
Beane, Ruth, 47–48
beauty contests, 249n60
Beckham, Daphne, 42
Belgian war brides, 42, 49–50, 143
Bennett, Robert, 163, 170
Bethel, W. A., 29–31, 242n52
Bevans, J. M., 152
bigamy cases, 244n64
Blackwell, Sean and Ehda'a, 235, 281n95
Bordeaux, France, holding camp for war
    brides at, 44, 45, 47
"Born in the U.S.A." (Springsteen), 203
Borstelmann, Thomas, 207
Bouguen, France, holding camp for war
    brides at, 44–45
Brest, France, hostess house in, 42, 46, 47
"bride schools," 213
Britain in World War I: desertion of wives
    and children by American soldiers, 35,
    244n4; Health Ministry, 85; Ministry
    of Information, 83–84; women's place
    in, 20
Britain in World War II, 81–85; American
    buildup in, 81–83, 252n25; Britons' view
    of Americans, 82, 83–84; dating in, 85;
    entertainment of American soldiers, 84;
    female Red Cross volunteers, 84; female
    workers, 83; GI visits to British homes,
    84; illegitimate birthrate, 85; intercul-
    tural marriage, 80; interracial marriages,
    discouragement of, 87; marriage rate
    per thousand U.S. soldiers in, 252n25;
    military suppression of brothels/prosti-
    tution, 77–78; venereal disease infection
    rate, 82, 96; wartime earning power of
    women, 86

British-American marriages: as antidote
    to upheaval, 85–86; chaplains' support
    for, 86–87; courtship in, 85, 253n38;
    educational attainment of partners,
    253n40; official support for, 86–87;
    parents' occupations, 253n40; rate of, 81;
    transportation to U.S., 254n44; in World
    War II, 85–87
British war brides: American women
    compared to, 141–142; bigamy cases,
    244n64; denial of entry to/deportation
    of, 63; educational attainments, 253n40;
    family life, 85–86, 92; foreign-born
    soldier husbands, 66, 67; as inappropri-
    ate wives for American soldiers, 49–50;
    maternalism of, 144–146; murder by,
    144–146; number of, World War II, 72,
    87; parents' occupations, 253n40; photos
    of, 121; press coverage of, 41–42; public
    approval of, 137–138; public protest by,
    116, 117; reasonableness of, 149–150;
    wartime work experience, 86
Brown, George, 184–185
Brown v. Board of Education of Topeka, 176,
    179, 192, 194
Budani, Donna, 98
bui doi, 233
Burgess, Ernest W., 191
Burns, John Horne, 2
Bush, George H. W., 235
Butler, Robert Olen, 227, 275n8
Butterfield, Fox, 228

California Supreme Court, 166, 167, 176
camptowns: erosion of military-sponsored
    programming and assistance for war
    brides, 213; image of women married to
    U.S. servicemen, 213; Korean War and
    afterwards in Korea, 204, 205, 206–214;
    locations overseas, 9, 204; prostitution
    across generations, 212; Time report on,
    211–212
Cannon, Poppy, 174
Carnegie Endowment for International
    Peace, 50
Carruthers, Susan, 159

Casablanca, prostitution in, 78–79
chaplains, 86–87, 88, 212, 224
Chicago Defender (newspaper), 176, 177, 186
Chicago Tribune (newspaper), 11, 157
Chicano serviceman, refusal of wake for, 198
Chicano veterans, discrimination against, 198
children of American soldiers: desertion of, 35–36; transportation to U.S., 41, 93–94, 223, 244n4; Vietnamese-American, 203, 231–234, 275n2
China-Burma-India in World War II, venereal disease in, 78, 96, 252n20
Churchill, Winston, 81, 94
citizenship, martial, 132, 134–135
Clement, Gloria Baldecano Santiago, 200–202
Clement, William, 201
Cleveland, Maude, 48–49
Coalition against Trafficking in Women, 238n8
Cohen, Lizabeth, 147
Cold War, 156–160, 204–207; American racism, 160; consumerism as economic and political tool, 147; containment policy, 206; institutionalization of military marriage, 204, 205–206, 213; military conflict during, 205; Soviet ban on emigration of war brides, 152, 159–160; U.S. foreign policy during, 207; war brides, rehabilitation of German and Japanese, 151, 156–159; "withdrawal" from conflicts, 9
Collier's (magazine), 153
Commission on Training Camp Activities (CTCA), 16, 22
Committee on Public Information, 51
condoms, 76
consumerism, 146–148
contract marriages, 52–54
Cott, Nancy, 31
Coudert Brothers (lawyers), 29
Creel, George, 51
"crossbreeding," fears of, 54
Cuba, American military in, 4, 15

Cumings, Bruce, 207–208
Curtin, John, 93, 139
Czechoslovakian war brides, 68, *120*

Dale, Enid (fictional war bride), 142
Daniels, Roger, 268n9
dating opportunities: AEF (American Expeditionary Force), 17–18, 25–26; Australia in World War II, 87, 89; Britain in World War II, 85; Italy in World War II, 98; modernity and, 72–73; Philippines, 105, 108; Vietnam War, 217; World War II, 72–73
Daughters of the American Revolution, 50–51
Daughters of the British Empire, 138
De Bogory, Natalie, 53
deployment, length and structure of, 73
Devola, Andrew, 63–64
Dickstein, Samuel, 135, 136
Domina, Norma, 147
Dower, John, 181
draft age, 14, 73
Duhig, James, 89
Dumlao, Felipe, 105
Dutch war brides, 143

Ebony (magazine), 175
economic survival, military marriage as tool for, 5
Eisenhower, Dwight D., 81–82, 163
Ellingston, John, 39, 40
Ellis Island, 63
Emerson, Gloria, 222, 232
endogamous relationships, 194
England. *See* Britain
English-Speaking Union (ESU), 138
Enloe, Cynthia, 3
Episcopal City Mission Society, 138
ESU (English-Speaking Union), 138
Europe: Jefferson on American visitors to, 14; as moral threat to American men, 12; venereal diseases cases per thousand WWII U.S. soldiers, 78, 252n20; women's political and economic inequality, 20–21

exogamous marriages, 191
"extenders," 228

family-centered domesticity in postwar
  U.S., 128
family reunification, military marriage as
  tool for, 5
Farrington, Joseph, 135–136
Feldstein, Ruth, 192
Fiancées Act (Public Law 471, 1946), 131,
  152
Filipina war brides, 106–109; in Angel
  Island detention center, 108; Asian war
  brides during Cold War, 109; estab-
  lishment of Filipino communities in
  U.S., 108–109; financial requirement
  for exiting Philippines, 107; military
  antagonism towards, 108; number of,
  108; poverty among, 106–107; status and
  identity of, 102
Filipina women, 81, 103, 108
Filipino-American marriages, 81, 105–106,
  257n101
Filipino immigration, 257n99
Filipinos, feelings of racial inferiority
  among, 201–202
Foch, Ferdinand, 55
Ford, Gerald, 231
Ford, Nancy Gentile, 67
A Foreign Affair (film), 153
foreign wars, intercultural marriage in,
  238n10
Fosdick, Raymond, 16
France: as moral threat to American men,
  12, 14; reputation for low life, 14; as
  source of prostitutes, 52, 62
France in World War I: abandonment of
  pregnant women by American soldiers,
  33–35; American attempts to sow racial
  prejudice, resistance to, 26, 61; billeting
  in French homes, 18; doughboys' view of
  French women, 19–20; female workers
  in, American, 47–48; "Franco-Yanko
  Romance" phenomenon, 17–21; marriage
  laws, 32; marriage opportunities for
  French women to French men, 21; sex-

ratio imbalance, 21, 241n29; war widows,
  number of, 21; women's place in, 20
"fraternazis," 151
French-American marriages, 39, 55
French war brides: of African American
  soldiers, 125; anti-immigrant sentiments
  directed at, 7; bigamy cases, 244n64;
  in Boston, 58; foreign-born soldier
  husbands, 67; "foreignness" of, 7; head
  shaving of, 101; holding camps for,
  World War I, 44–45, 47; hostility toward,
  62; as inappropriate wives for American
  soldiers, 49–50; infant deaths during
  transport, 143; number of, World War
  I, 244n1; photo of, 119; in postliberation
  France, 101; Red Cross on, 61–62; repa-
  triation/return migration of, 55–56
French women: American women compared
  to, 11, 47; doughboys' view of, 19–20; marriage opportunities in World War I, 21
Friedman, Barbara, 84
frugality, 149
Fullbright, J. W., 204

The Gallery (Burns), 2
Gandy, Charles, 59
"gangplank marriages," 4
Garcia, Hector and Wanda, 198–199
Gardner, Martha, 247n30
gender, military policies in defining, 5
German-American marriages, 181, 265n82
German war brides, 150–160; Cold War
  rehabilitation of, 151, 156–159; domestic
  perception of, 152, 156–158; as "escapees"
  from Communism, 159; foreign-born
  soldier husbands, 66, 67; as "fraternazis,"
  151; number of, 151, 160; photo of, 123; suspicion of/hostility toward, 48–49, 155–156;
  whiteness of, 151; World War I, 48–49
Germany, American Forces in (AFG), 48
Germany, postwar: GI's view of Germans,
  154–155; Marshall Plan aid, 157; nonfraternization policy, 152–153, 155; "occupation babies" of Allied fathers, 160;
  stigmatization of German women, 153;
  venereal disease infection rate, 96, 155

intercultural relations: Australian response to, 88–90; chaplains' view of, 88; as dishonorable and dangerous, 22; international relations and, 36; MACV's view of, 214–215; motives behind World War I, 21; spying on intercultural couples, 24–25; Vietnam War, 219–220, 221

international relations, intercultural relations and, 36

international understanding, intercultural marriage and, 57

interracial couples, 168–176; attacks on white wives/girlfriends, 173; liberal whites and, 200; marriage rights, 169; NAACP support for, 168–171, 173–175, 184–185; press coverage of, 175–176; prohibition on publishing photos of, 168; racism and segregation in lives of, 197–198; women's perceptions of, 172–173

interracial marriage, 163–179, 183–187; African Americans' ambivalence about, 174; as an act of resistance, 267n3; base assignment problems, 170; black servicemen husbands and Japanese wives, 183–187; commanding officer's approval, requirement for, 169; commitment to mental hospital for, 166; discouragement of in European Theater of Operations (ETO), 87; firing for, 165; as harbinger of racial future, 165; housing problems, 170; immigration, 136; imprisonment for, 165; as "laboratory" for study of racial integration, 192; legality of, 176–177; *Loving v. Virginia* decision, 166; military leaders' view of, 167; non-recognition of, 165; "normalcy" of, 177–179; *Perez* decision (California), 167; political awakening of white wives, 171–173; political meaning, 267n3; as a *problem* in World War II, 74; requests during World War I, 36; social science assessment of, 191–194; state laws against, 165–167; visibility of, 163–165; white supremacy, 267n3

Interracial Marriage in Hawaii (Adams), 193

interracial sex, AEF policies against, 25–26

intra-ethnic romance, military comfort with, 100

Iran, prostitution in, 78

Iraqi-American marriage, 1, 235, 237n2, 281n95

Irish war brides, 49–50

Italian-American marriages, 99–102

Italian war brides: age/youthfulness of, 101; bigamy cases, 244n64; in Brest hostess house, 42; community censure/ head shaving in Italy, 101; foreign-born soldier husbands, 66; independence and dependence, tension between, 110; number of, World War II, 102, 257n90; poverty among, 101–102

Italy in World War II, 94–99; African Americans prevented from dating, 97; American ambivalence about, 95; dating opportunities, 98; GI visits to Italian home, 98; marriage rate per thousand U.S. soldiers in, 252n25; military campaign in, 94; peak troop strength in, 252n25, 257n90; prostitution in, 78, 81, 94, 95–98; prostitution in, clandestine, 98–99; sexuality survey in, 95–99; social life for soldiers, regulation and organization of, 97; stigmatization of Italian women, 81, 99; venereal disease in, 95–98

Japan, "bride schools" in, 213

Japan, occupation of, 180–181

Japanese-American Citizens League (JACL), 187

Japanese-American marriages, 179–189; Asian exclusion provisions of immigration law, 181; black servicemen husbands, 183–187; blood rules, concern with, 181; husbands' *vs.* wives' framing of, 189; intraracial marriage, support for, 181–182; military's ban on, 179–183; between Nisei servicemen and Japanese women, 181–182, 187; "private" immigration legislation, 182–183; state antimiscegenation laws, 184; strife in, 211; white servicemen husbands, 183, 184

242n52; establishment of soldiers', 74; interracial couples, 169; "proxy marriage" for army personnel overseas, 242n52

Marsh, Billy, 145

Marsh, Edward, 144

"martial citizenship," 132, 134–135

Mason, Noah, 134, 135

May, Elaine Tyler, 128

May Act (1942)

Maye, Adam, 63, 64

Maye, Marlyse, 63–64

McBride, Margaret, 57–58

McCarran Walter Act (1952, Immigration and Nationality Act): Asian exclusion, 132, 167, 260n18; Asian immigration during life of, 268n9; Asian immigration following, 211; naturalization right for Asian immigrants, 182; reform elements, 268n9

McDonald, Joe and Dinh, 229

McKellway (Madison Barracks medical director), 58

McNarney, Joseph T., 155

Mead, Margaret, 84–85, 129

Menta, Steve and Leenie, 219–220

Mental Hygiene (journal), 191

Mexican American serviceman, refusal of wake for, 198

Mexican-American War, 238n10

Mexican border conflicts, 3, 14–15

Military Assistance Command Vietnam. *See* MACV

Military Defense Treaty (1954), 208

military marriage: arguments against, 29–30, 74; arguments for, 30–31, 175–179; commanding officer's approval, requirement for, 32, 74, 169; cultural and political functions of, 7; demographic patterns of, 225–227; establishment of permanent U.S. military bases, 204, 213; institutionalization of, 204, 205–206, 213; MACV discouragement of, 222, 223, 224–225; marriage benefits, officer's permission to wed and, 251n4; marriage laws of foreign nations in, 29, 32;

marriage rights, establishment of, 74; military inefficiency and, 29–30; non-marital relationships as context for, 75; the *problem* of, 74; prostitution balanced against, 79; race and, 6, 36, 175–179; relations with Allies, 31; soldier husbands, foreign-born among, 20, 41, 66–67; survivor benefits to common-law citizen wives of soldiers, 242n52; as tool for family reunification and economic survival, 5; during Vietnam War, 214–215; violence by GI husbands, 210–211; World War I compared to World War II, 73–75

"Miss Ho Chi Minh City" (Safire), 234–235

Miss Saigon (musical), 234

Moon, Katherine S., 207, 208, 210

murder, 144–146

Myrdal, Gunnar, 174

NAACP (National Association for the Advancement of Colored People): biracial babies in Japan, 186–187; case-by-case approach to marriage and discrimination cases, 173–175; support for interracial couples, 168–171, 173–175, 184–185

Nakashima, Hisao, 187

National American Red Cross. *See* Red Cross, American

National Catholic Welfare Conference, 212

Negro Digest (magazine), 175, 177

New York Times (newspaper), 51, 130–131, 159, 196

New York Times Magazine, 39, 150

New Zealand war brides, 138–139

Newman, Jill, 110–111, 115–116, 259n126

Newman, John, 111

Newport News, Virginia, 58

Newsweek (magazine): on Australian war brides, 138; Iraqi-American marriage, story about, 1, 235; on veterans' readjustment, 129–130; on Vietnamese "war orphans," 231

North Africa, prostitution in, 78

North Vietnamese Army (NVA), 203

51–52, 63; women's villages, 79. *See also* camptowns

Public Law 213 (Alien Brides Act, 1947), 132, 181, 187

Public Law 271. *See* War Brides Act

Public Law 450 (extension of Fiancées Act, 1948), 131

Public Law 471 (Fiancées Act, 1946), 131, 152

Public Law 717 (1950), *124*, 132, 181

Pyle, Ernie, 95, 100

"Quand La Guerre Est Fini" (song), 34

Queen Mary (ship), 142

Quezon, Aurora, 108

The Quiet American (Greene), 275n8

R & R program, Vietnam, 220–221

race: French resistance to American attempts to sow racial prejudice, 26, 61; Jim Crow, 26, 164, 166, 167; as *the* marriage *problem* in World War II, 74; military marriage and, 6, 36, 175–179; military policy toward brothels, 77–78, 271n48; venereal disease, 96; whiteness of German war brides, 151

Radcliffe, Cyril, 83

Rain, Rain, Go Away (Newman), 111, 115–116, 259n126

rape, 36, 215–216, 221. *See also* sexual violence

Reader's Digest (magazine), 127

Recreation and Amusement Association, 181, 271n48

Red Cross, American: American women working for, 47; in Australia and New Zealand, 89, 116–117; in Britain in World War II, 84; British war brides as model wives, 142; condoms, promotion of, 76; and Filipina war brides, 102, 106–107; in France in World War I, 47; on French war brides, 61–62; GI Bride Clubs, 116–117; imputations of sexual immorality among war brides, 43; information-gathering about betrothed American soldiers, 34; in Italy in World War II, 97; local volunteer workers, 84, 89; recre-

ation on war bride transports, 249n60; return migration of war brides, 56; shopping sprees for war brides, 146–147; in specifying "war bride," 5; testing of war brides for venereal disease, 50; in Vietnam, 217; in war bride narratives, 112; war bride programs, ending of, 204, 213; World War I war brides processed, 244n1

Red Cross, Australian, 93

Red Cross, Philippine, 102, 108

Red Scare, 45, 50

Redbook (magazine), 220

Reimers, Dave, 211

Republican National Committee, 52, 247n31

Reynolds, Quentin, 153–154

Rich, Frank, 235

Roosevelt, Eleanor, 93, 155–156, 160

Roosevelt, Franklin D., 94

Roosevelt, Theodore, 15

Rupeka, Peter and Erika, 265n82

Russian war brides, 42

Sabet, Bahereh, 71

Sackets Harbor, New York, 58

Sadowski, George, 133, 134–135

Safire, William, 234–235

Saint-Nazaire, France, holding camp for war brides at, 44

Saturday Evening Post (magazine), 54, 142

SCAP (Supreme Commander of the Allied Powers), 183, 186, 188, 271n48

The Scarlet Lily (play), 62

Schnepp, Gerald J., 192

Scott, Cleveland, 170–171

Scudder, Robert, 17

"Secret Information Concerning Black American Troops" (AEF memo), 26

Selective Service Act (1917), 13–14

Servicemen's Readjustment Act (GI Bill, 1944), 130

sexual immorality of war brides, imputations of, 43

sexual relations, military policies in defining, 5

xenophobia. *See* anti-immigrant
   sentiments

yang galbo, 209
yang gongju, 209
Yank (magazine), 76, 140
YMCA, 24, 25, 50, 66
Yu, Henry, 26 7n3
Yuh, Ji-Yeon, 209, 210–211
Yui, Agnes Masako, 192
YWCA: Czechoslovakian war brides, 68;
   Department on Work for Foreign-Born
   Women, 246n19; English-language

training, 57; female workers in France,
47; holding camps for war brides, 44–45,
47; "hostess houses" run by, 42; internationalism of, 46, 246n19; Migration
Service, 246n19; Pershing and, John J.,
42; services provided by, 42, 44–45, 46,
57; World War I war brides processed in
France, 244n1

Zebulon B. Vance (transport ship),
   143–144
Zinnemann, Fred, 160
Zschernitz, Edmund, 67–68

About the Author

SUSAN ZEIGER, a historian of gender, war, and peace movements in the United States, is author of *In Uncle Sam's Service: Women Workers with the American Expeditionary Force, 1917–1919*. Chair of the history department at Regis College for more than ten years, she now works as program director at Primary Source, an education nonprofit in the Boston area.